Studies in the Political Economy of Public Policy

Series Editors
Toby Carroll
Department of Asian and International Studies
City University of Hong Kong
Hong Kong

Paul Cammack
University of Manchester
Manchester, UK

Kelly Gerard
School of Social Sciences
The University of Western Australia
Crawley, Australia

Darryl S. L. Jarvis
Faculty of Liberal Arts and Social Sciences
The Education University of Hong Kong
Hong Kong

Studies in the Political Economy of Public Policy presents cutting edge, innovative research on the origins and impacts of public policy. Going beyond mainstream public policy debates, the series encourages heterodox and heterogeneous studies of sites of contestation, conflict and cooperation that explore policy processes and their consequences at the local, national, regional or global levels. Fundamentally pluralist in nature, the series is designed to provide high quality original research of both a theoretical and empirical nature that supports a global network of scholars exploring the implications of policy for society. The series is supported by a diverse international advisory board drawn from Asia, Europe, Australia, and North America, and welcomes manuscript submissions from scholars in the global South and North that pioneer new understandings of public policy.

International Advisory Board:
Caner Bakir, Koç University, Turkey
Jacqui Baker, Murdoch University, Australia
Shaun Breslin, University of Warwick, UK
Paul Cammack, University of Manchester, UK
Giliberto Capano, Bologna University, Italy
Sydney Calkin, University of Durham, UK
Paul Chambers, Naresuan University, Thailand
Barry Gills, University of Helsinki, Finland
Ruben Gonzalez-Vicente, Leiden University, Netherlands
Paul K. Gellert, University of Tennessee, USA
Penny Griffin, University of New South Wales, Australia
M. Shamsul Haque, National University of Singapore, Singapore
Pascale Hatcher, University of Canterbury, New Zealand
Heng Yee Kuang, GraSPP, University of Tokyo, Japan
Kevin Hewison, University of North Carolina at Chapel Hill, USA
Wil Hout, Institute of Social Studies, Erasmus University, Netherlands
Michael Howlett, Simon Fraser University, Canada
Kanishka Jayasuriya, Murdoch University, Australia
Lee Jones, Queen Mary University of London, UK
Zhang Jun, City University of Hong Kong, China
Max Lane, Victoria University, Australia
Kun-chin Lin, University of Cambridge, UK
Adrienne Roberts, University of Manchester, UK
Stuart Shields, University of Manchester, UK
Richard Stubbs, McMaster University, Canada
Silke Trommer, University of Manchester, UK
Philippe Zittoun, Science Po, France
Heng Yee Kuang, University of Tokyo, Japan
Heloise Weber, University of Queensland, Australia

All books in the series are subject to Palgrave's rigorous peer review process: https://www.palgrave.com/gb/demystifying-peer-review/792492.

For more information, or to submit a proposal, please contact one of the series editors: Toby Carroll (tcarroll@cityu.edu.hk), Paul Cammack (pcammack01@gmail.com), Kelly Gerard (kelly.gerard@uwa.edu.au), Darryl Jarvis (djarvis@eduhk.hk).

More information about this series at
http://www.palgrave.com/gp/series/14465

Toby Carroll • Shahar Hameiri
Lee Jones
Editors

The Political Economy of Southeast Asia

Politics and Uneven Development under Hyperglobalisation

Fourth Edition

palgrave
macmillan

Editors
Toby Carroll
Department of Asian and International Studies
City University of Hong Kong
Hong Kong, China

Shahar Hameiri
School of Political Science and International Studies
The University of Queensland
St Lucia, QLD, Australia

Lee Jones
School of Politics and International Relations
Queen Mary University of London
London, UK

ISSN 2524-7441   ISSN 2524-745X (electronic)
Studies in the Political Economy of Public Policy
ISBN 978-3-030-28254-7   ISBN 978-3-030-28255-4 (eBook)
https://doi.org/10.1007/978-3-030-28255-4

© The Editor(s) (if applicable) and The Author(s), under exclusive licence to Springer Nature Switzerland AG 2020
This work is subject to copyright. All rights are solely and exclusively licensed by the Publisher, whether the whole or part of the material is concerned, specifically the rights of translation, reprinting, reuse of illustrations, recitation, broadcasting, reproduction on microfilms or in any other physical way, and transmission or information storage and retrieval, electronic adaptation, computer software, or by similar or dissimilar methodology now known or hereafter developed.
The use of general descriptive names, registered names, trademarks, service marks, etc. in this publication does not imply, even in the absence of a specific statement, that such names are exempt from the relevant protective laws and regulations and therefore free for general use.
The publisher, the authors and the editors are safe to assume that the advice and information in this book are believed to be true and accurate at the date of publication. Neither the publisher nor the authors or the editors give a warranty, expressed or implied, with respect to the material contained herein or for any errors or omissions that may have been made. The publisher remains neutral with regard to jurisdictional claims in published maps and institutional affiliations.

Cover photograph by Chris Alexander (Slums and Skyscrapers, Jakarta, 5th April 2015). Original photograph at https://www.flickr.com/photos/mrcrisp/17232832745

This Palgrave Macmillan imprint is published by the registered company Springer Nature Switzerland AG.
The registered company address is: Gewerbestrasse 11, 6330 Cham, Switzerland

Preface

This book is the fourth edition in a series previously edited by Garry Rodan, Kevin Hewison and Richard Robison (1997, 2001, 2006). Together with two earlier books, *Southeast Asia: Essays in the Political Economy of Structural Change* (Higgott and Robison 1985a) and *Southeast Asia in the 1990s: Authoritarianism, Democracy and Capitalism* (Rodan et al. 1993), these texts established and consolidated what became known as the "Murdoch School" of political economy, with these scholars having established the Asia Research Centre at Murdoch University in Perth, Western Australia. The earlier volumes, together with other influential texts, like Robison's *Indonesia: The Rise of Capital* (1986), Rodan's *The Political Economy of Singapore's Industrialisation* (1989) and Hewison's *Bankers and Bureaucrats* (1989), challenged established literatures not just on Southeast Asia but on the nature of politics, institutions and social transformation under capitalism more broadly.

In the study of Southeast Asia, this scholarship constituted an important turn towards political economy, and an important departure from the work of those within area studies, comparative politics and orthodox economics. Murdoch School scholarship pointed to pivotal dynamics underway within the global political economy and how these trends were reshaping life in Southeast Asia. It focused on Southeast Asia not because it was unique but because, like any other region in a world interconnected for centuries by trade, colonialism and capitalism, it was an important point of entry from which to examine globally significant developments and the dynamics that shape their diverse local manifestations. In *Southeast Asia: Essays in the Political Economy of Structural Change*, Richard Higgott and Richard Robison (1985b) discussed countries in the region not as standalone entities to be studied in isolation, or categorised into different typologies; rather, they were considered in relation to the greater whole of the "New International Division of Labour" (NIDL): the dramatic shift in industrial production from developed to developing countries, the key aspect of what we now call "globalisation". Southeast Asia was host to several countries that looked to be following in the footsteps of other rare examples of late development, like Japan, South Korea and Taiwan. Their "developmental states" were at the very centre of scholarly debates on development, having seemingly disproven dependency theory, which never anticipated industrialisation beyond the established "core", while also posing thorny questions to orthodox economists and rational choice theorists. Notably, scholars battled over the degree to which states or markets were responsible for this unexpected but spectacular development (Amsden 1989; Johnson 1982; Rodan 1989: xiii).

The Murdoch School took a distinctive position in this debate, developing an analytical approach that, while universal in scope, was applied mostly to Southeast Asia. Like statists, Murdoch Scholars rejected many of the more deterministic positions within dependency theory and both rational choice and orthodox economics approaches. Inspired by Marxist understandings of capitalist social relations and development, the Murdoch School foregrounded *social conflict,* primarily between class forces, as central to explaining political and economic life. Southeast Asia—then undergoing dramatic economic growth and a manufacturing boom—was developing not because clever bureaucrats, isolated from deleterious social and political demands, were devising astute developmental policies, as the increasingly influential literature on the "developmental state" might have suggested, given its understanding of the Northeast Asian experience. Rather, state managers were being driven by contending social and political forces to develop their economies in particular ways, and their opportunities and constraints were heavily determined by global political and economic forces, notably the Cold War and the emerging NIDL. Rodan's description of his account of Singapore's startling development summarises the approach well:

> ...this study challenges the dominant understandings of Singapore as a case where "correct" policies have made rapid industrialisation possible and raises questions about the possibility and appropriateness of emulation. Rejection of the dominant perspective on Singapore is made possible by the

particular framework of this study which affords primary and thematic focus on the relationship between international capital and the Singapore state. It is this relationship which is both defined by, and at the same time helps to define, the emergence of a NIDL. Emphasis is also given to the social and political context of this relationship and the specific historical circumstances surrounding it. Within this framework, the successful implementation of the economic policies isolated by neo-classical economists and rational choice theorists as a fundamental cause of rapid industrialisation is seen here to be tied to various social and political conditions. These conditions make it possible to adopt policies which exploit the historically-unprecedented tendency of international capital to invest off-shore for the purpose of export manufacturing production (Rodan 1989: xiv).

Subsequent work by Murdoch Scholars investigated, dialectically, the consequences of this authoritarian, state-led development for political life in the region. While others waxed lyrical about the prospects of liberalisation and democratisation after the Cold War or the 1997–98 Asian financial crisis, Murdoch Scholars were sceptical. They studied and emphasised the class forces, power relations and ideologies arising from Southeast Asia's capitalist development: powerful politico-bureaucratic networks; dominant conglomerates, usually owned by small ruling cliques of families and "crony capitalists"; an illiberal, consumerist "new rich" and middle classes disinterested in democracy; a ravaged and disorganised working class and peasantry (Rodan et al. 1993). These were not propitious circumstances for democratisation, but conditions for authoritarianism and illiberalism to survive and thrive even amid economic liberalisation. Murdoch Scholars have subsequently shown that, given the weakness of socialist and liberal oppositions, ruling elites, most notably in Indonesia, have even managed to maintain their privileges following significant political liberalisation (Robison and Hadiz 2004). The first three editions of *The Political Economy of Southeast Asia* traced these developments across the region and, in particular, through country case studies.

As incoming editors of this path-breaking series, we faced formidable challenges. Thirteen years have elapsed since the third edition. Scholarly debates have changed—or even disappeared. China's rise as "factory of the world" has been a dramatic new phase of the NIDL. China's rapidly growing economy has provided stiff competition to Southeast Asia's manufacturing sector, but also new opportunities for investment, development financing and trade in raw commodities. And we have entered what the

United Nations Conference on Trade and Development calls "hyperglobalisation": the intensifying global spread of trade, production and finance, and associated vast imbalances in power and wealth. Our greatest challenge was to present an account of Southeast Asia's political and economic development that reflects the region's ever-greater enmeshment in pan-regional and global flows, as shown in Chap. 2, while not losing a sense of the considerable diversity that still characterises this part of the world. For example, we wanted to shed light on processes that we see across the globe, like the rise of populism, environmental degradation, and land-grabbing, and which can be seen holistically, as part of a specific era of capitalist social development. Yet we also want to convey a sense of why, for example, political regimes remain so heterogeneous.

Ultimately, we decided that the moment called for a thematic, rather than country-based, approach. Surveys of individual countries undoubtedly remain useful, but they can fall into the trap of methodological nationalism, whereby national-level analysis is overwhelmingly used to explain a given country's development. To the extent that this was ever true, it is certainly false in an era of hyperglobalisation. But neither do we wish to claim that international factors are more important than domestic ones. Rather, a thematic approach better captures the way that local, national developments are ultimately *intertwined* with regional and global ones, helping us to recognise both commonalities across societies and their shared causes.

Accordingly, this volume is divided into four parts. Part I, *Southeast Asia's Political Economy: Theory and Historical Evolution*, comprises two chapters: the first details competing theorisations of Southeast Asian political economy and explains the Murdoch School approach we use in this book; the second presents an overview of Southeast Asia's economic development from independence to hyperglobalisation. These chapters set up the wider theoretical and historical-sociological context for the rest of the volume. Part II—*Economic Development and Governance*—explores the main trends in economic and political governance across the region, discussing the evolution of domestic political regimes and contemporary political dynamics, and the transformation of statehood and regional governance. The third and fourth parts delve into particular areas of political economy, and how these relate to the evolving dynamic between economic and political development under conditions of hyperglobalisation. *Capital, State and Society* explores the nature of human society in Southeast Asia, discussing important themes like gender, migration, aid, and poor people's politics. These chapters are illustrated by case materials drawn from individual countries, some of them in comparative case studies. *Capital, State and Nature* explores how capitalist development occurs within, and is reshaping, the natural environment, covering issues such as environmental degradation, land use and agribusiness, and the extractives sector.

This melding of the theoretical, the thematic and the country-specific represents a cutting-edge approach in the study of Southeast Asia's political economy. Some of the material presented in this volume will naturally become outdated, as the conflicts and contradictions of hyperglobalisation, and increasing geopolitical tensions between the US and China, play out in the coming years. However, we hope that this volume will equip readers with the knowledge and theoretical tools to make sense of these future transformations. In 1986, Richard Robison opened his seminal book, *Indonesia: The Rise of Capital*, with the words: "The most revolutionary force at work in the Third World today is not communism or socialism but capitalism" (Robison 1986: vii). Although the term "third world" fell out of favour after the end of the Cold War, the substance of this statement remains as true now as it was then.

Toby Carroll
Shahar Hameiri
Lee Jones

References

Amsden, A. (1989). *Asia's next giant: South Korea and late industrialization*. New York: Oxford University Press.

Hewison, K. (1989). *Bankers and bureaucrats: Capital and state in Thailand*. New Haven: Yale University Press.

Higgott, R., & Robison, R. (Eds.). (1985a). *Southeast Asia: Essays in the political economy of structural change*. London: Routledge and Kegan Paul.

Higgott, R., & Robison, R. (1985b). Theories of development and underdevelopment: Implications for the study of Southeast Asia. In R. Higgott & R. Robison (Eds.), *Southeast Asia: Essays in the political economy of structural change* (pp. 16–61). London: Routledge and Kegan Paul.

Johnson, C. (1982). *MITI and the Japanese miracle: The growth of industrial policy, 1925–1975*. Stanford: Stanford University Press.

Robison, R. (1986). *Indonesia: The rise of capital*. Sydney: Allen and Unwin.

Robison, R., & Hadiz, V. R. (2004). *Reorganising power in Indonesia: The politics of oligarchy in an age of markets.* London: Routledge.

Rodan, G. (1989). *The political economy of Singapore's industrialisation.* London: Macmillan.

Rodan, G., Hewison, K., & Robison, R. (Eds.). (1993). *Southeast Asia in the 1990s: Authoritarianism, democracy and capitalism.* Sydney: Allen & Unwin.

Rodan, G., Hewison, K., & Robison, R. (Eds.). (1997). *The political economy of South-East Asia: An introduction.* Melbourne: Oxford University Press.

Rodan, G., Hewison, K., & Robison, R. (Eds.). (2001). *The political economy of South-East Asia: Conflict, crisis and change.* Melbourne: Oxford University Press.

Rodan, G., Hewison, K., & Robison, R. (Eds.). (2006). *The political economy of South-East Asia: Markets, power and contestation.* Melbourne: Oxford University Press.

Acknowledgements

This book would not have been possible without the intellectual and practical support of many people and organisations.

We are grateful for the generous funding we received from Murdoch University's Asia Research Centre, the School of Political Science and International Studies at the University of Queensland, and the Australian Research Council via Discovery Project grant DP170102647 ("Rising Powers and State Transformation").

We owe an enormous intellectual debt to Richard Robison, Kevin Hewison and Garry Rodan—the editors of the first three volumes of this series. Their leadership over three decades has been instrumental in the development of the "Murdoch School" approach, which this volume develops further. We have each benefited enormously from their intellectual legacy and personal mentorship. We thank them for their willingness to hand the series to us and for always respecting our editorial autonomy. In particular, we would like to thank Garry Rodan, who as Director of the Asia Research Centre played a particularly important role enabling this project. Without his encouragement and efforts to secure essential funding, this book simply could not have been produced. We also thank the contributing authors for participating in a workshop held at Murdoch University, Western Australia, in December 2018. Their receptivity to our vision for this volume, and the fine chapters they authored, were pivotal in making the volume what it is. Four other colleagues—Ed Aspinall, Chua Beng Huat, Kanishka Jayasuriya and Jeffrey Wilson—provided extremely valuable comments at the workshop, further supporting the editorial team.

We would like to thank our research assistants, Jan Mairhöfer and Ryan Smith, our copy-editor, Paula Bownas, and our indexer, Kate McIntosh. We are grateful for the support of our publishers, Palgrave Macmillan, especially Oliver Foster and Jemima Warren. The Asia Research Centre's administrator, Sia Kozlowski, deserves special acknowledgment, as her fine organisational skills were crucial in making the workshop a success.

Although universities are often caricatured as ivory towers and counterposed to the "real world", in fact, they are brutally exposed to the marketising forces that we explore in this book. Public funding is collapsing, while neoliberal managerialism is rampant. The space for critical inquiry is contracting, and academic standards are increasingly debased in the pursuit of income streams. It is a testament to the integrity and fortitude of the Murdoch School's founders and adherents that they have managed to carve out space for pioneering, critical scholarship over so many decades. They have created a large, thriving community of scholars, spanning generations and continents, far beyond its birthplace at the Asia Research Centre at Murdoch University. This volume testifies to the resilience and ongoing development of the Murdoch School, regardless of the travails of particular institutions. We hope that it inspires a new generation of researchers, particularly in Southeast Asia itself, to participate in its research agenda. Certainly, creating a better future for the region requires a clear-eyed understanding of the present.

Toby Carroll
Shahar Hameiri
Lee Jones
May 2019

Praise for *The Political Economy of Southeast Asia: Politics and Uneven Development under Hyperglobalisation*

"This is not only the best collection of essays on the political economy of Southeast Asia, but also, as a singular achievement of the "Murdoch School", one of the rarest of books that demonstrates how knowledge production travels across generations, institutions and time periods, thereby continually enriching itself. No course on Southeast Asia can afford to miss it as its core text."
—Professor Amitav Acharya, *American University, USA*

"This book—the fourth in a path-breaking series—demonstrates why a critical political economy approach is more crucial than ever for understanding Southeast Asia's transformation. Across a wide range of topics, the book explains how capitalist development and globalisation are reshaping the societies, economies and politics of a diverse group of countries, casting light on the deep sources of economic and social power in the region. This is a book that every student of Southeast Asia needs to read."
—Professor Edward Aspinall, *Australian National University*

"This book does what a work on political economy should do: challenge existing paradigms in order to gain a deeper understanding of the processes of social transformation. This volume is distinctive in three ways. First, it eschews methodological nationalism and focuses on how the interaction of national, regional, and global forces are shaping and reshaping systems of governance, mass politics, economies, labor-capital relations, migration, and gender relations across the region. Second, it is a bold effort to show how the "Murdoch School," which focuses on the dynamic synergy of internal class relations and global capitalism, provides a better explanatory framework for understanding social change in Southeast Asia than the rival "developmental state" and "historical institutionalist" approaches. Third, alongside established luminaries in the field, it showcases a younger generation of political economists doing pathbreaking work on different dimensions of the political economy of the region."
—Walden Bello, *State University of New York at Binghamton and Former Member of the Philippines' House of Representatives*

"This very timely fourth edition explores Southeast Asia's political economy within the context of hyperglobalisation and China's pronounced social-structural impacts on international politics, finance and economics over the past decade and a half. The volume successfully adopts a cross-cutting thematic approach, while also conveying the diversity and divergences among the Southeast Asian states and economies. This will be an important resource for scholars of International Relations and Comparative Politics, who need to take an interest in a dynamic and increasingly significant part of Asia."
—Professor Evelyn Goh, *Australian National University*

"This ambitious collection takes a consistent theoretical approach and applies it to a thematic, comparative analysis across Southeast Asia. The yield is impressive: the social, political and economic forces constituting the current conjuncture are not simply invoked, they are thoroughly identified and explained. By posing the deceptively simple questions of what is happening and why, the authors demonstrate the reciprocal relation between theory-building and empirical inquiry, providing a model of engaged scholarship with global resonance. Bravo!"
—Professor Tania Li, *University of Toronto*

"Counteracting the spaceless and flattened geography of much literature on uneven development, this book delivers a forensic examination of the unevenness of geographical development in Southeast Asia and the relations of force shaping capital, state, nature and civil society. This is the most compelling theoretical and empirical political economy book available on Southeast Asia."
—Professor Adam David Morton, *University of Sydney*

"A vital book for all scholars, students and practitioners concerned with political economy and development, this volume combines cutting-edge theory with rich and wide-ranging empirical analysis. It is terrific to see the continued success of this book with this fully revised fourth edition."
—Professor Nicola Philips, *Kings College London*

"*The Political Economy of Southeast Asia* has become a leading reference for students of the region. With its breadth of geographic scope, timely themes, clarity of prose and rigour of analysis, Carroll, Hameiri and Jones have ensured that with this fourth edition the volume will continue its landmark status. The book, which brings together prominent experts in the field, will not only be of immense interest to scholars studying Southeast Asia, but also those seeking to understand the multifaceted nature of the political economy of uneven development in contemporary capitalism."
—Professor Susanne Soederberg, *Queen's University, Canada*

"The Asia Research Centre at Murdoch University has long produced leading analyses of the social, economic and political developments in Southeast Asia. This volume carries on that wonderful tradition. It brings together top-class scholars to challenge our assumptions about one of the most dynamic parts of the world. This collection is a crucial read for anyone interested in understanding trends in Southeast Asia's development today and into the future."
—Professor Richard Stubbs, *McMaster University, Canada*

"This fourth volume in a distinguished series provides a welcome and timely update of the Murdoch School's distinctive approach to understanding the evolving political economy of Southeast Asia. Its theoretical depth and wide empirical scope will be of great value to scholars, students and practitioners seeking a systematic understanding of the political economy dynamics in the Asian region and, more broadly, of states and regions embedded in a complex, unstable global political economy."
—Professor Andrew Walter, *University of Melbourne*

Contents

Part I Southeast Asia's Political Economy: Theory and
Historical Evolution   1

1   Theorising Political Economy in Southeast Asia   3
    Shahar Hameiri and Lee Jones

2   The Political Economy of Southeast Asia's Development
    from Independence to Hyperglobalisation   35
    Toby Carroll

Part II Economic Development and Governance   85

3   Explaining Political Regimes in Southeast Asia: A Modes
    of Participation Framework   87
    Garry Rodan and Jacqui Baker

4   Transitions from State "Socialism" in Southeast Asia   111
    Caroline Hughes

5	The Post-war Rise and Decline of the Left Nathan Gilbert Quimpo	133
6	Populism in Southeast Asia: A Vehicle for Reform or a Tool for Despots? Richard Robison and Vedi R. Hadiz	155
7	The Internationalisation of Capital and the Transformation of Statehood in Southeast Asia Faris Al-Fadhat	177
8	Southeast Asian Regional Governance: Political Economy, Regulatory Regionalism and ASEAN Integration Lee Jones and Shahar Hameiri	199

Part III	Capital, State and Society	225
9	The Gendered Political Economy of Southeast Asian Development Juanita Elias	227
10	Labour Migration in Southeast Asia: The Political Economy of Poor and Uneven Governance Kelly Gerard and Charanpal S. Bal	249
11	Poor People's Politics in Urban Southeast Asia Jane Hutchison and Ian D. Wilson	271
12	The Changing Aid Landscape and the Political Economy of Development in Southeast Asia Andrew Rosser	293

Part IV Capital, State and Nature   315

13 The Political Economy of Southeast Asia's Extractive
    Industries: Governance, Power Struggles and
    Development Outcomes   317
    Pascale Hatcher

14 The Political Economy of Land and Agrarian Relations in
    Southeast Asia   341
    Philip Hirsch

15 The Political Economy of Environmental Degradation
    and Climate Disaster in Southeast Asia   367
    Paul K. Gellert

Index   389

Notes on Contributors

Faris Al-Fadhat is Lecturer in the Faculty of Social and Political Sciences at the Universitas Muhammadiyah Yogyakarta, Indonesia.

Jacqui Baker is Lecturer in Southeast Asian Politics at the College of Arts, Business, Law and Social Sciences, Murdoch University, Australia.

Charanpal S. Bal is Lecturer in Political Science at the School of Social Sciences at the University of Western Australia.

Toby Carroll is Associate Professor in the Department of Asian and International Studies at City University of Hong Kong, China.

Juanita Elias is Professor in International Political Economy at the University of Warwick, UK.

Paul K. Gellert is Associate Professor of Sociology at the University of Tennessee, USA.

Kelly Gerard is Senior Lecturer in the School of Social Sciences at the University of Western Australia.

Vedi R. Hadiz is Director and Professor in the Asia Institute, and assistant deputy vice-chancellor (Indonesia), University of Melbourne, Australia.

Shahar Hameiri is Associate Professor of International Politics in the School of Political Science and International Studies at the University of Queensland, Australia.

xxi

Pascale Hatcher is Senior Lecturer in the Department of Political Science and International Relations, University of Canterbury, New Zealand.

Philip Hirsch is Emeritus Professor of Human Geography in the School of Geosciences at the University of Sydney, Australia.

Caroline Hughes is the Rev. Theodore M. Hesburgh, C.S.C. Chair in Peace Studies at the Kroc Institute for International Peace Studies at the University of Notre Dame, USA.

Jane Hutchison is Associate Professor of Politics and International Studies in the College of Arts, Business, Law and Social Sciences, Murdoch University, Australia.

Lee Jones is Reader in International Politics in the School of Politics and International Relations at Queen Mary University of London, UK.

Nathan Gilbert Quimpo is Associate Professor at the Graduate School of Humanities and Social Sciences at University of Tsukuba, Japan.

Richard Robison is Honorary Professorial Fellow, Asia Institute, University of Melbourne, Australia.

Garry Rodan is Emeritus Professor in the College of Arts, Business, Law and Social Sciences, Murdoch University and an honorary professor in the School of Political Science and International Studies, the University of Queensland, Australia.

Andrew Rosser is Professor of Southeast Asian Studies in the Asia Institute at the University of Melbourne, Australia.

Ian D. Wilson is Senior Lecturer in Politics and Security, Terrorism and Counter-Terrorism Studies in the College of Arts, Business, Law and Social Sciences, Murdoch University, Australia.

LIST OF FIGURES

Fig. 2.1	Multidimensional and income poverty rates in selected Southeast Asian countries (percentages)	39
Fig. 7.1	OFDI stocks of selected Southeast Asian economies (US$, millions)	182
Fig. 8.1	Major Asia-Pacific Economic Cooperation Forums	200
Fig. 8.2	Average tariffs and number of non-tariff barriers in ASEAN	217
Fig. 10.1	Intra-ASEAN migration	251
Fig. 12.1	Traditional donor aid to Southeast Asian countries (commitments, US$ millions at constant prices)	297
Fig. 12.2	Percentage of traditional donor aid devoted to Southeast Asian countries (commitments, US$ millions at constant prices)	297
Fig. 12.3	Traditional donor aid to CLMV and emerging capitalist economies (commitments, US$ millions at constant prices)	298
Fig. 13.1	Total natural resources rents (percentage of GDP), 1981–2015: Brunei, Indonesia and Malaysia	324
Fig. 13.2	Total natural resources rents (percentage of GDP), 1981–2015, CLMV countries	324
Fig. 14.1	Expansion of selected boom crops in selected countries, 1990–2017	346
Fig. 14.2	Rurality, farm employment and agricultural GDP (percentages)	354

List of Tables

Table 2.1	Basic Southeast Asian country data	38
Table 2.2	General Southeast Asian developmental indicators	39
Table 2.3	Labour in Southeast Asia	40
Table 2.4	Basic economic data for Southeast Asian economies, 2016	40
Table 2.5	List of Southeast Asian dates of independence and colonial powers	41
Table 2.6	Southeast Asian FDI net inflows in perspective (current US$, millions), 1990–2016	58
Table 2.7	Southeast Asian stocks of foreign investment at home and abroad	59
Table 2.8	Indicators of ease of doing business, competitiveness and market interfacing in Southeast Asia	64
Table 2.9	Southeast Asian governance indicators	65
Table 2.10	Select indicators of intellectual property (IP) activity in Southeast Asia against select countries	69
Table 8.1	Bodies of the ASEAN Community	211
Table 8.2	ASEAN Community blueprints and action plans	212
Table 8.3	ASEAN Community-building projects, 2009–17	212
Table 8.4	AEC sectoral work-plans	214
Table 8.5	World Bank "ease of doing business" rankings	218
Table 9.1	Select gender inequality indicators	228
Table 10.1	Intra-ASEAN migrant stock by country of origin and destination	252
Table 12.1	Total net resource flows from OECD DAC countries to Southeast Asia (US$ millions at current prices)	299
Table 13.1	Production of selected mineral commodities in Southeast Asia, 2014	321

Table 13.2	Mineral fuels: Production and recoverable reserves in Southeast Asia	322
Table 14.1	Expansion of selected crops in CLMV economies (tonnes)	347
Table 15.1	Forest cover and deforestation in Southeast Asia, 1988–2017	370
Table 15.2	Coal-fired electrical power in Southeast Asia, China and India	377

PART I

Southeast Asia's Political Economy: Theory and Historical Evolution

CHAPTER 1

Theorising Political Economy in Southeast Asia

Shahar Hameiri and Lee Jones

Introduction

This chapter discusses contending theoretical approaches to political economy relevant to the study of Southeast Asia and outlines the approach taken in the rest of this book. Whatever their differences, all scholars investigating "political economy" share a belief that economics and politics cannot meaningfully be considered or studied as separate domains. Economic developments powerfully shape political ones, while politics has an enormous impact on markets. This distinguishes political economy from mainstream (neoclassical) economics, which tends to see politics as at best an unwanted intrusion into, or "distortion" of, the smooth operation of markets, and which seeks to understand economic life in an

S. Hameiri (✉)
School of Political Science and International Studies, The University of Queensland, St Lucia, QLD, Australia
e-mail: s.hameiri@uq.edu.au

L. Jones
School of Politics and International Relations, Queen Mary University of London, London, UK
e-mail: l.c.jones@qmul.ac.uk

© The Author(s) 2020
T. Carroll et al. (eds.), *The Political Economy of Southeast Asia*, Studies in the Political Economy of Public Policy,
https://doi.org/10.1007/978-3-030-28255-4_1

apolitical, technical manner. But it also distinguishes the field from much scholarship in politics and international relations (IR), which often ignores economic matters or treats them very simplistically. For example, many comparative politics scholars focus on the nature of party systems, manifestoes, political institutions, elections and regime types, neglecting the economy except as a domain of grievances and national policy-making, while some IR scholars still persist in viewing national economies as a property of states' national power.

For political economists, by contrast, the interconnections of politics and the economy are so obvious that they are perhaps too rarely specified. On the one hand, political conflict and decisions clearly shape how markets emerge and "mediate" their operation. Even if they do not seem to substantively "intervene" in economic matters, all states (and their agents, like international organisations) engage in or regulate the provision of the basic infrastructure—hard and soft—that allows economies to function. States issue currencies and typically regulate their value to some extent. They issue laws that create markets and regulate market exchange, covering everything from imports and exports to weights and measures. However unevenly, states enforce these rules and, crucially, defend private property, by maintaining laws, police, and judicial and penal systems. States are also often big taxers and spenders. Even in Southeast Asia, which is well behind the average for developed countries, tax revenues range from 12 to 25% of GDP, while government spending accounts for 15–30% (ADB 2018: 336–337). This withdrawal and expenditure of funds has a significant impact on economic activity. Moreover, Southeast Asian states have taken a major role in guiding and producing economic development, a fact grudgingly recognised even by organisations typically hostile to economic interference by the state, such as the World Bank (1993, 1997, 2002).

On the other hand, the reverse is also true: the economy strongly influences political conflict and decision-making. At the most basic level, states survive because they tax economic activity. If the economy falters, the state itself is in trouble. That could precipitate cuts in expenditure, which might provoke social unrest or shifts in perceptions of political legitimacy. To avoid this, in a very general sense political leaders must adopt policies that promote growth. Even setting aside the much-theorised relationship between the state and capital, and changes in the balance of forces over time, it should not be surprising that, under capitalism, states exhibit a systematic bias towards the interests of business. More broadly, economic development has a huge impact on society's basic composition. A highly industrialised economy is likely to have a large urban working class, for example, while a largely agrarian economy will have a substantial peasantry instead. An economy that has developed heavily through state leadership—as in Southeast Asia—will have a less independent capitalist class than one that developed primarily through private enterprise. A highly developed economy will have a bigger middle class, proportional to the overall size of the population, than a less developed one, and so on. This will naturally influence the kind of political actors that exist, and the strategies they can develop.

Beyond these uncontroversial truisms, however, political economists rarely agree on how to conceptualise the relationship between states and markets, and on how political outcomes shape economic outcomes and vice versa. This chapter surveys the three most important positions in debates on Southeast Asia: Weberian approaches; historical institutionalism; and the Murdoch School, also known as "social conflict theory". This survey cannot be exhaustive, and the groupings are to some extent analytical contrivances, but they do serve to provide a reasonable overview.

The major difference between these approaches concerns how they conceptualise institutions. Weberians have primarily focused on describing the institutions seen as necessary to promote economic development. Drawing implicitly or explicitly on Weber's conceptualisation of the state, they claim that institutions—like states or market regulators—can (and ideally should) be quite autonomous from society. Notably, for the purpose of this book, they have drawn attention to the emergence of "developmental states" in Asia, which, by virtue of their bureaucratic capacity and insulation from socio-political forces, have been able to make policies conducive to development, ostensibly underpinning the so-called "economic miracle" of the post-World War II era (e.g. Evans 1995; Johnson 1982). Historical institutionalism also broadly derives from a Weberian intellectual tradition. However, the apparent withering away of the institutions associated with the developmental state has led most historical institutionalists to shift attention away from evaluating state capacity and autonomy and towards explaining institutional dynamics and how they shape a range of political outcomes, including regime types and policymaking. By contrast, for the Murdoch School, which has always been concerned with explaining a wide range of political outcomes in Southeast Asia, institutions *reflect and entrench existing distributions of power among constellations of social forces—especially class forces—within particular historical junctures*. They evolve and operate not through autonomous political decision-making by enlightened and meritocratic bureaucracies, or specific historical legacies (paths), but through dynamic and evolving struggles for power and resources rooted in the structure of the wider national and global political economies.

This book takes the Murdoch School approach. As this chapter argues, there is little evidence that political or economic institutions are, or can be, autonomous from socio-political struggle, making Weberian approaches inadequate. Meanwhile, historical institutionalism's focus on institutional dynamics of stasis or change is hampered by an under-developed theorisation of the wider context shaping these dynamics. Especially problematic is their tendency to examine national institutional variegation in abstraction from global capitalist transformations, which shape class relations and conflict and hence institutional forms and outputs. A focus on social conflict—and in particular intra and inter-class conflict—is best placed to understand the forces that shape institutions and the ever-evolving relationship between politics and economics across multiple scales.

We have not devoted a section to neoliberal accounts of Southeast Asia's development, because we regard these as more ideological than theoretical. As Harvey (2005: 2) states, neoliberalism "proposes that human well-being can best be advanced by liberating individual entrepreneurial freedoms and skills within an institutional framework characterized by strong private property rights, free markets, and free trade". Neoliberals thus see unfettered markets as inherently superior to other forms of social and economic organisation, while politics is understood as "a set of external factors hampering the natural functioning of markets" (Rodan et al. 2006: 3). Hence, markets should be insulated from politics, to prevent their "distortion" by "vested interests" and "rent-seekers"—those able to extract disproportionate benefits for themselves due to their privileged position in the state or the economy.

This has led in practice to a rather conflicted view of the state and politics. Initially, neoliberals promoted the "rolling back" of state intervention to "free up" markets. They attacked the public delivery of services, like education, health and welfare, as inefficient, and derided the redistribution of wealth via progressive taxation as stifling entrepreneurial freedom and creativity. This approach shaped the international financial institutions' imposition of structural adjustment on many developing countries in the 1980s. However, this "roll-back neoliberalism" spurred widespread societal resistance and often failed to produce the buccaneering entrepreneurialism and liberated markets envisaged. Accordingly, from the late 1990s onwards, neoliberals have conceded that markets require institutional support to function properly. They have thus shifted from "rolling back" the state to specifying the sorts of institutions that should be crafted, intervening deeply within developing countries to support this (Carroll 2010, 2012; Rodan and Hughes 2014). Neoliberals thereby unconsciously adopted Weberian concepts of "state capacity" and "autonomy", while retaining a normative commitment to liberal markets. Unlike Weberians, however, they only value states' capacity to support liberal markets (see Carroll 2010; Hameiri 2009). Nonetheless, neoliberalism cannot be considered a unique *theoretical* approach for political economy analysis, notwithstanding its undoubted *ideological* force.

WEBERIAN APPROACHES AND THE DEVELOPMENTAL STATE DEBATE

Weberian approaches to Southeast Asia's political economy are part of an important stream of political science dating back to the German sociologist Max Weber (1864–1920). These approaches seek to explain development patterns by virtue of the variable capacity of states to generate and direct economic growth. In Southeast Asia, they have emerged as a subset of the wider, long-running debate over whether market liberalisation or state intervention explain capitalist East Asia's remarkable, though clearly uneven, post-war economic development.

The Weberian tradition is varied, but tends to converge around Weber's understanding of the modern state as a set of bureaucratic institutions standing above and dominating society, ultimately by virtue of its exclusive control of the legitimate means of violence (Anter 2014; Weber 1978: ch.11). Weber recognised that this "ideal type" did not always exist. However, Weberians typically postulate that if a state is effectively insulated from societal pressures and has sufficient bureaucratic capacity, this potentially allows it to play a major role in economic and social development. Indeed, some of the earliest thinking about political economy— from authors like Friedrich List and statesmen like Alexander Hamilton—argued that the state *must* do this in more "backwards" countries, were they to have any hope of "catching up" with more developed ones. Understandably, this interest was revived after decolonisation by authors including Gerschenkron, Kuznets and Myrdal, who saw the post-colonial state as a potential agent of economic modernisation. In his highly influential book, *Political Order in Changing Societies*, Samuel Huntington (1968) argued that the collapse of many post-colonial democracies into dictatorships was part of this process, whereby states would finally acquire the ability to control unruly societies and push forwards economic development.

Weberianism became prominent in political science and political economy from the mid-1980s and constituted the main opponent to ascending neoliberal positions—which emphasised the problematic relationship between the state and economy—and Marxist work which posited that the state was a reflection of particular constellations of class forces. A signal contribution was Evans et al.'s (1985) collection, *Bringing the State Back In*, which argued that earlier Marxist and pluralist approaches had wrongly depicted state policies as reflecting societal interest groups' preferences. Conversely, Skocpol (1985: 9) maintained:

> States conceived as organizations claiming control over territories and people may formulate and pursue goals that are not simply reflective of the demands or interests of social groups, classes, or society. This is what is usually meant by "state autonomy"... one may then explore the "capacities" of states to implement official goals, especially over the actual or potential opposition of powerful social groups or in the face of recalcitrant economic circumstances.

These key concepts of state "autonomy" and "capacity" became central to Weberian explanations of economic and political development, particularly late development in Asia. Put simply, where a state was "strong" (i.e. it enjoyed high "autonomy" from society and sufficient bureaucratic "capacity" to regulate it), political and bureaucratic elites could effect dramatic transformations (see Fukuyama 2013). Conversely, where a state was "weak" relative to its society, it would be overwhelmed by particularistic interests like rent-seeking elites or ethnic groups and therefore unable to prioritise the wider public good (Migdal 1988).

Applied to East Asia, this approach is most prominent in the literature on the "developmental state" (e.g. Amsden 1989; Johnson 1982; Wade 1990). Weberians explained the region's rapid economic growth by virtue of the emergence of "strong" states, insulated from particularistic interests and characterised by "centralised economic planning; elite technocracies; strong state involvement in seeding capital formation; and the use of industrial policy to allocate state credit and protection, and nurture fledgling industries" (Carroll and Jarvis 2017: 3). Skilled technocrats' institutional insulation from special interests ostensibly allowed them to redirect resources from rent-seeking and low value-added activities, like agriculture, towards manufacturing, industrial upgrading, and more recently services and even "green growth", thus maintaining national competitiveness (see Amsden 2001; Thurbon 2016). Conversely, the lagging behind of regions like sub-Saharan Africa was explained as a function of "weak" states lacking such institutional arrangements, instead producing neopatrimonial governance (e.g. Bratton and de Walle 1994). For Weberians, the strong Asian state has survived even the onset of globalisation. Against widespread arguments that globalisation weakened states, forcing them to adopt neoliberal policies, authors like Linda Weiss (1998) argue that states' "capacities" may allow them to steer industrial and institutional transformations so as to benefit from burgeoning trade and investment, while resisting harmful flows.

While Weberian approaches have been very powerful, especially in pushing back against neoliberal dogma throughout the 1980s and 1990s, they nonetheless have five serious drawbacks. First, it is never entirely clear where states' "capacities" come from. The implication is that they simply inhere in particular institutional arrangements, e.g. an economic planning unit that does not have to consult elected politicians or industrial interests, or a highly efficient tax-collection bureaucracy. However, if these "capacities" truly emerged merely from a particular institutional set-up, then it would be far easier to replicate them across states than has proven to be the case (see Routley 2014). In reality, efforts to "build" states encounter enormous socio-political contestation, which in practice determines state "capacity" (Hameiri 2009). For example, the routinisation of tax-collecting is a highly fraught process, with ruling elites struggling to extract resources from subjects (Martin et al. 2009). Today, powerful economic interests are using the threat or practice of offshore relocation to compel governments to reduce tax rates or weaken enforcement, even—indeed, especially—in the world's "strongest" states, shunting the tax burden onto poorer social groups (Palan et al. 2010). The Weberian "fetishism" of institutional arrangements incorrectly "decontextualise[s]" the state from the "underlying social relations of class and the distribution of power, production, and wealth" on which its particular institutional arrangements are always based (Carroll and Jarvis 2017: 8; Jayasuriya 2005).

Second, it is not clear how states can ever be truly "autonomous" from their societies. As early critics of the 1980s Weberian revival pointed out, efforts to empirically identify the exact demarcation between a state and its society always fail (Cammack 1989: 267–269; Jessop 1990: 287). On close inspection, the boundaries actually appear "elusive, porous, and mobile", with state officials enjoying close political, economic, personal or other relations with particular social groups (Mitchell 1991: 77). Indeed, it is difficult to see how a truly "autonomous" state could function, lacking any organic link to society. The Weberian scholar Peter Evans (1995) recognised this, noting that the bureaucrats of Asia's "developmental states" actually depended for their success on close working relationships with major industrial interests. He attempted to salvage Weberianism by calling this "embedded autonomy", but this is clearly a contradiction in terms.

Third, the "developmental state" model is arguably a poor empirical fit for Southeast Asia. It was designed predominantly to explain Northeast Asia's "tiger economies" (Japan, South Korea and Taiwan), and only latterly extended to Southeast Asia. However, it was immediately clear that only Singapore seems in any way to exhibit the venerated attributes of state "autonomy" and "capacity". Other Southeast Asian states are much more clearly in hock to special interest groups, leading to doubt as to whether they qualify (even the Singaporean case is dubious—see below) (Jomo 1997; Stubbs 2009). Since several of these states have, nonetheless, achieved remarkable growth rates, this undermines Weberians' core explanatory mechanisms (and, ironically, contemporary neoliberal positions, which also emphasise institutional integrity as necessary for economic development). Others have even argued that corruption has been beneficial for Southeast Asian development, completely inverting the Weberian model (e.g. Wedeman 2001).

Fourth, Weberian reliance on "ideal types" leads to an unproductive focus on charting deviation from idealised *models*. For example, since Malaysia does not conform entirely to the "developmental state" model, it is described as a "semi-developmental state" (Rhodes and Higgott 2000). This problem also occurs in the more recent institutionalist literature, discussed in the next section. Measuring deviation from some idealised standard, while tempting for those searching for developmental solutions, is a rather fruitless academic activity, producing endless typologies but very little in the way of explanation of why these regime forms exist and how they operate in practice.

Finally, Weberians' "institutional fundamentalism" (Carroll and Jarvis 2017: 8) leaves them increasingly unable to explain, or even adequately describe, the transforming nature of East Asia's developmental states. Particularly since the 1997 Asian financial crisis (AFC), there has been growing recognition that the "developmental state" form no longer describes many regional countries (Stubbs 2009). For example, many states have liberalised their financial sectors, moving away from state-directed credit allocation to market-based mechanisms (Rethel 2010). The corporations of Japan, South Korea and Taiwan, subjected to increasing competition under globalisation, are also less interested in maintaining the job-for-life workforce that was part of their earlier growth models (Kalleberg and Hewison 2013). Reflecting their reliance on "ideal types", Weberians have been torn between asserting the continuation of the "developmental state", or arguing that it has been replaced by a "neoliberal state" (see Hayashi 2010; Thurbon 2016; Wade 2018). This debate over whether "states" or "markets" drive Asian development today rests on a problematic distinction between the two, and does little to explain changing state–economy relations (Carroll and Jarvis 2017). In any case, the apparent withering away of the developmental state in Asia generally, and Southeast Asia specifically, has decreased scholarly interest in evaluating "state capacity" and "autonomy", and led to a partial convergence of the Weberian literature with the wider "new institutionalism" in political science, which is explicitly concerned with explaining institutional change.

Historical Institutionalism

The "new institutionalism" is a very large, diverse body of scholarship concerned with understanding how actors' behaviours are "shaped and conditioned by the institutional contexts in which they operate" (Bell 2002: 363). Unlike "old institutionalists", these scholars define institutions very broadly, as "any form of constraint that human beings devise to shape action" (North 1990: 4), including rules, laws, norms, routines, or conventions. However, they hark from different institutionalist traditions and, thus, disagree on key propositions, such as how to "construe the relationship between institutions and behaviour and how to explain the process whereby institutions originate or change" (Hall and Taylor 1996: 937). Hall and Taylor (1996) identify three distinct "schools of thought": rational-choice institutionalism, sociological institutionalism, and historical institutionalism (HI), with "discursive institutionalism" subsequently added to this list (Schmidt 2008). We focus on HI as the school most relevant for studies of Southeast Asia.

There are two basic HI approaches. The first sees institutions as "path-dependent"—relatively fixed structures, shaped by historical legacies, which strongly constrain agency. From this perspective, political and economic outcomes result from historically inherited institutional arrangements. Significant institutional change happens rarely, during "critical junctures", where some external "shock" causes disruption, allowing agents to reconfigure institutions (Capoccia and Kelemen 2007). When these institutions bed down, they go back to locking in certain patterned outcomes. Hence, historical change is seen as a "punctuated equilibrium" (Capoccia 2015: 148).

In political economy, this approach has been used to explain particular patterns of economic governance. In practice, HI analysis has often been quite Weberian; indeed, Evans et al.'s (1985) *Bringing the State Back In* is often considered an early HI publication (Hall and Taylor 1996: 938). The predominant application of HI in political economy, however, is the vast "Varieties of Capitalism" literature, which seeks to explain different patterns of development with reference to the institutionalised relationships between firms, governments and other actors. Hall and Soskice (2001), who launched this research agenda, distinguish between liberal market economies (LMEs) and coordinated market economies (CMEs). In LMEs, firms' relations with other actors, like governments, are mediated by markets, while in CMEs they are organised through non-market mechanisms, especially governmental institutions. Because neither ideal-type accurately describes national economies in Asia, studies of "Asian varieties of capitalism" have tended to add on more typologies, such as "hierarchical market economy" (Moore 2018: 12; see also Walter and Zhang 2012). In one extreme case, Andriesse (2015: 76) develops a unique typology for practically every Southeast Asian country. Vietnam is thus described as "post-state capitalism", Laos as "frontier capitalism", Singapore as "open-led state capitalism", Indonesia as "oligarchic capitalism", the Philippines as "inequality-trapped capitalism" and so on.

In Southeast Asia, this HI variant has been more commonly deployed to analyse political regime dynamics, particularly the longevity of authoritarianism. Optimism around the end of the Cold War that the "third wave" of democratisation would triumph in Southeast Asia has subsequently given way to the sober realisation that many regimes were not transitioning towards democracy (Carothers 2002). Institutionalists have tried to explain this by highlighting the existence of "hybrid regimes" combining democratic and authoritarian elements. The result has again been endless typologising, based on qualifying adjectives: "partial democracies" (Robinson 2003), "defective democracies" (Merkel and Croissant 2004), "deviant democracies" (Seeberg 2014), "competitive authoritarianism" (Levitsky and Way 2010), "semi-authoritarianism" (Ottaway 2003), and many more. Similarly, institutionalists have examined the use of rigged elections to perpetuate "electoral authoritarianism" (e.g. Morgenbesser 2016).

This approach has several interlinked weaknesses. First, owing to its Weberian roots it is predominantly descriptive and evaluative, not explanatory. Categorising a country as this or that kind of economy or regime, or measuring how far it departs from some idealised model, does not explain *why* particular institutional forms exist—it merely labels and describes them (Rodan 2018: 18; also Jayasuriya and Rodan 2007; Rodan and Jayasuriya 2012). Secondly, HI tends to give institutions primary causal status, while institutions themselves are only weakly explained as a legacy of historical development. This neglects the role of human agents in contesting and reshaping institutions. For example, the "electoral authoritarianism" literature clearly suggests that authoritarian regimes can *manipulate* institutions to perpetuate themselves (Pepinsky 2014). Thus, far from institutions determining the form of regime, it is actually forces within a regime that determine how institutions work in practice. Similarly, when HI political economists try to explain why Southeast Asian states diverge from the "developmental state" model, they ultimately point to the underlying political coalitions underpinning those regimes (e.g. Haggard 2004). For example, Doner et al. (2005) explain why developmental states emerged in Korea, Taiwan and Singapore, but not elsewhere in Southeast Asia, by highlighting elites' need to generate "side payments" for restive populations during the Cold War.

Third, this neglect of agency makes it hard for HI to explain change. As Thelen and Steinmo (1992: 15) note, institutions apparently explain everything except when, suddenly, in "critical junctures", they explain nothing, with attention switching entirely to agents and outcomes apparently entirely up for grabs. In reality, some "critical junctures" lead to radical change, others to continuity (Legro 2000: 419). For example, HI struggles to explain why the 1970s stagflation crisis in Western economies fundamentally transformed the institutions governing global capitalism (see Carroll, this volume), but the 2008 global financial crisis (GFC) did not. This reflects HI's limited engagement with the agential struggles shaping institutional developments, and its tendency to treat institutions as "external to—even if influenced by—broader power structures" (Jayasuriya and Rodan 2007: 775).

Finally, this variant of HI is restricted by its "methodological nationalism"—the tendency to take "national discourses, agendas, loyalties, and histories for granted without problematising them, or making them an object of an analysis in its own right" (Wimmer and Glick Schiller 2002: 304). It is simply assumed that national institutions follow distinctive pathways that produce national variation, which scholars then categorise and compare. This ignores, however, "evidence of systemic interdependence and contingent convergence" across countries, stemming from the structures of the capitalist system as a global whole (Peck and Theodore 2007: 761). Although local institutional variegation exists, it is grounded in wider capitalist structures and class relations, which also shape agents' relative power to effect change.

Attempts to remedy some of these problems are found in a second, "incrementalist" variant of HI, though this has been scantly applied in Southeast Asia. Rather than prioritising institutions, these scholars see agents and institutions as constantly shaping one another (Bell and Feng 2013). Accordingly, change can be small-scale and "incremental" over time, rather than large-scale and only during "critical junctures" (Mahoney and Thelen 2009). Institutions are still seen to exert considerable constraint, but agents are viewed as "strategic actors" that may exploit opportunities offered by "shifting contextual conditions" to change institutions in desired ways (Thelen and Steinmo 1992: 17). This approach usefully moves HI towards considering how institutions are politically produced. However, the wider "context" shaping this process is vaguely specified and "treated in an *ad hoc* way" (Bell and Feng 2014: 198). This problem, again, relates to HI's failure to locate particular institutional forms and agents' power within the wider structural context of capitalism (Peck and Theodore 2007: 761). The Murdoch School, on the other hand, approaches institutions very differently.

The Murdoch School

The "Murdoch School" is a label applied to a body of work originating with scholars initially based in the Asia Research Centre at Murdoch University in Perth, Western Australia. Whereas Weberian and institutionalist accounts have often neglected Southeast Asia, the Murdoch School has been primarily focused upon, and made a major impact on, the study of Southeast Asian politics, and the wider study of political economy, comparative politics, development and, most recently, international relations.

Foundational Assumptions

The Murdoch School is grounded in a humanist, flexible tradition of Marxist analysis traceable to the Italian theorist Antonio Gramsci (1891–1937) and subsequently developed by Nicos Poulantzas (1978) and Bob Jessop (1990, 2008), though early works also drew on non-Marxist scholars like Barrington Moore (1966), Alexander Gerschenkron (1962) and Karl Polanyi (1957 [1944]). At the heart of this approach is the insistence that political outcomes are primarily determined by struggles between socio-political forces, especially social classes and class fractions, but also ethnic, religious, gendered and state-based groupings. Such groups have different social, economic and political positions, resources and agendas, and they struggle against one another to obtain power and control over resources, forming coalitions to advance and defend their interests.

In this tradition, institutions are never neutral. Because they distribute power and resources, they are always fought over—sometimes violently—by social groups seeking to entrench their preferences as policy, to empower themselves and/or their allies, and to direct resources towards favoured entities. Institutions—most importantly, state institutions—are therefore seen as a contingent outcome of political struggle, or what Jessop (2008: 133), following Poulantzas, calls a "condensation of the balance of forces". Thus, institutional forms, such as political regimes or economic regulations, emerge from social conflict.

However, the "balance of forces" in a given society is rarely static, especially under capitalism. The constant revolutionising of the means of the production, the pressure to extract greater surplus value from labour, the onset of capitalist contradictions, the ceaseless expansion of commodity relations into new geographies and social domains, tend to generate rapid and significant social transformations, creating new classes and class fractions, "winners" and "losers", which may challenge existing institutional arrangements and hegemonic ideologies. Such changes in the "balance of forces" may generate changes in the form and content of institutions and policies, but this depends on the resources, strategies and struggles of the forces at work. Those benefiting from existing arrangements will resist change and may be able to limit reform, or subsequently stymie the operation of new institutions. In some cases, dominant elites may be able to lead institutional transformation without losing power to subordinate forces—what Gramsci called "passive revolution". By the same token, if institutions are reformed but the underlying "balance of forces" remains unchanged, we would expect reform outcomes to be limited, because dominant social forces are likely to ignore, evade, or undermine the reformed institutions.

Importantly, these struggles are always located within evolving, global social relationships. Even the most localised contest is ultimately nested within a wider set of power relations that now span the globe. As Marx and Engels (1848: 16) famously observed, 153 years before China joined the World Trade Organisation, capitalist development has spread investment, production and trade networks "over the entire surface of the globe… batter[ing] down all Chinese walls". In today's era of "globalisation", the world market is even more of a reality. Excepting a few isolated tribes, it leaves no community untouched. Capitalist development has fundamentally reshaped even apparently pre-capitalist social classes. Landlords, backed by state allies, enclose smallholders' farms into large plantations to grow cash crops for export, transforming themselves into export-oriented agrarian capitalists and former peasant farmers into agricultural workers, whose labour is suddenly priced globally against their peers. Other peasants move to cities, to work in factories supplying transnational production chains, or in the burgeoning informal services sector and insecure "gig" economy. Large middle classes have emerged across the developing world, including Southeast Asia, some of them servicing multinational enterprises. Capitalism's global development thus continually reshapes individual societies—the groups of which they are composed and their relations—and how societies relate to one another. Equally, the endless cycles of accumulation and crisis inherent to capitalist development create dislocations and opportunities to which domestic social groups and state managers must respond. It is impossible to pursue export-led growth, for example, without foreign investment to begin production, and effective demand in foreign countries to absorb what is produced. And as formerly national economies seek to attract foreign investment for export-led industrialisation, or integrate into transnational value chains, the range of choices available to policy-makers and social groups changes, providing new opportunities for some while severely circumscribing options for others. For the Murdoch School, then, the crucial "context"—only vaguely specified by institutionalists—is the global set of class relations attending capitalism, and the manner in which these relate to locally variegated patterns of investment, production and consumption, as well as geopolitical contestation.

Thus, scales such as "local", "national" or "global" should not be approached as discrete "levels of analysis", but as parts of a single "social whole" (Brenner et al. 2003: 16). In the early post-war decades, it was easy to lose sight of this fact, because local and global institutional arrangements were all focused on the consolidation of *national* states, societies, and economies. In the West, this involved "corporatist" compacts between business, labour and state managers, with Keynesian interventions used to reduce uneven development and share national wealth. In post-colonial countries, state managers focused on "nation-building", often adopting import-substituting industrialisation strategies to build up their own national economies. However, the 1970s' crises of capitalism led to intense social conflict and the breakdown of these arrangements. The victors of these conflicts—emblematised by Thatcher and Reagan—dismantled national protections, unleashing businesses to globalise. Post-colonial state managers increasingly adopted strategies to attract transnational enterprises and capital (see Carroll, this volume). The national scale thereby lost its taken-for-granted primacy, with power increasingly shifting to other scales, like city-regions, transnational production networks and regional economic groupings (Jessop 2009).

Accordingly, it is important to situate the analysis of any particular political economy development within its wider, global context. While earlier Murdoch School work focused on the development of particular national economies, societies and states, it is now clear that social relations are no longer contained within national boundaries, making such "methodological nationalism" inappropriate. This is a key motivation for our shift, in this book, from a country-based analysis to one based on issues and sectors. National states do remain crucial points where struggles for power and resources occur; they are not mere "transmission belts" for neoliberalism (see Bieler and Morton 2018: 119). Nonetheless, the transnationalisation of economic flows has also generated pressures to reconfigure the state, to attract and manage these flows. Accordingly, more recent Murdoch School scholarship has focused on "state transformation" as a key dynamic (e.g. Hameiri and Jones 2015), with social forces increasingly contesting the reassignment of authority to institutions beyond the national scale (see Al-Fadhat, and Jones and Hameiri, both this volume).

To illustrate how the Murdoch School framework is applied in practice, consider a simple, hypothetical example of government procurement rules. Such rules determine who will receive potentially lucrative state contracts, on what terms, and by what process. Given the resources at stake, the institutional arrangements are likely to be of considerable interest to businesses that could receive contracts, the political and bureaucratic elites who might selectively allocate them, and the taxpayers, banks, or aid donors who ultimately finance them. From a Murdoch School perspective, these contending interests will naturally seek to influence the development of procurement rules and how they are applied in practice. What ultimately emerges depends on the forces at work: their interests, resources, ideologies and strategies. And this will partly depend on the global power relations in which they are nested. For example, a highly aid-dependent state may be strongly pressured by donors to develop neoliberal policy templates favouring the private sector or even to open up bidding to foreign businesses, which are also likely to push strongly for such measures. Alternatively, international rankings and benchmarking of pro-market governance may create competitive pressures to conform, with deviation penalised by increased borrowing costs and diminished investment. Thus, "international" actors, resources and ideologies can be directly involved in apparently "local" struggles. Conversely, a regime that is strongly backed by overseas patrons, for ideological or geopolitical reasons, may be relatively insulated from any such pressures, allowing elites to craft institutions that funnel contracts to their domestic clients in exchange for political support. Cambodian leader Hun Sen's increasingly cosy relationship with China, involving military aid, loans and infrastructure investment, is emblematic here.

Understanding Institutions

From this perspective, crafting developmental institutions involves a process of socio-political contestation, whose outcomes will shape the form and operation of institutions. Given the economic and political resources at stake, it will take tremendous political struggle to create institutional arrangements approximating "Weberian" ideal types, where bureaucrats sit in splendid isolation, rationally allocating resources without any political "interference". Nor, contra institutionalism, is this simply a question of excluding "spoilers" through clever "institutional design". It is a question of power, strategy and struggle. If neoliberal technocrats were extraordinarily powerful, they *might* be able to craft procurement rules and processes that prioritise efficiency and value-for-money. However, where (local or international) businesses and political interests can influence the process, they may shape the rules so as to privilege particular interests, and/or influence decision-making institutions, formally or informally. This could take the form of measures explicitly designed to benefit particular social groups, such as ethnic quotas, or apparently innocuous requirements, such as levels of capitalisation, that funnel contracts towards a small number of dominant companies. Crucially, the Murdoch School views such outcomes as a normal, routine part of politics, not an aberrant deviation from an "ideal type". Murdoch Scholars have therefore sought to explain institutional forms and their operation *in their own terms*—as a product of socio-political struggle—rather than simply lamenting their "inefficiency" or trying to explain or remedy the gap between reality and an idealised model.

This perspective leads to a very different understanding of "developmental states" than that proposed by Weberians. For Murdoch Scholars, the state simply cannot be "autonomous" or "insulated" from society; whatever its appearance, it will always be shaped by socio-political conflict. Accordingly, it is always imperative to trace the institutional form of state and market arrangements to the interests and strategies of specific social forces, some of which lie beyond the nation-state. These institutions may be relatively autonomous from certain societal groups, but they will be heavily "penetrated" by, or skewed towards the interests of, others. Jessop (2008) calls this "strategic selectivity": institutions are always more open to, or biased towards, certain forces and agendas than others. From this perspective, Southeast Asia's "developmental states" cannot simply be understood as the invention of clever bureaucrats. Rather, they emerged from the often-violent social conflict that marked the post-independence decades. After the ravages of colonialism and World War II, radicalism and communism had widespread appeal across the region, terrorising the slender strata of elites that inherited Asia's post-colonial states. Their use of state institutions to promote economic "growth with equity" was a clear attempt to manage this unrest and avoid social revolution (Felker 2009). As noted above, some of the more critical institutionalists accept this point (e.g. Doner et al. 2005; Slater 2010), but the Murdoch School always gives such conflicts analytical primacy.

Crucially, moreover, these "local" struggles occurred within a global set of power relations, which strongly shaped their course. Economic development did not emerge simply because some inventive technocrats, shielded from politics by well-crafted institutions, could select "correct policies" that other countries might copy to achieve the same result. It occurred—indeed, it could *only* have occurred—within a highly specific set of global dynamics, specifically the Cold War and the onset of what we now call "globalisation" (see Carroll, this volume). In the early post-colonial period, like the rest of the Global South, Southeast Asian governments largely pursued import-substituting industrialisation (ISI) strategies, with rather modest results. However, they were tremendously boosted by the rapid emergence of "hot" Cold War conflicts—first in Korea, then Indochina—which spurred demand for commodities like tin, oil and rubber, plus agricultural produce (Stubbs 2005). The foreign exchange earned, coupled with extensive Western economic and military aid, allowed resources to be directed into domestic development projects. This laid the foundation for a gradual shift towards export-oriented development. However, for most regional states this could only occur fully following further global developments. First, the 1970s crisis of Western capitalism depressed Western demand, leading to a collapse in commodity prices, rendering existing development strategies defunct. Second, a longer-term consequence of this crisis—coupled with important techno-logistical developments—was the outsourcing of production from existing industrial centres to developing countries, especially in Asia, to benefit from lower wages and thus higher profitability. In Southeast Asia, this trend was reinforced by the appreciation of the yen against the dollar following the 1985 Plaza Accord. This made Japanese exports more expensive, prompting Japanese industrialists to offshore production to developing Asia, where wages were lower, to reduce costs. This played a major role in Southeast Asia's industrialisation (Stubbs 2005). Thus, it was only this new international division of labour that allowed Southeast Asian elites to adopt export-oriented development strategies, by inserting parts of their economies into globalising chains of investment, production and trade (Higgott and Robison 1985).

We can illustrate this alternative interpretation of the "developmental state" by considering the example of Singapore. Weberians and institutionalists depict Singapore as an archetypal developmental state, run by a highly autonomous, "quasi-authoritarian", technocratic and "meritocratic" political elite. Members of this elite happily take full credit for the city-state's transformation from "third world to first", parading around the globe to teach other countries how to copy them. In fact, as Rodan's (1989) pioneering study showed, the Singaporean state emerged from a highly peculiar, non-replicable set of social conflicts, and is not as autonomous as it superficially appears. In the 1960s, the People's Action Party (PAP) fought and destroyed the political left, suppressing and regulating independent political activity thereafter. However, the PAP leadership also consciously spurned the local, ethnic-Chinese bourgeoisie, suspecting their loyalty and doubting their capacity to industrialise Singapore. Instead, the PAP courted international capital, while establishing Government-Linked Companies (GLCs) as dominant business entities. They deliberately created widespread state dependency among ordinary citizens, particularly in housing and employment, and among many local businesses, which came to rely on government contracts and GLC activity. This constellation of forces, which occurred within a unique period of the global political economy, created considerable leeway for the PAP, generating the appearance of insulation and autonomy.

However, the PAP's strategy actually makes the regime heavily dependent on international and government-linked capital. Local growth depends critically on global market conditions, requiring recurring structural adjustments to maintain Singapore's "international competitiveness" (i.e. attractiveness to footloose international capital), usually at the cost of worker welfare. Hence, for example, economic downturns consistently result in wage suppression, tax cuts and investment incentives, rather than Keynesian pump-priming. For instance, in the late 1980s, as rising wages made Singapore less attractive for low-value-added manufacturing, the PAP adopted measures to close down inefficient industries and encourage higher-value-added production and the development of a services sector. This caused significant social dislocation, prompting working class voters to desert the PAP, though state control of trade unions restricted their capacity to express discontent. Conversely, the regime's dependence on GLCs and foreign capital gives rise to corporatist arrangements whereby businesses are incorporated directly into decision-making. For instance, Singapore's National Wages Council includes representatives of the US, German and Japanese chambers of commerce, and is designed to subordinate trade unions' wage demands to the requirements of long-term economic growth (Lim 2014). Similarly, the demand of transnational businesses for skilled labour produces a remarkably open immigration regime, such that a third of Singapore's workforce is foreign-born. GLCs' investment requirements, meanwhile, have resulted in the increasingly controversial sequestering of Singaporeans' pension funds. This systematic bias towards the interests of large-scale and foreign capital has generated a growing political backlash around welfare, wages and immigration, resulting in significant gains for opposition parties in the 2011 elections. Again, far from remaining "autonomous", the PAP has been compelled to respond to this upsurge in socio-political conflict, though the concessions it can make are constrained by the requirements of international capital, and the ideological tropes that the PAP uses to legitimise its domination: "meritocracy" and self-reliance (Rodan 2016).

Beyond Singapore, Southeast Asian regimes are far more clearly beholden to particularistic coalitions. For example, Indonesia's Suharto regime (1967–1998) came to power amidst bloody pogroms that destroyed the Indonesian Communist Party, pledging to restore market order after years of leftist turmoil. Suharto promoted his so-called "Berkeley boys"—Western-trained technocrats—to key policy-making institutions. However, this liberal-technocratic faction was largely outclassed by more dominant forces supporting Suharto, particularly military, political and bureaucratic elites and their business allies. State development policy was heavily skewed towards feeding the patronage networks that sustained the regime, creating massive networks of corruption, collusion and nepotism and a narrow oligarchy centred on Suharto's family and his predominantly ethnic-Chinese "cronies" (Robison 1986). Again, global dynamics were important to this consolidation of power. As an oil exporter, Indonesia benefited from surging oil prices in the 1970s, providing a bountiful patronage resource, and later the emerging new international division of labour allowed the regime to develop export-oriented industries. Meanwhile, the West strongly backed Suharto as an anti-communist bulwark, supplying extensive military aid and US$50bn in development assistance with negligible pressure for economic or political liberalisation (INFID 2007).

This focus on the historically evolving nature of social forces, coalitions and conflict also allows the Murdoch School to provide more compelling analysis of political developments than historical institutionalist accounts. One major research objective has been to explain the very limited development of liberal rights and democratic institutions despite rapid growth, urbanisation and the emergence of sizeable middle classes. Rather than merely labelling regimes as "hybrids", the Murdoch School explains why they exist, emphasising the historical development of Southeast Asia's social forces and coalitional dynamics.

Generally speaking, colonial rule and Cold War-era authoritarian developmentalism produced stark imbalances of social and political power across the region. The political left and even mainstream liberals were crushed, while peasant and workers' organisations were either destroyed or absorbed into the state and neutralised politically. Conversely, the main support bases of authoritarian regimes—the urban middle and capitalist classes, military, bureaucratic and political elites—were nurtured and supported through patronage and clientelism. Business elites who initially depended on political patronage—often called "crony capitalists"—eventually acquired so much wealth and influence that the power balance shifted, with businessmen being courted by politico-bureaucratic elites or even entering politics themselves, displacing their former patrons. State-led development has thus often produced "oligarchs": individuals or—often—families behind major conglomerates whose vastly disproportionate wealth empowers them to secure their interests under any regime (Winters 2011). As the editors of the third edition of this volume remarked, "one of the defining features of Southeast Asia… is the highly instrumentalist nature of capitalist control of state power" (Rodan et al. 2006: 25). Since authoritarian state power has served them exceedingly well, it is unsurprising that—contrary to liberal expectations and unlike their historical peers in democratising Europe—the region's capitalist and middle classes are typically bulwarks of authoritarianism rather than supporters of liberalisation (Bellin 2000). Indeed, with its main carriers crushed during the Cold War and yet to recover, socialism and liberalism have an exceedingly tenuous basis in Southeast Asia. Populist and moralistic (including religious) ideology is far more dominant, thanks to the survival of groups for whom these ideas are useful and attractive, such as oligarchic elites and the urban middle classes (Rodan 2018; Rodan and Hughes 2014). Hence, rather than institutions being used to explain political outcomes, institutions are instead explained as an artefact of historically evolving sociopolitical conflict.

This approach moves well beyond institutionalist accounts that frequently exaggerate the causal power of institutions and institutional change. As noted earlier, mainstream HI expects "critical junctures", where institutions break down, to generate substantial changes in politico-economic outcomes. Arguably the most dramatic "critical juncture" Southeast Asia has faced is the AFC. The crisis involved widespread economic collapse, leading to the fall of governments in Thailand and Indonesia and serious challenges to the Malaysian regime. Indonesia, in particular, experienced radical institutional change. In exchange for a bailout from the International Monetary Fund (IMF), the Suharto regime was forced to implement structural adjustment measures that some believed would end "crony capitalism". Thanks in part to this, Suharto was forced to resign, and his authoritarian, highly centralised regime was replaced by a newly democratic, highly decentralised institutional order. This led institutionalist commentators to proclaim that Southeast Asia's "democratic moment" had finally arrived (e.g. Acharya 1999). This was even mirrored within regional institutions, as emergent civil society networks were incorporated into the Association of Southeast Asian Nations (ASEAN), leading some to identify a "radical shift from the regional norms constituted in the ASEAN way" of regionalism, which traditionally emphasised authoritarian values (Caballero-Anthony 2005: 272).

Yet, two decades later, there is a striking continuity in the gross inequalities of wealth and power that characterise Southeast Asia's political economies, and even in the players populating the various stages. In Indonesia, for example, many of the individuals who dominated economic or political life under Suharto still haunt the polity. Suharto's son-in-law, General Prabowo Subianto, who was widely accused of horrific human rights abuses under the old regime, came a close second in the 2014 presidential election. The victor, Joko Widodo, rules at the head of a coalition of traditional politico-business elites, fronted by Megawati Sukarnoputri, daughter of Suharto's predecessor, and Vice-President Jusuf Kalla, one of Indonesia's leading businessmen, who made his fortune under Suharto. Other presidential candidates included Suharto's army chief, General Wiranto (also accused of serious human rights abuses, and now serving in Widodo's government), and Suharto crony Aburizal Bakrie, whose company is responsible for massive environmental devastation. Meanwhile, decentralisation has allowed a motley array of local politico-business elites to capture sub-national state power, some drawn from the lower tiers of the Suharto regime, others mobilising particularistic identities to win elections and funnel public resources to themselves and their allies (Hadiz 2010). Although civil and political freedoms have improved, corruption remains widespread, political parties offer substantially identical platforms framed in populist and nationalist rhetoric, and ordinary Indonesians rightly complain that they have little influence over policy-making (Aspinall and Berenschot 2019). Moreover, the Indonesian economy remains dominated by a small number of massive conglomerates established under Suharto's patronage regime (Hadiz and Robison 2013). In a sign of continued capitulation to the super-rich, the Widodo government issued a tax amnesty in 2017, offering discount rates of 90–98% for wealthy tax-dodgers including Suharto's son, Tommy, and Suharto's favourite crony capitalist, Liem Sioe Liong (Arshad 2017).

The Murdoch School explains such outcomes with reference to the underlying structure of social power relations and ongoing struggles over power and resources, which can remain remarkably consistent even amidst apparently dramatic institutional change. On the one hand, Indonesia's capitalist development has generated new social groups and created new contradictions, leading to the emergence of new forms of opposition to established power-holders, such as civil society organisations and Islamist groupings critical of corruption and cronyism. When the AFC shook the Suharto regime, these groups mobilised to push for change. Crucially, the oligarchy also split, with some key politico-business elites concluding that Suharto could no longer secure their material interests. However, as Robison and Hadiz (2004) show, these oligarchs were far better placed to shape and dominate the *reformasi* (reform) process, using their wealth and access to state power to mitigate the AFC's impact on their business empires and reorganise themselves into political parties to dominate the new institutional order. Although liberal reformers struggled for more thoroughgoing change, their relative weakness after decades of repression meant that they lacked a solid social base and the organisational capacity to successfully exploit the AFC. Similarly, Walter (2008) shows that extensive market reforms produced mostly "mock compliance" with international banking rules, as powerful business elites used their connections with political, bureaucratic and judicial figures to evade tougher regulation, without directly confronting the IMF. A similar focus on enduring structural power relations has helped to explain the limits of transitions from state "socialism" to capitalism, and from military or one-party dictatorships to ostensible multi-party democracies, in states like Cambodia and Myanmar (Hughes 2003; Jones 2014; also see Hughes, this volume). Thus, unlike institutionalists who can only descriptively categorise various types of "hybrid regime", Murdoch Scholars explain *why* these regimes exist, and whose interests they serve. They are revealed not as "deficient" with respect to some idealised model, but as highly functional for dominant interests—which explains their survival.

This approach can also explain the often-disappointing outcomes of international attempts to promote domestic or regional institutional change in Southeast Asia. Murdoch scholars have, for example, explained the frequent failure of Western donor projects to produce market-friendly institutions and "good governance" with reference to socio-political contestation in target states, which produces outcomes diverging from interveners' intentions (Carroll 2010; Hughes 2009; Hutchison et al. 2014). The same applies to international state-building interventions in jurisdictions like Cambodia, Timor-Leste and Indonesia's Aceh, where attempts to transpose liberal institutions have been strongly contested and warped by local interests (Hameiri et al. 2017; Jones 2010). Even where intervention is highly coercive, such as economic sanctions against Myanmar, local struggles for power and resources—not the degree or type of economic pain inflicted—ultimately determine the outcome (Jones 2015). At the regional level, the supposed liberalisation of the "ASEAN way" has likewise been shown to be exaggerated. There are certainly departures from traditional ASEAN norms like non-interference, but only when it serves the interests of dominant socio-political forces (Jones 2012). These same forces have also shaped the emergence of new, superficially liberal institutions, like the ASEAN Civil Society Conference and the Intergovernmental Human Rights Commission, "regulating" them to exclude serious contention and defend existing power relations (Gerard 2014).

As well as accounting for substantial continuity amidst apparently dramatic institutional change, the Murdoch School also attends to the more transformative dynamics of capitalist development in the region. Although the AFC did not produce the revolutionary change that some had hoped for, it nonetheless forced dominant social forces to shift their strategies to repair domestic support, reassure international capital that the region remained a stable and competitive place to invest, and shore up relations with important foreign powers (Jones 2012: 107–127). Most Southeast Asian governments adopted a "reformist" posture, ostensibly embracing "good governance" and reforms to improve "transparency" and political participation (Rodan 2004, 2018; Rodan and Hughes 2014). Many have also felt compelled to pursue economic reform. This reflects not merely a short-term response to particular crises, whether the AFC or the GFC, but more fundamentally the need to adapt constantly to the always-evolving international division of labour and changing geopolitical circumstances associated with global capitalist development. China's emergence as the "factory of the world" has posed a major competitive challenge to earlier

Southeast Asian industrialisers, like Malaysia, Thailand and Indonesia, as has the shift of formerly "communist" Vietnam and Cambodia into low-cost manufacturing. But more broadly, we have witnessed the ongoing "globalisation" of governance regimes, formerly domestic companies, investment, and value and production chains, and the growing concentration of production among powerful global conglomerates (Carroll and Jarvis 2017: 24).

These factors have created competitive pressures that make it increasingly difficult for Southeast Asian elites to resist liberalising reforms. Institutions like the World Bank and Asian Development Bank—unleashed from the Cold War imperative of protecting authoritarian regimes—have also continuously promoted "deep marketization" through a plethora of interventions (Carroll 2012). Alongside specific development and reform programmes, these agencies construct "naming and shaming" league tables, such as the *Doing Business* series, which benchmark countries on their attractiveness to international capital, sending signals that can be factored into the cost of borrowing and investment decisions. This creates a form of pressure for institutional reform that need not be tied to conditional lending but operates entirely through the market and access to capital (Carroll and Jarvis 2014).

The conflict-ridden responses to these pressures help explain institutional evolutions that historical institutionalists struggle to grapple with, particularly the transformation of states. HI focuses primarily on explaining local institutional variegation, which to be sure remains significant. However, in Southeast Asia, some national variegation has coincided with considerable institutional convergence, shaped by changes in the global political economy, that HI is incapable of capturing or explaining. Because the conditions that previously supported the emergence of "developmental states" have transformed, approaches to governance are also changing. As Carroll and Jarvis (2017: 9) argue, rather than being configured so as to produce broad, *national* development and "growth with equity", "state capacities have… been repositioned, repurposed and redeployed in instrumental ways to support marketization… reflect[ing] the transforming interests of specific classes… which are increasingly aligned with international regimes of accumulation". Indeed, Jayasuriya (2005) has charted the gradual decline of the old developmental state and the emergence of "regulatory statehood", whereby central authorities are less inclined to lead development directly than to "steer" it through broad, pro-market regulations (see Al-Fadhat, this volume). This is very difficult to explain from a Weberian or HI perspective. It is unclear why a state with supposed "capacity" to subordinate the market would simply lose or voluntarily relinquish it. Nor is this transformation the result of a "critical juncture", or even slow endogenous change, as neither helps explain why similar trends are apparent across the entire region, despite its institutional diversity. Understanding these developments demands an emphasis upon the continually evolving nature of capitalist accumulation and socio-political struggles.

The same applies for institutional change at the regional level. The increasing regionalisation of production and finance, for example, is a key driver behind the formation of new initiatives like the "ASEAN Plus Three" grouping, linking ASEAN to China, Japan and South Korea, the Trans-Pacific Partnership, and China's Belt and Road Initiative, for example. Similarly, the ASEAN Economic Community (AEC), ostensibly created in 2015, is an explicit attempt to transform Southeast Asia into an integrated production platform for transnational capital. The AEC involves a vast regulatory "blueprint" of pro-market policies that member-states should adopt, which are a far cry from the interventionist, developmentalist policy set of earlier decades. However, implementation is highly uneven and, again, a Murdoch School approach can explain why. Where powerful interests favour liberalisation—such as businesses that have outgrown their national cocoon and now seek new, regional scales of accumulation—it is likely to proceed. However, when influential social groups stand to lose, or where alternative, non-market sources of finance are available from a country such as China, they tend to resist, impeding progress (see Jones and Hameiri, this volume).

We conclude that the Murdoch School has superior explanatory power to either Weberian or HI approaches, which is why it is chosen as the framework for this volume. Whatever their differences, each chapter will show how evolving socio-political conflict, embedded in global social relations, explains outcomes in their issue area.

References

Acharya, A. (1999). Southeast Asia's democratic moment. *Asian Survey, 39*(3), 418–432.

ADB [Asian Development Bank]. (2018). *Asian development outlook 2018: How technology affects jobs*. Manila: ADB.

Amsden, A. (1989). *Asia's next giant: South Korea and late industrialisation.* Oxford: Oxford University Press.
Amsden, A. (2001). *The rise of "the rest": Challenges to the West from late-industrializing countries.* Oxford: Oxford University Press.
Andriesse, E. (2015). Regional dynamics of capitalism in the Greater Mekong Subregion: The case of the rubber industry in Laos. *Journal of the Korean Geographical Society, 50*(1), 74–90.
Anter, A. (2014). *Max Weber's theory of the modern state: Origins, structure and significance.* Basingstoke: Palgrave Macmillan.
Arshad, A. (2017, March 27). Tax amnesty: Indonesians repatriate $8.8bn from Singapore. *Straits Times.*
Aspinall, E., & Berenschot, W. (2019). *Democracy for sale: Elections, clientelism and the state in Indonesia.* Ithaca: Cornell University Press.
Bell, S. (2002). Institutionalism: Old and new. In J. Summers (Ed.), *Government, politics, power and policy in Australia* (7th ed., pp. 363–380). Sydney: Pearson Education.
Bell, S., & Feng, H. (2013). *The rise of the People's Bank of China: The politics of institutional development in China's monetary and financial systems.* Cambridge, MA: Harvard University Press.
Bell, S., & Feng, H. (2014). How proximate and "meta-institutional" contexts shape institutional change: Explaining the rise of the People's Bank of China. *Political Studies, 62*(1), 197–215.
Bellin, E. (2000). Contingent democrats: Industrialists, labor, and democratization in late-developing countries. *World Politics, 52*(1), 175–205.
Bieler, A., & Morton, A. D. (2018). *Global capitalism, global war, global crisis.* Cambridge: Cambridge University Press.
Bratton, M., & van de Walle, N. (1994). Neopatrimonial regimes and political transitions in Africa. *World Politics, 46*(4), 453–489.
Brenner, N., Jessop, B., Jones, M., & MacLeod, G. (2003). Introduction: State space in question. In N. Brenner, B. Jessop, M. Jones, & G. MacLeod (Eds.), *State/space: A reader* (pp. 1–26). Malden: Blackwell Publishing.
Caballero-Anthony, M. (2005). *Regional security in Southeast Asia: Beyond the ASEAN way.* Singapore: ISEAS.
Cammack, P. (1989). Bringing the state back in? *British Journal of Political Science, 19*(2), 261–290.
Capoccia, G. (2015). Critical junctures and institutional change. In J. Mahoney & K. Thelen (Eds.), *Advances in comparative-historical analysis* (pp. 147–179). Cambridge: Cambridge University Press.
Capoccia, G., & Kelemen, R. D. (2007). The study of critical junctures: Theory, narrative and counterfactuals in historical institutionalism. *World Politics, 59*(3), 341–369.

Carothers, T. (2002). The end of the transition paradigm. *Journal of Democracy*, *13*(1), 5–21.
Carroll, T. (2010). *Delusions of development: The World Bank and the post-Washington consensus in Southeast Asia*. Basingstoke: Palgrave Macmillan.
Carroll, T. (2012). Working on, through and around the state: The deep marketisation of development in the Asia-Pacific. *Journal of Contemporary Asia*, *42*(3), 378–404.
Carroll, T., & Jarvis, D. S. L. (2014). Theorising Asia's marketisation under late capitalism: Risk, capital and the new politics of development. In T. Carroll & D. S. L. Jarvis (Eds.), *The politics of marketising Asia* (pp. 1–23). Basingstoke: Palgrave Macmillan.
Carroll, T., & Jarvis, D. S. L. (2017). Disembedding autonomy: Asia after the developmental state. In T. Carroll & D. S. L. Jarvis (Eds.), *Asia after the developmental state: Disembedding autonomy* (pp. 3–48). Cambridge: Cambridge University Press.
Doner, R. F., Ritchie, B. K., & Slater, D. (2005). Systemic vulnerability and the origins of developmental states: Northeast and Southeast Asia in comparative perspective. *International Organization*, *59*(2), 327–361.
Evans, P. B. (1995). *Embedded autonomy: States and industrial transformation*. Princeton: Princeton University Press.
Evans, P. B., Rueschemeyer, D., & Skocpol, T. (Eds.). (1985). *Bringing the state back in*. Cambridge: Cambridge University Press.
Felker, G. (2009). The political economy of Southeast Asia. In M. Beeson (Ed.), *Contemporary Southeast Asia* (2nd ed., pp. 46–73). Basingstoke: Palgrave Macmillan.
Fukuyama, F. (2013). What is governance? *Governance*, *26*(3), 347–368.
Gerard, K. (2014). *ASEAN's engagement of civil society: Regulating dissent*. Basingstoke: Palgrave Macmillan.
Gerschenkron, A. (1962). *Economic backwardness in historical perspective*. Cambridge, MA: Harvard University Press.
Hadiz, V. R. (2010). *Localising power in post-authoritarian Indonesia: A Southeast Asia perspective*. Stanford: Stanford University Press.
Hadiz, V. R., & Robison, R. (2013). The political economy of oligarchy and the reorganization of power in Indonesia. *Indonesia*, *96*, 35–57.
Haggard, S. (2004). Institutions and growth in East Asia. *Studies in Comparative International Development*, *38*(4), 53–81.
Hall, P. A., & Soskice, D. (2001). An introduction to varieties of capitalism. In P. A. Hall & D. Soskice (Eds.), *Varieties of capitalism: The institutional foundations of comparative advantage* (pp. 1–68). Oxford: Oxford University Press.
Hall, P. A., & Taylor, R. C. R. (1996). Political science and the three new institutionalisms. *Political Studies*, *44*(5), 936–957.

Hameiri, S. (2009). Capacity and its fallacies: International state building as state transformation. *Millennium, 38*(1), 55–81.

Hameiri, S., & Jones, L. (2015). *Governing borderless threats: Non-traditional security and the politics of state transformation*. Cambridge: Cambridge University Press.

Hameiri, S., Hughes, H., & Scarpello, F. (2017). *International intervention and local politics*. Cambridge: Cambridge University Press.

Harvey, D. (2005). *A brief history of neoliberalism*. Oxford: Oxford University Press.

Hayashi, S. (2010). The developmental state in the era of globalization: Beyond the Northeast Asian model of political economy. *The Pacific Review, 23*(1), 45–69.

Higgott, R., Robison, R., with Hewison, K. J, & Rodan, G. (1985). Theories of development and underdevelopment: Implications for the study of Southeast Asia. In R. Higgott & R. Robison (Eds.), *Southeast Asia: Essays in the political economy of structural change* (pp. 16–61). London: Routledge and Kegan Paul.

Hughes, C. (2003). *The political economy of Cambodia's transition, 1991–2001*. London: RoutledgeCurzon.

Hughes, C. (2009). *Dependent communities: Aid and politics in Cambodia and East Timor*. Ithaca: Cornell Southeast Asia Press.

Huntington, S. P. (1968). *Political order in changing societies*. New Haven: Yale University Press.

Hutchison, J., Hout, W., Hughes, C., & Robison, R. (2014). *Political economy and the aid industry in Asia*. Basingstoke: Palgrave Macmillan.

INFID. (2007, August). *Profile of Indonesia's foreign debt* (Working paper). http://www.jubileeaustralia.org/LiteratureRetrieve.aspx?ID=22291. Accessed 18 Jan 2019.

Jayasuriya, K. (2005). Beyond institutional fetishism: From the developmental to the regulatory state. *New Political Economy, 10*(3), 381–387.

Jayasuriya, K., & Rodan, G. (2007). Beyond hybrid regimes: More participation, less contestation in Southeast Asia. *Democratization, 14*(5), 773–794.

Jessop, B. (1990). *State theory: Putting the capitalist state in its place*. Cambridge: Polity Press.

Jessop, B. (2008). *State power: A strategic-relational approach*. Cambridge: Polity.

Jessop, B. (2009). Avoiding traps, rescaling states, governing Europe. In R. Keil & R. Mahon (Eds.), *Leviathan undone? Towards a political economy of scale* (pp. 87–104). Vancouver: University of British Columbia Press.

Johnson, C. (1982). *MITI and the Japanese miracle: The growth of industrial policy, 1925–1975*. Stanford: Stanford University Press.

Jomo, K. S. (1997). *Southeast Asia's misunderstood miracle: Industrial policy and economic development in Thailand, Malaysia and Indonesia*. Boulder: Westview Press.

Jones, L. (2010). (Post-)colonial statebuilding and state failure in East Timor: Bringing social conflict back in. *Conflict, Security and Development, 19*(3), 547–575.
Jones, L. (2012). *ASEAN, sovereignty and intervention in Southeast Asia*. Basingstoke: Palgrave Macmillan.
Jones, L. (2014). The political economy of Myanmar's transition. *Journal of Contemporary Asia, 44*(1), 144–170.
Jones, L. (2015). *Societies under siege: Exploring how international economic sanctions (do not) work*. Oxford: Oxford University Press.
Kalleberg, A. L., & Hewison, K. J. (2013). Precarious work and the challenge for Asia. *American Behavioral Scientist, 57*(3), 271–288.
Legro, J. W. (2000). The transformation of policy ideas. *American Journal of Political Science, 44*(3), 419–432.
Levitsky, S., & Way, L. (2010). *Competitive authoritarianism: Hybrid regimes after the Cold War*. Cambridge: Cambridge University Press.
Lim, C. Y. (2014). *Singapore's National Wages Council: An insider's view*. Singapore: World Scientific.
Mahoney, J., & Thelen, K. (2009). A theory of gradual institutional change. In J. Mahoney & K. Thelen (Eds.), *Explaining institutional change: Ambiguity, agency, and power* (pp. 1–37). Cambridge: Cambridge University Press.
Martin, I. W., Mehrota, A. K., & Prasad, M. (Eds.). (2009). *The new fiscal sociology: Taxation in comparative and historical perspective*. Cambridge: Cambridge University Press.
Marx, K., & Engels, F. (1848). *Manifesto of the communist party*. https://www.marxists.org/archive/marx/works/download/pdf/Manifesto.pdf. Accessed 18 Jan 2019.
Merkel, W., & Croissant, A. (2004). Conclusion: Good and defective democracies. *Democratization, 11*(5), 199–213.
Migdal, J. S. (1988). *Strong societies and weak states: State–society relations and state capabilities in the third world*. Princeton: Princeton University Press.
Mitchell, T. (1991). The limits of the state: Beyond statist approaches and their critics. *American Political Science Review, 85*(1), 77–96.
Moore, B. (1966). *Social origins of dictatorship and democracy: Lord and peasant in the making of the modern world*. Boston: Beacon Press.
Moore, J. D. (2018). *Varieties of capitalism in Southeast Asia*. Cham: Palgrave Macmillan.
Morgenbesser, L. (2016). *Behind the façade: Elections under authoritarianism in Southeast Asia*. Albany: State University of New York Press.
North, D. C. (1990). *Institutions, institutional change and economic performance*. Cambridge: Cambridge University Press.
Ottaway, M. (2003). *Democracy challenged: The rise of semi-authoritarianism*. Washington, DC: Carnegie Endowment for International Peace.

Palan, R., Murphy, R., & Chavagneux, C. (2010). *Tax havens: How globalization really works*. Ithaca: Cornell University Press.
Peck, G., & Theodore, N. (2007). Variegated capitalism. *Progress in Human Geography, 31*(6), 731–772.
Pepinsky, T. (2014). The institutional turn in comparative authoritarianism. *British Journal of Political Science, 44*(3), 631–653.
Polanyi, K. (1957 [1944]). *The great transformation: The political and economic origins of our time*. Boston: Beacon Press.
Poulantzas, N. (1978). *State, power, socialism*. London/New York: Verso.
Rethel, L. (2010). The new financial development paradigm and Asian bond markets. *New Political Economy, 15*(4), 493–517.
Rhodes, M., & Higgott, R. (2000). Introduction: Asian crises and the myth of capitalist "convergence". *The Pacific Review, 13*(1), 1–20.
Robinson, N. (2003). The politics of Russia's partial democracy. *Political Studies Review, 1*(2), 149–166.
Robison, R. (1986). *Indonesia: The rise of capital*. Sydney: Allen & Unwin.
Robison, R., & Hadiz, V. R. (2004). *Reorganising power in Indonesia: The politics of oligarchy in an age of markets*. New York: RoutledgeCurzon.
Rodan, G. (1989). *The political economy of Singapore's industrialization: National state and international capital*. London: Macmillan.
Rodan, G. (2004). *Transparency and authoritarian rule in Southeast Asia: Singapore and Malaysia*. London: Routledge.
Rodan, G. (2016). Capitalism, inequality and ideology in Singapore: New challenges for the ruling party. *Asian Studies Review, 40*(2), 211–230.
Rodan, G. (2018). *Participation without democracy: Containing conflict in Southeast Asia*. Ithaca: Cornell University Press.
Rodan, G., & Hughes, C. (2014). *The politics of accountability in Southeast Asia: The dominance of moral ideologies*. Oxford: Oxford University Press.
Rodan, G., & Jayasuriya, K. (2012). Hybrid regimes: A social foundations approach. In J. Haynes (Ed.), *Routledge handbook of democratization* (pp. 175–189). London: Routledge.
Rodan, G., Hewison, K., & Robison, R. (2006). Theorising markets in Southeast Asia: Power and contestation. In G. Rodan, K. Hewison, & R. Robison (Eds.), *The political economy of Southeast Asia Vol 3: Markets, power and contestation* (pp. 1–38). Oxford: Oxford University Press.
Routley, L. (2014). Developmental states in Africa? A review of ongoing debates and buzzwords. *Development Policy Review, 32*(2), 159–177.
Schmidt, V. A. (2008). Discursive institutionalism: The explanatory power of ideas and discourse. *Annual Review of Political Science, 11*(1), 303–326.
Seeberg, M. (2014). Mapping deviant democracy. *Democratization, 21*(4), 634–654.

Skocpol, T. (1985). Bringing the state back in: Strategies of analysis in current research. In P. B. Evans, D. Rueschemeyer, & T. Skocpol (Eds.), *Bringing the state back in* (pp. 3–38). Cambridge: Cambridge University Press.

Slater, D. (2010). *Ordering power: Contentious politics and authoritarian leviathans in Southeast Asia.* Cambridge: Cambridge University Press.

Stubbs, R. (2005). *Rethinking Asia's economic miracle: The political economy of war, prosperity, and crisis.* London: Palgrave.

Stubbs, R. (2009). What ever happened to the East Asian developmental state? The unfolding debate. *The Pacific Review, 22*(1), 1–22.

Thelen, K., & Steinmo, S. (1992). Historical institutionalism in comparative politics. In S. Steinmo, K. Thelen, & F. Longstreth (Eds.), *Structuring politics: Historical institutionalism in comparative analysis* (pp. 1–32). Cambridge: Cambridge University Press.

Thurbon, E. (2016). *Developmental mindset: The revival of financial activism in South Korea.* Ithaca: Cornell University Press.

Wade, R. H. (1990). *Governing the market: Economic theory and the role of government in East Asian industrialization.* Princeton: Princeton University Press.

Wade, R. H. (2018). The developmental state: Dead or alive? *Development and Change, 49*(2), 518–546.

Walter, A. (2008). *Governing finance: East Asia's adoption of international standards.* Ithaca: Cornell University Press.

Walter, A., & Zhang, X. (Eds.). (2012). *East Asian capitalism: Diversity, continuity, and change.* Oxford: Oxford University Press.

Weber, M. (1978). *Economy and society.* Berkeley: University of California Press.

Wedeman, A. (2001). Development and corruption: The East Asian paradox. In E. T. Gomez (Ed.), *Political business in East Asia* (pp. 34–61). London: Routledge.

Weiss, L. (1998). *The myth of the powerless state.* Ithaca: Cornell University Press.

Wimmer, A., & Glick Schiller, N. (2002). Methodological nationalism and beyond: Nation-state building, migration and the social sciences. *Global Networks, 2*(4), 301–334.

Winters, J. A. (2011). *Oligarchy.* New York: Cambridge University Press.

World Bank. (1993). *The East Asian miracle: Economic growth and public policy.* Oxford: Oxford University Press.

World Bank. (1997). *World development report 1997: The state in a changing world.* Oxford: Oxford University Press.

World Bank. (2002). *World development report 2002: Building institutions for markets.* Oxford: Oxford University Press.

CHAPTER 2

The Political Economy of Southeast Asia's Development from Independence to Hyperglobalisation

Toby Carroll

INTRODUCTION

While policy-makers and mainstream scholars emphasise "the market" and market-friendly governance as key to generating economic development, the real story of what "makes" a particular political economy in a developmental sense is far less savoury and far more complex.[1] Whether it involves innovations in technology and knowledge that enabled advanced seafaring and the securing of territory for colonial plunder, or a firm's position at the top of global value chains despite owning no physical factories at all, explaining developmental outcomes from a political economy perspective demands a focus on the revolutions in and ownership of the means of production, and the conflicts between and within social classes. Southeast

[1] I am grateful for comments from Garry Rodan, Darryl Jarvis, Max Lane, Lee Jones, Shahar Hameiri and Danny Marks on earlier drafts. The usual disclaimers apply.

T. Carroll (✉)
Department of Asian and International Studies, City University of Hong Kong, Hong Kong, China
e-mail: tcarroll@cityu.edu.hk

© The Author(s) 2020
T. Carroll et al. (eds.), *The Political Economy of Southeast Asia*, Studies in the Political Economy of Public Policy, https://doi.org/10.1007/978-3-030-28255-4_2

Asia has been emblematic of this reality: first as a prominent site of colonial occupation and extraction; secondly, as an important set of newly independent countries in the context of the Cold War and emerging patterns of transnational production and exchange; and, finally, as host to highly varied sites within evolving regional and global value chains, under what the United Nations Conference on Trade and Development now dubs "hyperglobalisation" (UNCTAD 2017).

This chapter locates the political economy of Southeast Asia's development within the context of capitalism generally and, in particular, capitalism in its most recent, albeit incomplete and highly uneven and competitive, "world market" stage—a "sub-mode" of production that David Harvey (2007) has dubbed "flexible accumulation" (see also Cammack 2017). The chapter concentrates on what I call *substantive economic development*; that is development defined in a classic post-war/pre-neoliberal sense *well beyond* contemporary definitions that conflate it with economic growth, market-oriented governance and official development assistance (ODA). Historically, substantive economic development has entailed perpetual revolutions in the means of production and concomitant transformations in the social relations of production, often following large-scale processes of primitive accumulation and colonial extraction. In the post-war period, these revolutions combined with the ability of working classes to challenge capital's leverage, leading to the constitution of welfare states and massive improvements in material conditions. Such outcomes, which were associated with large-scale industrialisation, attracted both veneration and efforts towards replication in the under-developed world using various forms of *development policy*. While earlier studies of capitalist Southeast Asia pointed to impressive industrialisation (which, as we shall see, is better described in hindsight as an increase in *manufacturing*), this chapter makes clear the manner in which such substantive economic development has been deeply constrained by the broader historical, and highly uneven, relations of global capitalism. This said, Southeast Asia has played host to important ideological and political struggles over how best to advance material conditions and, importantly, the distribution of spoils.

The current juncture, characterised by unprecedented competition between countries to become sites of labour-intensive manufacturing (with vast pools of labour having been added to the global political economy over the last three decades) and the concentrated ownership and/or control of advanced manufacturing, technology and services, poses a serious developmental challenge to Southeast Asia. Across many accepted measures, including foreign investment flows, patents filed, and basic developmental and aggregate economic indicators, the picture is one of economies that, while continuing to grow and attract investment, have largely failed to progress beyond low value-added economic activity, remaining subordinated to the prerogatives and vagaries of global value chains, international financial capital, commodity prices and new state-linked investment from China. Tellingly, as illustrated in Table 2.1, seven of Southeast Asia's 11 countries remain classed as "lower-middle-income countries" by the World Bank, with annual per capita incomes between US$1006 and US$3955. Removing tiny Singapore and Brunei from the picture, the regional per capita income rests at US$3368, less than a tenth of the OECD average. Inequality in the region is also generally high, with Indonesia, Malaysia and Singapore all manifesting Gini coefficients above 0.40. Seven countries—including the region's biggest economy, Indonesia—still have active programmes with the World Bank, and remain important "clients" and hosts for myriad other development organisations. Southeast Asia's key exports continue to be dominated by primary commodities, simple products, final assembly and basic services, unlike most OECD economies (see Appendix).

None of this is to deny that there have been at times impressive increases in growth and per capita incomes, declines in privation and absolute poverty (although see Fig. 2.1 and Tables 2.1 and 2.3 for an important corrective to overly glossy analyses). Likewise, the data reveal enhanced health outcomes, increased electrification, and manufacturing employment (see Tables 2.2, 2.3 and 2.4).[2] Despite China's rise as "factory to the world", and the increasing prominence of countries such as Bangladesh in garment production, manufacturing in electronics, garments, footwear and automobiles has been, and continues to be, statistically important in Southeast Asia in terms of employment, growth and investment in the region. Looking at increased car ownership and production (which relative to population remain diminutive) or the number of shopping malls and the percentage of the population holding credit cards in countries such as Indonesia, also demonstrates important shifts in purchasing power and consumption. However, as this chapter will make clear, developmental gains also need to be put in context, for example, against countries that

---

[2] These measures also need to be treated with nuance. For example, accepted definitions of industry can include construction and extremely basic activities within the global hierarchy of production.

Table 2.1 Basic Southeast Asian country data

	Per capita GDP Current US$, 2016, World Bank	Absolute GDP Millions, current US$, 2016, World Bank/OECD	Inequality GINI, latest available, multiple sources, 0 = perfect equality, 100 = maximal inequality World Bank/CIA	Population Thousands, 2016, World Bank	World Bank country classification[a]
Brunei	26,939.4	11,400.65	–	423.20	High-income
Cambodia	1269.9	20,016.75	36 (2013)	15,762.37	Lower-middle-income
Indonesia	3570.3	418,976.68	38.1 (2017)	261,115.46	Lower-middle-income
Laos	2338.7	15,805.71	36.7 (2013)	6758.35	Lower-middle-income
Malaysia	9508.2	296,535.93	41 (2015)	31,187.26	Upper-middle-income
Myanmar	1195.5	63,225.10	38.1 (2015)	52,885.22	Lower-middle-income
Philippines	2951.1	304,905.41	40.1 (2015)	103,320.22	Lower-middle income
Singapore	52,962.5	296,975.68	45.9 (CIA, 2017)	5607.28[b]	High-income
Thailand	5910.6	407,026.13	36.5 (2017)	68,863.51	Upper-middle-income
Timor-Leste	1405.4	1782.97	28.7 (2014)	1268.67	Lower-middle-income
Vietnam	2170.6	205,276.17	35.3 (2016)	94,569.07	Lower-middle-income
Southeast Asia	10,020.2	2,041,927.18	38.51	641760.61	
OECD	42,438.29	54,664,115.01	31	1,289,872.63	

Sources: World Bank (2018a), OECD (2019), CIA (2019)

[a]Based on per capita GDP: Low-income: $1005 or less; Lower-middle-income: $1006–$3955; Upper-middle-income: $3956–$12,235; High-income: over $12,235

[b]Includes large numbers of foreign workers

Fig. 2.1 Multidimensional and income poverty rates in selected Southeast Asian countries (percentages)

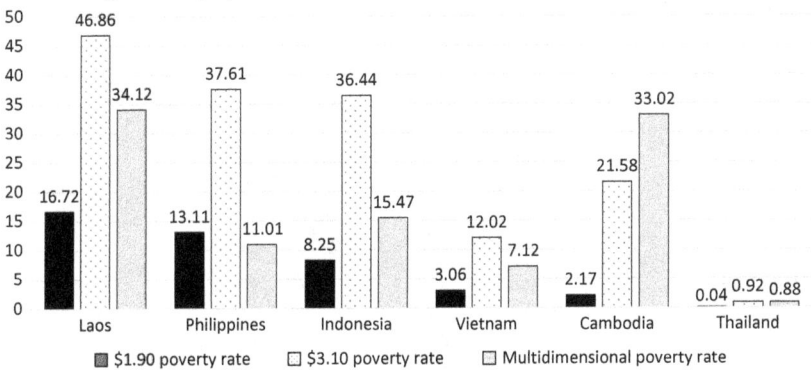

Country	$1.90 poverty rate	$3.10 poverty rate	Multidimensional poverty rate
Laos	16.72	34.12	46.86
Philippines	13.11	37.61	11.01
Indonesia	8.25	15.47	36.44
Vietnam	3.06	12.02	7.12
Cambodia	2.17	21.58	33.02
Thailand	0.04	0.92	0.88

Source: ADB 2017: 10

Table 2.2 General Southeast Asian developmental indicators

	Life expectancy at birth, years, 2017 World Bank	Current health expenditure as a percentage of GDP, 2015, World Health Organization	Electric power consumption (kWh per capita), 2014 World Bank	Population living in slums (% of urban population), 2014 World Bank
Brunei	77	2.6	10,243	–
Cambodia	69	6	271	55
Indonesia	69	3.3	812	22
Laos	67	2.8	–	31
Malaysia	75	4	4596	–
Myanmar	67	4.9	217	41
Philippines	69	4.4	699	38
Singapore	83	4.3	8845	–
Thailand	75	3.8	2540	25
Timor-Leste	69	3.1	–	–
Vietnam	76	5.7	1411	27

Source: World Bank (2018a), WHO (2019)

have experienced substantive economic development. Southeast Asia may have leveraged low labour costs to attract low value-added manufacturing, but the transfer, use and domestic development of more advanced forms of productive technology remain limited, with ownership and operation of such technology dominated by multinational companies (MNCs) and

Table 2.3 Labour in Southeast Asia

	Proportion of population employed by sector, male/female			Labour force participation rate, [a]male/female, 15+	Vulnerable employment, [b]male/female
	Industry	Services	Agriculture		
Brunei	23/10	76/89	1/0	75/59	5/5
Cambodia	28/26	45/48	27/26	89/81	45/57
Indonesia	25/16	42/53	32/29	82/51	42/56
Laos	12/7	28/30	59/63	80/77	77/89
Malaysia	32/20	54/74	14/7	77/51	20/25
Myanmar	18/14	31/38	51/48	80/51	56/62
Philippines	23/10	45/74	32/17	75/50	32/40
Singapore	20/12	80/88	0/0	77/60	10/6
Thailand	25/19	40/50	35/30	77/60	49/52
Timor-Leste	19/6	57/66	24/28	52/25	48/52
Vietnam	29/21	32/37	39/42	83/73	50/62

Source: 2017 estimates modelled by ILO (2017)
[a]Proportion of working-age population engaged in work or looking for work
[b]Defined as the sum of own-account and contributing family workers, presented as a share of total employment, including wage and salaried workers

Table 2.4 Basic economic data for Southeast Asian economies, 2016

	Value added by sector (percentage GDP)			Trade (percentage GDP)		Total external debt (public and private, current US$ millions)	Tax revenue (% GDP)
	Industry	Agriculture	Services	Exports	Imports		
Brunei	57	1	42	50	38	–	–
Cambodia	32	27	42	61	66	10,230	15.3
Indonesia	41	14	45	19	18	316,431	10.3
Laos	19	19	48	35	42	14,160	12.9
Malaysia	38	9	53	68	61	200,364	13.8
Myanmar	35	25	40	17	28	6453	6.4
Philippines	31	10	60	28	37	77,319	13.7
Singapore	26	0	74	172	146	–	14.3
Thailand	36	8	56	69	54	121,497	15.7
Timor-Leste	19	18	64	4	58	–	13.9
Vietnam	36	18	45	94	91	86,952	19.1[a]
OECD average							34.26

Source: World Bank (2018a), OECD (2019)
[a]Falls outside of precise period

their affiliates. Likewise, basic commodity exports remain central to many regional economies, leaving them vulnerable to frequent shifts in global market prices and other repercussions of resource dependence.

To understand Southeast Asian development and its limits, this chapter charts the historical evolution of economic development across three key phases, paying careful attention to how these patterns have shaped, and been shaped by, the relative power and leverage of social forces within the ever-shifting relations of production of the world market.

From Colonial Economies to National Development During the Cold War (1945 to Mid-1970s)

This section discusses the largely shared beginnings of the region's political economies within the colonial division of labour and the shift from this to various forms of nationally centred *late* development. With the exception of Thailand (which was not immune from foreign influence), all Southeast Asian countries were colonised, most securing independence soon after World War II, often after long-running anti-colonial struggles that in several cases morphed into Cold War conflicts (see Table 2.5). The post-war period was key to development worldwide, with the emergence of new nation-states, grand ideologies (communism, socialism and a variegated Western technocratic capitalist assemblage), and superpower rivalries all shaping developmental strategies. Southeast Asia was particularly emblematic in this respect, with Cold War ideological rivalry

Table 2.5 List of Southeast Asian dates of independence and colonial powers

	Date of independence	Previous colonial power
Brunei	1984	United Kingdom
Cambodia	1953	France
Indonesia	1945/49	The Netherlands
Laos	1953	France
Malaysia	1963	United Kingdom
Myanmar	1948	United Kingdom
Philippines	1898/1946	Spain/United States
Singapore	1965	United Kingdom
Thailand	–	–
Timor-Leste	1975/1999	Portugal/Indonesia
Vietnam	1945/1954	France

and conflict figuring prominently both before and after decolonisation, together with various national developmentalist approaches.

At independence, the region's political economies were typically poor, inheriting low productive capacities from their colonisers. Economic activity was largely based around primary commodities (notably tin, rubber, sugarcane, spices and oil), some limited forms of primary processing and traditional "small-scale craft work" (Rasiah 1994: 198). Colonial exploitation had frequently been vast: Gordon (2018) estimates that the Netherlands extracted perhaps something over US$200bn from Indonesia from 1880 to 1939, for example. The low productive capacity of these countries, together with often sizeable populations, translated into poor relative development indicators. Even by 1967, the earliest year for which the World Bank holds comparable data, per capita incomes (in current US dollars) were remarkably low: Indonesia, US$57; Thailand US$166; the Philippines US$207; Malaysia US$317; Singapore, US$625. The figure for high-income countries at the time was US$2212 (World Bank 2018a).

After independence, new governments and opposition forces in the region grappled with how to advance late economic development, with often ferocious struggles over the path forward, sometimes with the involvement of the superpowers and/or previous colonisers. A common approach, as in many post-colonial states, was to pursue import-substitution industrialisation (ISI). This involved establishing tariffs against imports and nurturing domestic industry to produce goods instead. At the time, this strategy generally enjoyed strong support from a range of mercantilists, Keynesians and influential development economists, such as Raul Prebisch. And, indeed, ISI was indicative of the understandable desperation of nascent, poor countries thrust into late development after long periods of colonial exploitation and extraction. ISI approaches were particularly important in Southeast Asia's capitalist economies. Rasiah dates their dominance as follows: 1958–67 in Malaysia; 1960–71 in Thailand; 1950–70 in the Philippines; 1965–75 in Indonesia (Rasiah 1994: 199). Singapore represented a different case, being a small entrepôt economy with few natural resources other than its rather fortuitous geography.

Nonetheless, it is important to note that exports were not entirely neglected even in this early period, despite development practitioners arguing at the time that protectionism created a "bias" against export-oriented manufacturing. In fact, mirroring the strategies of Northeast Asian developmental states, various pilot agencies and investment boards were established throughout Southeast Asia to encourage export-oriented development. Examples include Singapore's Economic Development Board, Thailand's National Economic Development Board, the Philippines' Board of Investment, Malaysia's Federal Industry Development Authority and Vietnam's Centre for Industrial Development. Notably, countries such as Singapore and Malaysia explicitly adopted subsidies to encourage the development of export industries (Hughes 1970: 16–28).

This strong role for governments in shaping development trends reflected the global post-war tendency to view countries—*national* economies—as key units of development (Berger 2004: 38), to be nurtured with the "right set" of policies, steered by able technocrats and enlightened leaders (of various ideological persuasions), towards late development. This was a period in which Keynesian and other technocrats were prominent in managing Western capitalist economies within an emerging "golden age", with state forms, heavily conditioned by the relatively strong power of organised labour, tailored towards protecting and even owning the commanding heights of industry, reducing uneven development across national economies, and establishing redistributive taxation, national health and welfare systems, and strong regulatory standards, including robust workers' rights. This was also the high-point of the Fordist mode of production in the developed world. "Fordism", named for US industrialist Henry Ford, involved making significant concessions to workers, in terms of pay and welfare, facilitating high levels of consumption, which created the demand for more industrial output, thereby also securing capitalist profits. It was underpinned by certain technological innovations—notably the introduction of assembly lines and standardised production techniques—but also by a class compromise between workers and the owners of capital. Crucially, this compromise was struck at the *national* level, frequently giving rise to "corporatist" state forms, where representatives of *national* labour unions and *national* business elites shaped broad economic policy outlines alongside *national* bureaucrats (Schoenberger 1988: 247). This compromise was aided by global institutions that supported national-level economic planning, and by the spectre—underpinned by the Soviet Union's existence and industrialisation—of communist revolution if workers' demands were not met. Ruggie (1982) famously described these arrangements as "embedded liberalism", reflecting the way that capitalist markets had become embedded within, and limited by, broader socio-political considerations. Japan and Europe's post-war reconstruction quickly demonstrated what this approach could achieve, albeit in places where industrialisation was already considerably advanced (Hewison and Rodan 1994: 246).

Southeast Asian governments' attempts to copy something of this model were perhaps even more powerfully shaped by the emerging Cold War. Importantly, the Korean War (1950–53) propelled demand for Southeast Asian commodities such as rubber, while also creating "a ripple of apprehension" as fears mounted of Communism "sweeping down" through Indochina and beyond (Stubbs 1989: 521). The increasingly hot Cold War drove powerful states to buy up necessary strategic commodities, sending prices surging: tin prices increased 400% and rubber prices rose by 200%. This commodity boom was particularly crucial for Indonesia, Malaya and Singapore (the latter as a key trader and entrepôt), but also mattered for Thailand and Vietnam. For example, the economy of colonial Malaya was described as "entirely dependent on rubber and tin", with over a third of the workforce connected in some way to rubber production (ibid.: 521). Importantly, rather than being used for the purchase of foreign manufactures, British-imposed import restrictions meant that much more of the surpluses generated from commodity exports remained in the territories than might have otherwise been the case. Moreover, the devolution of administrative financing allowed local colonial administrations to raise significant revenues (the highest in percentage of GDP terms in the region) through income taxes and export duties, permitting an expansion in key social and economic infrastructure (ibid.: 521–525).

Even before its large-scale troop commitments during the Vietnam War, US efforts to contain communism also had important but highly variable impacts on parts of Southeast Asia. Thailand was viewed as particularly strategically important, and consequently received large aid flows (US$650 million from 1950 to 1975) and military assistance (US$940 million from 1951 to 1971), and saw the construction of US military bases (whose occupants brought with them purchasing power, driving local consumption). Both Singapore, which split from Malaysia in 1965, and the Philippines also saw significant economic gains from US military-linked trading and tourism, and, in the case of the Philippines, the expansion of military facilities (ibid.: 528–530). Across Indochina, however, Cold War-related conflict had devastating impacts upon largely poor peasant populations, with communist parties sweeping to power in Vietnam, Cambodia and Laos by 1975. Burma had been under "socialist" rule since a military coup in 1962. Bequeathed minimal productive capacity by extractive colonial regimes, and forced to organise war economies, on this side of the Cold War divide central planning and the disappearance of the private sector became the norm. In Vietnam, for example, with help from communist China and the Soviet Union, attempts were made to transition from subsistence agriculture to socialist industrialisation through the First Five Year Plan (1961–65), which focused on building heavy industrial capacity (Nguyen et al. 2016: 4).

In capitalist Southeast Asia, governments adopted a variety of approaches, ranging from liberal to highly heterodox and interventionist, to promote Fordist development. While the tendencies associated with the developmental state in Northeast Asia were less pronounced in Southeast Asia, neither were they completely absent. They emerged after often bitter struggles between social forces that, although typically united in the need to pursue development, not least to stave off communist revolution, were divided over the precise form that this should take. In Indonesia, this was first exemplified by President Sukarno's efforts to establish an alliance with the Indonesian Communist Party (PKI), couple nationalism with socialism, and nationalise industry during a period of "Guided Democracy" (1957–65) (Lane 2008: 29–30; Pluvier 1970: 13; Robison 1986: 213; Vickers 2005: 144). This approach generated economic instability and mounting resistance from Islamists, urban elites and the military, culminating in the 1965–66 mass slaughter of members of the PKI, other leftists and Indonesians of Chinese descent, by the army and militias.[3] This—the region's most systematic example of anti-communist efforts— led to Sukarno's fall and the rise of Suharto's "New Order" (*Order Baru*).

However, the eradication of oppositional and other social forces did not mean the arrival of unbridled liberalism. Indeed, this period of authoritarian rule—in which a politically demobilised population was reinterpreted in a corporatist sense as a "floating mass"—fused state command of the corporate sector (especially early on), nationalism, anti-communism and neo-sultanistic patronage, with liberal technocrats only exercising sporadic influence during times of economic crisis. As Robison (1986) noted, in the early New Order period, the state-owned sector constituted "the largest and most crucial element of domestic capital", keeping the means of production out of the hands of foreign capital and playing an important role in industrialisation efforts throughout the 1970s. The con-

---

[3] Estimates vary, but recent scholarship has found that 500,000–1,000,000 members of the PKI and affiliated organisations were killed, with many more detained, some for decades and often without charge (Melvin 2017: 487; Robinson 2018: 1).

trol of this apparatus also allowed the regime to nurture favoured private enterprises, and maintain a vast patronage system directing resources to the army and allied elites (Robison 1986: 211–212). Thus, contrary to dependency theory expectations, Suharto's New Order was not simply a comprador arrangement for foreign exploitation. Rather, it combined mercantilist elements (echoing countries in Northeast Asia), with patrimonialism, albeit in a way that would ultimately fail to transcend key technological barriers to moving up value chains.

In Malaysia, the colonial state's violent suppression of "communists, left-wing nationalists, former wartime partisans, radical sections of the working class, and squatter farmers" translated initially into a brief *laissez faire* period (Khoo 2001: 181–182). However, increasing inequality, rising unemployment and declining fortunes for many would demand active state intervention "to manage class pressures and ethnic demands that an unregulated market had not satisfied" (ibid.: 183–184). After a period of significant unrest, including Malay riots directed at the economically dominant ethnic-Chinese population, the ruling *Barisan Nasional* adopted the far more interventionist New Economic Policy in 1971, which promoted Malay economic empowerment. Early state intervention was designed to encourage foreign direct investment (FDI) into textiles, garment manufacturing and electronics (ibid.: 178). However, as in Indonesia, state intervention was also associated with extensive patronage to regime-linked business interests.

The Philippines in the late 1960s—in marked contrast to its present-day economy characterised by dependence on foreign worker remittances, a depreciating currency and lacklustre productive capacity (see for example *Financial Times* 2018)—was a regional leader in terms of absolute value-added in manufacturing, only outclassed in per capita terms by Singapore and Malaysia (Hughes 1970: 6–7). The use of protectionist policies, such as import licensing (up until 1962), protected domestic capitalists from import competition and forced foreign—mostly US—companies to set up operations as a pre-emptive strategy to fend off international rivals also eyeing the country as a possible production site. A World Bank working paper of the time noted that this strategy succeeded in realising "easy import substitution opportunities" in "food processing, textiles, electrical appliances and automobile assembly", producing "rapid growth in investment and output in manufacturing" (ibid.: 15). As elsewhere in the region, import licensing later gave way to tariff collection as the protectionist method-of-choice—one that lent itself to the extraction of bribes and considerable smuggling.

Singapore's development story is more unusual. Like other leaders in the region, Prime Minister Lee Kuan Yew perennially touted the threat of communist and leftist social forces to late development, a fact that had made him particularly attractive to the British. This was used to justify the rounding up and suppression of opponents, bolstering Lee's political power and achieving victory for his People's Action Party (PAP) in the 1963 elections (Jones 2000: 86–87). However, also like other anti-communist elites in the region, Lee was cognisant of the need to secure economic stability and deliver developmental gains to restive populations to offset incentives for revolutionary alternatives: "We needed stability and growth to counter and deny the communists the social and economic conditions for revolutions" (Lee 2000: 369–370; also Jones 2012: 46). Having purged and crushed leftist elements, Lee and the PAP consolidated power, constructing a vast bureaucratic apparatus. Unlike other Southeast Asian regimes, the PAP did not enjoy close relations with domestic business elites, doubting their loyalty and their capacity to industrialise Singapore, particularly following the contraction in Singapore's domestic market size after it was expelled from Malaysia (Rodan 2001: 142–143). This soon led the PAP to pursue a quite different developmental strategy, focused on attracting FDI to develop export-oriented industrialisation (EOI). In so doing, the Singaporean party-state developed clear affinities with several Northeast Asian "developmental states". The Economic Development Board became a key "pilot agency", government-linked corporations played a dominant role, and development and post office banks channelled funds towards developmental purposes. Government provision of key infrastructure, targeted non-market lending (echoing South Korea and Japan) and the control and incorporation of organised labour within an overarching "soft-authoritarian" framework also figured prominently (ibid.: 145). Workers were kept quiescent through the state control of labour unions, the provision of public housing, a large civil service that served as an important employer, gerrymandering, social surveillance and sanctions for those still daring to challenge the PAP's legitimacy and strategy (Hughes 1970: 15).

Overall, Southeast Asian countries' developmental strategies and fortunes in the immediate post-war period significantly reflected the externally conditioned challenges and opportunities facing developing countries worldwide, albeit with regional specificities, notably the presence of Cold

War "hot wars" and the looming spectre of communism as an alternative to capitalism. Capitalist countries in the region—as hosts to large pools of cheap labour—also started to become important sites for offshore manufacturing production for first-world markets, a process that would become even more important as the world economy gravitated further towards what would later be called globalisation.

Flexible Accumulation, Japanese Investment and the Rise of Offshore Manufacturing (Mid-1970s to Mid-1990s)

The late 1960s and 1970s saw the conditions for Southeast Asia's development transformed dramatically by a deep crisis within, and restructuring of, global capitalism. This period saw the end of the great post-war boom in industrialised countries and the emergence of massive contradictions that cast doubt on the notion that national economies could perpetually be steered developmentally in relative autonomy by able technocrats. Crisis in Europe and North America initially threw Southeast Asian economies into disarray, while the oil crises benefited some and threatened to bankrupt others. By the late 1970s, as in many developing countries, Southeast Asian development strategies were in serious trouble, with several governments being driven to seek assistance from the International Monetary Fund (IMF). However, unlike other regions, Southeast Asia ultimately benefited from the resolution of the West's economic crisis in favour of globalising fractions of capital, which increasingly relocated their industrial production to low-wage economies. This created the basis for the so-called "economic miracle" of the 1980s.

The 1970s saw the emergence of a set of interlinked structural crises in global capitalism. First, industrialised economies experienced a radical economic slowdown. In the US, for example, average growth from 1968 to 1973 was close to half what it had been from 1960 to 1968. In Japan, then seen as a post-war reconstruction and industrialisation model *par excellence*, growth fell from over 10% to just 3.6% over the same periods (Harvey 1990: 130, 140–143). Second, the US's abandonment of the gold standard—rendered unaffordable by increasing economic competition from Europe and Japan, and the rising costs of domestic welfare and Cold War conflicts—sent global economic governance into disarray. Initially, the value of post-war currencies had been fixed relative to the US dollar, allowing national governments to manage their economies through negotiated adjustments in exchange rates. The replacement of this system with floating exchange rates made national economic management far harder, with terms of trade fluctuating wildly and inflation spiralling. Third, a series of "oil crises" erupted, as oil producers responded to the end of the dollar standard by restricting production, sending prices of this crucial commodity sky-rocketing. Combined, these pressures created a massive crisis of profitability in developed capitalist states and gave rise to prolonged "stagflation": low growth and rising prices. This compelled systemically important rethinks in government policy and corporate strategy, a renaissance in neoliberal ideology, and the rise of pro-capital politicians in leading Western economies, such as Margaret Thatcher and Ronald Reagan, who put this ideology into practice. Post-war "social compacts" between capital and labour were torn up, with labour unions crushed, corporatist state institutions dismantled, and states reconfigured in relation to *global* competitiveness, rather than *national* development (Ruggie 1982).

This crisis and its outcome had variable and evolving effects on Southeast Asia. Initially, the region experienced very negative impacts, compounding the withering of gains from Cold War conflict as the Indochina Wars wound down. Northern stagflation depressed demand for, and hence the income earned from, raw commodity and manufactured exports, whilst also increasing the prices of imports from developed countries, notably the capital goods needed to establish manufacturing. The region's oil-producing countries—Malaysia, Indonesia and Brunei— benefited from surging global oil prices. However, Southeast Asia's oil-importing countries experienced serious dislocation, and the oil boom did not last, with Northern stagflation sparking a general collapse in commodity prices in the early 1980s. Many regional governments sought aid and loans through the 1970s to compensate for falling export revenues and maintain investment in social and industrial infrastructure, and several now found themselves unable to service their loans, entering a "debt crisis" like so many similarly positioned developing countries. Some, like Indonesia, the Philippines and Thailand, were forced to turn to the IMF for assistance, which demanded structural adjustments in exchange (Hart-Landsberg 1998).

Unlike many other developing countries, however, Southeast Asia's capitalist economies were rescued from this crisis by the arrival of investment from developed economies, led initially by Japan. Japanese capital was experiencing intensifying competitive pressures to lower the costs of production relative to rising Northeast Asian challengers Taiwan and South Korea. From the late 1970s, Japanese companies increasingly shifted production to Southeast Asia to secure cheaper labour, new supplies of raw materials and access to markets shielded by protectionist methods. Importantly, Japanese policy-makers abandoned their policy of "severely restricting" outbound investment into Southeast Asia, where companies often formed joint ventures with majority-holding local affiliates (Stubbs 1989: 531–532). This process was further spurred by the 1985 Plaza Accord, whereby Japan agreed to increase the value of the yen's value relative to the dollar, creating further pressure on Japanese businesses to cut costs to maintain international competitiveness (Urata 2002: 3). As neoliberal deregulation occurred in Western economies, American and European firms increasingly followed suit, producing a veritable boom in manufacturing in Southeast Asia (Felker 2003: 261).

This global transformation was enabled by earlier-established production trends and crucial techno-logistical transformations that were rapidly "compressing time and space", making the reorganisation of production along transnational lines increasingly feasible (Harvey 1990; Hobsbawm 1994: 277). Improved modes of data transmission (through the expansion of telex and, later, facsimile services) and more efficient forms of logistics and production (such as containerised shipping and "just-in-time" production) made it possible for production to be "offshored", with manufacturing and assembly of components into finished goods parcelled off to multiple locations. Competitive fractions of capital able to reorganise along such transnational lines moved labour-intensive production to areas with lower labour costs, thereby cutting costs and boosting profits. Together with the "soft infrastructure" of neoliberal policy reforms from the 1980s onwards, this gradually led to the emergence of a new mode of accumulation that dealt a near terminal blow (though not everywhere all at once) to nationally oriented production and, accordingly, notions of nationally centred development, whether ISI, EOI, or anything else. This accumulation regime has been dubbed "flexible accumulation", given the "flexibility" it afforded international capital "with respect to labour processes, labour markets, products and patterns of consumption". It was also "characterized by the emergence of entirely new sectors of production, new ways of providing financial services, new markets, and, above all, greatly intensified rates of commercial, technological, and organizational innovation" (Harvey 1990: 147). Crucially, this shift would also foist ever-greater competitive pressures upon states, labour and, indeed, fractions of capital.

This global surge in the offshoring of manufacturing created new but uneven opportunities for export-oriented economic growth in Southeast Asia. By the late 1970s, the majority of Japanese investment (52%) still went into resources, with the bulk of all FDI (up until 1987) mostly going to Indonesia, followed, in order, by Singapore, Malaysia, Thailand[4] and the Philippines. The expansion in productive capacity stemming from the economic activity associated with the Korean and Vietnam Wars had created favourable conditions for manufacturing investment in countries like Singapore, Malaysia and Thailand, but investment in Indonesia was still heavily resource-related, with Japan accounting for as much as 70–80% of oil exports and 80–90% of timber exports (Stubbs 1989: 531–535; Weinstein 2001: 95).[5] Japan had also become the dominant trading partner of Thailand, Indonesia, the Philippines and Malaysia by 1975 (Weinstein 2001: 93). By the early 1990s, Singapore had become a major recipient of Japanese FDI, receiving almost 10% of all Japanese FDI, rising to 15% by 1997, propelled by multiple large investments in chemicals and semi-conductors (Urata 2002: 4). This increase was reflected to differing degrees across the major Southeast Asian economies, even with the bursting of the Japanese bubble, with steady and regularly increasing flows between the late 1980s up until the 1990s. In absolute terms, Indonesia and Thailand were the biggest recipients by far, with the latter receiving record flows from 1993 until 1997 (ibid.).

As always, Southeast Asia's capitalist development was conflict-prone. While some authoritarian regimes had earlier made great gains in terms of socio-political consolidation, social conflict escalated during the 1970s, as opposition forces pushed to expand political space, prompting new responses from those in power. Notably, Burma, the Philippines and Thailand experienced increasingly emboldened, communist-led armed struggles, and student-led activity across the region expressed grievances on a host of issues, including political repression and, in places like

---

[4] Thailand's receipt of Japanese investment increased significantly throughout the mid-to-late 1980s.

[5] Investments into the electronics industry by US and Japanese companies were important from the 1970s on in Singapore, Malaysia and the Philippines. These industries' contribution to local economies has declined in many (though not all) Southeast Asian countries (see the final section) and the exports of all regional economies in this sector now constitute single digit and lower contributions to total world exports (Rasiah et al. 2014: 646–647).

Indonesia, rapidly increasing Japanese foreign investment.[6] Even in Singapore, the bite of the mid-1970s recession and the state-linked union's inability to represent workers' interests led to an active, though short-lived, student movement (Hewison and Rodan 1994: 249–250). These developments terrified elites, who cracked down hard.

> [T]he growth of solidarity movements between students, workers, peasants and the downtrodden was greatly feared by the governments of the region, especially as students were seen as allies of the communists. But, by the late 1970s, authoritarian governments had again moved to close the political opening, and repressive regimes dominated the political stage throughout the late 1970s and into the 1980s: the Marcos dynasty and its lackeys kept the pressure on through martial law, although some concessions were made; Thailand had a military government again, although limited elections were introduced in the 1980s; New Order Indonesia was still under a military dominated government, and Suharto appeared stronger than ever; Lee and the PAP had further entrenched themselves in Singapore, having arrested 100 "communists" and harassed all legal opposition; and the Malaysian government had cracked down on opposition groups (ibid.: 250–251).

While many of these authoritarian regimes relied on nationalism to help legitimise strategies of repression, in an economic sense the story was far more complicated. On the one hand, embracing export-oriented FDI allowed Southeast Asia's capitalist states to avoid the fate of many poor countries: enforced structural adjustment at the hands of the World Bank and IMF, which forcibly dismantled the institutions of ISI and essentially terminated national development projects based on ISI and other non-liberal measures. Dependence on the international financial institutions was often—though not always—postponed throughout the 1980s as the Japanese-led investment boom gathered momentum (Carroll 2017). Nonetheless, Southeast Asia's capitalist regimes' wholesale turn towards export-oriented growth also involved increasingly inserting parts of their economies into transnational production networks. They supplied low-wage labour—kept disciplined and cheap by ruthless repression—infrastructure and political stability; but they became increasingly dependent

---

[6] Importantly, while Japanese investment often attracted political resistance and action, the Japanese government met this challenge with significant aid programmes that had their antecedents in post-war reparations, economic grants and technical assistance (Stubbs 1989: 531–535).

on overseas capital, technology, management and export markets to varying degrees. Moreover, to attract investors, governments deregulated their economies, often beginning with export-processing and special economic zones but increasingly spreading beyond these hubs. Crucially though, despite increased investment into manufacturing, this economic internationalisation was not amenable to delivering the sort of substantive *national* development, evident in developed countries, which depended upon earlier forms of primitive accumulation and developing a commanding advantage in the means of production. In the all-too-rare cases of late developers such as South Korea, such advantages were developed within the unique historical conditions of the post-war economic expansion and the Cold War and the political and economic advantages—such as market access and technology transfer—attending these. No equivalent development in the means of production occurred in Southeast Asia, with the region largely continuing to serve as a repository of low value-added manufacturing and supplier of commodities to international markets.

That said, Southeast Asia's insertion into emerging global production networks was never total, and the apparent turn towards economic liberalisation often remained selective, as dominant social forces struggled to secure their wealth and power amid changing global conditions. Burma, Cambodia, Laos and Vietnam remained relatively isolated from capitalist investment and trade until Burma's "socialist" regime collapsed in 1988, and the Indochinese regimes—abandoned by their Soviet sponsors in 1986—undertook pro-market reforms. Moreover, even Southeast Asia's capitalist regimes practised selective liberalisation (Felker 2009). Domestically oriented sectors, especially those dominated by regime-linked interests, remained shielded from foreign competition. Business elites within ruling coalitions were the primary beneficiaries of a wave of dubiously arranged privatisations of state assets in the 1980s, and some also became leading partners in foreign joint ventures. This period cemented the rise of "crony capitalism" in the region, with most of the top banks and companies led by politically connected families. Furthermore, in places like Indonesia and Thailand, crony capitalists increasingly outgrew their politico-bureaucratic patrons, becoming political actors in their own right, and even "oligarchs" capable of dominating the state despite a change of political leadership (Winters 2011). Thus, Rodan et al. commented in the third edition of this series, "one of the defining features of the political economy of Southeast Asia, with the exception of Singapore, is the highly instrumental nature of capitalist control of state power"

(Rodan et al. 2006: 25). To capture the symbiotic existence of these highly corrupt, politically shielded sectors alongside considerably liberalised, internationally oriented sectors, Jayasuriya developed the term "embedded mercantilism" (Jayasuriya 2004). Export-oriented FDI generated economic growth and revenues that helped to sustain networks of patronage. Thus, even as Southeast Asian economies liberalised, political and economic governance remained highly illiberal in many respects.

The 1997–98 Asian financial crisis (AFC) brought this so-called "economic miracle" to an end, reminding the region once again that it was located in a global system in a subordinate and, indeed, conditional role. Described by Higgott (2000: 262) as the first crisis of globalisation, the AFC was initially triggered by the effective bankruptcy of Thai financial institutions in mid-1997, spreading quickly to other countries that had also liberalised their investment and capital account regimes. From the late 1980s, Southeast Asian banks had tapped into resurgent global capital markets, borrowing overseas and re-lending the money domestically at higher interest rates. This fuelled massive speculation, especially in real estate, enriching many politically linked business interests, who often acquired large loans with inadequate oversight. However, many of these investments proved unprofitable. This was compounded by the mismatch in loan maturities: banks' overseas borrowing was typically short-term, often requiring repayment within six months, whereas their domestic re-lending was longer-term, making banks unable to demand repayment to pay off their foreign creditors. When the latter realised that many Southeast Asian banks were unable to service their loans, they stampeded from the region (Radelet and Sachs 1997: 47). Regional currencies plummeted, making it even harder to repay dollar-denominated loans. Thailand and Indonesia were forced to seek record-breaking bailouts from the IMF and World Bank, which—often in league with usually marginalised domestic reformers—demanded dramatic pro-market reforms in exchange. There had obviously been earlier crises, as in the early 1980s, that required reforms to shore up investor confidence and maintain economic growth. But these had not fundamentally challenged embedded mercantilism. The AFC was of a much larger scale. Protected fractions of domestic capital and policy elites were forced to grapple with the neoliberal "Washington consensus", while unemployment and poverty soared, generating widespread unrest.

In Indonesia, the crisis profoundly disrupted the social fabric. Family-centred networks of power and patronage were particularly impacted by compounded corporate, banking and fiscal crises (Robison 2001: 118).

The IMF demanded the dismantling of signature developmentalist efforts such as national car and aircraft projects, subsidies on fuel and rice, and state trade monopolies, and the closing down of insolvent banks (ibid.). The shifting fortunes at the very highest level of the patronage apparatus were visible to everyone when then IMF Managing Director Michel Camdessus stood, arms folded, behind the dictator Suharto as he signed a Letter of Intent, capitulating to these demands in exchange for receiving emergency funds. The crisis led to turmoil and violence on the streets, massive student-led protests and the emergence of the *reformasi* (reformation) movement, the latter demanding institutional reform, including a diminution of the military's role, and attacking the corruption, nepotism and collusion endemic to the New Order. Eventually, key politico-business and military elites, realising that Suharto could no longer secure their interests, abandoned him, forcing him to resign and ushering in an era of democratic and decentralising reforms.

Malaysia was less adversely impacted by the crisis than Indonesia and Thailand, but also experienced massive social unrest. A *reformasi* movement also erupted there, though it was effectively contained by the ruling *Barisan Nasional* regime. The Malaysian government also refused to adopt IMF-mandated reforms, instead containing the economic crisis by imposing capital controls and other interventionist measures, and various fiscal and monetary tools. However, this did not signal any kind of retreat into autarky or ignorance of the realities of the global political economy: the government exempted exports from currency restrictions and removed foreign ownership restrictions in manufacturing (Felker 2015: 138–139).

Even after the crisis abated and growth had resumed, the region was a significantly changed place. Although the newer ASEAN economies had been relatively shielded from the AFC by virtue of their relatively insulated, weakly developed banking systems, on the whole, the crisis spurred not a retrenchment from global economic flows but a quest to restore them by undertaking pro-market governance reforms. Southeast Asian governments strove to reassure investors by liberalising investment rules and embarking on the formation of a business-friendly ASEAN Economic Community in 2003 (see Jones and Hameiri, this volume). However, even when investment did return, it was often in a different form. For example, Japanese investors exploited changing ownership rules to take over their local affiliates, creating vertically integrated production chains with far less opportunity for local ownership and substantive development (Urata 2002).

More important, perhaps, was mounting competition arising from the emergence of new low-cost sites of production for global markets, creating intense competitive pressures. In 2001 China was admitted into the World Trade Organization (WTO). Its ongoing transformation into "the factory of the world" created great demand for commodities from Southeast Asia, helping the region to export its way back to growth, but also generated intense competition as a supplier of low-cost labour for foreign investment (see below). Anderson (1998: 302) offered a pithy corrective to the more bullish sentiments common prior to the economic turmoil: "Seen retrospectively, the South-East Asian miracle was thus in part the product of an extraordinary forty-year sequestration from the global market of the greatest power in Asia". China was joined by other regional economies, too, as ASEAN expanded to include Vietnam (1995), Myanmar (1997), Laos (1997) and Cambodia (1999). Myanmar remained largely isolated from global markets due to intensifying Western economic sanctions (notwithstanding a brief boom in garment exports in the early 2000s) and, with Laos, remained heavily reliant on basic commodity exports. But Vietnam and Cambodia, having embarked on pro-market reforms in the late 1980s, quickly copied their neighbours' earlier strategies, using their low-cost labour to lure foreign investors to establish manufacturing facilities in sectors like garments and electronics. From 1989 to 1996, Vietnam's foreign trade surged from 46% of GDP to almost 100%, with the share of manufactures in exports rising from 2 percent in 1990 to nearly 30 percent by 1996 (Masina 2006: 65–67). This was accompanied by large amounts of ODA that largely overlooked heterodox policy elements and instead attributed Vietnam's success rather simplistically to its supposed embrace of market relations (see Carroll 2010: ch.7).

Southeast Asian policy-makers—including newer converts to market relations—knew where comparative advantage lay. Facing demands for higher wages in the mid-1990s, Vietnam's labour minister remarked that "Vietnam cannot set its minimum wage higher than other regional countries... Otherwise foreign investment will... go elsewhere" (quoted in Rigg 1997: 26). Deyo (1997: 213) captured well the growing competitive pressures on producers, states and, of course, labour in this period:

> Compounding... [the] EOI-linked structural demobilisation of labour are continuing international pressures, often associated with ongoing regional and global trade agreements to further open domestic markets to imports. Trade liberalisation has, in turn, subjected firms to intensified competition in both domestic and international markets. In developing countries, with

their relatively labour-intensive, export oriented industrial structures, managers have sought to meet these new competitive pressures through cost-cutting measures directed in large part at reducing labour costs. Such measures have, in turn, both reflected and reinforced labour's already weakened bargaining position, for competitive pressures have created a credible threat of shutdowns, retrenchments and relocation of production to cheaper labour sites in the absence of effective labour cost containment.

What had previously appeared to be a Southeast Asian extension of the late development "miracle" in Northeast Asia now looked like something more contingent and fleeting. Countries in capitalist Southeast Asia, especially dominant domestic fractions of capital, had initially benefited from the global reorganisation of production. However, as Jayasuriya noted, the AFC and ongoing transformations in the world market presented a fundamental, though not entirely terminal, challenge to the sustainability of "embedded mercantilism" (Jayasuriya 2004: 48).

Hyperglobalisation, the Commodities Boom and the Limits to Development (1998 to Present)

Soon after the AFC, Greg Felker provided a sober summary of the development challenge facing Southeast Asia:

> The same historical forces that propelled Southeast Asia's development "miracle" now cast a shadow across the region. The globalization of manufacturing... transformed the region's resource-based economies into export dynamos in a mere two decades. Since the crisis, political instability and partial economic reforms, recurrent slumps in global electronics markets and China's emergence as the premier offshore manufacturing platform have curtailed the flow of new [FDI] into Singapore, Malaysia, Thailand, the Philippines and Indonesia. Has Southeast Asian industrialization run out of steam? Has the region's FDI-reliant strategy led to a high-level dependency trap, leaving its economies without the capabilities required to chart a new development course as MNCs shift their attention to new and greener pastures (Felker 2004: 82)?

It was now abundantly clear that the world economy was a deeply interconnected place and that mobile capital was ascendant. Southeast Asian elites had long recognised that foreign investment was the life-blood of their growth model, but Cold War dynamics and instability elsewhere had allowed them to combine the economic liberalisation needed to

Table 2.6 Southeast Asian FDI net inflows in perspective (current US$, millions), 1990–2016

	1990	2000	2010	2016
Brunei	–	61[a]	481	–151
Cambodia	33[a]	118	1342	2287
Indonesia	1093	–4550	15,292	4469
Laos	6	34	279	997
Malaysia	2332	3788	10,886	13,516
Myanmar	163	255	901	3278
Philippines	530	1487	1070	8280
Singapore	5575	15,515	55,076	74,253
Thailand	2444	3366	14,747	3063
Timor-Leste	–	1[a]	30	5
Vietnam	180	1298	8000	12,600
Regional total	12,356	21,373	108,104	122,597
China	3487	42,095	243,703	174,750
All developing economies[b]	34,649	233,821	642,690	646,030
All developed economies[b]	170,185	1,120,509	677,451	1,032,373
World total[b]	204,905	1,360,254	1 383,779	1,746,424

Source: World Bank (2018a), UNCTAD (2018)
[a]Data from closest year
[b]Reported figures from UNCTAD

attract it with protectionism, in a heterodox mix of policies. However, the new context of intense global competition for investment—hyperglobalisation—has made it increasingly difficult to sustain this heterodoxy or to achieve substantive development, despite the formal continuation of economic growth.

The scale of the challenge can be illustrated by considering China's entry into world markets. In 1990, China attracted approximately US$3.5bn in FDI, less than Singapore at US$5.58bn,[7] but considerably more than Malaysia (US$2.3bn) or Indonesia (US$1.09bn) (see Tables 2.6 and 2.7). However, by 2010, China was receiving US$243.7bn in FDI (over a third of all developing country FDI), outweighing all of

[7] Singapore has long attracted relatively large amounts of FDI, but much of this is routed through the city-state's financial institutions to other countries, and hence does not necessarily contribute to production (or substantive development) in Singapore itself. For example, in 2014 almost half of India's FDI came from Singapore and Mauritius. FDI to Singapore can also be involved in "round tripping", flowing back to the country of origin in order to benefit from tax breaks and other incentives (Aykut et al. 2017; Sjöholm 2013: 11–12).

Table 2.7 Southeast Asian stocks of foreign investment at home and abroad

	Estimated stock of foreign investment at home		Estimated stock of foreign investment abroad	
	Value, US$ (year)	World rank	Value, US$ (year)	World rank
Brunei	–	–	–	–
Cambodia	29.17bn (2014)	70	–	–
Indonesia	247.7bn (2017)	25	19.96bn (2017)	53
Laos	15.14bn (2012)	90	–	–
Malaysia	133.2bn (2017)	41	137.9bn (2017)	32
Myanmar	–	–	–	–
Philippines	67.25bn (2017)	54	47.58bn (2017)	44
Singapore	1.158tr (2017)	10	725.9bn (2017)	15
Thailand	112.3bn (2017)	34	112.3bn (2017)	34
Timor-Leste	–	–	–	–
Vietnam	128.3bn (2017)	42	7.7bn (2009)	66

Source: CIA (2019)

Southeast Asia's FDI combined, by a wide margin. When China joined the WTO in 2001, official growth stood at 8.34 percent per annum; it skyrocketed to 14.23 in 2007 before tapering to a still impressive 10.64 percent in 2010. Yet, tellingly, Southeast Asia's 2016 intake of FDI was only a modest increase on its 2010 performance, although declining flows to countries like Indonesia and Thailand were offset by increases for newly important manufacturing sites like Vietnam.

China's emergence as the "factory of the world" has had highly contradictory consequences for Southeast Asia's development, providing both benefits and costs to different social forces. On the one hand, the need for inputs to fuel China's manufacturing boom propelled a massive surge in commodity prices in the period 2003–11. This allowed Southeast Asian economies to export their way back to growth after the AFC, benefiting especially the domestic interests positioned to allocate licences and derive income from this activity. This continued despite the 2008 global financial crisis (GFC), which dramatically impacted global demand. The emptying container terminals at Singapore's port—then one of the world's busiest—were yet another stark reminder of how the fortunes accruing from global economic integration could rapidly be wound back. However, the GFC's impact on the region was somewhat offset by returning demand for commodities and by "quantitative easing" (QE) in developed countries, which drove capital flows to "emerging markets".

On the other hand, however, China's emergence as a rival site of low-cost manufacturing—alongside other competitors—has further disrupted substantive development in Southeast Asia, with economies remaining largely mired in low to intermediate value-added production. Southeast Asian economies have remained important within emerging "regional production networks", wherein components are produced and combined into a finished product at multiple sites, across several regional economies. For example, simple components for a smartphone may be produced in low-cost economies like Southeast Asia, shipped to South Korea to be combined with more high-tech components requiring higher-skilled, more capital-intensive production, then shipped to China for assembly with other elements into the finished product, which is then transported to, say, Japan, Europe or the United States to be sold. The "value added" at each stage—i.e. the difference in market price before and after a part of the production process is undertaken—can vary enormously. The labour used to, say, assemble cloth pieces into garments or combine parts into an automobile, is obviously essential to making a finished product. However, because low-skilled workers are both abundant and politically weak within a highly competitive world market where capital can relocate production, their wages have been driven down by employers and governments seeking to attract low-cost manufacturing investments. Accordingly, the "value added" of their labour is low (indeed countries are competing on the basis of just how low this is for a certain mix of basic skill sets). Conversely, higher-skill, more capital-intensive processes add more value. Furthermore, some firms—including many not even involved in physically producing an item—capture the lion's share of the final retail price via their ownership of "intellectual property". For example, Apple does not produce any physical part of an iPhone, but it controls research, design and development, owns various patents to the technology and designs used and, of course, owns the brand itself. This allows Apple to capture 42 percent of the retail price of each iPhone 7 sold, while just 1 percent goes to the Chinese workers who actually assemble the components (Dedrick and Kramer 2017: 17).

While Southeast Asian economies remain important in the *intermediate* phases of production in regional production networks, they are clearly struggling to move towards higher value-added activities. Today, development practitioners frequently refer to the "value-added ladder", suggesting that economic development should involve efforts to "climb" this ladder by shifting from low-skill, low value-added activities towards higher-skill, higher value-added ones. However, it is increasingly obvious that this is easier said than done. While scholars have recently identified some cases of upgrading in high-technology industries in Southeast Asia, the share of value retained from this production remains small, because of a continued reliance on high-value foreign inputs. Indeed, a recent, detailed study concludes that it is "far-fetched" to suggest that increasing regional production and growth signalled the development of domestic value-adding advantage in high-technology and innovation (Kam 2017: 705–711).

For many countries in Southeast Asia, these contradictory dynamics have brought rising per capita incomes, declining absolute poverty and expanded consumption, but also burgeoning private debt, rising inequality, further elite capture of key economic sectors, environmental destruction, and an underlying failure to deliver substantive development. Indonesia emblematises all of these contradictions. As the World Bank's 2015 "Systematic Country Diagnostic" noted:

> There is strong evidence that growth and poverty reduction were strongly influenced by global commodity markets in the first decade of the new millennium. Indeed, the significant rise in commodity prices in 2003–11 led to massive income and wealth effects in Indonesia. These fed into corporate revenues, household incomes and government revenues, lending to a significant jump in domestic demand for goods and services. On the supply side, the (largely non-tradeable) services sector rose considerably, contrasting with a quasi-stagnant manufacturing sector, which lost competitiveness due to sharp appreciation of the real exchange rate and high logistics and trade costs (World Bank 2015: 7).

Unsurprisingly, the commodities boom, like earlier booms, led to a fresh economically illiberal push from dominant oligarchic interests. Well-positioned domestic capitalists led calls for "resource nationalism" in an attempt to grab a larger share of the rents from commodity exports from the foreign capitalists who had increasingly dominated the extractives sector in particular. A capitalist class "more powerful, more liquid, and more engaged in resource industries than ever before"—combined with Indonesia's nationalist-developmentalist tradition and an environment of patronage politics "largely devoid of ideological differences and substantive policy debate"—was able to realise such demands, even as commodity prices subsequently fell (Warburton 2017: 2–3). Laws passed under President Yudhoyono (2004–14) increased opportunities for state control of natural resources, generating gains for oligarchs deeply embedded in party-political life and close to the state (ibid.: 10). High commodity prices also contributed to significant windfalls for domestic producers, like the state oil company and the oligarchs controlling the environmentally ruinous palm oil industry. Yet this bounty for certain leading enterprises did little to change the overall picture of an economy that remained heavily dependent upon the exogenous drivers of commodity prices.

Moreover, Indonesia also epitomised the struggle to maintain wider economic growth amid the competitive pressures of hyperglobalisation. Even as powerful interests successfully pushed "resource nationalism", policy-makers were promoting a near-diametrically opposed liberalisation drive in other crucial areas. This was particularly noticeable after the 2014 election of President Joko Widodo, despite his campaign rhetoric being similarly nationalistic to his populist opponent, Suharto's former son-in-law, Prabowo Subianto. Poor manufacturing performance and rising inequality—the country's Gini coefficient increased from 0.30 to 0.42 in parallel with the commodities boom—combined with wider global dynamics impacting emerging markets, such as the US Federal Reserve's "taper tantrum" (winding back QE, increasing interest rates and drawing money out of emerging markets and bonds) and a rising dollar (making the servicing of dollar-denominated debt costlier).

Indeed, much of Southeast Asia—like China—now finds itself firmly within what is often called the "middle income trap". This concept was defined by Gill and Kharas (2007: 5) in their World Bank report, *An East Asian Renaissance*, to characterise countries "squeezed between low-wage poor-country competitors that dominated in mature industries and rich-country innovators that dominated in industries undergoing rapid technological change". Growth and capital accumulation, especially relative to population, has slowed significantly. Accordingly, while limited protectionist measures have been evident, and the legacy of developmentalist and central planning still have an impact, Southeast Asian states have been vocally committed to improving the "business environment" to maintain foreign investment. This manifests in a quest to rise up rankings tables, such as the World Bank's *Doing Business* ratings, and the World Economic Forum's *Competitiveness Report*, which penalise deviations from neoliberal economic governance. Southeast Asian policy-makers' pursuit of higher rankings reflects the interests of more competitive fractions of domestic capital, and political and bureaucratic forces that recognise the constraints of illiberal policies on investment and growth (see Al-Fadhat, this volume). Despite occasional nationalist rhetoric, and political mediation that continues to privilege certain domestic actors, then, the overall trend is towards pro-market reforms, reflecting the ever-more competitive international environment and the dearth of developmental alternatives in the post-Cold War context.

For example, while Vietnam's communist party remains firmly in power, that country's impressive growth and investment track record is significantly, though not entirely, explained by a combination of ongoing market reforms started over three decades ago, a literate and healthy workforce (the product of many non-market measures) and the global reorganisation of production. In 2018, Vietnam was ranked 68 in *Doing Business*, above Indonesia and the Philippines, and 55 in the *Competitiveness Report* (see Table 2.8). Despite often egregious corruption and the ability of powerful fractions of domestic capital to secure continued protection and patronage, both Thailand and Malaysia also do well on both indices, while Singapore has often topped such rankings. Indonesia, long targeted for its corruption and burdensome bureaucracy, has recently improved its *Doing Business* standing considerably—Widodo has targeted a ranking of 40 for the country—rising 19 places in 2018. Notably, the country does even better on the WEF rankings, placing it closer to Thailand and Malaysia, and frequently receives favourable coverage in the quality financial media, such as the *Financial Times*.

This does not, of course, mean there has been a wholesale shift towards delivering what international development organisations call an "enabling environment" for the private sector. Notably, the newer ASEAN members and Timor-Leste come well down the *Doing Business* index, with Cambodia at 135, Laos at 141, Myanmar at 171 and Timor-Leste at 178. Surveying other governance indicators is also revealing, with many of the latter countries in particular also doing poorly in terms of regulatory quality, rule of law and control of corruption (see Table 2.9). Combined with intensely unequal and resource-driven economies that permit relatively easy capture and rent-seeking opportunities, this bodes poorly for prospective developmental outcomes. That said, the areas that these markers refer to are often precisely where critical elements within domestic and international civil society currently target their efforts.

While such rankings are far from perfect measures of governance, they do reflect genuine efforts to provide "enabling environments" for capital, particularly transnational capital and competitive fractions of domestic capital that can operate profitably without state protection. Governments under pressure to attract capital have had to embrace liberalising strategies, such as those associated with the Washington consensus (Williamson 1990), and later-generation neoliberal reforms that target both the "soft" (institutional) and "hard" infrastructure deemed necessary to maintain competitiveness, the former including limited social safety nets to manage the politics of reform.

Table 2.8 Indicators of ease of doing business, competitiveness and market interfacing in Southeast Asia

	Doing business rank, 2018 (/190)	WEF global competitiveness report rank, 2016–17	WTO/WIPO membership (year joined)	Average tariff rate, 2016[a]	Capital account liberalisation[b]	Currency rate regime[c]
Brunei	56	46	Yes (1995)/Yes (1994)	5.57	–	Currency board
Cambodia	135	94	Yes (2004)/Yes (1995)	14.23	Other	Other managed
Indonesia	72	36	Yes (1995)/Yes (1979)	10.04	Gate	Floating
Laos	141	98	Yes (2013)/Yes (1995)	9.02	Wall	Stabilised
Malaysia	24	23	Yes (1995)/Yes (1989)	15.66	Gate	Other managed
Myanmar	171	–	Yes (1995)/Yes (2001)	7.41	Other	Other managed
Philippines	113	56	Yes (1995)/Yes (1980)	7.45	Gate	Floating
Singapore	2	3	Yes (1995)/Yes (1990)	0	Gate	Stabilised
Thailand	26	32	Yes (1995)/Yes (1989)	17.21	Gate	Floating
Timor-Leste	178	–	Observer/Yes (2017)	–	–	No separate legal tender
Vietnam	68	55	Yes (2007)/Yes (1976)	15.44	Other	Stabilised

Source: IMF (2016), World Bank (2018b), World Trade Organization (2018), World Economic Forum (2016)

[a]Simple averages (WTO tariff line averaging method), most favoured nation, all products
[b]Wang-Jahan Index, based on IMF data (Jahan and Wang 2016)
[c]IMF Annual Report on Exchange Arrangements and Exchange Restrictions, 2016 (IMF 2016: 6–8)

Table 2.9 Southeast Asian governance indicators

	Voice and accountability	Political stability and absence of violence/terrorism	Government effectiveness	Regulatory quality	Rule of law	Control of corruption
Brunei	−0.95/23.15	1.26/93.81	1.07/81.25	0.59/71.15	0.59/71.15	0.66/72.60
Cambodia	−1.14/17.73	0.18/52.38	−0.69/24.52	−0.47/34.13	−0.47/34.13	−1.30/8.17
Indonesia	0.14/50.25	−0.38/33.33	0.01/53.37	−0.12/50.00	−0.12/50.00	−0.39/42.79
Lao PDR	−1.73/4.43	0.50/62.38	−0.98/39.42	−0.73/24.52	−0.73/24.52	−0.93/15.38
Malaysia	−0.47/33	0.10/50.00	0.88/75.96	0.71/75.48	0.71/75.48	0.11/61.54
Myanmar	−0.85/24.14	−0.63/23.33	−0.98/16.35	−0.87/18.75	−0.87/18.75	−0.65/30.77
Philippines	0.14/50.74	−1.30/10	−0.01/51.92	0.00/53.85	0.00/53.85	−0.53/34.13
Singapore	−0.28/36.95	1.53/99.52	2.21/100.00	2.18/100.00	2.81/100.00	2.07/97.12
Thailand	−1.10/20.69	−0.93/15.71	0.34/66.35	0.17/60.10	0.17/60.10	−0.40/40.87
Timor-Leste	0.24/54.19	−0.08/43.33	−1.03/13.94	−0.98/13.94	−0.98/13.94	−0.51/34.62
Vietnam	−1.41/9.85	0.17/51.43	0.01/52.88	−0.45/35.10	−0.45/35.10	−0.40/41.83

Source: World Bank (2017)

Note: Each column shows the estimate, ranging from −2.5 (weak) to 2.5 (strong) and percentile rank, from 0 (lowest) to 100 (highest)

Indicative of this, Malaysia's government has faced a formidable set of headwinds relating to declining FDI (attributed to relatively high wage rates and skills constraints), a depreciating currency, slowing growth in China (Malaysia's top trading partner), and significant productivity challenges for small and medium enterprises. Declining oil revenues, which account for around a third of government income, have also limited the government's capacity to dispense patronage to key social groups. Overall, the government seems set to miss its target of turning Malaysia into a high-income country by 2020 (World Bank 2019). No doubt driven by the need to attract more (and more diverse) investment, government statements have repeatedly emphasised the need to improve Malaysia's *Doing Business* rankings, targeting the top 20 by 2020. Moreover, the 2010 New Economic Model—with its avowedly neoliberal line—contrasts markedly with earlier state-led, developmentalist efforts, such as the New Economic Policy (National Economic Advisory Council 2010: 13).

Similar dynamics can be seen in other Southeast Asian countries facing challenges in terms of productivity, fixed-capital formation, declining social mobility and rising inequality. In wealthier countries, like Singapore, governments have been able to respond to social unrest with new fiscal transfers, yet even these have often failed to ameliorate popular angst regarding price rises, declining social mobility and rising inequality (Rodan 2016). Moreover, lacklustre attempts by the government to move up value chains and generate opportunities for citizens have now given way to yet more efforts towards "managing expectations". An example of this was when Prime Minister Lee Hsien Loong took to Twitter to propose that young Singaporeans become "hawker-preneurs", a remark that recast remaining opportunities for social mobility around establishing one of the city's cheap food stalls. In the larger and poorer regional economies, however, the policy choice has narrowed around further liberalising efforts, regularly paired with attempts to attract Chinese investment. This combination is often awkwardly fused with nationalist rhetoric and even violent populism, as in the case of Rodrigo Duterte's contortions in the Philippines that have combined courting Chinese investment with nationalist machismo, extra-judicial killings and liberal tax reform. Thompson describes this as an extreme example of policy and politics emanating from the death of national development (Thompson 2016, 2018: 20–21). In Indonesia, the first major policy switch after Widodo's 2014 election was to increase fuel prices and then remove fuel subsidies, provoking outrage from the urban poor. This was ostensibly done in a bid to free up money for infrastructure spending, a central focus of the *Masterplan for the Acceleration and Expansion of Indonesia's Economic Development* (2011–2025), which placed public–private partnerships—a key neoliberal modality—at its core. Widodo has regularly spoken of "big bang" liberalisation and elevated numerous reform-minded technocrats to senior government positions. In 2016, a revised Negative Investment List abolished restrictions on foreign investment entirely for 35 industries, and significantly relaxed them for a further 40 (Chilkoti 2016; Lane 2015; *The Wall Street Journal* 2016). In the region's "frontier" states, well-placed elites have disproportionately benefited from processes of marketisation, significantly shaping reform agendas and the realities of market relations. For example, in Myanmar, Jones—echoing earlier studies of countries within the region[8]—has described a transition from "state socialism to state-mediated capitalism", and the cronyism that has emerged from this process (Jones 2014: 148).

All of the above speaks to the contemporary constraints upon capitalist development in Southeast Asia and, indeed, more generally. It is particularly instructive that there are no Southeast Asian companies in the key global ranking lists of companies, issued by the likes of Forbes, Bloomberg and PricewaterhouseCoopers (PwC). Rankings by market capitalisation are completely devoid of a Southeast Asian presence, yet South Korea, Taiwan, Brazil, Denmark, Belgium and Ireland are all present (PricewaterhouseCoopers 2017: 16). In Forbes's Global List of largest publicly traded companies, the first Southeast Asian entry is Thailand's state-linked oil and gas company, PTT, at 156. This brings us back to questions about where value lies within the global political economy and where Southeast Asia's economies are situated in relation to this. PwC's 2017 ranking of companies by market capitalisation is not dominated by old industrial behemoths: there are only six industrial companies in the top 100, led by General Electric at 11th place (PricewaterhouseCoopers 2017). Unsurprisingly, the picture that emerges from these lists is the dominance of technology, finance and telecommunications firms: companies at the heart of flexible accumulation. Comparable ASEAN-only tables are instead dominated by state-linked and family-controlled (as opposed to fully publicly listed) companies; national and regional finance; national and regional telecommunications service providers; firms involved with

---

[8] Many Murdoch Scholars have offered similar analyses: in addition to others cited earlier, see Hughes (2003) and Hutchison et al. (2014).

primary resources (oil, gas, palm oil), cement, chemicals, steel, foodstuffs, retail, tourism, and real estate; and just a few prominent industrial actors (Nikkei Asian Review 2014). Importantly, almost all of these companies are concentrated in "first tier" Southeast Asian economies—countries that became globally important manufacturing sites during the 1980s.

What does this mean in terms of substantive developmental possibilities and outcomes in Southeast Asia? The numbers related to filed patents, an indicator that says a lot regarding the ownership of high-value productive knowledge, are revealing (see Table 2.10). Combined with the global company rankings just discussed, they are suggestive of economies mired in low-value activities. For example, recent headlines have trumpeted Mercedes Benz's decision to assemble cars from start to finish in Indonesia. This is not actually new: Japanese manufacturers have long done this through local affiliates in the country. However, in a substantive developmental sense, this is very different to, say, the formation of the German automotive industry in the last century, or even the development of this sector in Northeast Asia. Mercedes Benz retains control of all aspects of design, software engineering, branding and plant design/organisation, allowing it to capture the lion's share of the cars' final retail price. As Doner and Wad (2014: 668–669) state:

> Southeast Asia's success is less impressive when compared to auto sectors in South Korea, China and Taiwan. Automotive growth in Southeast Asia is "extensive": consisting largely of vehicle and component assembly and export, almost totally under the auspices of foreign producers. Extensive growth has altered the production profile of these countries; it has generated jobs and local value added; but it has not involved much if any increase in substantive contributions from local producers and institutions. In contrast, automotive production in Northeast Asia has been more "intensive" in that it has been based on national—indigenous—ownership as well as indigenous firms' technical capacities and inputs in the form of design, (product and process) engineering, and management.

Thus, Thailand and Indonesia have developed significant automotive sectors, but producing mostly finished vehicles for Japanese brands for both domestic consumption and (particularly in Thailand's case) export. Malaysia constitutes the only partial exception to this, maintaining a protected domestic market to shelter the national car company, Proton (Wijeratne and Lau 2016).

Similarly, the assembly of processors for Advanced Micro Devices (AMD) in Malaysia (or anywhere else) means something very different

Table 2.10 Select indicators of intellectual property (IP) activity in Southeast Asia against select countries

	Rankings of total (resident and abroad) IP filing activity by origin	Patent applications resident/non-resident
Brunei	–	–
Cambodia	–	–
Indonesia	45	1058/8095
Laos	–	–
Malaysia	35	1272/6455
Myanmar	–	–
Philippines	51	375/3359
Singapore	26	1469/9345
Thailand	42	1006/6924
Timor-Leste	–	–
Vietnam	50	582/4451
China	1	968,252/133,612
South Korea	4	167,275/46,419
Germany	5	47,384/19,509

Source: World Intellectual Property Organization (2016)

developmentally to the formation of such companies in their home domiciles. AMD dominates the value chain due to its competitive advantage in designing processors that place increasing numbers of transistors on silicon wafers. Indeed, since 2009, AMD does not manufacture any physical product at all (having gone "fabless"), limiting itself to design and branding. Where value is captured is now increasingly delinked from where production takes place. Where many things are made is now largely dependent on the cost of labour, remaining trade barriers, and proximity to large and increasingly consumer-led growth markets. The difficulty Southeast Asian economies have in shifting towards higher value-added production is reflected in the numbers of patent filings for Southeast Asia. Both those filed for residents (domestic companies) and non-residents (foreign companies) are incredibly low when set against those in industrial powerhouses. Moreover, non-resident filings well and truly eclipse resident filings, even in Southeast Asia's most advanced economies, like Singapore, Malaysia and Thailand (see Table 2.10).

Not surprisingly then, given declining commodity prices and concerns over continuing FDI-led development, many regional governments have recently juggled the prospects of attracting increasing public and private Chinese investment, including that associated with the nebulous Belt and Road Initiative (BRI), with broader neoliberal efforts, in a bid to attract more FDI. The latest regional entrants to the world capitalist system (typically at much lower levels of development than their regional peers)—Cambodia, Laos and Myanmar—have been especially indicative (though not alone) in this juggling act. All three have been increasingly incorporated into regional and broader relations of production and accumulation in a manner that has indelibly impacted their particular patterns of development. They manifest the persistence of subsistence farming and high poverty rates alongside fast but highly uneven growth, increased manufacturing, and intensive extractive activity often associated with "land grabbing". In Cambodia, this combination has seen Hun Sen, now one of the world's longest serving heads of government, bolster his long-running political domination based upon a deeply entrenched patronage apparatus, suppressing opposition forces. China is a significant supporter of Hun Sen, extending military aid and loans for infrastructure in Cambodia, alongside substantial commercial investment in low-wage industry (especially garments) and the extractives sector. The legal dissolution of the main opposition party ahead of the 2018 elections, leading to the ruling party capturing every parliamentary seat, is a sad commentary on the limited impact of two decades of donor programmes on "good governance" (Reed 2018a, b).[9]

Chinese state-linked and private (though often still state-connected) investments are undoubtedly becoming important in shaping patterns of governance and prominent developmental projects in Southeast Asia (see Rosser, this volume). This influence differs from that of earlier Japanese aid and investment, which occurred in the absence of China from global markets. China is significant in exporting surplus capital into projects that often involve large numbers of Chinese workers and which are now seen as possible "debt traps" and "white elephants" associated with poor governance and corruption. For example, Chinese investment played a prominent role in the lead-up to the shock 2018 election defeat of the ruling *Barisan Nasional* in Malaysia, an outcome that also stemmed from rising living costs and declining economic fortunes for much of the population (Palma 2018). The award of the contract for the US$5.5bn Jakarta–Bandung high speed railway to a Chinese state-owned firm has also symbolised the growing prominence of Chinese state investment and generated diplomatic tensions with Japan, a seasoned rival bidder and long-standing

---

[9] Some have also speculated that the 2018 election involved Chinese hackers targeting political opponents of the incumbent regime.

donor and investor in Indonesia (Negara and Suryadinata 2018).[10] Importantly, in the region's "frontier states", such as Myanmar, Chinese investment has often involved sub-national Chinese state agencies and economic enterprises combining to create a "rapacious form of development", which has heightened insecurity in many ways on both sides of the border (Hameiri et al. 2018). In several countries, especially those with long-standing resentments towards economic dominance by ethnic-Chinese entrepreneurs, the social, environmental and political consequences of such projects are generating new vectors of resistance and conflict. For example, enemies of Indonesia's President Widodo have seized upon his engagement with the BRI, branding him part of a "Beijing axis" and positioning themselves as a "Mecca axis" in an effort to mobilise support in the majority-Muslim country, where ethnic-Chinese have long been both crony capitalists and ethnic scapegoats.

Conclusion

At this end of the short century of development that began in 1945, with the reorganisation of production and revolutions in the means of production at such an advanced state, underdeveloped countries find themselves in a difficult position. At worst, they are grappling with realising elements of the first industrial revolution; at best, they are often stuck between the second and third industrial revolutions. Growth figures fail to capture the real developmental story of asymmetrical, non-linear and uneven development that can often disappear as quickly as it arrived, with processes of creative destruction, the arrival of new and cheaper labour forces, or increasing automation and "reshoring". Contemporary development policy, now almost completely delinked from the sorts of substantive development processes evident in the post-war era, focuses upon the often modest gains possible from improvements in governance and further public–private partnerships—the main method made responsible for delivering on infrastructure to further support growth—within the ostensibly inevitable context of the world market.

It was not always thus. In the post-war/pre-neoliberal period, policymakers, politicians, scholars and revolutionaries struggled over the potential of different development strategies, as part of "hot" and "cold" conflicts. Yet an underlying argument of this chapter is that the present

[10] The project has also been plagued by questions over economic prudence and safeguards and issues relating to land acquisition.

trajectory was largely set in place a long time ago, albeit with important battles and shifts in leverage for capital, the state and labour shaping outcomes. Some scholars blame developmental divergences between Southeast Asia and Northeast Asian developmental states on the lack of what Peter Evans (1995) famously described as "embedded autonomy"—the relative insulation of bureaucrats from vested interests, which ostensibly permitted effective dirigiste policies; Southeast Asia failed to achieve this, so the argument goes, thereby descending into crony capitalism and patrimonialism. While such analyses are tempting they are perhaps somewhat unfair, obscuring the developmentalist efforts of multiple Southeast Asian governments and downplaying the historically inscribed constraints associated with capitalist development, assigning the lion's share of blame, explicitly or implicitly, to poor governance.

Re-telling the story of Southeast Asia's development with one eye firmly on the evolving nature of global capitalism reveals a rather different narrative. It emphasises that, from the outset, capitalist Southeast Asia's comparative advantages were, first, its natural resources and, second, its large pool of disciplined labour—both located in a region that was a primary Cold War theatre and intimately joined to two of the world's most important economies, Japan and the US. However, an advantage in commodities and cheap labour has made the region particularly susceptible to particular patterns of development, including those associated with the "resource curse" and "crony capitalism", wherein a small elite has often gained overwhelming advantage. Despite the often negative outcomes of these processes for many people, political elites have proven adept at developing new ways to manage political conflict (Rodan 2018). The addition of new repositories of labour, with Eastern Europe, China and Indochina joining the world market, and histories involving the systematic suppression of workers and peasants, have also massively weakened the leverage of those social forces—workers, the left and civil society more broadly—traditionally at the forefront of struggles for progressive economic and political development. Moreover, the possibility of pursuing national developmental strategies of any shade within capitalism has largely disappeared with the rise of flexible accumulation. This perhaps speaks to the emergence of various forms of populism that typically comprise contradictory agendas centred on morality, identity issues and vocal right-wing nationalism, but which also often include efforts—however limited—to reverse the neoliberal economic and social policy sets that have become the norm almost everywhere (see Hadiz and Robison, this volume; Gonzalez-Vicente and Carroll 2017).

Appendix: Southeast Asian Economic Composition by Country

	Main industrial products of economic importance	Main agricultural products of economic importance	GDP composition by sector of origin	Labour force by occupation	Exports	Export partners	Imports	Import partners
Brunei	Petroleum, petroleum refining, liquefied natural gas, construction, agriculture, aquaculture, transportation	Rice, vegetables, fruits, chickens, water buffalo, cattle, goats, eggs	Agriculture: 1.2% industry: 56.5% services: 42.3% (2017 est.)	Agriculture: 4.2% industry: 62.8% services: 33% (2008 est.)	Mineral fuels, organic chemicals	Japan 36.5%, South Korea 16.8%, Thailand 10.6%, India 9.8%, Malaysia 6.6%, China 4.6% (2016)	Machinery and mechanical appliance parts, mineral fuels, motor vehicles, electric machinery	US 28.4%, Malaysia 24%, Singapore 7.1%, Indonesia 5.7%, Japan 5.3%, China 4.9%, Australia 4.3% (2016)
Cambodia	Tourism, garments, construction, rice milling, fishing, wood and wood products, rubber, cement, gem mining, textiles	Rice, rubber, corn, vegetables, cashews, cassava (manioc, tapioca), silk	Agriculture: 25.3% industry: 32.8% services: 41.9% (2017 est.)	Agriculture: 48.7% industry: 19.9% services: 31.5% (2013 est.)	Clothing, timber, rubber, rice, fish, tobacco, footwear	US 21.3%, UK 9.4%, Germany 9%, Japan 8.2%, Canada 6.5%, China 6%, Thailand 4.2%, Spain 4% (2016)	Petroleum products, cigarettes, gold, construction materials, machinery, motor vehicles, pharmaceutical products	China 35.3%, Thailand 14.8%, Vietnam 11%, Singapore 4.4%, Japan 4.1%, Hong Kong 4% (2016)

(continued)

(continued)

	Main industrial products of economic importance	Main agricultural products of economic importance	GDP composition by sector of origin	Labour force by occupation	Exports	Export partners	Imports	Import partners
Indonesia	Petroleum and natural gas, textiles, automotive, electrical appliances, apparel, footwear, mining, cement, medical instruments and appliances, handicrafts, chemical fertilizers, plywood, rubber, processed food, jewellery, and tourism	Rubber and similar products, palm oil, poultry, beef, forest products, shrimp, cocoa, coffee, medicinal herbs, essential oil, fish and fish products, spices	Agriculture: 13.9%, industry: 40.3% services: 45.9% (2017 est.)	Agriculture: 32%, industry: 21% services: 47% (2016 est.)	Mineral fuels, animal or vegetable fats (includes palm oil), electrical machinery, rubber, machinery and mechanical appliance parts	China 22.1%, Japan 14.7%, US 13.6%, India 10.8%, Singapore 10%, Malaysia 6.4%, South Korea 5.1% (2017)	Mineral fuels, boilers, machinery, and mechanical parts, electric machinery, iron and steel, foodstuffs	China 22.9%, Singapore 10.8%, Japan 9.6%, Thailand 6.4%, US 5.4%, Malaysia 5.4%, South Korea 5% (2016)
Laos	Mining (copper, tin, gold, gypsum); timber; electric power, agricultural processing, rubber, construction, garments, cement, tourism	Sweet potatoes, vegetables, corn, coffee, sugarcane, tobacco, cotton, tea, peanuts, rice; cassava (manioc, tapioca), water buffalo, pigs, cattle, poultry	Agriculture: 20.9% industry: 33.2% services: 39.1% (2017 est.)	Agriculture: 73.1% industry: 6.1% services: 20.6% (2012 est.)	Wood products, coffee, electricity, tin, copper, gold, cassava	Thailand 40.1%, China 28.5%, Vietnam 13.7% (2016)	Machinery and equipment, vehicles, fuel, consumer goods	Thailand 64.6%, China 16.5%, Vietnam 9.4% (2016)

Malaysia	Peninsular Malaysia — rubber and oil palm processing and manufacturing, petroleum and natural gas, light manufacturing, pharmaceuticals, medical technology, electronics and semiconductors, timber processing; Sabah — logging, petroleum and natural gas production; Sarawak — agriculture processing, petroleum and natural gas production, logging	Peninsular Malaysia — palm oil, rubber, cocoa, rice; Sabah — palm oil, subsistence crops; rubber; timber; Sarawak — palm oil, rubber, timber; pepper	Agriculture: 8.4% industry: 36.9% services: 54.7% (2017 est.)	Agriculture: 11% industry: 36% services: 53% (2012 est.)	Semiconductors and electronic equipment, palm oil, petroleum and liquefied natural gas, wood and wood products, palm oil, rubber, textiles, chemicals, solar panels	Singapore 14.7%, China 12.6%, US 10.3%, Japan 8.1%, Thailand 5.7%, Hong Kong 4.8%, India 4.1% (2016)	Electronics, machinery, petroleum products, plastics, vehicles, iron and steel products, chemicals	China 19.4%, Singapore 9.8%, Japan 7.7%, US 7.6%, Thailand 5.8%, South Korea 5%, Indonesia 4% (2016)
Myanmar	Agricultural processing, wood and wood products, copper, tin, tungsten, iron, cement, construction materials, pharmaceuticals, fertiliser, oil and natural gas, garments, jade and gems	Rice, pulses, beans, sesame, groundnuts, sugarcane, fish and fish products, hardwood	Agriculture: 24.8%, industry: 35.4% services: 39.9% (2017 est.)	Agriculture: 70% industry: 7% services: 23% (2001 est.)	Natural gas, wood products, pulses and beans, fish, rice, clothing, minerals, including jade and gems	China 40.6%, Thailand 19.1%, India 8.8%, Singapore 7.6%, Japan 5.7% (2016)	Fabric, petroleum products, fertilizer, plastics, machinery, transport equipment, cement, construction materials, food products, edible oil	China 33.9%, Singapore 14.3%, Thailand 12.5%, Japan 7.9%, India 6.9%, Malaysia 4.3% (2016)

(*continued*)

(continued)

	Main industrial products of economic importance	Main agricultural products of economic importance	GDP composition by sector of origin	Labour force by occupation	Exports	Export partners	Imports	Import partners
Philippines	Semiconductors and electronics assembly, business process outsourcing, food and beverage manufacturing, construction, electric/gas/water supply, chemical products, radio/television/communications equipment and apparatus, petroleum and fuel, textile and garments, non-metallic minerals, basic metal industries, transport equipment	Rice, fish, livestock, poultry, bananas, coconut/copra, corn, sugarcane, mangoes, pineapple, cassava	Agriculture: 9.4%, industry: 30.8%, services: 59.8% (2017 est.)	Agriculture: 26.9%, industry: 17.5%, services: 55.6% (2016 est.)	Semiconductors and electronic products, machinery and transport equipment, wood manufactures, chemicals, processed food and beverages, garments, coconut oil, copper concentrates, seafood, bananas/fruits	Japan 16.2%, US 14.8%, Hong Kong 13.7%, China 11.1%, Singapore 6.1%, Thailand 4.2%, Germany 4.1%, South Korea 4% (2017)	Electronic products, mineral fuels, machinery and transport equipment, iron and steel, textile fabrics, grains, chemicals, plastic	China 18.1%, Japan 11.4%, South Korea 8.7%, US 8%, Thailand 7.1%, Indonesia 6.8%, Singapore 5.9%, Taiwan 5.3% (2016)
Singapore	Electronics, chemicals, financial services, oil drilling equipment, petroleum refining, biomedical products, scientific instruments, telecommunications equipment, processed food and beverages, ship repair, offshore platform construction, entrepôt trade	Vegetables, poultry, eggs, fish, ornamental fish, orchids	Agriculture: 0%, industry: 26%, services: 74% (2016 est.)	Agriculture: 0.96%, industry: 15.5%, services: 83.5% note: excludes non-residents (2016 est.)	Machinery and equipment (including electronics and telecommunications), pharmaceuticals and other chemicals, refined petroleum products, foodstuffs and beverages	China 12.8%, Hong Kong 12.6%, Malaysia 10.5%, Indonesia 7.8%, US 6.8%, Japan 4.5%, South Korea 4.4% (2016)	Machinery and equipment, mineral fuels, chemicals, foodstuffs, consumer goods	China 14.3%, Malaysia 11.4%, US 10.8%, Japan 7%, South Korea 6.1%, Indonesia 4.8% (2016)

Thailand	Tourism, textiles and garments, agricultural processing, beverages, tobacco, cement, light manufacturing such as jewellery and electric appliances, computers and parts, integrated circuits, furniture, plastics, automobiles and automotive parts, agricultural machinery, air conditioning and refrigeration, ceramics, aluminium, chemical, environmental management, glass, granite and marble, leather, machinery and metal work, petrochemical, petroleum refining, pharmaceuticals, printing, pulp and paper, rubber, sugar, rice, fishing, cassava, world's second-largest tungsten producer and third-largest tin producer	Rice, cassava (manioc, tapioca), rubber, corn, sugarcane, coconuts, palm oil, pineapple, livestock, fish products	Agriculture: 8.2% industry: 36.2% services: 55.6% (2017 est.)	Agriculture: 31.8% industry: 16.7% services: 51.5% (2015 est.)	Automobiles and parts, computer and parts, jewellery and precious stones, polymers of ethylene in primary forms, refined fuels, electronic integrated circuits, chemical products, rice, fish products, rubber products, sugar, cassava, poultry, machinery and parts, iron and steel and their products	US 11.4%, China 11.1%, Japan 9.6%, Hong Kong 5.3%, Australia 4.8%, Malaysia 4.5%, Vietnam 4.4% (2016)	Machinery and parts, crude oil, electrical machinery and parts, chemicals, iron and steel and products, electronic integrated circuits, automobile parts, jewellery including silver bars and gold, computers and parts, electrical household appliances, soybean, soybean meal, wheat, cotton, dairy products	China 21.6%, Japan 15.8%, US 6.2%, Malaysia 5.6% (2016)

(*continued*)

(continued)

	Main industrial products of economic importance	Main agricultural products of economic importance	GDP composition by sector of origin	Labour force by occupation	Exports	Export partners	Imports	Import partners
Timor-Leste	Printing, soap manufacturing, handicrafts, woven cloth	Coffee, rice, corn, cassava (manioc, tapioca), sweet potatoes, soybeans, cabbage, mangoes, bananas, vanilla	Agriculture: 9.4% industry: 57.8% services: 31.3% (2017 est.)	Agriculture: 64% industry: 10% services: 26% (2010 est.)	Oil, coffee, sandalwood, marble	–	Food, gasoline, kerosene, machinery	–
Vietnam	Food processing, garments, shoes, machine-building; mining, coal, steel, cement, chemical fertilizer, glass, tires, oil, mobile phones	Rice, coffee, rubber, tea, pepper, soybeans, cashews, sugar cane, peanuts, bananas, pork, poultry, seafood	Agriculture: 15.9% industry: 32.7% services: 41.3% (2017 est.)	Agriculture: 48% industry: 21% services: 31% (2012 est.)	Clothes, shoes, electronics, seafood, crude oil, rice, coffee, wooden products, machinery	US 19.4%, China 16.6%, Japan 7.9%, South Korea 6.9% (2017)	Machinery and equipment, petroleum products, steel products, raw materials for the clothing and shoe industries, electronics, plastics, automobiles	China 27.6%, South Korea 22.1%, Japan 7.9%, Taiwan 6%, Thailand 5%, US 4.4% (2017)

Source: CIA (2019)

REFERENCES

Anderson, B. R. (1998). *The spectre of comparisons: Nationalism, Southeast Asia and the World*. London: Verso.

Asian Development Bank. (2017). *Key indicators for Asia and the Pacific*. Manila: ADB.

Aykut, D., Sanghi, A., & Kosmidou, G. (2017). *What to do when foreign direct investment is not direct or foreign: FDI round tripping* (Policy research working paper no. 8046). Washington, DC: World Bank.

Berger, M. T. (2004). *The battle for Asia: From decolonization to globalization*. London: Routledge.

Cammack, P. (2017). Capitalist development in the 21st century: States and global competitiveness. In T. Carroll & D. Jarvis (Eds.), *Asia after the developmental state: Disembedding autonomy* (pp. 124–147). Cambridge: Cambridge University Press.

Carroll, T. (2010). *Delusions of development: The World Bank and the post-Washington consensus in Southeast Asia*. Basingstoke: Palgrave Macmillan.

Carroll, T. (2017). Multilateral development policy and neoliberalism in Southeast Asia. In A. McGregor, L. Law, & F. Miller (Eds.), *Routledge handbook of Southeast Asian development* (pp. 69–84). London: Routledge.

Central Intelligence Agency. (2019). *The World Factbook*. https://www.cia.gov/library/publications/the-world-factbook/geos/sn.html. Accessed 20 May 2019.

Chilkoti, A. (2016, February 11). Indonesia launches "big bang" liberalisation. *Financial Times*. http://www.ft.com/cms/s/0/52390634-d087-11e5-92a1-c5e23ef99c77.html. Accessed 6 July 2016.

Dedrick, J., & Kramer, K. L. (2017). *Intangible assets and value capture in global value chains: The smartphone industry* (Economic research working paper no. 41). Geneva: World Intellectual Property Organization.

Deyo, F. C. (1997). Labor and post-fordist industrial restructuring in East and Southeast Asia. *Work and Occupations, 24*(1), 97–118.

Doner, R. F., & Wad, P. (2014). Financial crises and automotive industry development in Southeast Asia. *Journal of Contemporary Asia, 44*(4), 664–687.

Evans, P. B. (1995). *Embedded autonomy: States and industrial transformation*. Princeton: Princeton University Press.

Felker, G. (2003). Southeast Asian industrialisation and the changing global production system. *Third World Quarterly, 24*(2), 255–282.

Felker, G. (2004). Global production and Southeast Asia's industrlialization. In K. Jayasuriya (Ed.), *Asian regional governance: Crisis and change* (pp. 82–104). London: Routledge.

Felker, G. (2009). The political economy of Southeast Asia. In M. Beeson (Ed.), *Contemporary Southeast Asia* (2nd ed., pp. 46–73). Basingstoke: Palgrave Macmillan.

Felker, G. (2015). Malaysia's development strategies: Governing distribution-through-growth. In M. Weiss (Ed.), *Routledge handbook of contemporary Malaysia* (pp. 133–147). London: Routledge.

Financial Times. (2018, July 9). Why the Philippine peso's slump is worrying. *Financial Times.* https://www.ft.com/content/678fd198-7ed1-11e8-bc55-50daf11b720d

Gill, I., & Kharas, H. (2007). *An East Asian renaissance: Ideas for economic growth.* Washington, DC: World Bank.

Gonzalez-Vicente, R., & Carroll, T. (2017). Politics after national development: Explaining the populist rise under late capitalism. *Globalizations, 14*(6), 991–1013.

Gordon, A. (2018). A Last Word: Amendments and Corrections to Indonesia's Colonial Surplus 1880–1939. *Journal of Contemporary Asia, 48*(3), 505–518.

Hameiri, S., Jones, L., & Zou, Y. (2018). The development–insecurity nexus in China's near-abroad: Rethinking cross-border economic integration in an era of state transformation. *Journal of Contemporary Asia.* https://doi.org/10.1080/00472336.2018.1502802.

Hart-Landsberg, M. (1998). *Causes and consequences: Inside the Asian crisis.* https://www.marxists.org/history/etol/newspape/atc/1837.html. Accessed 23 Aug 2018.

Harvey, D. (1990). *The condition of postmodernity.* Cambridge, MA: Blackwell.

Harvey, D. (2007). *A brief history of neoliberalism.* New York: Oxford University Press.

Hewison, K., & Rodan, G. (1994). The decline of the left in Southeast Asia. In R. Miliband & L. Panitch (Eds.), *Socialist register 1994* (pp. 235–262). London: Merlin.

Higgott, R. (2000). The international relations of the Asian crisis: A study in the politics of resentment. In R. Robison, M. Beeson, K. Jayasuriya, & H.-R. Kim (Eds.), *Politics and markets in the wake of the Asian crisis* (pp. 261–282). London: Routledge.

Hobsbawm, E. (1994). *Age of extremes: The short twentieth century, 1914–1991.* London: Michael Joseph.

Hughes, H. (1970). *Southeast Asia's economy in the 1970s.* Washington, DC: World Bank.

Hughes, C. (2003). *The political economy of Cambodia's transition, 1991–2001.* London: RoutledgeCurzon.

Hutchison, J., Hout, W., Hughes, C., & Robison, R. (2014). *Political economy and the aid industry in Asia.* Basingstoke: Palgrave.

International Labour Organization. (2017). *ILOSTAT*. https://www.ilo.org/ilostat. Accessed 20 May 2019.

International Monetary Fund. (2016). *Annual report on exchange arrangements and exchange restrictions*. Washington, DC: IMF.

Jahan, S., & Wang, D. (2016). *Capital account openness in low-income developing countries: Evidence from a new database* (IMF working paper WP/16/252). Washington, DC: IMF.

Jayasuriya, K. (2004). Southeast Asia's embedded mercantilism in crisis: International strategies and domestic coalitions. In R. C. Thakur & E. Newman (Eds.), *Broadening Asia's security discourse and agenda: Political, social, and environmental perspectives* (pp. 47–71). Tokyo: United Nations University Press.

Jones, M. (2000). Creating Malaysia: Singapore security, the Borneo territories, and the contours of British policy, 1961–63. *The Journal of Imperial and Commonwealth History, 28*(2), 85–109.

Jones, L. (2012). *ASEAN, sovereignty and intervention in Southeast Asia*. Basingstoke: Palgrave Macmillan.

Jones, L. (2014). The political economy of Myanmar's transition. *Journal of Contemporary Asia, 44*(1), 144–170.

Kam, A. (2017). Dynamics of trade in value-added in "Factory Asia". *Journal of Contemporary Asia, 47*(5), 704–727.

Khoo, B. T. (2001). The state and the market in Malaysian political economy. In G. Rodan, K. Hewison, & R. Robison (Eds.), *The political economy of South-East Asia* (pp. 178–205). South Melbourne: Oxford University Press.

Lane, M. (2008). *Unfinished nation. Indonesia before and after Suharto*. London: Verso.

Lane, M. (2015). The politics of Widodo's prioritisation of accelerated infrastructure construction. *Perspective* 2015(43). Singapore: ISEAS–Yusof Ishak Institute.

Lee, K. Y. (2000). *Third world to first: The Singapore story 1965–2000*. Singapore: Singapore Press Holdings.

Masina, P. (2006). *Vietnam's development strategies*. Abingdon: Routledge.

Melvin, J. (2017). Mechanics of mass murder: A case for understanding the Indonesian killings as genocide. *Journal of Genocide Research, 19*(4), 487–511.

National Economic Advisory Council. (2010). *New economic model for Malaysia*. Putrajaya: National Economic Advisory Council.

Negara, S. D., & Suryadinata, L. (2018). *Jakarta–Bandung high speed rail project: Little progress, many challenges* (ISEAS perspective 2018 no. 2). Singapore: ISEAS-Yusof Ishak Institute.

Nguyen, T. T. A., Minh, D. L., & Trinh, D. C. (2016). *The evolution of Vietnamese industry* (Learning to compete working paper no. 19). Washington, DC: Brookings Institution.

Nikkei Asian Review. (2014). *The region's top companies: ASEAN 100.* Tokyo: Nikkei. https://asia.nikkei.com/Business/The-regions-top-companies-ASEAN-1002. Accessed 11 June 2018.

Organisation for Economic Co-operation and Development. (2019). *OECD data.* https://data.oecd.org. Accessed 20 May 2019.

Palma, S. (2018, June 5). Malaysia finance minister suggests China connection to 1MDB. *Financial Times.* https://www.ft.com/content/40bb3ddc-68a6-11e8-8cf3-0c230fa67aec

Pluvier, J. (1970). Indonesia before the holocaust. *Journal of Contemporary Asia, 1*(2), 5–21.

PricewaterhouseCoopers. (2017). *Global top 100 companies in 2017.* PricewaterhouseCoopers.

Radelet, S., & Sachs, J. (1997). Asia's reemergence. *Foreign Affairs, 76*(6), 44–59.

Rasiah, R. (1994). Capitalist industrialisation in ASEAN. *Journal of Contemporary Asia, 24*(2), 197–216.

Rasiah, R., Yap, X.-S., & Chandran Govindaraju, V. G. R. (2014). Crisis effects on the electronics industry in Southeast Asia. *Journal of Contemporary Asia, 44*(4), 645–663.

Reed, J. (2018a, July 8). Chinese hackers target Cambodia opposition ahead of elections. *Financial Times.* https://www.ft.com/content/4d4482e6-84a0-11e8-96dd-fa565ec55929

Reed, J. (2018b, July 26). Hun Sen sounds death knell for Cambodian democracy. *Financial Times.* https://www.ft.com/content/7fca2394-8e44-11e8-b639-7680cedcc421

Rigg, J. (1997). *Southeast Asia: The human landscape of modernization and development.* London: Routledge.

Robinson, G. (2018). *The killing season: A history of the Indonesian massacres, 1965–66.* Princeton/Oxford: Princeton University Press.

Robison, R. (1986). *Indonesia: The rise of capital.* Singapore: Equinox.

Robison, R. (2001). Indonesia: Crisis, oligarchy and reform. In G. Rodan, K. Hewison, & R. Robison (Eds.), *The political economy of South-East Asia: Conflict, crisis and change* (pp. 104–137). Melbourne: Oxford University Press.

Rodan, G. (2001). Singapore: Globalisation and the politics of economic restructuring. In G. Rodan, K. Hewison, & R. Robison (Eds.), *The political economy of South-East Asia: Conflict, crisis and change* (pp. 138–177). Melbourne: Oxford University Press.

Rodan, G. (2016). Capitalism, inequality and ideology in Singapore: New challenges for the ruling party. *Asian Studies Review, 40*(2), 211–230.

Rodan, G. (2018). *Particpation without democracy: Containing conflict in Southeast Asia.* Ithaca/London: Cornell University Press.

Rodan, G., Hewison, K., & Robison, R. (Eds.). (2006). *The political economy of South-East Asia: Markets, power and contestation.* Melbourne: Oxford University Press.

Ruggie, J. (1982). International regimes, transactions, and change: Embedded liberalism in the postwar economic order. *International Organization*, *36*(2), 379–415.
Schoenberger, E. (1988). From Fordism to flexible accumulation: Technology, competitive strategies, and international location. *Environment and Planning D: Society and Space*, *6*, 245–262.
Sjöholm, F. (2013). *Foreign direct investments in Southeast Asia* (Lund University Department of Economics, Working paper no. 987). Lund: Lund University.
Stubbs, R. (1989). Geopolitics and the political economy of Southeast Asia. *International Journal*, *44*(3), 517–540.
The Wall Street Journal. (2016, February 18). Indonesia's economic opening. *The Wall Street Journal*. http://www.wsj.com/articles/indonesias-economic-opening-1455841349. Accessed 6 July 2016.
Thompson, M. R. (2016). The early Duterte presidency in the Philippines. *Journal of Current Southeast Asian Affairs*, *35*(3), 39–68.
Thompson, M. R. (2018). Duterte's violent populism in the Philippines. Association of Asian Studies annual conference, 22–25 March. Washington, DC.
UNCTAD. (2017). *Trade and development report 2017. Beyond austeriety: Towards a global new deal*. Geneva: Secretariat of the United Nations Conference on Trade and Investment.
UNCTAD. (2018). *UNCTADstat*. https://unctadstat.unctad.org. Accessed 20 May 2019.
Urata, S. (2002). *Japanese foreign direct investment in East Asia with particular focus on ASEAN4*. Conference on foreign direct investment: Opportunities and challenges for Cambodia, Laos, and Vietnam, 16–17 August. Hanoi: International Monetary Fund.
Vickers, A. (2005). *A history of modern Indonesia*. Cambridge: Cambridge University Press.
Warburton, E. (2017). *Resource nationalism in post-boom Indonesia: The new normal?* Sydney: Lowy Institute for International Policy. https://think-asia.org/bitstream/handle/11540/7088/Warburton_Indonesia_FINAL%20WEB.pdf?sequence=1
Weinstein, F. B. (2001). Multinational corporations and the third world. In W. Mendl (Ed.), *Japan and Southeast Asia* (pp. 88–120). London: Routledge.
Wijeratne, D., & Lau, S. (2016). *Riding Southeast Asia's automotive highway*. PricewaterhouseCoopers.
Williamson, J. (1990). What Washington means by policy reform. In J. Williamson (Ed.), *Latin American adjustment: How much has happened?* (pp. 5–20). Washington, DC: Institute for International Economics.
Winters, J. A. (2011). *Oligarchy*. Cambridge: Cambridge University Press.
World Bank. (2015). *Indonesia: Systematic country diagnostic*. Jakarta: World Bank Group.

World Bank. (2017). *Worldwide governance indicators.* https://info.worldbank.org/governance/wgi/#home. Accessed 20 May 2019.

World Bank. (2018a). *World development indicators.* https://databank.worldbank.org. Accessed 20 May 2019.

World Bank. (2018b). *Doing Business 2018: Reforming to create jobs.* Washington, DC: World Bank.

World Bank. (2019). *Malaysia overview.* https://www.worldbank.org/en/country/malaysia/overview. Accessed 17 May 2019.

World Economic Forum. (2016). *Global competitiveness report 2016–17.* Geneva: WEF.

World Health Organization. (2019). *Current health expenditure (CHE) as percentage of gross domestic product (GDP) (%) Data by country.* http://apps.who.int/gho/data/node.main.GHEDCHEGDPSHA2011. Accessed 20 May 2019.

World Intellectual Property Organization. (2016). *World intellectual property indicators 2016.* Geneva: WIPO.

World Trade Organization. (2018). *Tariff analysis online.* https://tao.wto.org. Accessed 20 May 2019.

PART II

Economic Development and Governance

CHAPTER 3

Explaining Political Regimes in Southeast Asia: A Modes of Participation Framework

Garry Rodan and Jacqui Baker

INTRODUCTION

Modernisation theorists expected capitalism and liberal democracy to be partners in Southeast Asia's development, as they supposedly were in Europe and North America. Economic development was meant to generate new middle classes that would eventually demand and support democratic institutions. Yet, in a region boasting some of the world's fastest capitalist development in the last half century, no regimes approach liberal democracy; rather, assorted authoritarian regimes have consolidated or emerged, and oligarchies dominate in both democratic and authoritarian regimes. Explaining such outcomes need not involve abandoning the idea

G. Rodan
College of Arts, Business, Law and Social Sciences, Murdoch University, Perth, WA, Australia

School of Political Science and International Studies, The University of Queensland, St Lucia, QLD, Australia

J. Baker (✉)
Asia Research Centre, Murdoch University, Perth, WA, Australia
e-mail: Jacqui.Baker@murdoch.edu.au

© The Author(s) 2020
T. Carroll et al. (eds.), *The Political Economy of Southeast Asia*, Studies in the Political Economy of Public Policy,
https://doi.org/10.1007/978-3-030-28255-4_3

that capitalism and political regimes are linked. Rather, a political economy framework with a very different theorisation of this complex and contingent relationship is required to explain political regimes in Southeast Asia, and elsewhere.

Southeast Asia's political regimes reflect the particular historical development of the region's political economies. The Cold War and authoritarian rule first destroyed the left, while the region's late insertion into globalised capitalist production systems has militated against the emergence of powerful, cohesive and independent civil society organisations (see Quimpo, Carroll, this volume). The region's growing middle and business classes are typically directly or indirectly dependent upon the state, and lack the will and/or capacity to challenge oligarchic power. Nonetheless, capitalism's inherently dynamic and conflictual nature (see Hameiri and Jones, this volume) means that Southeast Asia's oligarchs continually face challenges of political management from new or emerging social forces, often manifesting as struggles over political institutions.

To explain Southeast Asia's political regime dynamics, this chapter uses a Modes of Participation (MOP) framework, building on the Murdoch School. The MOP approach draws attention to struggles over who can participate in political decision-making, how and on what basis, as the principal issue at stake in both democratic and authoritarian regimes. Whereas some MOPs entrench oligarchic power, others may challenge existing power relations more substantially. The emergence and operation of specific MOPs are a function of struggles between coalitions of sociopolitical forces, rooted in evolving political economy dynamics. The ideologies of representation around which these coalitions form are of crucial importance. In Southeast Asia, an especially powerful role is played by non-democratic—consultative and particularlist—ideologies of representation, which often constrain the emergence of serious competition to dominant interests.

Following a brief critical evaluation of modernisation theory and institutionalist explanations of regime dynamics, we elaborate on the MOP framework. We then proceed to examine two cases: Singapore's expansion of consultative institutions, and how struggles over Jakarta's neighbourhood associations shaped the outcomes of the provincial elections in 2017.

Economic Development and Political Institutions

Early modernisation theorists understood liberal economics and politics as evolving in a functional relationship. This involved a cultural shift from traditional to modern practices favouring law-based, rational systems and values—including democratic politics. The bourgeoisie and middle class were viewed as strategic vectors of these modern values. From a more structuralist perspective, Moore (1966) argued that democracy resulted where a strong bourgeoisie emerged to play a leading political role; otherwise, authoritarianism accompanied capitalism. However, in Southeast Asia and elsewhere, bourgeois and middle classes have supported a range of political regimes and taken varying stances on legal-rational authority. This led Samuel Huntington (1968) to argue that the path to modernisation might benefit from authoritarian regimes facilitating social integration, economic growth and political order. Nonetheless, Huntington (1991) subsequently rebooted modernisation theory with his influential claim that a "third wave" of democratisation was accompanying capitalist globalisation in the late 1980s.

By the turn of the twenty-first century, though, many of these "transitions" had collapsed or had democratic credentials that could not withstand close scrutiny. China and Russia demonstrated, too, that capitalism and authoritarianism might be viable long-term partners. Carothers (2002) thus declared the end of the "democratic transitions" paradigm. However, instead of a decisive break from this paradigm, what followed was popular recourse to the concept of so-called "hybrid regimes", comprising a mixture of democratic and authoritarian elements. A wide range of political regimes in Southeast Asia have thus been characterised as "hybrid", including Singapore, Malaysia, Thailand and the Philippines (see Case 2002; Levitsky and Way 2002).

Most hybrid regime analyses focus on scrutinising political and related institutions, identifying deviations from ideal-typical democratic regimes and evaluating the "quality" of nominally democratic institutions (Morlino et al. 2011). Thus, rather than providing a genuinely new framework for better conceptualising and explaining regime diversity, this literature *reinforces* the "democratic transition" problematic, endlessly measuring how far countries have yet to go before "democracy" is achieved, and assuming that the only real change is movement along this spectrum. Some analyses are also narrowly focused on technical aspects of institutional design and elite choices (e.g. Henderson 2004). Such classifications merely *describe* "deficiencies" in regimes; they do not *explain why* regimes look and operate as they do.

Some analysts who examine relationships between institutions, structure and history from a historical institutionalist perspective come closer to this goal (e.g. Carothers 2006; Slater 2010). However, ultimately historical institutionalism portrays political institutions as mechanisms to elevate political engagement beyond societal or intra-party conflict (Pepinsky 2014; Rodan and Jayasuriya 2012). The social foundations of institutions remain under-explored. For example, Brownlee's (2008: 112) comparison of third-wave transitions in Malaysia and the Philippines argued that "the maintenance of hybrid regimes may depend less on the elections they hold than on the coalitions they hold together", highlighting the role Malaysia's dominant party plays in managing inter-elite contestation. This starts to move beyond a narrow fixation on institutions to consider the social forces behind particular regimes. However, as with historical institutionalism more generally (see Hameiri and Jones, this volume), this framework is better at explaining continuity—so-called "authoritarian resilience"—than change. For example, Malaysia's 2018 elections led to the first change of government in 61 years, despite no change in party organisation. To understand this, we need to examine how contradictions in Malaysian capitalism culminated in the corruption scandal of the state investment company 1MDB and rising inequalities that paved the way for a pro-reform coalition to take power. By the same token, the persistence of oligarchic power can explain the subsequent limits to the new government's reform agenda (Gomez 2019).

CAPITALISM, CONFLICT AND POLITICAL INSTITUTIONS

The Murdoch School accords a pivotal place to capitalism in explaining the form and function of political institutions and regimes. Its approach starts from the observation that capitalism is inherently dynamic and conflict-ridden. Interests among elites can alter with development, resulting in intra-elite struggles and new coalitions. The emergence of new social forces, and unequal distribution of the costs and rewards of development, also generate new contentions. These dynamics create pressures and opportunities for elites and their opponents, who variously seek to contain or progress conflict over the distribution of power and resources. Ethnic, religious and other identities, and struggles with pre-capitalist roots, also continue to provide bases for political struggles over state power. Yet the conditions under which these and other conflicts play out, and the coalitions that are possible in the process, are profoundly influenced by capitalist development's transformative and contradictory nature.

Crucially, exactly how struggles over the limits to institutionalised conflict play out is highly contingent on the specific historical and geopolitical context of capitalist development. This includes how capitalism is organised and controlled, which shapes the precise social contradictions generated by development and potential new coalitions that may form. There is no assumption here that democracy is naturally or functionally most suited to accompany capitalist development or to contain or resolve the contention generated by it. Instead, the Murdoch School seeks to "explain the forces and interests that are historically thrown up in the evolution of capitalism and how conflicts between these shape economic and political life and the institutions in which they operate" (Hadiz and Robison 2013: 41). This approach places political institutions within a broad and inseparable struggle over state power; they are sites of struggle over whose interests and agendas will prevail. This is quite different from evaluating institutions against their ideal-typical democratic credentials. What matters are the interests served by institutions, how, and why.

Today, Southeast Asia's regimes are highly diverse, but there are clearly significant limits on the forms and extent of institutionalised conflict in all countries, democratic or otherwise. Despite some major regime transformations, Southeast Asian countries are broadly ruled by oligarchies. In oligarchies, economic and political power is extremely concentrated, allowing a narrow elite to dominate public policy-making—often for their own pecuniary interests—and to secure their interests and preferences, typically regardless of formal changes of government or even regime. This includes countries where: communist and non-communist parties control state power; authoritarian regimes take either civilian form or involve significant military control over state power; new democracies have replaced authoritarian rule; historical links between contemporary oligarchs and traditional landowning elites have been woven; and new state capitalists or bourgeoisies have transformed elite structures (Robison 2012).

Possibly the two most significant examples of the durability of oligarchic rule are the Philippines and Indonesia. Both countries experienced popular uprisings, spurring transitions from authoritarian to democratic political systems. However, in the Philippines, the 1986 "People Power" uprising was soon followed by an emphatic reassertion of oligarchic dominance in which—as under earlier electoral democracy—a narrow elite of politico-business families harnessed its wealth to dominate Congress. Similarly, in Indonesia, after *reformasi* and the fall of Suharto, oligarchs reorganised, using connections, wealth and extra-legal means to outcompete oppositional forces in the new electoral system (Hadiz 2003). Political decentralisation also provided fresh avenues for patronage and corruption that had been more centralised under Suharto (Hadiz 2010).

In former socialist countries like Cambodia, Vietnam, Laos and Myanmar, capitalist development has variously privileged the interests of party officials, state capitalists, bureaucrats, the military and select private capitalists, giving rise to highly authoritarian regimes (see Hughes, this volume). Yet, in all Southeast Asian countries, capitalism's social contradictions continue to generate conflicts that require political management—if only to protect the interests of capitalist oligarchs as others bear the uneven distribution of the social and environmental costs of development.

The pervasiveness of oligarchies in Southeast Asia reflects the particular historical context within which the region's political economies developed (see Carroll, this volume). The Cold War's political legacy looms large. In the ideological struggle between socialism and capitalism, liberals, leftists, peasants and workers were suppressed under both left- and right-wing governments (see Quimpo, this volume). The space for independent civil society organisations was severely limited, especially for labour movements linked to reformist political parties. Direct or indirect dependence on the state by middle and business classes for commercial contracts, employment or access to other resources is also widespread where political patronage flourishes, leaving these forces generally reluctant to challenge authoritarianism. Various small, middle-class-led non-governmental organisations have emerged, especially in the Philippines and Indonesia, but they generally remain marginal and have compounded political fragmentation.

Cohesive civil societies and social democratic reform movements in particular failed to (re)emerge following the end of the Cold War or even the overthrow of authoritarian regimes. This was not just due to the breadth and depth of damage inflicted by decades of authoritarian rule, but also the advent of globalised capitalist production systems from the 1970s onwards, which further strengthened capital's hand over labour (Hutchison and Brown 2001). As Carroll (this volume) details, evolving global value chains heighten the structural and ideological challenges in contesting oligarchic power. The rise of Chinese investments in infrastructure and property development, and the activities of Singaporean government-linked companies and sovereign wealth funds, have also been unhelpful for social and political forces seeking to arrest or contest oligarchic rule.

Nevertheless, capitalism's dynamic and inherently conflictual nature ensures that oligarchs continually face challenges of political management, as recent developments in Malaysia highlight. This directs attention to *struggles* over political institutions. Institutions are not merely reflections of existing structural power relations; they are shaped by conflict. The precise forms of conflict ensuing from capitalist development, or amplified by it, vary widely, as do the options open to oligarchs seeking to contain such conflict. Yet, in all cases, what is at stake is whose interests prevail through the resulting institutional arrangements.

In contrast to hybrid regime theory, the Murdoch School has taken non-democratic institutions seriously, analysing them not against an idealised "democracy" benchmark but asking in whose interests they operate (Rodan 2004, 2018; Rodan and Hughes 2014; Rodan and Jayasuriya 2007). This has generated a comprehensive MOP framework for explaining different forms and political outcomes of conflicts arising from capitalist development. The term "mode of participation" denotes an institutional arrangement defining who can participate in political decision-making, how, and on what basis. MOPs are crucial because they shape the permissible bounds of political contestation: some may facilitate genuine challenges to deeply entrenched social power relations; others may channel participation in ways that actually protect these relationships (Rodan 2018). Murdoch Scholars explain the specific MOPs that emerge in particular contexts with reference to struggles between socio-political forces, rooted within evolving political economy dynamics.

Recent MOP scholarship has argued that these struggles involve different *ideologies* of representation, around which contending coalitions often form, whether for principled or tactical reasons. Four kinds of ideologies are commonly observed. Democratic ideologies emphasise popular sovereignty and political equality, insisting on MOPs that make political elites accountable to citizens. Populist ideologies divide society rhetorically into "the people" and "elites" and typically promote MOPs that empower strong leaders, ostensibly to act directly on behalf of "the people" against "elites". Consultative ideologies emphasise technocratic, apolitical rationales for who should be involved in political participation and representation and how. Particularist ideologies emphasise the claims of discrete identities and communities to participation and representation, based on race, religion, ethnicity, geography, gender and/or culture. These ideologies are present, to some extent, in many societies; but crucially the forces that mobilise around them, and their chances to realise their desired MOPs in practice, vary enormously depending on the social formations arising from capitalist development in particular contexts (Rodan 2018).

This framework applies across all capitalist societies. It enables us to better understand why new institutions of participation emerge, or established ones might change—and what directions they take. These questions are just as important for comprehending differences within, as well as across, authoritarian and democratic regimes. We demonstrate this through examining authoritarian Singapore and democratic Indonesia. In each case, capitalist development has generated specific social contradictions and conflicts, resulting in struggles over MOPs. The actors and interests necessarily differ, but the core struggle in both cases is over who should be able to participate, how and on what issues. The MOPs involved all constrain or advance particular societal interests.

Singapore: State Capitalism, Technocrats and Consultation

In Singapore, rising social conflict over the last 15 years is rooted in spiralling inequality produced by state capitalism dominated by technocratic politico-bureaucratic elites under the ruling People's Action Party (PAP). Here, neoliberal globalisation and foreign investment-led growth have aided the consolidation and extension of state capitalist enterprises and entrenched related interests in bureaucratic and political power. However, the PAP's capital accumulation strategies—involving the exploitation of low-wage migrant labour in sectors like construction and domestic services, alongside extremely highly-paid "foreign talent" in higher value-added service sectors—fuelled rampant inequality, surging living costs, and a growing anti-immigration backlash. This generated unprecedented pressure on the PAP's legitimation strategy: an ideological myth of meritocracy rationalising the acute concentration of power in the hands of a narrow politico-bureaucratic elite.

As in previous periods of rising social conflict, the PAP has sought to develop state-controlled MOPs involving non-democratic consultative representation to contain conflict and reduce support for opposition political parties. PAP leaders ideologically rationalised these new MOPs in technocratic terms supportive of their own political authority and control over state power. They projected these MOPs as functional for sound policy precisely because they bypassed partisan politics (i.e. democratic contestation) in favour of rational, problem-solving deliberations. Previous MOP initiatives included the establishment in 1985 of the Feedback Unit (later renamed Reaching Everyone for Active Citizenship @ Home, or REACH) and the introduction in 1990 of nominated members of parliament.

Through such consultative institutions, avenues for individuals and groups to participate in public policy discussions have significantly expanded. However, those purportedly represented in these discussions do not enjoy the power to endorse or discipline those projected as acting on their behalf, unlike in democratic representation. Nor are policy-makers obliged to implement the feedback submitted. Below we examine the latest such institutional initiative, Our Singapore Conversation (OSC), held during 2012–13. First, though, this must be set in its historical and political economy context.

Roots of Technocratic Elite Power in Singapore

During Singapore's anti-colonial struggle, the most profitable elements of the domestic bourgeoisie shared little enthusiasm for independence. The PAP was different. Formed in 1954, it was the vehicle that brought together popular forces with grassroots organisations and English-educated, middle-class elements in a broad independence movement. This alliance proved a winning electoral formula, sweeping the PAP to power in 1959.

However, there were tensions between more radical, Chinese-educated forces—variously seeking to advance socialist and economic-nationalist agendas—and the comparatively conservative, English-educated faction headed by Lee Kuan Yew. The PAP split in 1961, leaving Lee's faction in total control of the PAP and government. This power was used to systematically repress PAP opponents and critics, including the dismantling of independent labour. Subsequently, the state and the PAP were effectively merged and democratic participation downgraded. This was rationalised as part of an allegedly apolitical developmental agenda needed to improve Singaporeans' social and economic conditions. This ostensibly required the elevation of skilled technocrats able to craft cohesive administrative structures and rational policy solutions, whose domination was legitimated with reference to their supposed "merit" rather than to their popular support, notwithstanding regular—but highly constrained—elections.

Inequality with Growth

Given the domestic bourgeoisie's dubious loyalties and small scale, and Singapore's tiny domestic market, the PAP embarked on export-oriented industrialisation (EOI), driven by government-linked companies (GLCs) and the courting of foreign investment. This combination of state capitalism and EOI delivered broadly egalitarian outcomes in the 1960s and 1970s. However, by the 1980s, rising wages and the emergence of rival sites for low-cost industrial production began to challenge this strategy's sustainability (Rodan 1989). The ascendancy of technocratic elites within the PAP state and the structural demobilisation of organised labour—with the PAP-dominated National Trades Union Congress providing the only avenue for workers' representation—favoured selective neoliberal policy solutions, which struck at workers. Low value-added factories were closed down or offshored to lower-wage neighbouring economies (see Al-Fadhat, this volume), and industrial policy shifted towards promoting higher value-added industries and services.

This has increasingly bifurcated the Singaporean economy, increasing reliance on migrant workers and spurring inequality. On the one hand, the push to develop high-end industries and services like biotechnology and finance has sharply increased demand for high-wage skilled professionals, prompting employers to turn to "foreign talent". On the other, residual low-cost manufacturing, construction, hospitality and domestic services require low-wage labour. To maintain high growth rates, the PAP allowed employers to meet labour shortages by recruiting foreign workers, such that, by 2010, they comprised one-third of Singapore's total workforce,[1] with the population surging by around 32% from 2000 to 2010. Although growth intensified, so too did income inequality: Singapore's Gini coefficient increased from 0.42 to 0.48 from 2000 to 2012, while absolute poverty was estimated at 11–12% in 2011 (Rodan 2018: 48).

Unsurprisingly, this generated intensifying conflict ahead of the 2011 elections. Tensions were high over government policies on immigration, welfare, housing, transport, health, education, pensions and wages. Many

---

[1] This did not include the vast number of domestic helpers, or maids, from overseas.

voters regarded heavy dependence on low-cost guest workers as a strain on social and physical infrastructure and a threat to both social cohesion and domestic workers' incomes. The PAP's ideological emphasis on meritocracy was also subject to growing critical scrutiny. Thus, despite the considerable usual impediments to a level electoral playing field—including extensive electoral gerrymandering, tight media controls, and restrictions on freedom of speech and assembly—the PAP's support dropped to 60% at the May 2011 polls, the lowest since independence in 1965.

Refining Consultative Representation

In response, the government developed a new MOP that sought to channel socio-political conflict in ways that bolstered PAP hegemony. Prime Minister Lee announced that there would be a "national conversation on Our Singapore to define what sort of country we want to be and how we can achieve it" (Lee 2012). This was the OSC, a 12-month enquiry that began in October 2012, led by then Education Minister Heng Swee Keat. The OSC was a consultative MOP. The public was allowed to participate in deliberations over Singapore's future, but only through invitations to join depoliticised conversations, dominated by regime-friendly interests—rather than, say, through elected representatives. This allowed surging popular discontent to be reframed in a consensual manner, with PAP technocrats retaining discretion over concrete policy formulation and implementation.

The OSC comprised a 26-member committee including figures from business, academia, media, the legal profession and community groups. It engaged around 47,000 people through diverse mechanisms; 660 dialogues were organised by the OSC committee, government organisations, grassroots organisations and state-linked unions, as well as select interest groups, civic and civil society organisations and companies. Engagements and consultations were conducted in 75 different locations, including small groups in coffee shops. Other feedback was obtained through 1331 email threads, 4050 Facebook wall posts, 211 Facebook private messages, and 73 YouTube videos (OSC Committee 2013: 3).

The OSC's first six-month phase was loosely structured around questions of Singapore's overall direction. According to Heng (quoted in Wong and Sim 2012), "some general consensus around where we would like Singapore to go" was a necessary basis for detailed policy discussion. The OSC committee distilled the feedback received into 12 thematic perspectives. This guided the second phase, which focused on healthcare, housing, education and old-age policy issues. The final report—*Reflections of Our Singapore Conversation: What Future Do We Want? How Do We Get There?*—offered no specific policy recommendations but identified five "core aspirations" of citizens: opportunities for all; communities with purpose; assurance of basic needs; spirit for a compassionate society; and trust in engagement with policy-makers (OSC Committee 2013: 4). By implication, these core aspirations embodied a consensus. How to translate this into policy was left to the PAP government's discretion.

Arguably, all five core aspirations could be linked to conflicts over inequalities and elitism, around which opposition parties had already submitted concrete policy proposals, helping to boost their support at the 2011 election. However, understandably, opposition parties boycotted the OSC. The OSC committee was not just unrepresentative of Singapore's political diversity, but strategically dominated by PAP politicians and other members of the PAP establishment, many imbued with technocratic worldviews including apolitical notions of consultation.

Nevertheless, ahead of the 2015 election, the PAP linked OSC processes to key policy reform announcements. Prime Minister Lee and other leaders also invoked the OSC in announcing a purported embrace of greater social redistribution, declaring a shift towards "compassionate meritocracy" (Ong 2014). Policy changes included major new commitments in areas like healthcare for the elderly, public housing affordability, and education and income supplements for disadvantaged families. Chief among the reform announcements was the Pioneer Generation Package for senior citizens, announced in 2014 at a cost of S$8bn. Importantly, this redistributive spending was made possible in part by Singapore's state capitalist model, which allowed the PAP to tap returns from GLCs and sovereign wealth funds.

These changes helped the PAP to boost its support to 69% at the 2015 election, delivering 83 of the total 89 parliamentary seats under Singapore's first-past-the-post voting system. Crucially, competing ideologies of political representation were at the fore in the election campaign. Workers' Party (WP) leader Low Thia Khiang linked government policy changes to greater opposition support in 2011, urging voters to consolidate their empowerment by further increasing opposition numbers "to supervise the Government" (quoted in Chong 2015). Many voters, however, swung back to the ruling party, appearing to validate the PAP's "compassionate meritocracy" and revitalised consultative representation.

Nonetheless, there are both ideological and material limits to the PAP's "compassionate meritocracy". These limits are revealed by the fact that, 3 years on, in 2018, Singapore was still ranked as the world's second-most unequal high-income economy in the United Nations Development Programme's Human Development Index, while Oxfam ranked Singapore at 149 among 157 countries for efforts to address inequality (Rahim and Yeoh 2019: 97–101). The PAP's ideological insistence on "meritocracy" is essential to legitimise the ongoing domination of a narrow politico-bureaucratic elite, but it implies limits to wealth redistribution. As Teo (2018) observes, by definition, meritocracy generates inequality: those with merit will do better than those without. The addition of "compassion" shores up an elitist political paternalism: the PAP dispenses welfare out of kindness, not because it recognises social citizenship rights that might embody a different—more democratic—power relationship between citizens and political representatives. Accordingly, social welfare remains a problematic concept for the PAP, even as more budget allocations to social spending unfolded in 2019.

Constraints on PAP redistributive policies are also related to the structural preconditions of prevailing capital accumulation strategies. Official concerns that a minimum wage could erode the competitiveness of certain low-skilled industries dominated by international and national capital, including GLCs, are not unfounded. Alternative employment opportunities for displaced workers are not immediately apparent. Reducing the number of foreigners working in Singapore—by 32,000 in 2017—also risks severe skills shortages that would undermine the PAP's emphasis on maximising economic growth.

Rationalising the uneven social and economic outcomes arising from capitalist development and state power will thus require continuing political management. This will mean more pressure on consultative representation MOPs and other PAP strategies intended to limit the permissible bounds of institutionalised political conflict.

Indonesia: Predatory Capitalism and Particularism

This case study examines how the institution of Indonesia's neighbourhood associations (*Rukun Tetangga*, RT) and their elected neighbourhood heads (*Kepala Rukun Tetangga*, KRT) became intensely politically contested from 2012 onwards, reflecting underlying social conflict over land in Jakarta under the administration of Basuki Purnama Tjahaja (aka

"Ahok"), from 2012 to 2017.[2] The RTs, and elections of KRTs by community consensus or vote, have survived the transition to independence and four subsequent regime changes. The RT and KRT elections are often held up as evidence of Indonesia's grassroots democratic culture. However, the MOP framework instead directs attention to how these institutions are contested. While KRT elections are suggestive of democratic, "bottom up" representation, the selection of some KRT by community consensus also resonates with particularist, organicist ideologies of hierarchy, harmony and social order, where the village head is seen as the purest and most authentic representative of the community (Bourchier 2014). Moreover, RTs/KRTs have non-democratic roots in consultative ideologies, which have historically allowed them to function as "top down", state-controlled forums. This suggests that social power relations and contestation, invoking competing ideologies, are crucial in explaining what these institutions actually do and whose interests they serve.

This is very clear in the Ahok era. In 2016, in the context of accelerating neighbourhood displacements of Jakarta's urban poor for luxury property developments, Ahok's administration promoted reforms of the KRT/RT that intensified their non-democratic, consultative function. As with Singapore's OSC, Ahok's proposals sought to redirect and contain underlying social conflict. However, unlike Singapore, where new consultative institutions effectively consolidated PAP rule, Ahok's reforms ignited deep conflict over who the KRTs represent and how, animating social actors and political alliances that drew on a range of democratic, consultative, populist and particularist ideological visions. Ultimately, the promise of KRTs as democratic representatives for the urban poor evaporated as a more powerful coalition emerged, harnessing particularist and populist ideologies, ultimately to win the 2017 Jakarta elections.

The following sections detail the significance of Jakarta's property development in the unique formations of local capitalist development and social conflict, and then explore how these conflicts were institutionally expressed under Ahok.

---

[2] Ahok became Jakarta's deputy governor in 2012, under Joko Widodo ("Jokowi"), succeeding him as governor in 2014.

Property and Unequal Growth

As in Singapore, Indonesia's capitalist development combines aspects of neoliberal globalisation and state capitalism, but very different forces dominate: a strong bureaucratic class and a capitalist class nurtured by state power (Robison 1986). This trajectory, developed under the authoritarian Suharto regime, which ruthlessly suppressed workers, peasants and the left, generated a predatory form of capitalism wherein large-scale capital accumulation depends on access to domestic economic rents rather than increased efficiency and competition (Robison and Hadiz 2004). The boundaries between public and private interests are routinely blurred for the benefit of a rapacious oligarchic class, which is increasingly leveraging domestic rents to expand into regional and global markets (see Al-Fadhat, this volume). Indonesia's post-1998 democratisation and decentralisation introduced powerful new ideological frames to support the redistribution and opening up of political power. However, the forces that became dominant under Suharto were also in prime position to exploit these new opportunities, allowing a wider, fractious cohort of bureaucratic, political and business elites at the national and provincial levels to consolidate power. Hadiz and Robison (2013) call this Indonesia's oligarchical democracy.

Land acquisition, speculation and development, especially in Jakarta, has been an important strategy for rapid capital accumulation for much of Indonesia's nascent national business elite. Under Suharto's New Order, licences for property development, notably the conversion of agrarian land in peri-urban Jakarta into gated middle- to upper-class housing estates, financed corporate diversification schemes for some of the country's biggest conglomerates, including Lippo, Sinar Mas and Salim Group. By 1998, nine of Indonesia's richest 14 tycoons had significant investments in property development (Suryadinata 2012).

State-owned enterprises (SOEs), which gained significant property holdings from Sukarno-era nationalisation and forced acquisitions under Suharto, have also played a pivotal role in shaping the political economy of Jakarta's real estate. SOEs have developed state-owned land, sold it cheaply to private developers, and incubated an elite class of property developers as joint venture partners and board members. Thus, state and private actors have formed a property oligarchy (Arai 2015), whose development of Jakarta's real estate sector supports capital formation for the wider national economy.

This development is highly predatory and increasingly internationalised. Haila (2016) describes Singapore as a "property state," a regime of land ownership, auction and sales that suppresses speculation and concentrates land under government control, with rents comprising a significant proportion of national wealth. This has enabled the ruling PAP to supply public housing to around 80% of the population, reinforcing PAP claims to meritocratic rule. The political economy of Jakarta's real estate appears the polar opposite: land speculation is rife and property development has produced a contrasting spatial order. Luxury housing has been developed by systematically displacing the urban poor who inhabit neighbourhoods (*kampung*) with poor infrastructure and insecure land tenure. Moreover, while Singapore's domestic land management is sheltered from marketisation, Singapore provides a tax haven base for Indonesian, Singaporean and other foreign developers to invest in Jakarta's real estate market (Haila 2000).[3] Hence, Singapore's internationalised state capitalism and Indonesia's private, predatory capitalism are mutually constituted through property development.

New Coalition, New Conflict

Eviction and displacement have been contested by Jakarta's urban poor for decades. But, prior to 2017, municipal elections had not produced a political coalition willing to challenge the power relations underpinning predatory property development. Successive city administrations only further embedded these relations by continuing to support neighbourhood displacements and evictions. In this regard, Jakarta's first ethnic-Chinese, Christian governor, Ahok (2014–17), was not unique, though the sheer scale of his promised urban transformation was unprecedented. Ahok presented an all-embracing, technocratic vision of spatial and infrastructural development that would turn Jakarta into one of the world's "global cities" (Leitner and Sheppard 2018). He was backed by a coalition of property oligarchs, tech entrepreneurs, young bureaucratic elites, and pro-Jokowi cabinet ministers and power-brokers.

Much of Ahok's vision for Jakarta openly drew on a selective, self-interested portrayal of Singapore, emphasising technocratic efficiency to a

---

[3] In 2018, Singapore remained Indonesia's top source of foreign direct investment, with US$6.7bn (Anya 2018). The data are not disaggregated by sector, but property is consistently among the most popular FDI destinations.

cheering middle class. Amidst the far-reaching plans for canal dredging, city greening and footpath widening, the most ambitious infrastructure project was the National Capital Integrated Coastal Development (NCICD). This US$40bn sea wall, ostensibly designed to protect the sinking city from coastal flooding, would also enable the construction of 17 artificial islets, to be populated by luxury commercial and residential properties for international, predominately mainland Chinese, investors (Sherwell 2016).

Islet development licences were held by a range of property development firms, including the Suharto family, a transnational Singaporean property developer financed by Singaporean sovereign wealth funds, and two prominent ethnic-Chinese developers, PT Agung Podomoro and PT Agung Sedayu, emblematic of Jakarta's new property oligarchy. Significantly, an equal number of islet development licences were held by municipal SOEs, including PT Jakarta Propertindo.

Neighbourhood Representation in Conflict

Displacement of Jakarta's *kampung* was critical to achieving the Governor's vision and this proceeded at an accelerated pace. Jakarta Legal Aid estimated that, from 2015 to 2016, there were over 306 rounds of evictions affecting some 16,000 families (Wilson 2016). For Ahok, the role of the KRT was to support the administration to displace targeted neighbourhoods. But urban poor fighting displacement increasingly pressured their elected KRT to fight the administration and defend neighbourhood interests. While the KRT is not essential to a neighbourhood's removal, or indeed its resistance, the KRTs control important organisational, informational, political and material resources that could meaningfully advance group interests on either side. This set the scene for contestation between social forces over who should be represented and how through the position of the neighbourhood association head, drawing on non-democratic and democratic ideologies of representation.

In 2016, at the height of public anger about displacement and the NCICD, the Ahok administration presented a new "reconsolidated" set of guidelines on the role of the neighbourhood heads. These changes, announced in Gubernatorial Decree 1/2016, were ostensibly designed to modernise the KRT, which Ahok had scorned as a feudal relic. The decree emphasised a consultative role for KRTs, where association heads would empower communities by providing "two way communication between local government and the community" (Article 16). Heads would still be democratically elected by their neighbourhoods, but the administration claimed the authority to fire inefficient or poorly performing heads. For KRTs and the neighbourhoods they represented, this downgraded their democratic authority, reducing them to city-appointed officials. The administration's clear goal was to co-opt the KRTs as a top-down institution and prevent their use by those resisting Ahok's plans.

In response, for the first time in Jakarta's political history, the KRTs consolidated politically into a series of territorially organised bodies known as the Forum RT. These fora staged a series of protests from the second half of 2016 that attracted hundreds of KRTs and evinced rival ideologies of representation. For example, some held placards reading: "RTs are formed by the community, from the community and for the community", expressing a clear democratic ethos (*Suara Muhammadiyah* 2016). Others drew on particularist ideologies of representation by emphasising that KRTs should be respected as they represented the vestiges of traditional village authority, where rulers and ruled should supposedly be in harmony.

By mid-2016, this conflict had become tactically important in mobilisations ahead of the February 2017 Jakarta elections. In this election, the Gerindra Party—the main nationalist-populist rival to Jokowi's ruling coalition—fielded Anies Baswedan as their candidate for governor. Baswedan rallied considerable support by appealing to racialised (anti-Chinese) Islamic populism, promising to stop the displacement of urban poor and to end the reign of Jakarta's ethnic-Chinese property oligarchy by cancelling the NCICD (see also Robison and Hadiz, this volume). In addition to courting Islamists, who were accusing the Governor of blasphemy, Baswedan also openly appealed to the KRTs. His approach framed neighbourhood heads not as democratic representatives of the city's residents, but in particularistic ideological terms, as the legitimate leaders of a harmonious social and political order threatened by Ahok's reforms (Hidayat 2018). Particularist ideologies of representation of the KRTs resonated with the election campaign's wider ethno-nationalist and ethno-religious populist rhetoric. Seeing an opportunity to advance their goals, Forum-allied KRTs managed their neighbourhoods to support Baswedan, organising political contracts with Gerindra candidates, disallowing pro-Ahok campaign material and, in some instances, threatening pro-Ahok residents.[4] This was critical in helping Baswedan into office, while Ahok was jailed for blasphemy.

Since then, the KRTs have been co-opted into Baswedan's ruling coalition, but changes to Jakarta's property oligarchy remain partial, reflecting the current balance of social power within this coalition. Governor Baswedan has rewarded the KRTs with expanded budgets and greater autonomy, effectively incorporating the KRTs into patron–client relationships that serve the interests of his coalition. He also cancelled the NCICD, sending stock in ethnic-Chinese property development companies plummeting. But Baswedan also issued 10-year licences for the four islets thus far developed to the city-owned property enterprise, PT Jakarta Propertindo, one of the original NCICD developers, drawing objections from some of the city's urban rights activists (Wijaya 2018). Baswedan's moves to date have thus been more about reorganising Jakarta's property oligarchy than dismantling it, illustrating the broader constraints on challenges to the political economy of property development in Jakarta.

Conclusion

This chapter has set out a distinctive Murdoch School approach to the analysis and explanation of political institutions and regimes. Our argument is that political regimes are fundamentally shaped by conflict between socio-political forces, rooted in evolving political economy dynamics. Rather than just classifying regimes as more or less democratic, or as some sort of "hybrid", which merely describes their form and tells us what they are not, this approach allows us to explain why regimes and institutions take this form, and the precise interests that they serve. This reveals these institutions not as dysfunctional but, rather, as functional for specific social forces, as they facilitate or constrain scrutiny and reform of social power relations. Everywhere, struggles over who should be able to participate, how, and on what issues, are fought by forces with concrete interests and concerns that are fundamentally shaped by capitalist dynamics. Yet the precise forces involved necessarily vary across cases, as does the predisposition towards, and utility of, different ideologies of representation for contending forces. Some struggles are more effectively contained than others.

In Singapore, conflict over rising inequality played out in a context where authoritarian controls over political competition are reinforced

---

[4] Reja Hidayat, interview with Jacqui Baker, Jakarta, November 2018.

through state capitalism. Here the absolute political ascendance of technocratic politico-bureaucrats was consolidated and extended through growth. Consequently, refinements to strategies of political management amidst tension over rising inequality invariably resulted in yet another state-sponsored initiative in consultative representation—the OSC. In the absence of substantive measures towards reducing extreme inequality, however, the effectiveness of this strategy will face continued challenges.

In Indonesia, state power is more contested not just because there is greater independent political space for civil society forces, but also because alliances among political and economic elites are less cohesive. The coalitions of interest reflected in state power are more factious, complex and dynamic under predatory capitalism. In this context, we have seen how conflict over capital accumulation strategies in property development precipitated the emergence of competing coalitions that looked to the RTs to advance their respective interests. This institutional site of struggle historically privileged particularist cultural ideologies of representation, now emphasised by a new Islamic populist coalition arising out of the wider urban land conflict. While the conflict delivered the governorship to Baswedan's coalition, its ability to challenge Jakarta's property oligarchy remains constrained.

References

Anya, A. (2018, November 13). Indonesia eyes more investment from Singapore. *Jakarta Post*. https://www.thejakartapost.com/news/2018/11/13/indonesia-eyes-more-investment-singapore.html. Accessed 14 Nov 2018.

Arai, K. (2015). Jakarta "since yesterday": The making of the post-new order regime in an Indonesian metropolis. *Southeast Asian Studies, 4*(3), 445–486.

Bourchier, D. (2014). *Illiberal democracy in Indonesia: The ideology of the family state*. Abingdon: Routledge.

Brownlee, J. (2008). Bound to rule: Party institutions and regime trajectories in Malaysia and the Philippines. *Journal of East Asian Studies, 8*(1), 89–118.

Carothers, T. (2002). The end of the transition paradigm. *Journal of Democracy, 13*(1), 5–21.

Carothers, T. (2006). *Confronting the weakest link: Aiding political parties in new democracies*. Washington, DC: Carnegie Endowment for International Peace.

Case, W. (2002). *Politics in Southeast Asia: Democracy more or less*. London: Curzon.

Chong, Z. L. (2015, August 27). Entrench opposition presence, urges WP chief. *Straits Times*. https://www.straitstimes.com/singapore/entrench-opposition-presence-urges-wp-chief. Accessed 1 Mar 2019.

Gomez, E. T. (2019, March 12). Business as usual: Regime change and GLCs in Malaysia. *New Mandala*. https://www.newmandala.org/business-as-usual-regime-change-and-glcs-in-malaysia. Accessed 18 Mar 2019.

Hadiz, V. R. (2003). Reorganising political power in Indonesia: A reconsideration of so-called "democratic transitions". *Pacific Review, 16*(4), 591–611.

Hadiz, V. R. (2010). *Localising power in post-authoritarian Indonesia: A Southeast Asia perspective*. Stanford: Stanford University Press.

Hadiz, V. R., & Robison, R. (2013). The political economy of oligarchy and the reorganization of power in Indonesia. *Indonesia, 96*, 35–58.

Haila, A. (2000). Real estate in global cities: Singapore and Hong Kong as property states. *Urban Studies, 37*(12), 2241–2256.

Haila, A. (2016). *Urban land rent: Singapore as a property state*. Chichester: Wiley.

Henderson, K. (2004). The Slovak Republic: Explaining defects in democracy. *Democratization, 11*(5), 133–155.

Hidayat, R. (2018, January 5). Kekuatan Forum RT/RW dalam Pilkada Jakarta 2017. *Tirto*. https://tirto.id/kekuatan-forum-rt-rw-dalam-pilkada-jakarta-2017-cCMj. Accessed 1 Mar 2019.

Huntington, S. P. (1968). *Political order in changing societies*. New Haven/London: Yale University Press.

Huntington, S. P. (1991). *The third wave: Democratization in the late twentieth century*. Norman: University of Oklahoma Press.

Hutchison, J., & Brown, A. (2001). *Organising labour in globalising Asia*. London: Routledge.

Lee, H. L. (2012). Prime Minister Lee Hsien Loong's National Day Rally speech. Speech delivered at the 2012 National Day Rally. Singapore, 26 August. http://www.pmo.gov.sg/mediacentre/prime-minister-lee-hsien-loongs-national-day-rally-2012-speech-english. Accessed 1 Mar 2019.

Leitner, H., & Sheppard, E. (2018). From Kampungs to Condos? Contested accumulations through displacement in Jakarta. *Environment and Planning A: Economy and Space, 50*(2), 437–456.

Levitsky, S., & Way, L. A. (2002). Elections without democracy: The rise of competitive authoritarianism. *Journal of Democracy, 13*(2), 51–65.

Moore, B. (1966). *Social origins of dictatorship and democracy: Lord and peasant in the making of the world*. Boston: Beacon Press.

Morlino, L., Dressel, B., & Pelizzo, R. (2011). The quality of democracy in Asia-Pacific: Issues and findings. *International Political Science Review, 32*(5), 491–511.

Ong, A. (2014, January 8). Consider what compassionate meritocracy entails. Singapolitics. *Straits Times*. http://www.singapolitics.sg/news/consider-what-compassionate-meritocracy-entails-lim-siong-guan. Accessed 1 Mar 2019.

OSC Committee. (2013). *Reflections of our Singapore conversation: What future do we want? How do we get there?* Singapore: Our Singapore Conversation Secretariat.
Pepinsky, T. (2014). The institutional turn in comparative authoritarianism. *British Journal of Political Science, 44*(3), 631–653.
Rahim, L., & Yeoh, L. K. (2019). Social policy reform and rigidity in Singapore's authoritarian developmental state. In L. Rahim & M. Barr (Eds.), *The limits of authoritarian governance in Singapore's developmental state* (pp. 95–130). Singapore: Palgrave Macmillan.
Robison, R. (1986). *Indonesia: The rise of capital*. Singapore: Equinox Publishing.
Robison, R. (2012). Interpreting the politics of Southeast Asia: Debates in parallel universes. In R. Robison (Ed.), *Routledge handbook of Southeast Asia* (pp. 5–22). London: Routledge.
Robison, R., & Hadiz, V. R. (2004). *Reorganising power in Indonesia: The politics of oligarchy in an age of markets*. London: Routledge.
Rodan, G. (1989). *The political economy of Singapore's industrialization: National state and international capital*. London: Macmillan.
Rodan, G. (2004). International capital, Singapore's state companies, and security. *Critical Asian Studies, 36*(3), 479–499.
Rodan, G. (2018). *Participation without democracy: Containing conflict in Southeast Asia*. Ithaca: Cornell University Press.
Rodan, G., & Hughes, C. (2014). *The politics of accountability in Southeast Asia: The dominance of moral ideologies*. New York: Oxford University Press.
Rodan, G., & Jayasuriya, K. (2007). The technocratic politics of administrative participation: Case studies of Singapore and Vietnam. *Democratisation, 14*(5), 795–815.
Rodan, G., & Jayasuriya, K. (2012). Hybrid regimes: A social foundations approach. In J. Haynes (Ed.), *Routledge handbook of democratization* (pp. 175–189). Abingdon: Routledge.
Sherwell, P. (2016, November 22). $40bn to save Jakarta: The story of the Great Garuda. *The Guardian*. https://www.theguardian.com/cities/2016/nov/22/jakarta-great-garuda-seawall-sinking. Accessed 1 Mar 2019.
Slater, D. (2010). *Ordering power: Contentious politics and authoritarian leviathans in Southeast Asia*. New York: Cambridge University Press.
Suara Muhammadiyah. (2016, September 17). Forum RT/RW Se-DKI Jakarta Demo Ahok. http://www.suaramuhammadiyah.id/2016/09/17/forum-rtrw-se-dki-jakarta-demo-ahok/. Accessed 1 Oct 2016.
Suryadinata, L. (2012). Ethnic Chinese in Southeast Asia and their economic role. In M. Jocelyn Armstrong et al. (Eds.), *Chinese populations in contemporary Southeast Asian societies: Identities, interdependence and international influence* (pp. 55–74). Abingdon: Routledge.
Teo, Y. Y. (2018). *This is what inequality looks like*. Singapore: Ethos Books.

Wijaya, C. A. (2018, June 14). Critics slam Anies' decision to form agency on reclamation project. *Jakarta Post*. https://www.thejakartapost.com/news/2018/06/14/critics-slam-anies-decision-to-form-agency-on-reclamation-project.html. Accessed 14 June 2018.

Wilson, I. (2016, November 3). Making enemies out of friends. *New Mandala*. https://www.newmandala.org/making-enemies-friends/. Accessed 1 Mar 2019.

Wong, T., & Sim, B. (2012, August 9). "No sacred cows" in review of policies. *Straits Times*. https://www.facebook.com/notes/reachsingapore/no-sacred-cows-in-review-of-policies/10151012580338795. Accessed 1 Mar 2019.

CHAPTER 4

Transitions from State "Socialism" in Southeast Asia

Caroline Hughes

INTRODUCTION

Cambodia, Laos, Myanmar (Burma) and Vietnam (the CLMV countries) were all dominated by "socialist" regimes during the Cold War.[1] In practice, their experiments with state socialism were uniformly unsuccessful and short-lived. Cambodia's disastrous collectivisation and state violence under Pol Pot killed up to 1.5 million people and destabilised the whole region, prompting invasion by Vietnam in 1979 and a Western international aid and trade embargo that undercut the economic prospects of both countries. Laos's post-1975 collectivisation began to be reversed in 1979 following devastating droughts and emigration. The Soviet Union's withdrawal of foreign aid after 1986, and its collapse soon thereafter, compelled the states of Indochina to embark on pro-market reforms. Vietnam

---

[1] Quotation marks are used because the Stalinist regimes that emerged in Southeast Asia (and elsewhere) bear no resemblance to socialist precepts. For readability the quotation marks are not used hereafter.

C. Hughes (✉)
Kroc Institute for International Peace Studies, University of Notre Dame, Notre Dame, IN, USA
e-mail: chughe11@nd.edu

© The Author(s) 2020
T. Carroll et al. (eds.), *The Political Economy of Southeast Asia*, Studies in the Political Economy of Public Policy, https://doi.org/10.1007/978-3-030-28255-4_4

withdrew from Cambodia and opened its economy, and the 1991 Paris Peace Accords facilitated a United Nations-led transition to multi-party market democracy in Cambodia. Meanwhile, Burma's socialist regime collapsed in 1988, following two decades of stagnation and a pro-democracy uprising.

However, the economic liberalisation that ensued has not been matched by political liberalisation. Cambodia formally adopted a liberal, democratic constitution with regular multi-party elections, but the country remains dominated by the authoritarian Cambodian People's Party (CPP), a reconstituted version of the old communist regime. Communist parties remain in power in Vietnam and Laos. Myanmar's pro-market reforms in the 1990s were (successfully) aimed at bolstering a military regime against tightening Western sanctions, and the post-2011 transition to greater democracy remains heavily constrained by military domination and continued ethnic civil war.

Despite failing to conform to Western prescriptions for liberal democracy, the CLMV countries—especially Vietnam and Cambodia—are often viewed as developmental success stories, thanks to consistently high economic growth rates. Yet these have been achieved predominantly through dispossession and asset-stripping, facilitated by post-socialist contexts in which privileged, state-linked groups gained control over land, natural resources and business opportunities through often-violent privatisation processes. China's proximity and the associated commodities boom contributed to this success. Meanwhile, decades of authoritarian control over civil society meant that farmers, workers and other subordinated groups found it difficult to defend their customary or legal rights. This has permitted the emergence of an extremely wealthy elite spanning the politico-bureaucratic, business and military spheres, fuelling inequality and corruption and motivating continued repression of critical civil society movements. Conflicts have emerged around environmental degradation, factory wages, land-grabbing and corruption, reflecting a growing legitimacy crisis. Dominant forces have responded by intensifying authoritarianism, sometimes combined with populist policies, including promises of welfare in Cambodia, anti-corruption show trials in Vietnam, cultural nationalism in Laos, and the fanning of Buddhist nationalism in Myanmar.

There are signs of tentative transnational alliances amongst political, economic and military elites across the region. Post-socialist infrastructure projects focused on integration of the Greater Mekong Subregion and reorientation of transport and energy networks towards southwest China have promoted opportunities for transnational investment and cooperation.

This has produced new economic landscapes of deforestation, plantation agriculture, tourism, exploitation and energy generation, sometimes policed through cross-border security cooperation on behalf of hybrid state–private interests. Heavy investment by Vietnamese state-owned businesses in Cambodian and Laotian plantations and logging ventures, and Thai and Chinese hydropower, timber and mining operations across the region have been facilitated by state-sponsored expulsions of local and indigenous people in a transnational politics of expropriation.

With resource extraction so lucrative, industrial development remains limited, with the partial exception of Vietnam. Domestic elites have invested in easy, state-protected extraction schemes and avoided the more risky task of building an internationally competitive industrial base in the difficult context of late development. Low wages have attracted foreign investment to particular sectors, notably garments. Vietnam has had broader success in export-oriented manufacturing, including IT and electronics components, but industry remains overwhelmingly labour-intensive, low value-added, and dependent on multinational corporations (Black 2018; Eckardt et al. 2018; Ekaphone 2018; Kikuchi and Vo 2016; Lee and Huang 2018). Economic activity is predominantly informal and small-scale. Although statistics are somewhat unreliable, 73% of workers in Myanmar are estimated to be informal (World Bank 2014a); 77% in Vietnam (VGSO and ILO 2016); 81% in Cambodia (DTUC 2015); and 83% in Laos (Ministry of Planning and Investment Lao Statistics Bureau 2017).

The chapter begins by reviewing the transition from state socialism to market economy in each country, showing how economic liberalisation empowered ruling elites, helping them to secure alliances with the military and bureaucrats, and enabling strategies of primitive accumulation. It then shows how policies of subregional integration have fostered transnational connections between these elite alliances, protected by cooperating security services. It concludes by discussing the nature and extent of opposition social movements.

STATES, BUSINESS AND COMMODITIES

In each CLMV country, the transition to a market economy was steered by social forces concerned with maintaining political power and control of significant economic assets. These assets could be extracted and sold to raise money that enriched loyal groups, thereby consolidating power in the hands of dominant elites. The means used reflected both regional commonalities (see Carroll, this volume)—notably, the decline of Cold War confrontation, the rise of foreign investment, and burgeoning demand for natural resources in neighbouring industrialising economies—and each state's specific circumstances.

Cambodia

In Cambodia, the Vietnamese-backed communist party converted itself into the CPP, ostensibly accepting electoral competition after the UN-led transition. In reality, CPP leaders used their long-standing control of state power to consolidate an alliance between the party, the bureaucracy, the military and leading Cambodian and regional business tycoons. Their control of key resources allowed them to maintain the loyalty of the bureaucracy and military and marginalise their political opponents. The offer of control of land, mining operations and logging concessions to defecting insurgent commanders was successful in ending the civil war and binding the newly integrated army to the CPP, while tolerance of bureaucratic corruption maintained civil servants' loyalty. The sale of natural resources—state-owned, a legacy of socialist rule—also funded some rural development schemes, which, coupled with extensive repression, consolidated the CPP's main electoral base.

Business has played a critical role in these developments. The Indochina wars left Cambodia with no significant industrial sector; accordingly, the key mechanism the CPP has used to generate patronage has been the asset-stripping of natural resources. Millions of hectares of state or common land have been privatised, handed to regime-linked businessmen for logging or agribusiness or, less commonly, for special economic zones (SEZs) and tourist resorts. In peripheral areas where deforestation and de-mining[2] made large areas available for plantation development, relationships between provincial military chiefs, local tycoons, international companies and CPP politicians were consolidated through business partnerships burdened with minimal regulation or taxation (Hughes 2008, 2011; Verver and Dahles 2015). In urban areas, informal settlers were expelled to facilitate the entry of property development companies with military and/or CPP links. Especially during the commodities boom, these strategies provided windfall profits to CPP-linked companies.

[2] During the Indochina wars, anti-personnel landmines were placed over large areas.

In exchange, business elites have supported the regime, donating to CPP development schemes and even bankrolling military operations. Teng Bunma of the Thai–Cambodian Thai Boon Rong trading company, and Vietnamese-Cambodian Sok Kong, chairman of Sokimex, helped to fund the recapture of Pailin from the Khmer Rouge in 1994 and the ousting of FUNCINPEC from the coalition government in 1997 (Pisani 1996; Post Staff 2000). Both then received lucrative state contracts and monopolies. More recently, tycoons were invited to sponsor particular military units. Among those involved are Sok Kong; CPP Senator Ly Yong Phat, who has been embroiled in controversy over land allocations for sugar plantations (Davies 2017); and Try Pheap, allegedly a key node in a network of political-business alliances organised around illegal logging (Global Witness 2007). Interestingly, Prime Minister Hun Sen's bodyguard unit, which has backstopped his personal dominance of the CPP since the late 1990s, is reportedly sponsored by a Chinese company, Unite Group, through a "military-commercial alliance" formed in 2010. Unite Group was rewarded with a stretch of Cambodia's coastline to convert into a tourist resort, including land inside a national park (Kynge et al. 2016).

Indeed, Chinese investors have been a significant feature of the elite alliance more widely. China is Cambodia's largest source of imports, fifth largest export market, largest creditor, largest bilateral donor and largest foreign investor, with interests in plantation agriculture, energy, property development and tourism. China's accumulated investments in Cambodian hydropower alone are estimated at US$7.5bn. Cambodia is considered a core area in China's Belt and Road Initiative, which will supposedly involve building new roads and railways to link southwest China to Indochina and the Gulf of Thailand (Lin 2018). China's close relationship with the CPP will secure this deal, despite the likely negative impacts on many Cambodian farmers.

Myanmar

Myanmar's post-2010 transition from direct military rule has opened up political space for the previously outlawed National League for Democracy and its leader Aung San Suu Kyi to participate in politics, but its top-down implementation also ensured that significant power remained in military hands. The 2008 military-drafted constitution reserves 25% of parliamentary seats and the ministries of defence, home affairs and border affairs for military appointees; the army remains under military, not civilian command; and ex-military personnel still dominate the bureaucracy (Kyaw 2018). This continued grip on state power is justified by the military's self-proclaimed role in securing Myanmar's integrity in the face of ethnic-minority insurgencies that have operated in the country's border areas since independence.

As in Cambodia, however, state–business relationships have been crucial to entrenching the military's power, despite the imposition of Western sanctions from 1989 (see Jones 2015: ch.3). The privatisation of state economic enterprises in the 1990s privileged private companies linked to, or owned by, the army. The military established its own holding companies, which dominated in primary commodity production and heavy industry, and cultivated so-called "national entrepreneurs": crony capitalists selected for their political loyalty (Jones 2014). Subcontracting arrangements also allowed the state to reduce its direct ownership of firms while maintaining tight control of the economy. State control was maintained in key resource sectors, notably oil and gas, exports of which to neighbouring Thailand and China netted the regime about US$2bn annually.

The borderlands saw similar developments. After 1988, the army expanded rapidly, using Chinese arms imports, intensifying pressure on war-weary rebels. Those who agreed to ceasefires were rewarded with economic concessions, leading to a "ceasefire capitalism" which tied rebel leaders to regional military commanders and foreign, especially Chinese and Thai, investors (Woods 2011). This typically involved the exploitation of natural resources—notably in logging, mining, hydropower and agribusiness—with assets stripped and exported. This has underpinned what Callahan (2007) calls "emerging political complexes", incorporating local headmen, warlords and drug barons, national and foreign investors, military officers, NGOs and political parties. These deals extended state power into the borderlands to an unprecedented extent, but failed to address the deep-seated grievances underpinning the world's longest-running ethnic insurgencies. Indeed, these have often been exacerbated by the violent expropriation frequently involved.

These military–business ties have survived the post-2010 transition intact. Reflecting their structural power, Aung San Suu Kyi has cosied up to military elites and crony capitalists, and extended the practice of "ceasefire capitalism" as part of her efforts to pacify the borderlands. The international financial institutions have supported a limited process of economic reform, but have been unable to effect deep-seated change that would untangle the complex military–business ties undergirding state power.

Vietnam

Vietnam entered the post-Cold War era in the best state of any CLMV state, despite a decade of Western sanctions and war in Cambodia. Following its defeat of the US and reunification in 1975, the Vietnamese government made some progress in promoting healthcare, electrification and education, making it the most advanced among the CLMV states. Relations between the state and the private sector have also developed differently to Cambodia and Myanmar, as socialism has, somewhat awkwardly, remained the regime's official ideology. Crony capitalism has consequently become embedded in hybrid state–private conglomerates that incorporate elements of the Communist Party, the bureaucracy and the private sector. These were created ostensibly to promote development but have, in reality, facilitated the corruption and patronage that continue to cement intra-elite alliances (Abuza 2017).

Despite the abandonment of central planning and the emergence of a significant private sector, the Vietnamese government has maintained substantial state control of the economy. International investors were keen to tap into Vietnam's low-paid yet literate workforce in the 1990s, spurring international engagement even ahead of the US lifting its embargo in 1994. Soon thereafter, Vietnam welcomed international donors to support pro-market reforms and prepare the country for ASEAN and World Trade Organisation membership. However, while many orthodox economists guiding such efforts lambasted state-owned enterprises (SOEs) for "crowding out" private investment and hoped for their demise (Nguyen and Freeman 2009), change has been constrained. While many smaller SOEs were privatised, large SOEs—which still accounted for a quarter of state revenues in 2003 (Painter 2003)—remained under government control. A 2001 party resolution described SOEs as "the leading role in the socialist-oriented market economy, and… the main force in international economic integration", while also allowing "the state to orient and regulate the macroeconomy" (Vu-Thanh 2017).

Accordingly, Vietnam's embrace of globalisation has been state-led and state-mediated. The government merged SOEs in key sectors into state economic groups (SEGs): conglomerates, organised sectorally, initially in textiles, telecommunications, shipbuilding, minerals and finance. Each

SEG was dominated by an SOE as parent company, with controlling shares in subsidiaries allowed to form joint stock companies, joint ventures or limited liability companies (Nguyen 2016). Thirteen SEGs were created in 2006–07 and, by 2015, SEGs controlled, among other things, 99% of fertiliser production, 97% of coal mining, 94% of electricity and gas output, and 91% of the media (Vu-Thanh 2017). This approach has allowed Vietnamese businesses to survive trade and investment liberalisation, permitting contributions from private equity and foreign investment without eradicating state control. SOEs also remained vehicles for government policies, from stabilization of employment to assuring food security, supplying the military and promoting particular regions (Nguyen 2016; Sjöholm 2006).

State control also allowed the Vietnamese Communist Party to establish a state–party–business alliance through the distribution of benefits. SOE managers formed a significant and influential constituency, as other sections of the 1980s' administration were dismantled (Painter 2003). The demise of central planning created "state business interests", with "strong roots in provincial and local state and party circles", constituting a powerful political force (ibid.). These interests used SOEs as vehicles to amass wealth and forge patronage links, leading to signs of "large scale corruption within the ranks of the party" (ibid.). By the mid-2000s, many government officials had personal interests in SOEs, using SOE capital to fund their own "backyard businesses" (Tran et al. 2016).

Coupled with continued authoritarian political structures, these networks allow SOEs to evade oversight from citizens, lenders or even political managers. SOEs are routinely exempted from, or flout, Vietnam's competition laws. Expanding into new sectors, including banking, finance and insurance, allowed SEGs effectively to borrow from themselves, cheaply and with little transparency, facilitating massive debt-driven expansion, especially under Prime Minister Nguyen Tan Dung from 2006 to 2016, allowing him to build patronage networks under the guise of economic nationalism. By 2016, SOEs owned 32% of Vietnam's total capital, and 39% of fixed assets and long-term investment (VietnamNet 2017).

Laos

In Laos, as in Cambodia, industrial under-development entailed that post-socialist transition largely involved the de-collectivisation of agriculture and the opening of natural resource sectors to foreign investment. As in

Vietnam, one-party rule was maintained. In practice, this meant perpetuating a party–state–army "symbiosis" (Soukamneuth 2006: 19) resting on clan-based patronage links to different regions, supported through the party-mediated distribution of proceeds from resource extraction. This has been facilitated by large-scale infrastructure investment from Thailand, China and Vietnam, including road construction and hydropower. Logging has been a mainstay, while mining, particularly of gold and copper, also surged during the commodity boom.

Relations between Lao People's Revolutionary Party (LPRP) leaders, bureaucrats, the military and provincial governors—who enjoy significant autonomy—are mediated within closed-door party forums. Through the 1990s, politicians and their families developed provincial conglomerates with wide-ranging interests, which gate-keep foreign investment schemes, generating large kickbacks and bribes, while the military controls lucrative logging concessions. By 2000, around a dozen families had cemented their political position and accumulated massive wealth (ibid.: 63). This allows them to control leading positions within national LPRP structures, while their patronage networks—often more effective than the corrupt, demoralised bureaucracy—organise subordinate forces to support them (Creak and Barney 2018; Sayalath and Creak 2017).

This ruling elite's entrenchment, and the ongoing marginalisation of subordinate groups, have been fundamentally aided by Laos's insertion into the regional economy as a hydropower and mineral resources exporter. The LPRP's development plans aim to convert Laos into a "battery" for neighbouring industrialised economies. Hydropower megaprojects, though central to the achievement of 7% average GDP growth from 2005 to 2015, and to Laos's designation as a middle-income country in 2011, have generated little local employment (World Bank 2017a). However, they have also extended ruling elites' grip over local populations, by permitting local electrification and irrigation projects (Blake and Barney 2018). Between 2000 and 2011, almost half of foreign investment was focused on mining (29%) and electricity generation (20%), with China, Vietnam and Thailand the top three investors. The World Bank estimates that this accounts for over a third of Laos's annual growth (2.5 of 7%) and contributes about a fifth of government revenues (Keovilignavong and Suhardiman 2018: 345–346). Mining has been environmentally and socially unsustainable, with profits appropriated by elites (World Bank 2017a), and profoundly negative social, livelihoods and health impacts for the poor (Keovilignavong and Suhardiman 2018; see also Hatcher, this volume). Plantation agriculture, focused on rubber and eucalyptus, has also destroyed rural livelihoods (Keovilignavong and Suhardiman 2018).

Meanwhile, productivity in non-plantation agriculture—which sustains the vast majority of the population—has stagnated. Some villages regarded as under-developed, particularly those in forested, upland areas practising swidden agriculture, have been subjected to forced relocation into "focal sites" for cash crop production, in a process of "de-agrarianism" that immediately harmed livelihoods and well-being (Rigg 2006). Although poverty has fallen, inequality has widened and malnutrition remains a factor in a third of child deaths under the age of five (World Bank 2017a: ii). Such indicators prompted characterisation of the post-socialist transition in Laos as "pro-rich" (Kakwani 2001, quoted in Rigg 2006: 126).

Transnational Dimensions

In Southeast Asia's post-socialist transitions, emerging regional investment and trade networks have been critical to shaping illiberal political economy dynamics. These party, state, military and familial transnational networks reflect complex ties of solidarity and hostility among communist movements from the 1950s, which evolved into smuggling and logging networks in the 1980s and 1990s before becoming more formalised business partnerships.

Consider the example of Vietnam Rubber Group (VRG), which produces 85% of Vietnam's rubber exports and controls 40% of its rubber plantations. VRG also controls extensive plantations in Laos and Cambodia, obtained under controversial "economic land concession" schemes, widely understood to erode customary livelihoods and resource rights (see also Hirsch, this volume). Thanks to close relations with Cambodia's ruling elites, VRG has circumvented legal limits on concession sizes by using subsidiaries, and engaged in illegal logging outside of concession areas in league with local timber companies owned by relations of Cambodia's prime minister. Similar activities are alleged in Laos (Global Witness 2013). Cambodian officials have also granted large agribusiness concessions to a company belonging to the Vietnamese military (Blomberg and Roeun 2015), and been involved, alongside Vietnamese officials, in illegally smuggling timber into Vietnam (Tatarski 2017).

Across the region, then, post-socialist transition has been conducted in a way that has strengthened and consolidated the power of socialist-era elites. Revenues from privatisation, corruption, asset-stripping and resource exports have allowed these elites to flourish despite the loss of socialist legitimation ideologies. Transnational connections between them are consolidating despite the nationalist tensions that have long divided the region, facilitated by "connectivity" policies, funded by regional powers, development banks and donors (Hughes 2011).

CONTRADICTIONS AND OPPOSITION

Post-socialist economies, like all capitalist economies, are contradictory and crisis-ridden, generating periodic socio-political ferment. The weakness of civil society in the CLMV states, stemming from years of war and authoritarian control, means that resistance to entrenched elites remains weak and sporadic, with the important exception of Myanmar where ethnic-minority armed groups—in active insurgencies or tense ceasefires—deprive the state of full territorial control. Central themes for opposition are issues of dispossession, corruption and exploitation, frequently intertwined in the politics of land (see also Hirsch, this volume).

Contradictions, crises and simple tussles over spoils are typically managed within elite structures. For example, the monopolisation of lucrative smuggling rackets by the intelligence network around General Khin Nyunt, Secretary-1 of Myanmar's military regime, led to this network being purged from the state apparatus in 2004, significantly weakening the regime's surveillance capacity. Similar but stronger tensions emerged in the VCP after 2010, beginning with the collapse of Vinashin—a shipbuilding SEG run by a close ally of Prime Minister Dung—with debts of US$4.5bn. Eight executives were jailed for economic mismanagement and corruption, with two sentenced to death. Other SEG scandals followed in what appeared to be a factional struggle against Dung, resulting in his resignation in 2016 and a government pledge to privatise most SEGs by 2020 (Al Jazeera 2016a; Brown 2017; Hutt 2018). These struggles, while contained within VCP structures, signal a wider legitimacy crisis in a context where increasingly evident inequality and corruption has rendered ideological legitimacy bases—a mixture of nationalism, developmentalism, paternal benevolence and Ho Chi Minh thought—increasingly threadbare (Thayer 2009).

Land conflicts symbolise this wider crisis. Across the Mekong River watershed, 5.1m hectares of land have been granted as land concessions for plantation agriculture since 1991, 80% of which produce just six export crops: rice, cassava, maize, sugar cane, palm oil and rubber (Ingalls et al.

2018). The result has been declining forest cover, shrinking smallholdings, increased landlessness, and social and environmental costs borne by the poor. Granted by incumbent political elites, upheld by the courts, cleared of previous inhabitants by the military and police, and operated by private business, land concessions are a visible manifestation of the elite coalitions empowered by post-socialist transition and the strategies of primitive accumulation they have employed at the expense of common and customary forms of land use (see also Hirsch, this volume).

Plantation agriculture's rampant expansion also reflects peasant producers' political weakness. The extraordinary militarisation of Southeast Asia during the Cold War, the devastating impact of war on farming communities, and disruptive legacies of land mines and collectivisation have meant peasant farmers have struggled to resist land-grabbing effectively. Local, on-site protests have occasionally involved violent resistance, but are easily crushed by military units routinely dispatched to defend company interests. Dispossessed farmers frequently converge on capital cities to petition higher-ranking officials to dispense justice, often invoking smallholding farmers' special status in past nationalist and socialist rhetoric (Kerkvliet 2014). As the commodity boom wanes, there is some evidence of a slowdown in land-grabs and a more conciliatory approach to protestors from regimes increasingly concerned about social unrest.

In Phnom Penh, isolated land protests were commonplace but ineffective from the early 1990s to the mid-2000s. Ahead of the 2013 election, however, land became an electoral issue, partly because of high-profile evictions of middle-class communities in the capital city itself, and partly because a dramatic expansion of social media access—thanks to mobile telephony—allowed images of violent expropriation to be circulated for the first time. The government responded by issuing a moratorium on economic land concessions and attempting a (poorly executed) land titling programme. Nonetheless, the CPP performed poorly in the 2013 elections, in part due to discontent over land.

A major land issue in Vietnam's development has been the reclassification of rural land as urban, as in the 2008 expansion of Hanoi's city limits. Such re-zoning displaces farmers, jeopardising their livelihoods and pushing them into the informal urban economy, causing significant discontent (Kerkvliet 2014; Nguyen 2017). Land protests became increasingly common (Kerkvliet 2014) and, in 2017, there was a rare climb-down by Hanoi authorities after villagers kidnapped police sent to secure a contested site and held them in the municipal hall for a week (The Economist 2017).

Disruption of traditional livelihoods from the effects of foreign-owned factories has also been central to oppositional politics. In 2016, mass fish deaths off the coast of Vietnam's Ha Tinh province sparked protests in Hanoi and Ho Chi Minh City, as the deaths were blamed on pollution from a nearby Taiwanese-owned steel plant. The protests erupted after the plant's spokesman stated that Vietnam needed "to choose whether to catch fish and shrimp or to build a state-of-the-art steel mill. You cannot have both" (Al Jazeera 2016b). This enraged local fishermen, amid wider public concern about government failure to regulate environmental damage caused by foreign factories. Such unrest has fed into Secretary General Nguyen Phu Trong's anti-corruption campaign, but also reflects the discursive link between traditional rural livelihoods, land, natural resources and national sovereignty that was prominent in the region's socialist rhetoric (Kieng 2017).

Although, outside Vietnam, significant industrial development remains confined to small pockets of Cambodia and Myanmar, there are also stirrings of urban labour unrest in post-socialist Southeast Asia. Export-oriented investments, often in SEZs, are drawing—or forcing—young people off the land and into industrial centres to work in mainly low-skill and low-wage manufacturing for foreign companies, where conditions are often abysmal. In Cambodia, industrial discontent centres on the garment industry, which employs 800,000 workers, mostly young women from rural areas. They work in poor conditions for below-subsistence pay, and have been highly militant, repeatedly striking for better pay and conditions and forming a dedicated support-base for the opposition party, the Cambodian National Rescue Party (CNRP). The emergence of this young and mobile industrial workforce has been problematic for the CPP, which is organised around a patronage and surveillance network focused on rural villagers.

The CPP's near-loss in the 2013 general election was attributed largely to the impact of the youth vote. Both young workers and the unemployed were alienated by CPP policies that have offered them scant economic prospects and, in 2013, were newly mobilised by opposition campaigning on Facebook, which had become quite widely available for the first time in Cambodia in 2012 (Hughes and Eng 2018). In response, the CPP has refocused its political efforts on this constituency. After violently crushing garment workers' demonstrations in 2014, killing four workers, the party shifted to a more conciliatory approach. Annual minimum wage bargaining was introduced, delivering significant wage increases, along with promises of cheaper social insurance, maternity pay and pensions. Alongside these promises, the government outlawed the CNRP in 2017 ahead of the 2018 national elections, while also passing a trade union law which significantly restricts rights to organise and entrenches "yellow unions" in factories.

Another form of industrial-related resistance involves nationalist protests against mounting foreign investment, which can often become racialised. In 2018, protests broke out simultaneously in several Vietnamese cities against a law permitting Chinese firms to obtain 99-year SEZ leases. The ferocious nationalist backlash prompted the government to delay legislation and reassure the populace (Parameswaram 2018). This echoed protests in 2009 over plans to develop bauxite mining in the Central Highlands in a joint venture with Chinese companies, which prompted a widespread mobilisation by environmental groups and eventually included revered wartime general Vo Nguyen Giap. Giap issued open letters to Vietnam's leadership, opposing the plan and emphasising national security concerns associated with the influx of Chinese into the Vietnamese uplands (Thayer 2009). Anti-Chinese riots were also sparked in 2014 by Chinese actions in the South China Sea, resulting in the destruction of several mostly Taiwanese factories. Anti-Chinese sentiment is also intense in Myanmar, reflecting widespread resentment at growing Chinese domination of the economy under military rule, and the social and environmental consequences imposed on poor farming communities. Widespread protests caused the suspension of the Chinese-backed Myitsone dam in 2011, seriously disrupting bilateral ties. However, protests by peasants and monks at the Letpadaung copper mine—a joint venture between a Chinese SOE and the Myanmar military—have been brutally repressed, with Aung San Suu Kyi telling farmers to stop protesting and accept "development". In Cambodia, nationalist sentiment is typically anti-Vietnamese, and opposition parties have channelled deep-seated racism to protest against corrupt bilateral deals. However, as the CPP relies increasingly on Chinese support, the opposition is starting to rethink its traditional orientation.

The fiercest resistance to any CLMV regime is in Myanmar, where several ethnic-minority armed groups are engaged in active warfare against the government and many others are in tense ceasefires. This is partly a result of the failure of "ceasefire capitalism", pursued through the 1990s and early 2000s, to deliver either widespread economic benefits or a resolution of political and social grievances. The concentration of benefits in the hands of corrupt militia and military elites, while poor communities bore mounting social, economic and environmental costs, eventually contributed directly to the breakdown of a key ceasefire in Kachin state, with fighting spreading to Shan state (Brenner 2015). The roots of these insurgencies lie in decades of Bamar-Buddhist supremacist policies implemented brutally by the armed forces. The immediate cause of the breakdown of some ceasefires was the government's increasing determination to exercise greater control over the border with China, as the Belt and Road Initiative began to bring remote areas into the economic development mainstream. Controversial dam and other infrastructure policies implemented from the centre have caused displacement in ethnic-controlled ceasefire areas, putting pressure on local leaders to lead a new round of armed resistance (Brenner 2015; Kelleher 2018). The expulsions and massacres of the Rohingya from Northern Rakhine state represent similar tensions further fuelled by a long history of exclusionary ethnic and religious nationalism (Jones 2017).

The picture emerging from this account of post-socialist transitions reinforces the message of this volume. Although transitions from state socialism in each country have taken particular forms, influenced by the history, geography and institutional landscape of the different national contexts, they also share a strong transnational aspect. In each country, networks of business, state and military elites collaborate internally and across borders to escape national state regulation or pressures for redistributive policies, in an asset-stripping economy organised on a regional scale and oriented towards the Chinese demand for commodities and a broader regional demand for cheap, exploitable labour. Aside from ethnic insurgencies in Myanmar, the devastated post-Cold War civil society of the poor in these countries has found it difficult to reorganise and respond, as governments in the region routinely mobilise their extensive security apparatuses, sometimes in collaboration (Hughes 2011), to repress organised oppositions.

Where concessions have been made to popular protest, they reflect corrections rather than fundamental shifts. In Cambodia, the CPP faced a real threat of being voted out of office in the 2018 elections as its heavy-handed approach to patronage-based government failed to impress the swelling ranks of young voters who do not remember the war. The party responded with a reform programme aimed at improving public financial management to release money for improved social protection, regarded as a vote-winning policy. However, to achieve this, it would have to tackle corruption rings embedded within the party and the ministries, and the leadership was unwilling to take serious action to achieve this. As reforms floundered, the party changed tack, disbanding the opposition party, imprisoning its leaders and using repressive legislation to limit trade unions, NGOs and internet use. It seems to have been successful in stabilising its position. There has been little organised protest in response, since civil society's organisational mechanisms, re-established since the war ended in 1998, remain too weak to effectively combat the repressive power of the party, military and state.

In Vietnam, similarly, VCP General Secretary Trong's purge of his predecessor's cronies through corruption show trials reflects less an attack on the power of the political–business–bureaucratic alliance in the interests of a more inclusive approach to development than a greater opening towards Chinese investment at the expense of corrupt economic nationalists. Trong's shift towards an SEZ development model to attract Chinese investment threatens to further undermine workers' rights rather than advance them (Bloomberg Law 2018). A 2018 World Bank evaluation praised Vietnam's low wages, deregulation, reduction of corporation tax and "relentless focus on competitiveness" as the key to its "manufacturing miracle" and its climb in the ranks of World Bank Ease of Doing Business Surveys after the fall of Dung (Eckardt et al. 2018). But such developments suggest an intensification of exploitation of Vietnam's workers. So far, despite sporadic anti-Chinese outbursts, there is little organised opposition that can significantly challenge such a strategy. However, the rising expectations of young Vietnamese, following massive and successful investment in education, may prove difficult for the government to manage. For the reasons outlined by Carroll (this volume), Vietnam has struggled to diversify away from low-end manufacturing, such that it faces the prospect of millions of educated Vietnamese emerging from its universities with no jobs to go to. Eroding long-term legitimacy, virulent anti-Chinese sentiment and environmental disaster combined with high vulnerability to climate change represent significant future challenges, even if the organisational base for a sustained political movement is not currently evident.

Conclusion

Transitions from state socialism in Cambodia, Laos, Vietnam and Myanmar occurred largely in response to external shocks rather than from domestic mobilisations of opposition forces capable of capturing state power. Consequently, existing power-holders had considerable latitude to mould reforms to suit their own self-interest and regime security concerns. In the context of a commodities boom and resource-hungry China, this has prompted the emergence of economies organised to facilitate asset-stripping of natural resources and land-grabbing for plantation development. Authoritarian and semi-authoritarian states have presided over the construction of state–private networks of investors and entrepreneurs, including or supported by the national security forces, sweeping aside ordinary citizens' attempts to enforce legal or customary claims to land or resources.

Although part of the proceeds from resource exploitation have been reinvested in poverty-reduction schemes and services such as universal education, with positive effects on statistical indicators, large sections of the population, with the exception of Vietnam, remain vulnerable to poverty. In Cambodia, for example, absolute poverty fell from 53% in 2004 to 20% in 2014, but a fifth of the population are less than 30 cents a day above the official poverty line (World Bank 2014b). Similarly, in Laos, poverty declined from 33.5% to 23.2% in the period 2003–13, but 80% of the population remain on incomes below US$2.50 a day (World Bank 2015). In Myanmar, 37% of people are in poverty or vulnerable to it (World Bank 2017b). Conditions in manufacturing industries are oppressive and environmental degradation is rife. Civil society organisations have remained weak, as media is censored and protests are routinely violently suppressed.

Increasingly, regional tycoons' business interests are transnational, linking states and militaries together in a cross-regional exploitative violence and expropriation nexus, organised around the demands of regional capital. The regional nature of this nexus has itself attracted protest. In Vietnam and Myanmar in particular, the presence of Chinese businesses has prompted rising nationalist sentiment, while in Cambodia, the presence of Vietnamese state-owned rubber plantations has prompted opposition parties to claim the country's "annexation" by Vietnamese imperialists. As internet access and social media use have spread, the possibility of circulating such views has grown, although increasingly effective internet censorship and the use of Facebook by the Myanmar military to incite genocide suggest the limits to social media as a tool of the oppressed.

These trends have been significant in prompting an erosion of legitimacy across the region, despite success in growth and poverty-reduction terms. In Cambodia, the reversion to authoritarian rule in 2018 reflected the CPP's conviction that it was about to be voted out of office, while in

Vietnam, corruption show-trials and a reassertion of "Ho Chi Minh Thought" reflect concern within the VCP that the scandals of the Dung years were threatening political stability. In Myanmar, the appalling spectacle of massacres and ethnic cleansing of Rohingya, and Aung San Suu Kyi's apparent unwillingness to confront Buddhist nationalism, suggest a failure to establish more compelling legitimacy sources. Given the weaknesses of non-state organisations, it is difficult to see these ad hoc protests transforming into sustained anti-regime challenges. However, the youthful demographic of populations in the region, rising mobility, and the rapid expansion of information and education may combine to create better conditions for the emergence of non-state social movements in the near future. One implication of states' reorganisation around the interests of regional capital, rather than local populations' demands, and the powerful corruption networks that militate against reform, may be that, if a well-organised, regime-threatening social movement were to emerge, governments in the region would find it difficult to come up with an effective reformist response.

References

Abuza, Z. (2017, May 8). A top comrade's fall underlines divisions in Vietnam. *Asia Times*. https://www.asiatimes.com/2017/05/article/top-comrades-fall-underlines-divisions-vietnam/. Accessed 1 Mar 2019.

Al Jazeera. (2016a, April 6). Vietnam's Assembly "dismisses" prime minister. *Al Jazeera*. https://www.aljazeera.com/news/2016/04/vietnam-assembly-dismisses-prime-minister-160406133834975.html. Accessed 2 Mar 2019.

Al Jazeera. (2016b, May 9). Vietnam police break up protest after fish deaths. *Al Jazeera*. https://www.aljazeera.com/news/2016/05/vietnam-protest-fish-deaths-160509041334507.html. Accessed 2 Mar 2019.

Black, E. (2018, May 1). Rising costs pose new challenges for Cambodia's garment sector. *Southeast Asia Globe*. http://sea-globe.com/rising-costs-pose-new-challenges-for-cambodias-manufacturing-sector/. Accessed 1 Mar 2019.

Blake, D., & Barney, K. (2018). Structural injustice, slow violence? The political ecology of a "best practice" hydropower dam in Lao PDR. *Journal of Contemporary Asia, 48*(5), 808–834.

Blomberg, M., & Roeun, V. (2015, December 24). Special report: Grand concessions. *Cambodia Daily*. https://www.cambodiadaily.com/news/grand-concessions-103731/. Accessed 2 Mar 2019.

Bloomberg Law. (2018, August 24). Vietnam: Special economic zones may endanger workers' rights, expert worries. *Bloomberg Law*. https://www.bna.com/vietnam-special-economic-n73014482154/. Accessed 2 Mar 2019.

Brenner, D. (2015). Ashes of co-optation: From armed group fragmentation to the rebuilding of popular insurgency in Myanmar. *Conflict, Security & Development*, *15*(4), 337–358.

Brown, D. (2017, September 18). Vietnamese conservatives purge former Dung allies. *Asia Sentinel*. https://www.asiasentinel.com/politics/vietnam-conservatives-purge-former-pm-dungs-allies/. Accessed 2 Mar 2019.

Callahan, M. (2007). *Political authority in Burma's ethnic minority states: Devolution, occupation and co-existence*. Singapore: ISEAS.

Creak, S., & Barney, K. (2018). Conceptualising party-state governance and rule in Laos. *Journal of Contemporary Asia*, *48*(5), 693–716.

Davies, J. (2017). "Europe's Blood Sugar," *Politico*, 3/4/17. https://www.politico.eu/article/europe-blood-sugar-cambodia-human-rights-trade/. Accessed 24 Dec 2019.

DTUC [Danish Trade Union Council for International Development]. (2015). *2015 labour market profile, Cambodia*. Copenhagen: LO/FTF Secretariat. http://www.ulandssekretariatet.dk/sites/default/files/uploads/public/PDF/LMP/LMP2015/lmp_cambodia_2015_final_version.pdf. Accessed 1 Mar 2019.

Eckardt, S., Mishra, D., & Viet, T. D. (2018). *Vietnam's manufacturing miracle: Lessons for developing countries*. Brookings Future Development Blog. https://www.brookings.edu/blog/future-development/2018/04/17/vietnams-manufacturing-miracle-lessons-for-developing-countries/. Accessed 1 Mar 2019.

Ekaphone, P. (2018, May 29). Lao industrial sector sees 11 per cent growth. *Asia News Network*. http://annx.asianews.network/content/lao-industrial-sector-sees-11-percent-growth-73705. Accessed 1 Mar 2019.

Global Witness. (2007). *Cambodia's family trees*. Phnom Penh: Global Witness. https://www.globalwitness.org/en/reports/cambodias-family-trees/, Accessed 1 Mar 2019.

Global Witness. (2013). *Rubber barons: How Vietnamese companies and international financiers are driving a land-grabbing crisis in Cambodia and Lao*. https://www.globalwitness.org/en/campaigns/land-deals/rubberbarons/. Accessed 2 Mar 2019.

Hughes, C. (2008). Cambodia in 2007: Development and dispossession. *Asian Survey*, *48*(1), 69–74.

Hughes, C. (2011). Soldiers, monks, borders: Violence and contestation along borderlines in the Greater Mekong Subregion. *Journal of Contemporary Asia*, *41*(2), 181–205.

Hughes, C., & Eng, N. (2018). Facebook, contestation and poor people's politics: Spanning the urban–rural divide in Cambodia? *Journal of Contemporary Asia*. https://doi.org/10.1080/00472336.2018.1520910.

Hutt, D. (2018, May 19). Vietnam drives to revive its "moral" revolution. *Asia Times.* https://www.asiatimes.com/2018/05/article/vietnam-on-a-drive-to-revive-its-moral-revolution/. Accessed 2 Mar 2019.

Ingalls, M. L., Diepart, J.-C., Truong, N., Hayward, D., Niel, T., Sem, T., et al. (2018). *State of land in the Mekong.* Bern: Bern Open Publishing.

Jones, L. (2014). The political economy of Myanmar's transition. *Journal of Contemporary Asia, 44*(1), 144–170.

Jones, L. (2015). *Societies under siege: Exploring how international economic sanctions (do not) work.* Oxford: Oxford University Press.

Jones, L. (2017, September 26). A better political economy of the Rohingya crisis. *New Mandala.* https://www.newmandala.org/better-political-economy-rohingya-crisis/. Accessed 2 Mar 2019.

Kelleher, G. (2018, February 8). Beyond the Rohingya: Myanmar's other crisis. *The Diplomat.* https://thediplomat.com/2018/02/beyond-the-rohingya-myanmars-other-crises/. Accessed 2 Mar 2019.

Keovilignavong, O., & Suhardiman, D. (2018). Characterizing private investments and implications for poverty reduction and natural resource management in Laos. *Development Policy Review, 36*(S1), O341–O359.

Kerkvliet, B. (2014). Protests over land in Vietnam: Rightful resistance and more. *Journal of Vietnamese Studies, 9*(3), 19–54.

Kieng, T. K. (2017, December 29). Crony capitalism subverts socialist aspirations. *Vietnam News.* https://vietnamnews.vn/opinion/op-ed/420212/crony-capitalism-subverts-socialist-aspirations.html#XF7FXbmJpt6GYr6X.97. Accessed 2 Mar 2019.

Kikuchi, T., & Vo, H. (2016, July 30). Keeping Vietnam's textile and garment industry competitive. *East Asia Forum.* https://www.eastasiaforum.org/2016/07/30/51375/. Accessed 1 Mar 2019.

Kyaw, Z. M. (2018, September 22). Will the Tatmadaw still be in control 30 years from now? *The Irrawaddy.* https://www.irrawaddy.com/dateline/will-tatmadaw-still-control-30-years-now.html. Accessed 1 Mar 2019.

Kynge J., Haddou, L., & Peele. M. (2016, September 8). FT investigation: How China bought its way into Cambodia. *Financial Times.* https://www.ft.com/content/23968248-43a0-11e6-b22f-79eb4891c97d. Accessed 1 Mar 2019.

Lee, J. Y., & Huang, X. (2018, October 5). Manufacturing key to Myanmar's growth. *Myanmar Times.* https://www.mmtimes.com/news/manufacturing-key-myanmars-growth.html. Accessed 1 Mar 2019.

Lin, Q. (2018, January 7). Money talks: China's Belt and Road Initiative in Cambodia. *Global Risk Insights.* https://globalriskinsights.com/2018/01/money-talks-chinas-belt-road-initiative-cambodia. Accessed 1 Mar 2019.

Ministry of Planning and Investment Lao Statistics Bureau. (2017). *Lao PDR labour force survey 2017, survey findings report.* Vientiane: Ministry of Planning and Investment Lao Statistics Bureau.

Nguyen, T. B. (2016). *State economic groups in Vietnam: Characteristics, roles and development trends.* Ho Chi Minh National Academy of Politics Political Theory Forum, 24 November. http://lyluanchinhtri.vn/home/en/index.php/forum/item/393-state-economic-groups-in-vietnam-characteristics-roles-and-development-trends.html. Accessed 1 Mar 2019.

Nguyen, M. Q. (2017, February 8). Is Vietnam in for another devastating drought? *The Diplomat.* https://thediplomat.com/2017/02/is-vietnam-in-for-another-devastating-drought/. Accessed 2 Mar 2019.

Nguyen, T., & Freeman, N. (2009). State-owned enterprises in Vietnam: Are they "crowding out" the private sector? *Post-Communist Economies, 21*(2), 227–247.

Painter, M. (2003). The politics of economic restructuring in Vietnam: The case of state-owned enterprise "reform". *Contemporary Southeast Asia, 25*(1), 20–43.

Parameswaram, P. (2018, July 13). What's behind Vietnam's anti-China protest? *World Politics Review.* https://www.worldpoliticsreview.com/articles/25055/what-s-behind-vietnam-s-anti-china-protests. Accessed 2 Mar 2019.

Pisani, E. (1996, March 12). Cambodia's top investor scoffs at rumours about a shady past. *Asia Times.* http://www.ternyata.org/journalism/features/teng_boonma_profile.html. Accessed 2 Mar 2019.

Post Staff. (2000, April 28). All that glitters seems to be… Sokimex. *Phnom Penh Post.* https://www.phnompenhpost.com/national/all-glitters-seems-be-sokimex. Accessed 1 Mar 2019.

Rigg, J. (2006). Forests, marketization, livelihoods and the poor in the Lao PDR. *Land Degradation and Development, 17*(2), 123–133.

Sayalath, S., & Creak, S. (2017). Regime renewal in Laos: The Tenth Congress of the Lao People's Revolutionary Party. *Southeast Asian Affairs, 2017,* 179–200.

Sjöholm, F. (2006). *State owned enterprises and equitization in Vietnam* (EIJS working paper 228). Stockholm: Stockholm School of Economics/European Institute of Japanese Studies.

Soukamneuth, B. (2006). *The political economy of transition in Laos: From peripheral socialism to the margins of global capitalism.* PhD dissertation. Cornell University. https://ecommons.cornell.edu/handle/1813/3430. Accessed 2 Mar 2019.

Tatarski, M. (2017, May 19). Report details graft, illegal logging on Vietnamese border with Cambodia. *Asia Times.* https://www.asiatimes.com/2017/05/article/report-details-graft-illegal-logging-vietnamese-border-cambodia/. Accessed 1 Mar 2019.

Thayer, C. (2009). Political legitimacy of Vietnam's one-party state: Challenges and responses. *Journal of Current South East Asian Affairs, 28*(4), 47–70.

The Economist. (2017, June 15). Property disputes are Vietnam's biggest political problem. *The Economist.* https://www.economist.com/asia/2017/06/15/property-disputes-are-vietnams-biggest-political-problem?zid=306&ah=1b164dbd43b0cb27ba0d4c3b12a5e227. Accessed 2 Mar 2019.

Tran, D. M., Fallon, W., & Vickers, M. (2016). Leadership in Vietnamese state-owned enterprises (SOEs): Exploring multi-stakeholder perceptions—A qualitative study. *Asia-Pacific Journal of Business Administration, 8*(1), 21–36.

Verver, M., & Dahles, H. (2015). The institutionalisation of Okhna: Cambodian entrepreneurship at the interface of business and politics. *Journal of Contemporary Asia, 45*(1), 48–70.

VGSO & ILO [Vietnam General Statistics Office & International Labour Organisation]. (2016). *2016 report on informal labour in Vietnam*. Hanoi: Hong Duc.

VietnamNet. (2017, December 27). SOE scandals unveiled, Vietnam speeding up SOE reform. *VietnamNet*. https://english.vietnamnet.vn/fms/business/192460/soe-scandals-unveiled%2D%2Dvietnam-speeding-up-soe-reform.html. Accessed 2 Mar 2019.

Vu-Thanh, T. (2017). Does WTO accession help domestic reform? The political economy of SOE reform backsliding in Vietnam. *World Trade Review, 16*(1), 85–109.

Woods, K. (2011). Ceasefire capitalism: Military–private partnerships, resource concessions and military–state building in the Burma–China borderlands. *Journal of Peasant Studies, 38*(4), 747–770.

World Bank. (2014a). *Myanmar: Ending poverty and boosting shared prosperity in a time of transition. A systematic country diagnostic*. Yangon: World Bank.

World Bank. (2014b). *Where have all the poor gone? Cambodia poverty assessment, 2013*. Washington, DC: World Bank. http://documents.worldbank.org/curated/en/824341468017405577/Where-have-all-the-poor-gone-Cambodia-poverty-assessment-2013

World Bank. (2015). *Lao People's Democratic Republic: Drivers of poverty reduction in Lao PDR*. Washington, DC: World Bank. http://documents.worldbank.org/curated/en/590861467722637341/pdf/101567-REPLACENENT-PUBLIC-Lao-PDR-Poverty-Policy-Notes-Drivers-of-Poverty-Reduction-in-Lao-PDR.pdf

World Bank. (2017a). *Lao People's Democratic Republic: Systematic country diagnostic. Priorities for ending poverty and boosting shared prosperity*. Washington, DC: World Bank. http://documents.worldbank.org/curated/en/983001490107755004/Lao-PDR-Systematic-Country-Diagnostic-Priorities-for-Ending-Poverty-and-Boosting-Shared-Prosperity. Accessed 2 Mar.

World Bank. (2017b). *An analysis of poverty in Myanmar. Trends between 2004/5–2015*. Yangon: Ministry of Planning and Finance and World Bank. http://documents.worldbank.org/curated/en/556581502987486978/pdf/118851-REVISED-v2-PovertyReportPartEng.pdf

CHAPTER 5

The Post-war Rise and Decline of the Left

Nathan Gilbert Quimpo

INTRODUCTION

Leftist movements and parties played prominent roles in Southeast Asia's politics before, during and after World War II. Communists and socialists were in the forefront of anti-colonial struggles, resistance against Japanese occupation, and revolutionary movements against post-colonial elite rule. In the 1960s and 1970s, Southeast Asia became a focal point of the Cold War, as the Vietnam War—in which the US and US-backed forces sought to crush Vietnamese revolutionaries—sparked worldwide protests. Since the 1980s, however, leftist forces have faded and, despite recent but variable expansions of political space, they have not significantly recovered. This chapter asks why, despite their significant contribution in developing civil society, did leftist forces in Southeast Asia (excepting the three countries of Indochina, and Timor-Leste) fail to seize state power and enact revolutionary change? More recently, why have leftist groups been largely unable to gain power through the electoral route, or even to perform creditably in elections?

N. G. Quimpo (✉)
Graduate School of Humanities and Social Sciences, University of Tsukuba, Tsukuba, Japan
e-mail: quimpo.nathan.fn@u.tsukuba.ac.jp

© The Author(s) 2020
T. Carroll et al. (eds.), *The Political Economy of Southeast Asia*, Studies in the Political Economy of Public Policy,
https://doi.org/10.1007/978-3-030-28255-4_5

Much has been written about the left's decline in Southeast Asia, but the usual focus is on domestic movements and parties, neglecting possible trends or patterns at the regional level. Among the few exceptions are Hewison and Rodan (1994, 2012). They argue that, while the left played a pivotal role in developing civil society from the 1920s to the 1970s, other non-state actors—non-governmental organisations (NGOs) and civil society groups—promoting bourgeois reformism rather than genuine social transformation have since taken the leading role in expanding political space. They attribute this to rapid capitalist development: "a shift from import-substitution to export-oriented and low wage manufacturing development", followed by "increased competition between economies, companies and workers", which created extensive, albeit low-paid, employment, and eroded the left's appeal. Authoritarian rulers "used economic success to boost political regime legitimacy and to justify repression" (Hewison and Rodan 2012: 34).

Hewison and Rodan are right to highlight increased repression and the economic success of capitalist Southeast Asian countries as important factors. But this chapter argues that the left's decline also stemmed from strategic errors made by leftist forces themselves. Most of the region's major revolutionary left groups (excepting those of Vietnam and Laos) were strongly influenced by Maoist tenets, which proved unsuitable to their countries' conditions. While some Southeast Asian states—namely, Singapore, Malaysia, Thailand and Indonesia—made tremendous gains in their pursuit of authoritarian developmentalism from the 1960s to the 1980s, the revolutionary left, stirred by advances in Indochina and by the Chinese Cultural Revolution, launched or revitalised "protracted people's wars", which all failed to progress beyond guerrilla warfare. The revolutionary left's dogmatism and inflexibility subsequently prevented it from shifting successfully from armed to electoral/parliamentary struggle, and from playing a significant role in popular uprisings in the region from the mid-1980s onwards. Meanwhile, in Indochina, the communists who did seize power failed to make their centralised economies work, ultimately embracing capitalism under the guise of "market socialism" (see Hughes, this volume). A final explanatory factor is the capacity of dominant sociopolitical forces to shape political life. Some leftist political forces—mostly social democratic parties and non- or pre-party formations[1]—have

---

[1] Some groups, like SocDem Asia (see below) refer to themselves as "pre-party" formations, signalling their intention to become political parties in the future. Other NGOs have no such intention.

emerged to challenge entrenched politico-economic elites. However, the latter, alongside their usual strategies of patronage and corruption, have also shaped modes of participation and representation in ways that prevent effective contestation for power by progressives.

THE LEFT IN THE EARLY POST-WAR DECADES (MID-1940S TO MID-1960S)

In the first two post-war decades, Southeast Asian leftist movements and parties continued their pre-war struggles against colonialism or neo-colonialism, striving for a socialist or more egalitarian social order. In Indochina, Indonesia, Burma (now Myanmar) and Malaya/Singapore, communists and socialists took leading or prominent roles in the struggles against French, Dutch and British rule. Communists in the Philippines, Burma and Malaysia[2] took up arms against the post-colonial state, while avowed socialists gained power in Burma and Singapore. In Indonesia, the *Partai Komunis Indonesia* (PKI) grew rapidly, especially after joining the ruling coalition under Sukarno.

Although these struggles all had strong domestic roots, they quickly became tied up with the emerging Cold War, following the 1949 Chinese Revolution and the outbreak of the Korean War (1950–53). The boundary between Asia's communist and non-communist states was dubbed the "Bamboo Curtain", echoing Europe's "Iron Curtain". US policy-makers expounded the "domino theory", suggesting that if communists seized power in one non-communist country, neighbouring countries would fall like dominoes to communism. To avert this, in 1955, the US and its allies established the Southeast Asia Treaty Organisation (SEATO), envisaged as a regional version of the North Atlantic Treaty Organisation, although only three of its nine members were countries from the region—the Philippines, Thailand and South Vietnam. SEATO was dissolved in 1977. By then, the domino theory had justified US interventions across Southeast Asia, internationalising many domestic struggles.

This occurred first in Indochina. In August 1945, as Japan faced defeat in the Pacific war, the Vietnamese League for Independence (Viet Minh) spearheaded the August Revolution, a general insurrection that liberated

---

[2] Malaya, Singapore, North Borneo and Sarawak merged to form the Federation of Malaysia in 1963. Singapore was expelled from the Federation in 1965.

the entire country. The Viet Minh was a broad front organised by Ho Chi Minh's Communist Party of Vietnam (CPV). The return of the French colonialists, who had been ousted by the Japanese, triggered a resistance war that quickly spilled into Cambodia and Laos—the First Indochina War (1946–54). In May 1954, the Vietnamese decisively defeated the French at the Battle of Dien Bien Phu. The 1954 Geneva Conference temporarily divided Vietnam into North and South, with reunification elections set for 1956. When the elections did not materialise, armed hostilities ensued between the Viet Minh and forces of the US-backed South Vietnamese government, which quickly escalated into the Vietnam War (or Second Indochina War, 1955–75).

Indonesia's domestic struggles were also drawn into Cold War dynamics. The 1945 "August Revolution" initiated a four-year war of independence from Dutch rule, led by the nationalists Sukarno and Mohammad Hatta, but also involving Indonesian communists and socialists. The PKI's participation was marred, however, by the September 1948 "Madiun Affair", when PKI forces in East Java rebelled following growing tensions with rightists in Sukarno's government. The army brutally quelled the revolt, killing thousands of PKI cadres. Thereafter, the PKI returned to legal struggle, spreading across the country to build electoral support, seeking nationalist allies and wooing President Sukarno. This bore fruit, as Sukarno integrated communism in the "Nasakom" ideology[3] of his "Guided Democracy" in 1960, and made the PKI a junior partner in his government in 1962. The PKI's membership swelled from 10,000 in 1951, to one million in 1961, and three million by 1965 (Kuntjoro-Jakti 1984), making it the world's third largest communist party after the Soviet Union and China. However, the Sukarno regime's leftward trajectory—expressed internationally by Indonesia hosting the anti-neo-colonialist Bandung Conference (1955), which led to the development of the Non-Aligned Movement, and announcing a new "Jakarta–Phnom Penh–Hanoi–Peking–Pyongyang axis" in 1965—led to increasing tensions with right-wing nationalists, Islamists and capitalists.

These tensions ended in disaster for the Indonesian left. On 30 September 1965, a group of progressive army officers, allegedly anticipating a planned anti-communist coup in October, arrested and killed six leading generals. Major General Suharto, taking command of the

---

[3] Nasakom combined *nasionalisme* (nationalism), *agama* (religion), and *komunisme* (communism) into an Indonesian form of socialism.

US-trained and -funded army, quickly crushed the rebellion. Although the rebels had received guidance from a few PKI leaders, the PKI itself was not involved in planning or executing the "30 September Movement". However, Suharto accused it of masterminding a coup as a prelude to a communist takeover. As the US ambassador at the time later remarked, the US viewed this "attempted communist coup" as one of the most dangerous moments of the Cold War, saying: "what is now the fourth largest nation in the world... was about to go communist, and almost did" (Roosa 2006: 13). This led Washington to support a ferocious military reaction: the massacre of between 500,000 and one million "communists" by the army and allied militias in 1965–66. Suharto gradually ousted Sukarno, seizing the presidency in March 1967 and establishing a right-wing dictatorship that lasted for 30 years.

The Philippine left encountered US-backed bloodshed even earlier. Shortly after the US granted independence to the Philippines in July 1946, the Philippine government, dominated by landed elites, launched an all-out campaign against the *Partido Komunista ng Pilipinas* (PKP) and the Huks, a PKP-organised peasant army that had resisted the Japanese invasion in World War II. The Huks resisted, launching a rebellion spanning 10 provinces in the Philippines' biggest island, Luzon. With US military assistance and advice, government forces crushed the rebellion in the mid-1950s. Kerkvliet (1977) attributed the outcome to weariness among peasant rebels and their supporters, as well as government reforms, and the state's more effective use of force. PKP leader Jesus Lava (1978) cited US intervention as the main factor, while Pomeroy (1978) blamed PKP errors in strategy and tactics, lack of international support, their incorrect perception that a "revolutionary situation" existed in 1950, and their failure to build a broad anti-imperialist front.

Post-war Burmese politics was initially dominated by leftist forces, but political and ethnic fragmentation quickly led to civil war, Cold War interventions and, eventually, military dictatorship. Tensions initially erupted between the socialists and communists who had fought together against the Japanese under the Anti-Fascist People's Freedom League (AFPFL). The Communist Party of Burma (CPB) favoured militant mass action to achieve independence. A radical faction, the CPB-Red Flag, split off to begin armed struggle in February 1946. By December, the AFPFL, which was dominated by the Burma Socialist Party (BSP), expelled the CPB, earning the confidence of the British and a rapid decolonisation. In March 1948, less than three months into Burma's independence, civil war broke out between the BSP-led government and the CPB. Ethnic minorities dissatisfied at their incorporation into Burma had also launched insurgencies. The BSP began receiving aid from communist China, which was itself combatting remnant, US-backed nationalist forces in Burma's Shan state. The grinding civil war, and political splits in the AFPFL/BSP, steadily empowered the military (Tatmadaw), allowing General Ne Win to seize power, first in a "caretaker" regime from 1958 to 1960, and then permanently in March 1962. Ne Win set out on a programme for economic development and national independence, "The Burmese Way to Socialism"—purportedly a middle way between capitalism and socialism but, in reality, a recipe for authoritarian, statist domination of the economy and society and continued civil war.

The Communist Party of Malaya (CPM) proved even less successful. Having led the armed anti-Japanese resistance during World War II, the CPM disarmed and pursued a united front with non-communist forces to achieve independence from Britain. The CPM soon gained dominance in the trade union movement of Malaya, including Singapore. Amid growing labour unrest, the British declared a state of emergency in June 1948 and violently suppressed the CPM and its allies, forcing the CPM back into armed struggle. Inspired by revolutionary advances in China, the CPM adopted a Maoist "protracted people's war" strategy supposedly best suited to "colonial (or semi-colonial) and semi-feudal societies" (Tupaz 1991). This involved "encircling the cities from the countryside", entailing a long process of organising peasants and workers, building bases and a revolutionary "people's army" in the countryside, de-emphasising the building of urban mass movements (ibid.). British forces quickly gained the upper hand and felt sufficiently confident to hand power to a postindependence government dominated by Malay aristocrats in August 1957. Continued repression drove the CPM to the border with Thailand by 1960, and its leader, Chin Peng, fled to Beijing. Leftist forces in Borneo also revolted in 1962–63 to resist the incorporation of Brunei and Sarawak into the Malaysian federation.[4] British troops quickly quashed the Brunei insurrection, but the communist insurgency in Sarawak stretched on.

The left fared similarly poorly in Singapore. Founded in 1954, the People's Action Party (PAP), which has ruled Singapore since independence (in 1965), has long described itself as a "democratic socialist" party.

---

[4] Sarawak joined Malaysia, but Brunei remained a British protectorate until independence in 1984.

In reality, the PAP was captured by right-wing forces ahead of the 1963 elections, with the expulsion of the left and the subsequent suppression of the *Barisan Sosialis* (Socialist Front).

In the immediate post-war period, then, the left was prominent across Southeast Asia, having played a leading role in struggles against Western and Japanese imperialism. However, in the context of the Cold War, the Americans, French and British were unwilling to see communists take power in Southeast Asia, leading to brutal repression and political splits. Opposition to leftist agendas from propertied social forces reinforced this repression, which escalated into civil war and massacres in several states.

Revolutionary High Tide, Then Decline (Late 1960s to Late 1980s)

The late 1960s and early 1970s witnessed a dramatic intensification of Cold War conflicts in Southeast Asia. The Vietnam War became a massive "hot" conflict, with communists and their opponents fighting an internationalised civil war. Meanwhile, Sino–Soviet relations deteriorated and, with the onset of China's tumultuous Cultural Revolution (1966–76), Beijing's assistance to revolutionary forces in Asia and Africa increased sharply. In this tussle for local support, China gained the upper hand, reinforcing Southeast Asian communist parties' embrace of Maoism—which proved disastrous for their fortunes outside of Indochina.

Facing intense domestic repression, and internationalist by orientation, Southeast Asia's communist parties had always sought international support, though they never received as much assistance as their ruling-class opponents did from Western powers. After 1949, communist China loomed particularly large as a potential ally. The presence of sizeable ethnic-Chinese communities in several countries contributed to China's influence. The radio stations of the CPB, CPM and Communist Party of Thailand all broadcast from southern China. Moreover, as the Sino–Soviet split widened, regional parties were forced to take sides. Most sided with Beijing, excepting those in Vietnam and Laos, which remained neutral until the mid-1970s, when they allied with Moscow.

Throughout the Vietnam War, the Democratic Republic of Vietnam (communist-led North Vietnam) secured support, including military assistance, from both communist giants, and Beijing allowed Soviet assistance to travel through Chinese territory to North Vietnam. The North

Vietnamese used the Ho Chi Minh Trail—a vast, complex network of mountain and forest paths running through Laos and Cambodia to South Vietnam—to transport weapons, supplies and personnel to communist forces and supporters in South Vietnam. The US, which had succeeded France as the main sponsor of anti-communism in Indochina, backed the increasingly authoritarian and corrupt South Vietnamese regime. Its military involvement grew, with US troops fighting a ground war, bombing the Ho Chi Minh Trail, and supporting anti-communist forces, coups and regimes in Laos and Vietnam. The CPV and the National Liberation Front (aka "Viet Cong") coordinated closely with the Lao People's Revolutionary Party (LPRP) and its broad front, the Pathet Lao, and the Communist Party of Kampuchea (CPK) and its network, the Khmer Rouge.

The CPV's eventual victory stemmed in part from its adoption of non-Maoist strategies. Following its defeat of the French in 1954, the CPV had shifted to a protracted people's war strategy by the 1960s, but this was very different from the Maoist model. Instead of prioritising military struggle, the CPV regarded it as equal to political struggle—ranging from open mass movements to popular insurrections. And instead of prioritising rural over urban areas, Vietnamese revolutionary forces sought to "attack the enemy in all three strategic areas (hill forests, plains, and cities)", employing different forms of struggle in each (Le Duan 1971: 44–45). Thus, in the 1968 Tet Offensive, Vietnamese revolutionaries combined military offensives with popular uprisings across South Vietnam. Although they sustained great military losses, the Tet Offensive was a huge political victory. By drawing critical worldwide attention to American intervention in Vietnam, it helped to turn the tide of the war, especially by fomenting domestic opposition within the US. This eventually compelled American forces to withdraw, allowing revolutionary forces to sweep to power in Saigon in 1975, unifying Vietnam under CPV rule. In the same year, Vietnam's allies, the CPK and LPRP, also seized power in Cambodia and Laos. The Second Indochina War claimed an estimated 1,450,000–3,595,000 lives across the three countries, including 605,000–1,389,000 civilians in Vietnam alone (Rummell 1994: ch.11). The US, which sustained just 58,318 battle deaths, had dropped around 500,000 tons of bombs on Indochina, leaving these impoverished societies ravaged.

Beyond Indochina, Beijing won over all the main communist parties, leading them to embrace Maoist ideology and strategy. Despite supposedly undertaking concrete analysis of their respective countries' conditions, they all came to the same conclusions: their societies were "semi-colonial and semi-feudal", and the ruling classes—big landlords, compradors and bureaucratic capitalists—exploited and oppressed the broad masses of peasants and workers. This was virtually identical to Mao's analysis of China in the 1930s and 1940s. Southeast Asia's Maoist parties dismissed ruling elites' national developmentalist programmes, asserting that national development could only be achieved after the revolutionary overthrow of the "reactionary classes" following a protracted people's war. For them, the tragic end of the PKI's parliamentary struggle was incontrovertible proof of the Maoist dictum, "political power grows out of the barrel of a gun".

These insurgencies initially received political and material support, including arms, from China, but this was sharply reduced in the early 1980s (Mysicka 2015). This reversal stemmed from the demise of the Cultural Revolution and the re-emergence of communist splits in Indochina, in the broader context of Sino–Soviet rivalry. By 1976, the destructive effects of Maoist mobilisation on Chinese society had prompted a *de facto* counter-revolution; following Mao's death, Deng Xiaoping steered China from communism towards capitalist transformation, and Beijing's support for foreign revolutionary groups declined dramatically. The sole exception was Cambodia's Khmer Rouge, which remained strongly influenced by Mao's disastrous domestic policies:

> The forced evacuation of the cities; the execution of former government officials, military officers, and the educated; the rapid creation of communes; and the frontal assault upon religion and individualism constituted an application and extension of Maoist ideology to the most extreme degree (Morris 1999: 71).

By the most reliable estimates, these policies killed around 1.7 million Cambodians from 1975–78. The Khmer Rouge were also motivated by extreme anti-Vietnamese nationalism, persecuting ethnic Vietnamese and launching raids into Vietnamese territory. This drove Hanoi into a formal alliance with Moscow. In December 1978, the Vietnamese army, allied with a Khmer Rouge splinter group, invaded Cambodia, overthrew Pol Pot's regime—which fled to the Thai border—and installed a pro-Vietnamese government. The Chinese regime perceived this development as an instance of Soviet "social imperialism" and attacked Vietnam, occupying part of its territory until the early 1990s.

These events fostered a radical reorientation of forces in Southeast Asia. To rescue its Khmer Rouge clients, China essentially allied with Southeast Asia's capitalist regimes against Vietnam, which the latter perceived as initiating a revolutionary advance that threatened toppling "dominoes" in the Association of Southeast Asian Nations (ASEAN). To contain the Vietnamese and their Cambodian allies, Thailand's ferociously anti-communist regime hosted the Khmer Rouge and non-communist Cambodian guerrillas on its territory, funnelling Chinese aid to them, while ASEAN backed these groups materially and diplomatically—even helping the ousted Pol Pot regime to retain Cambodia's UN seat, with Western backing. In exchange, the Chinese severed aid to ASEAN's communist parties through 1980–81. The US joined this anti-Vietnamese crusade, known as the Third Indochina War, increasing military aid to ASEAN regimes and even funding Khmer Rouge activities for a time (Jones 2012: ch.4).

Although national experiences varied, these developments underpinned a general trend in the left's fate in Southeast Asia. The 1960s and early 1970s were marked by apparent revolutionary upticks, as communist parties turned to or intensified armed struggle, with Chinese backing. However, despite provoking genuine terror among Southeast Asia's propertied classes, their practical advances were actually rather limited and, when the Chinese withdrew their (always modest) moral and material support, they were left badly exposed. Conversely, capitalist regimes' development successes, coupled with enhanced US military aid, empowered anti-communist forces to defeat their enemies. In Indochina, efforts to build state socialism were stymied by the demands of war in Cambodia and Western sanctions. Moreover, the Stalinist nature of these states led—as in Burma—to the eradication of all non-state centres of power, entailing the effective demobilisation of workers and peasants. When the Soviet Union itself cut aid to its overseas allies after 1986, these regimes were all forced to embrace so-called "market socialism", just to survive (see Hughes, this volume). Thus, any genuinely leftist qualities they had once possessed were effectively eradicated.

In Indonesia and neighbouring East Timor, Maoist rebellions were harshly repressed. PKI remnants split into pro-Soviet and Maoist factions, the latter launching armed struggle and being quickly crushed by Suharto's forces. When neighbouring Portuguese Timor began to be decolonised in 1974, the Suharto regime feared a possible PKI comeback and quickly moved to absorb the territory, initially by stealth and, when this failed, through a wholescale military invasion in December 1975. East Timor was then annexed by Indonesia (until 1999), with the invasion, subsequent counter-insurgency and associated famine killing up to 245,000 Timorese—about a quarter of the population (Jones 2012: 73). Timor's leading anti-colonial force, the Revolutionary Front for an Independent East Timor (FRETILIN), adopted a Maoist protracted people's war strategy (Kiernan 2017). China briefly extended modest support to FRETILIN, mainly through its government-in-exile in Mozambique, but abandoned it after 1979 to shore up relations with ASEAN. FRETILIN's armed wing, isolated from external support, formally abandoned Marxism-Leninism in 1984, maintaining a guerrilla army but also cultivating support among urban youth.

In Malaysia, communist forces escaped such bloody outcomes but enjoyed no greater success. Suharto's rise deprived the North Kalimantan Communist Party (NKCP) of its safe havens in Indonesian territory, undermining its insurgency in Malaysian Borneo. More importantly, the NKCP remained largely composed of ethnic Chinese, failing to make significant inroads into the majority Dayak and Malay communities. After fruitless decades in the jungle, it surrendered in October–November 1990. In peninsular Malaysia, the CPM also reinvigorated its "people's war" from 1968 but, following suspected infiltration by the police special branch, the party split into three parts, which competed with each other through to the 1980s as their forces dwindled (Cheah 2009). In 1983, the two breakaway groups merged into the Communist Party of Malaysia (MCP). The CPM never managed to build a sizeable army or develop beyond guerrilla warfare; nor, crucially, could it build support beyond the ethnic Chinese. The MCP was also unable to shift to urban warfare, despite being more theoretically disposed towards it, being confined to the Thai borderlands. In April 1987, the MCP's guerrillas surrendered to the Thai military while the CPM laid down its arms in December 1989, after negotiations with the Malaysian and Thai governments.

In Burma, the CPB initially fared better, thanks in part to its proximity to China and the ethnic-minority insurgencies against the Burmese state. In 1967, amid the frenzy of the Cultural Revolution, Mao openly backed their armed struggles, prompting thousands of ethnic-Chinese Burmese to march on the streets of Rangoon, shouting slogans against the military regime, but they were soon attacked by anti-Chinese mobs (Tucker 2001). The CPB thus remained confined to rural insurgency, with arms, training and other material support coming from China. However, intensified counter-insurgency operations eliminated the CPB-Red Flag faction in 1970, and cleared central Burma of communist guerrillas by 1975. The CPB and Beijing-backed ethnic-minority rebels were thus confined to the north-eastern borderlands. In 1981, China severed all aid to the CPB, severely weakening the party (Mysicka 2015; Tucker 2001). In April 1989, thousands of CPB rank-and-file members hailing from various ethnic-minority groups rebelled against the ethnic-Chinese leadership. The once-mighty CPB fragmented into multiple ethnic-minority armed groups, most of which swiftly entered ceasefires with the country's post-1988 military regime (Lintner 1990).

The Communist Party of Thailand (CPT) was also defeated by the mid-1980s. Founded in 1942 and proscribed by the Thai government since 1952, the CPT had initially pursued parliamentary struggle but, facing increasing repression, it launched armed struggle in August 1965, adopting Mao's protracted people's war strategy. Initially, the CPT and its guerrilla army grew quickly, drawing logistical, financial, military and food support from China and revolutionary forces in neighbouring Indochina (Hobday 1986; Rousset 2009). A 1976 military coup, accompanied by vicious crackdowns on the left, also drove thousands of socialists and students to seek refuge in the CPT's guerrilla bases. The CPT forged an alliance with various socialist and progressive groups, the Coordinating Committee for Patriotic and Democratic Forces (CCPDF). However, the Third Indochina War dealt the CCPDF a terrible blow. The CPT sided with China against Vietnam. It therefore lost its bases and support in Indochina, only to then lose Chinese aid when Beijing effectively allied itself with Thailand's anti-communist regime. Moreover, pro-Vietnamese members of the CPT and CCPDF became disenchanted, with many increasingly questioning the CPT's Maoist dogma. Thousands deserted the CPT and CCPDF, many tempted by government amnesties. Meanwhile, government-led development efforts aimed at north-eastern peasants, coupled with counter-insurgency campaigns strengthened by US and Chinese aid, gradually eroded the CPT's support base. In 1986, Thailand's military regime declared victory over the CPT.

The only Maoist party to survive the brutal 1980s was the Communist Party of the Philippines (CPP), which broke away from the PKP in 1968 and launched armed struggle in 1969. After riotous, anti-government student demonstrations in early 1970, protests spread to other sectors and CPP-aligned organisations became ascendant in a broad mass movement. In September 1972, President Ferdinand Marcos declared martial law, driving tens of thousands of activists underground or into the CPP's revolutionary army. After massive initial setbacks, the CPP adjusted to the repressive conditions, reviving mass movements of workers, the urban poor and youth, and establishing liberated zones in virtually all areas favourable to guerrilla warfare, except the Muslim areas in the south. The CPP and its allies became the biggest, best-organised force resisting the Marcos dictatorship. However, this lead was squandered through strategic errors. After the assassination of parliamentary opposition leader Benigno Aquino in August 1983, hundreds of thousands of people protested in the streets, forcing Marcos to call elections for February 1986. The CPP urged an electoral boycott, correctly anticipating widespread fraud. However, after the corrupt elections, mass protests again erupted, triggering military defections that enabled a peaceful "people power" regime transition, with Marcos resigning and fleeing to the US. Having boycotted the elections, the CPP and its allies were left out of the uprising, ceding control to establishment politicians.

Explaining the Left's Defeat

By the 1990s, then, the left was unquestionably a marginal political force in Southeast Asia. In almost all of the countries where revolutionary forces had adhered to Maoism, they were not just defeated but virtually obliterated. Some former revolutionaries became active in emergent civil society groups, and some were even absorbed into government bureaucracies. But no significant leftist parties—legal or illegal—emerged from these defeated groups. Following the collapse of the Soviet Union, the region's only surviving Maoist party, the CPP, suffered a debilitating split in 1992–93. The only other major socialist/social democratic groups that persisted were FRETILIN and Malaysia's Democratic Action Party (DAP).

There were therefore hardly any major leftist groups remaining to participate in the popular uprisings against authoritarian rule that rocked Southeast Asia from the late 1980s: the 1986 "people power" revolution in the Philippines; the mass uprisings in Burma in 1988 that toppled Ne Win; Thailand's "Black May" protests in 1992 that forced General Suchinda Kraprayoon to resign as prime minister; the 1998 *reformasi* protests that ended Suharto's dictatorship; or the so-called "Saffron Revolution"—the failed, monk-led protests against Myanmar's military regime in 2007. The Philippines again constituted a partial exception. In the "People Power II" uprising that forced corrupt President Joseph

Estrada from office in January 2001, various left groups, including CPP allies, played a major role in the mass mobilisations. But, once again, traditional politicians tied to oligarchic interests were in the driver's seat, resulting in Estrada's replacement by establishment politician Gloria Arroyo.

Some of the blame for the failure of the armed revolutions in Southeast Asia outside of Indochina can be laid squarely on the revolutionary forces themselves. By the 1980s, large areas of Southeast Asia remained mired in poverty and under-development. Sticking to Maoist dogma, however, the revolutionary forces were oblivious to significant changes stemming from state-led development. With growing urbanisation, the peasant sector, upon which the Maoists' guerrilla base-building greatly relied, was shrinking, while the urban working and middle classes were expanding. Unlike Vietnam's revolutionaries, who had devised their own revolutionary strategy, Southeast Asia's other communist parties remained largely fixated on Mao's protracted people's war, without seriously considering other strategies—military or political—that might be better suited to their countries' concrete conditions. The Maoist strategy of building "stable base areas"—"liberated" zones, virtually impregnable "rear" bases for the "front" where guerrillas are actually fighting—might have suited a large country such as China in the 1930s and 1940s. But modern technology made large military formations, even in Southeast Asia's mountainous areas, more easily perceptible and the areas themselves more pregnable. Moreover, Southeast Asian countries are far smaller than China. In smaller countries, such as Cuba and Nicaragua, revolutionaries had more success by mobilising popular insurrections to topple dictators and seize power. The "people power" revolutions of the Philippines (1986), Tunisia and Egypt (2011), among others, showed that *unarmed* popular uprisings could also bring down dictators.

Beyond questions of strategy, several other factors were important. The left's reputation and appeal were obviously tarnished by the totalitarian rule of Stalin and Mao, which had led to terrible famines and violent purges, not to mention the horrors perpetrated by the Khmer Rouge in Cambodia. Sustained repression by Southeast Asia's authoritarian regimes—and the extensive economic and military assistance they received from the West and Japan—were also critical, as was the relative success of state-led development in building popular support for these regimes. The Sino–Soviet split, and China's later retreat from revolutionary internationalism, also severely limited the sources of international support for revolutionary movements, as did the decline and fall of the Soviet Union. The dramatic empowerment of transnational capital in the process of globalisation also dramatically weakened the power and leverage of forces struggling for radical alternatives (see Carroll, this volume).

The left's decline in Southeast Asia contrasts starkly with the situation in Latin America, providing an instructive comparison. After waging armed struggle against military and other authoritarian regimes from the 1950s to the 1970s, the Latin American left largely shifted to parliamentary struggle in the 1980s, transforming their mass bases in guerrilla zones into electoral bases, or building new electoral bases from below. After winning some parliamentary seats and capturing some local governments, including those of several major cities in the 1980s, left parties emerged as major—if not the main—opposition in the 1990s. By the 2000s, left parties had swept to power in half of Latin American countries, including Brazil, Argentina, Venezuela and Chile (though some later embraced neoliberalism).

To be sure, the Latin American left mostly did not have to contend with some of factors that crippled the Southeast Asian left: successful state-led developmentalism; massive pogroms like those in Indonesia (directed against communists) and Cambodia (directed by communists); and the Sino–Soviet split (the Latin American left was much more variegated, with major pro-Moscow, pro-Beijing and neutral parties and movements). Western counter-insurgency experts and operatives were also more violently engaged with the "frontline states" of Southeast Asia than with South American countries. Moreover, while democratisation swept almost all countries of Latin America in the 1980s and 1990s, authoritarian rule proved much more durable in Southeast Asia.

Compared to Southeast Asian revolutionaries, however, Latin American leftists were also much more imaginative and inventive in their strategies for capturing power. They experimented with various strategies: these included "foco strategy", in which a small guerrilla band inspires popular uprising (Cuba and Bolivia); urban guerrilla warfare (Uruguay and Brazil, 1960s and early 1970s); parliamentary struggle (Chile, 1960s to early 1970s); insurrectional strategy (Nicaragua, 1970s); Maoist protracted people's war (Peru's Shining Path, 1980s); Vietnamese-style protracted people's war (El Salvador, 1980s); and *coup d'etat* (Venezuela, 1992). Most of these strategies ultimately failed, but the broadmindedness and flexibility of the Latin American leftists helped them considerably when they shifted, in large numbers, to the parliamentary/electoral road in the 1980s and 1990s. Conversely, all of Southeast Asia's Maoist parties remained mired in hopeless insurgencies—including today's only surviving example, the CPP.

The Shift to Electoral Politics

After the Cold War, there was little support for armed struggle, particularly of a protracted nature, not least because this leads to much death and destruction. Peaceful popular uprisings have sometimes toppled dictators, but such events are often spontaneous, making them difficult to predict and plan for. Consequently, to gain power and achieve its objectives of social justice and a more egalitarian society, what remains of the left in contemporary Southeast Asia has had few other options than to take the legal, democratic route: elections. Unfortunately, however, this involves competing in electoral regimes that have typically been crafted by, and remain dominated by, entrenched politico-economic elites.

With the exception of the CPP, Southeast Asia's Maoist groups have failed to make the transition into electoral politics. The CPP has done so without abandoning armed struggle. CPP-aligned, open, legal parties have regularly managed to secure six to eight seats in the lower house of Congress through a "party list" system for "marginalised" sectors. But because the CPP's primary aim remains the revolutionary overthrow of the state, rather than participation in "bourgeois" governance, it engages in elections only for tactical or instrumental reasons, and has not made further progress in electoral politics.

More broadly, contending with entrenched elites in the electoral arena has posed a formidable challenge for democratic left groups in Southeast Asia. This is partly because the balance of forces is profoundly unpromising: workers and peasants demobilised, left forces crushed, and oligarchic elements ascendant. This context allows entrenched socio-political elites to shape the contours of contemporary political participation. As Rodan (2018: 1) states, they no longer simply resort to crude strategies of repression:

> Rather, both elites and their opponents are moving… to construct or pursue their own models of participation, representation, and democracy with vastly different objectives in mind. For many entrenched elites, these initiatives are designed as political instruments to enforce and consolidate deepening concentrations of power and wealth and to domesticate opposition.

For those on the margins of power, they are intended as the political vehicles for these concentrations to be dismantled.

Although socio-political contestation determines particular outcomes, the overwhelming power of elite forces has allowed them to devise increasingly sophisticated modes of participation that channel popular pressures in ways that do not fundamentally challenge oligarchic domination (see Rodan and Baker, this volume). Thus, "increasing political participation has often been accompanied by a narrowing of the channels for political contestation" (Jayasuriya and Rodan 2007: 773).

The emergence of quite extensive networks of civil society or non-government organisations is instructive. The left has historically been pivotal in developing civil society in Southeast Asia and, banking on their strong embeddedness in social movements, some leftists have sought to build up political parties from this mass base. However, as Rodan (2018) points out, politicians and political parties of traditional or entrenched politico-economic elites have constructed their own modes of participation, representation and democracy, seeking to domesticate opposition forces by drawing them into these modes. Furthermore, parties of the elite have enjoyed superior resources during campaigning, and wooed voters, including those in the left's base, through patronage and corruption. Thus, left parties have been unable to mount a significant challenge to parties of the elite.

For example, in 1998, some leftist groups—mostly CPP breakaways that had turned towards open, legal political struggle—began fielding candidates for the Philippines' lower house of Congress under the party list system, which had been established after Marcos's fall by traditional elite politicians, supposedly to accommodate representatives of "marginalised sectors." A few groups on the democratic left did win seats, but most failed to retain them in subsequent elections, as groups linked to the politico-economic elite slowly took effective control of the party list vote. Similarly, in Indonesia, the People's Democratic Party (PRD), a democratic socialist group which had been in the forefront of the anti-Suharto movement in the 1990s, contested the 1999 legislative election, but garnered only 0.07% of the vote, with parties linked to various oligarchic elements dominating instead. Afterwards, the PRD experienced a series of splits and faded away.

The most spirited—and the broadest—challenge to the rule of entrenched politico-economic elites appears to be coming from social democrats, which have emerged as the dominant leftist force in the region. Social democratic parties or pre-party formations now operate in six Southeast Asian countries and are affiliated with the Network for Social Democracy in Asia (SocDem Asia), and the Progressive Alliance (PA). Established in May 2013, the PA is an international association of social democratic, progressive and socialist parties, most of which have left the Socialist International. It includes many of the most prominent social democratic parties of Europe and Latin America. SocDem Asia is an associate network of PA.

Malaysia's DAP is one of the few social democratic parties in Southeast Asia to have successfully surmounted the great constraints on contestation imposed by dominant elites. An opposition party since its founding in 1965, the DAP is now in government as part of the ruling coalition, *Pakatan Harapan*, which ousted the previously undefeated but corruption-tainted *Barisan Nasional* in the May 2018 elections. It also holds a good number of seats in the State Legislative Assemblies of Penang, Perak, Selangor and Johor. The DAP, whose vision is to establish a multi-ethnic social democracy that, among other goals, distributes wealth equitably and fights corruption, has intensified its organising and training efforts. However, in a country where political parties have long been organised along racial/ethnic lines, the DAP remains predominantly identified with the ethnic Chinese, having yet to make significant inroads in the Malay majority and other ethnic communities.

The Philippines' *Akbayan*, a member of PA and SocDem Asia, has had at least one party list representative in Congress since 1998. In 2010–16, it even became a junior partner in the ruling coalition during the administration of President Benigno Aquino III, holding two Cabinet positions. In 2016, an Akbayan candidate also won a seat in the Senate, the legislature's upper house. However, although some Akbayan candidates have been elected to government posts in various municipalities, cities and provinces, its voter base remains thinly spread.

Elsewhere in the region, the global power relations of neoliberalism and deeply entrenched patterns of patronage present substantial barriers for even moderate social democracy. Although FRETILIN became Timor-Leste's first ruling party after independence in 2002, it was unable to pursue radical policies: there was simply no international support for the war-torn, cash-strapped country to pursue even modest state-led development. Competition for incredibly scarce resources prompted a split in the security forces in 2006, precipitating the return of international peace-keepers. Since 2007, Timor-Leste has been ruled by coalitions led by the National Congress for Timorese Reconstruction (CNRT), which has consolidated a highly corrupt regime. As Aspinall et al. (2018: 154, 160) note: "a new politics of patronage and distribution has emerged, facilitated by oil wealth". CNRT "combines the features of a personalistic party, built around charismatic leader Xanana Gusmão, and [those] of a patronage machine". FRETILIN was even temporarily drawn into these arrangements after 2013, being granted control over lucrative mega-projects in the Oecussi enclave (Scambary 2015).

Indonesian leftists confront similar challenges in their efforts to build new parties or to reform mainstream ones, in a political economy dominated by oligarchy. The most energetic, perhaps, have been social democratic activists espousing more progressive politics within the Indonesian Democratic Party of Struggle (PDI-P) and the National Democratic Party (NasDem)—senior and junior parties, respectively, in Indonesia's current ruling coalition—and the Indonesia Solidarity Party (PSI), a newly established entity. Largely through these activists' endeavours, the PDI-P and NasDem have joined both PA and SocDem Asia as observers. However, with figures identified with the entrenched elite still playing major roles in PDI-P and NasDem, it remains to be seen how far these activists can genuinely transform these parties into truly social democratic entities.

Conclusion

In the decades immediately before and after World War II, the left was a major political force in Southeast Asia. Revolutionary movements, inspired in part by the Chinese and Vietnamese revolutions, became a marked feature of the region's political dynamics. Maoism became the dominant force in the left in Southeast Asia (outside of Vietnam and Laos) from the 1960s to 1980s, as revolutionary forces sought to copy Mao's protracted people's war strategy by "encircling the cities from the countryside". One by one, these groups were defeated, as Southeast Asian governments, backed by the West, stepped up counter-insurgency operations, and as Maoist tenets proved unsuitable to concrete conditions in the region.

The Maoist spell has now been broken. Unlike in post-authoritarian Latin America, however, Southeast Asia's leftist revolutionaries have not been able to transform themselves into political parties capable of battling effectively with entrenched politico-economic elites in the electoral arena. Since the decline of the revolutionary left in the 1980s, some leftist political forces—mostly social democratic parties and pre-party formations—have emerged. The often-dire material conditions and staggering inequality within the region still offer ripe opportunities for revitalising the left. But aside from having to contend with a variegated neoliberalism and the legacy of Cold War authoritarian rule, these forces must also grapple with both the patronage and corruption of the entrenched elites, and the more sophisticated modes of participation and representation that the latter now employ. Moreover, the democratic leftist forces have to deal with a global downturn in the fortunes of the left, which is currently reeling from populist and ultra-nationalist onslaughts. To succeed, leftist forces would need to operate in a coordinated way, both within the region and internationally.

References

Aspinall, E., Hicken, A., Scambary, J., & Weiss, M. (2018). Timor-Leste votes: Parties and patronage. *Journal of Democracy, 29*(1), 153–167.

Cheah, B. K. (2009). The communist insurgency in Malaysia, 1948–90: Contesting the nation-state and social change. *New Zealand Journal of Asian Studies, 11*(1), 132–152.

Hewison, K., & Rodan, G. (1994). The decline of the left in South East Asia. *Socialist Register, 30*, 235–262.

Hewison, K., & Rodan, G. (2012). Southeast Asia: The left and the rise of bourgeois opposition. In R. Robison (Ed.), *Routledge handbook of Southeast Asian politics* (pp. 25–39). London: Routledge.

Hobday, C. (1986). *Communist and Marxist parties of the world*. Essex: Longman.

Jayasuriya, K., & Rodan, G. (2007). Beyond hybrid regimes: More participation, less contestation in Southeast Asia. *Democratization, 14*(5), 773–794.

Jones, L. (2012). *ASEAN, sovereignty and intervention in Southeast Asia*. Basingstoke: Palgrave Macmillan.

Kerkvliet, B. J. (1977). *The Huk rebellion: A case study of peasant revolt in the Philippines*. Berkeley: University of California Press.

Kiernan, B. (2017). *Genocide and resistance in Southeast Asia: Documentation, denial, and justice in Cambodia and East Timor*. New Brunswick: Transaction Publishers.

Kuntjoro-Jakti, D. (1984). Armed communism in Indonesia: Its history and future. In J. Lim & S. Vani (Eds.), *Armed communist movements in Southeast Asia* (pp. 3–28). Aldershot: Gower Publishing.

Lava, J. (1978). Review: The Huk rebellion. *Journal of Contemporary Asia, 9*(1), 75–81.

Le Duan. (1971). *The Vietnamese experience*. New York: International Publishers.

Lintner, B. (1990). *The rise and fall of the Communist Party of Burma*. Ithaca: Cornell University Press.
Morris, S. J. (1999). *Why Vietnam invaded Cambodia: Political culture and the causes of war*. Stanford: Stanford University Press.
Mysicka, S. (2015). Chinese support for communist insurgencies in Southeast Asia during the Cold War. *International Journal of China Studies*, 6(3), 203–230.
Pomeroy, W. (1978). The Philippine peasantry and the Huk revolt. *Journal of Peasant Studies*, 5(4), 497–517.
Rodan, G. (2018). *Participation without democracy: Containing conflict in Southeast Asia*. Ithaca: Cornell University Press.
Roosa, J. (2006). *Pretext for mass murder. The September 30th movement and Suharto's coup d'état in Indonesia*. Madison: University of Wisconsin Press.
Rousset, P. (2009). Thai Communist Party. In I. Ness (Ed.), *The international encyclopedia of revolution and protest*. Wiley Online Library. https://onlinelibrary.wiley.com/doi/10.1002/9781405198073.wbierp1445
Rummell, R. J. (1994). *Death by government*. New Brunswick: Transaction Publishers.
Scambary, J. (2015). In search of white elephants: The political economy of resource income expenditure in East Timor. *Critical Asian Studies*, 47(2), 283–308.
Tucker, S. (2001). *Burma: The curse of independence*. London: Pluto Press.
Tupaz, O. (1991). Toward a revolutionary strategy of the 90s. *Kasarinlan*, 7(2–3), 58–89.

CHAPTER 6

Populism in Southeast Asia: A Vehicle for Reform or a Tool for Despots?

Richard Robison and Vedi R. Hadiz

INTRODUCTION

While discussions of contemporary populism have focused on the United States and Europe, populism is not merely a Western phenomenon. Populist leaders such as Recep Tayyip Erdogan in Turkey, Narendra Modi in India and Jair Bolsonaro in Brazil have also swept to power through resounding electoral victories, with the same promises to end the rule of self-seeking elites and to restore national greatness. In Southeast Asia, Thailand's Thaksin Shinawatra (prime minister from 2001 to 2006), Indonesia's Joko Widodo (president from 2014 to present), and the Philippines' Rodrigo Duterte (president from 2016 to present) have all mobilised resentful populations with calls to put an end to chaos, corruption and inequality and to rebuild a strong national identity.

R. Robison (✉)
Asia Institute, University of Melbourne, Melbourne, Australia
e-mail: r.robison@iinet.net.au

V. R. Hadiz
Asia Institute, University of Melbourne, Melbourne, VIC, Australia
e-mail: vedi.hadiz@unimelb.edu.au

© The Author(s) 2020
T. Carroll et al. (eds.), *The Political Economy of Southeast Asia*, Studies in the Political Economy of Public Policy,
https://doi.org/10.1007/978-3-030-28255-4_6

Given its global scope, it is difficult to dismiss contemporary populism as essentially idiosyncratic, reliant on the charismatic appeal or the tactical skills of individual, opportunistic leaders. It must be understood, we argue, in the context of the struggles for power and wealth that accompany deeper structural crises in society and politics. The primary question is whether populism opens the door for long-supressed popular demands for the redistribution of wealth and social justice or acts as a vehicle to protect the interests of established oligarchies and ruling classes. The answer is forged not within processes of institutional decay and regeneration but rather in the conflicts between the cross-class alliances that emerge in periods of crisis, and the forces and interests that are mobilised within them.

Understanding Global Populist Stirrings

Analysing populism is difficult because it is such a slippery concept. It is not enough to understand populism in terms of inherent ideas, as some of the literature has tended to do (Urbinati 2014). As Sheri Berman has argued with respect to the rise of right-wing populism in the US and Europe, contemporary populism does not necessarily equate with fascism just because it may share xenophobic or nationalist ideas with fascist movements in 1930s Europe (Berman 2016). In the same way, despite neoliberal arguments to the contrary, labour movements and social democratic parties cannot be dismissed as populist merely because they argue for redistribution of wealth (Australian Financial Review 2016: 38).

Populism is defined by specific ideas about legitimacy and authority that override alternative ideologies of patronage or liberal ideas of representative politics. Populist leaders base their legitimacy on claims that they embody the common will of the people. This paves the way for cross-class alliances that enable populist rulers to outflank established political vehicles and networks and build new pathways to power. Such alliances are usually buttressed by political symbols and imageries associated with national solidarity, religious sentiment or racial and ethnic identity. It is through such political vocabularies that social justice issues or outright resentment of "elites" are articulated together with conceptions of "masses" formed by a common experience of being systematically marginalised or exploited (Canovan 1981; Laclau 2005; Mouzelis 1985; Mudde 2004).

The important question is whether and under what circumstances populist movements can emerge as a liberating force for repressed classes, as theorists like Laclau (2005) and Mouffe (2018) have envisaged. Conversely, under what circumstances do they descend into a vehicle for autocracy and oligarchy to legitimise arbitrary authority and to bypass demands for reform by diverting the poor and disenchanted into culture wars?

Few studies of populism in Southeast Asia have addressed these questions. In his insightful study of populism in Asia, Mietzner (2019) warns us to be wary of accepting linear or general interpretations of populism or trying to identify a common global strand. He argues that it is "increasingly important to study differences between the various forms of populism; the successes or failures they record in different societies; the competition between different types of populism; and the response of elites and populations towards populist experiments" (ibid.: 370). He develops categories of populism according to four distinct leadership types, ranging from the "movement populism" of Modi, premised on mass-based political organisations rooted in a well-established Hindutva political tendency, to the "authoritarian populism" of mavericks like Duterte, which mobilises popular support through fiery assaults on self-seeking elites and a rhetoric of extra-legal violence against criminal gangs. These differ from the "technocratic" populism of Indonesia's Joko Widodo (aka "Jokowi"), who came to power with promises to reform government from within by imposing technocratic principles of public administration. Jokowi's main opponent, Prabowo Subianto, represents a different category, "oligarchic populism", where nationalist appeals for a return to a romantic past mask an agenda to re-establish the rule of oligarchs and autocrats (Mietzner 2019; see also Aspinall 2015).

While this sort of typology provides important descriptive insights, it lacks broad explanatory power. Categorising populism in terms of the behaviour of individual leaders and their personalities or their organisational, tactical and strategic abilities does not explain why populism is a widespread contemporary political phenomenon. In contrast, this chapter looks at populism in the context of larger political upheavals that accompany crises of market capitalism at a global scale. This renders debates about whether populism is an ideology or a strategy of political mobilisation somewhat inconsequential (see Barr 2019; Hawkins 2019; Mudde 2016; Weyland 2017). What is more important is understanding populism as a response to a deeper structural malaise that can combine social interests into cross-class alliances, however tenuous or fractious. These variations tend to define the agendas—and limits—of different populisms.

From this standpoint, we can more productively ask why mass-based movements became effective political vehicles for Erdogan in Turkey or Modi in India when they had played a more marginal—though growing—

role in previous decades. What sort of circumstances allowed a populist alliance deploying the vocabulary of Islamic politics, in Turkey's case, to launch a successful and almost frontal assault on Kemalism since 2002, after decades of being on the political defensive? In India, how did Hindutva politics develop so robustly so as to, once again, break the dominance of Congress in 2014—even winning an outright majority of seats in parliament?[1] In Indonesia, why was Jokowi able to mobilise such enthusiastic support behind calls for efficient administration and good governance when previous presidents had made similar promises and failed? Why did large sections of the Philippine population embrace Duterte, for decades a provincial politician whose noisy rhetoric was largely ignored? Why were his supporters now prepared to swap the norms of a well-established, if flawed, tradition of Philippine democracy for more autocratic government, including through state-sponsored and extra-legal violence? After all, political disorder and endemic crime and corruption have been established parts of Philippine society throughout its history.

To answer such questions, we must foreground the structural crises confronting societies and the new political conflicts these produce. As Heydarian (2018) has noted, populism seems to find particularly fertile ground where such crises have created an interregnum of profound social and political disorder; where, in the words of Gramsci (1971: 276), "the old is dying and the new cannot yet be born".

Many analysts of populism in Southeast Asia recognise that populism can emerge in periods of political decay and dysfunction. However, drawing on Huntington (1968), and more recent theories of democratic transition, they see this as largely a problem of institutional decay and regeneration. They await the emergence of leaders who will build new institutions and political coalitions (O'Donnell et al. 1986). Mietzner (2019: 378) notes, for example, that populist leaders in Southeast Asia have commonly "exploited a widespread sense of frustration among voters with the way contemporary democracies function" and speculates that populism has emerged as a project to overcome democratic crisis.

In contrast, we see these interregna as the products of continual and wrenching social upheavals that accompany the spread of market capitalism and globalisation. These are inevitably accompanied by intense

---

[1] In the late 1970s, the Janata Party briefly ruled India with the support of such organisations as the militantly Hindu Nationalist RSS, which also serves as a major base of power for the Modi government.

conflicts over power and resources as established interests struggle to survive and new ones have not yet entrenched their power. This approach draws on a different literature, that of political economy. In relation to Southeast Asia, it borrows from the works of Hadiz (2016), Robison and Hadiz (2004), Rodan and Hewison (2004), and more generally from Oxhorn's (1998) work on Latin America as well as some earlier studies led by Ionescu and Gellner (1969).

While neoliberalism and globalisation can be linked to the rise of populism, this is not necessarily because they increase levels of poverty. Populism often emerges as incomes and GDP rise. Rather, neoliberalism can promote social resentment by disorganising and uprooting large sections of society, deepening inequalities, destroying old certainties and communities, forcing people into new forms of work and into different ways of confronting power and authority (Mishra 2016). For example, the introduction of property rights, industrial monoculture and global markets can make farmers vulnerable to land-grabbing and expropriation by governments, officials and crony capitalists (see Hirsch, this volume). Rural populations then flood into the cities as disengaged and precarious workers, while the world of rural elites, traders and small-scale manufacturers is turned on its head. At the same time, neoliberalism has resulted in the expansion of a vast and precarious—and often significantly youthful and educated—middle class, increasingly exposed to the uncertainty of the labour market and state authority and the dysfunction and corruption of the administrative apparatus, and fearful of demands from below.

Neoliberalism also fractures ruling elites and creates new and contending forces within them. The privatisation of state-owned enterprises and the transfer of public monopolies into private hands, together with trade and financial liberalisation, have concentrated the power of oligarchic ruling elites in Southeast Asia (Robison and Hadiz 2004: 71–102), as they did in Russia under the IMF's "shock therapy". But new fractures emerge, including between larger, corporatised interests plugged into the global economy and more regional and middle-ranking businesses, vulnerable to the competitive power of global investors and producers (see Al-Fadhat, and Jones and Hameiri, both this volume).

Yet, even the spread of uncertainty and resentment is not enough to produce populist insurgencies. A necessary factor, as Berman (2016) has argued, is the ongoing failure of rulers to deal with crises confronting societies, as they often cling to the very neoliberal prescriptions that promoted dissatisfaction in the first place. Governments find themselves increasingly unable to deal with new demands for welfare assistance, public education and health services, public order and rule of law, and effective public administration. It is telling that, despite decades of rapid economic growth, most governments in developing countries still cannot provide safe drinking water or deal with growing housing shortages or gridlocked roads in new cities.

This is not simply a problem of weak institutions or bad governance or constraints on markets that can be resolved by policy or institutional fixes (World Bank 1991, 2001). Efficient and honest government might seem a technical matter, but reform also threatens the very systems of predatory power that support oligarchs. As Jokowi has found in Indonesia, even the seemingly technocratic tasks of clamping down on corruption or providing public infrastructure and services meet with obstruction and resistance from the ruling class, its police and politicians. Institutions and policies that can appear objectively dysfunctional are often efficient mechanisms for consolidating power and wealth for elites, especially when they are reliant on the private plunder of public assets and authority. As Chabal and Daloz (1999) have argued in the case of Africa, seemingly dysfunctional states are "states (and governments) that work"—for dominant social forces.

For entrenched elites, the existential question is how to protect and preserve their power and wealth from demands for reform, especially where these imply a fundamental reordering of political and social power. In some instances, simply marginalising reformers runs the risk of leaving the field open to populist cross-class alliances, as Mubarak discovered in Egypt. These can articulate grievances on behalf of what are claimed to be the common interests of a unified mass, whether defined in terms of opposition to elites or through ethnic, religious or nationalist sentiments, or some sort of combination of these.

It is therefore crucial to understand the forces that support and oppose populist leaders. Does a leader like Duterte have a real interest in dismantling the inherently corrupt and inept oligarchy that rules the Philippines? Or is he a leader who will actually rescue it, on behalf of disgruntled and marginal regional elites and the middle classes that cling to the margins of power? Looking at things in this way, it is possible to understand Duterte not just as a demagogue but as a typically "petty bourgeois" populist, resentful of upper elites but, in the last instance, fearful of the masses. Similarly, it is problematic to define Jokowi simply in terms of his technocratic approach to administrative reform. It is more pertinent to ask where he fits into the growing contradiction between the reformist demands of his popular political base and the very elites that aided and abetted his rise, and whose interests are embedded in corrupt and predatory governance. This question is also critical in the case of Thaksin, whose eventual overthrow by the military and continuing political marginalisation suggest that his popularity, welfare and redistributive agendas had become too threatening to the dominant military and business alliances.

The usefulness of a political economy analysis of populism has perhaps been most thoroughly illustrated with respect to Donald Trump in the US. Despite the important differences in context to Southeast Asia, the Trump experience shows us that larger-than-life, narcissist personalities do not simply emerge from nowhere. Trump draws on the same old historical resentments that defined the populism of Huey Long or the John Birch Society (Kazin 2016), just as contemporary European populism inherits ideas from fascism in the 1920s and 1930s. We also see the cathartic impact of economic crises on the rise of populism. In the US, the vast deindustrialisation of the 1970s and the 2008 global financial crisis of provided a political constituency for Trump among those former blue-collar and lower-wage professional workers and small businesses of the South and Midwest now "left behind" by globalisation. His rise was also enabled by the failure of established political parties to provide answers: the Republican moderates and the Democrats could only offer more of the same market prescriptions that had created these resentful and angry populations in the first place. The US case also shows how populist politics can enable a reformulation of power among elites rather than its real redistribution. The Tea Party's rise in the 1990s was to be the vehicle for counter-revolution. By throwing the red meat of nationalism and white identity to the increasingly frustrated and resentful mass, Trump built a political base to consolidate the interests of the an ultra-rich plutocracy. Once in power, Trump sought to further dismantle the public sphere and its bureaucracy, including the public school and health systems, to hand over public lands to private opportunists, to slash taxes for the rich, and to dismantle key regulatory constraints, notably in environmental protection.

Many of the same factors are also at work in Southeast Asia. Old political certainties have been upset as neoliberal globalisation and economic crises created new social constituencies of seemingly abandoned sections of the population. Power and public trust has slipped, at different junctures, from the hands of established political parties in Thailand, Indonesia and the Philippines as they failed to offer avenues for social or political reform. And while populism has often taken the form of outwardly bizarre political coalitions between the rich and the poor, redistributive and reformist agendas have generally failed to undo the existing foundations of power and wealth.

Nevertheless, populism in this region has been shaped by different historical legacies. It has been incubated within the context of a ramshackle, family-based oligarchy in the Philippines, while in Indonesia it exists within a blend of crude money politics and the residual system of centralised and bureaucratised state power forged under Suharto. In both countries, as in Thailand, authoritarian rule and the Cold War client relationship with the West had resulted in extraordinary concentration of power within the state and widespread hollowing out of opposition politics, whether liberal reformist or revolutionary leftist (see Quimpo, this volume). The advance of neoliberalism and democracy in the 1980s and 1990s was built upon this concentration of wealth and power.

The critical question is how these different circumstances fed into the rise of different forms of populism. Once again, the answer principally lies in the nature of the cross-class alliances that emerged as the basis of populist challenges. In the US, populism became a vehicle for oligarchs and plutocrats to dismantle the remnants of social democracy. In Europe, populism has been the vehicle for marginal or rising elements within the elites themselves who may have more petit bourgeois or fascist agendas. Southeast Asia presents a complex fusion of these.

How Social and Economic Upheavals Created the Conditions for Southeast Asian Populism

As political opposition was hollowed out and leftist movements defeated in Indonesia, the Philippines and Thailand during the Cold War, the remnants of reformist movements made little headway. However, the depredations of the 1997–98 Asian financial crisis (AFC) and the failure of governments to address the concerns of an increasingly anxious and unequal society opened the door for new political challenges.

Such a vacuum has been partly filled in Thailand by the Thai Rak Thai (TRT) party and its successors. Thailand presents the seeming puzzle of why a billionaire businessman, Thaksin Shinawatra, would build and maintain a populist political movement drawing on the support of the rural and urban poor, in government from 2001 to 2006 and subsequently from political exile. The answer lies in the framework of political authority and class power within which Thaksin's political career operated and, more specifically, how the AFC weakened and fractured these structures. The Thai system of power was built around the long-standing alliance between the military, the royal household and leading business interests, supported and reinforced during the Cold War by Thailand's Western allies. This ruling alliance allowed periodic democratic elections and tolerated progressive elements of the middle class. For decades, the West had feted Thailand as the ideal of a successful and sustainable democratic transition. All this began to unravel with the AFC and the decisions by the coalition governments under Chavalit Yongchouyudh and Chuan Leekpai to persist with IMF prescriptions of even more market liberalisation, fiscal austerity and privatisation (Hewison 2005: 313). This resulted in deepening poverty and unemployment in rural areas, especially in the more impoverished northeast region and among the urban working classes. At the same time, neoliberal reforms threatened important and highly indebted elements within the Thai bourgeoisie, exposing them to fire sales of assets and competition from foreign companies (ibid.: 317). As Hewison has argued (2017: 429) the dispersed and globalised production networks, flexible labour markets and precarious work that came with neoliberalism made it possible to forge multi-class coalitions. As an increasingly moribund Thai government clung to neoliberal orthodoxy, Thaksin was able to consolidate an apparently unlikely alliance between the increasingly marginalised rural and urban poor and powerful elements within the crisis-ridden bourgeoisie.

Similarly, in Indonesia, populist rhetoric and mass mobilisations have become entangled in conflict between factions of an oligarchy initially nurtured under the authoritarian New Order era (1966–98). Fusing public authority and private interest, this oligarchy now dominates the key institutions of Indonesian democracy, including major political parties (Robison and Hadiz 2004). Like in Thailand and the Philippines, these parties are not so much common policy platforms as mechanisms to control the levers of the state and to access and distribute tangible resources. Indonesia has also experienced near-continual economic growth since the advent of the New Order, except during and in the aftermath of the AFC. Yet, while producing wealth, this growth has also produced social inequalities that recently reached their highest recorded levels (World Bank 2016). By 2018, absolute poverty affected only 9.82 per cent of Indonesians, down from 19.1 per cent in 2000 (BPS 2018a; OECD

2006). Yet, from 1990 to 2012, the Gini coefficient, which measures income inequality, grew from 0.33 to 0.41 (Yusuf et al. 2013), while the World Bank (2016) shows that Indonesia's richest 1% now has more wealth than the poorest 50%. Even the transition to democracy in 1998 did nothing to arrest this trend. In the meantime, new generations who had bought into the promises of development have seen their aspirations for quick upward social mobility thwarted, while they are simultaneously exposed to the conspicuous consumption of the rich in everyday life. Even their more mundane expectations of employment are not always fulfilled. While official unemployment hovers around 6%, youth unemployment stands at 20% while under-employment regularly affects a third of the workforce (BPS 2018b). These circumstances undoubtedly provide fertile ground for a politics of resentment associated with populist emergence.

In the Philippines, the rise of Duterte re-focused attention on populism, years after President Estrada (1998–2001) had briefly punctuated decades of comfortable rule by family-based oligarchs. Estrada had gained popularity not simply as the result of his "tough guy" or "everyman" image, cultivated in a prior career as a movie star, but also because he appealed to widespread disenchantment with the patronage politics controlled by big political families. This was reinforced as broader social changes affected the urban social landscape in particular, with the growth of urban poor slums and "economically insecure clients" within the general population (Hedman 2001). There had also been other attempts to challenge the power of the traditional oligarchy, the most significant being the presidency of Ferdinand Marcos (1965–86). Marcos, who hailed from minor oligarchic origins himself, consolidated his regime by centralising state power at the expense of the big families in the 1970s and 1980s. But he was undone by the almost ungovernable and entrenched autonomy of local oligarchic interests and the violent political "bossism" that defined local political relations (Lacaba 1995). Long after the Marcos era, we can still find evidence of the weakness of the central state, such as the 2009 Maguindanao massacre, where dozens of journalists opposing the local ruling clan were murdered with apparent impunity. More recently, the Battle of Marawi saw a disorganised Philippine military struggle to deal with a low-level takeover of a regional city by Islamist insurgents (Crisis Group 2018).

It was in this context that Duterte achieved a stunning electoral victory in 2016, with his tough "law and order" approach—most infamously seen in a brutal "war on drugs" (a tactic also used by Thaksin in Thailand). This appealed to a broad segment of Philippines society, including the middle class and the poor who had suffered from the chaos and violence of crime-infested cities (Keenan 2013), as well as the ineffectiveness of governance more generally. Nevertheless, Duterte did not emerge in the context of economic malaise—quite the opposite. Economic growth had in fact burgeoned, reaching levels of 6–7 per cent per annum, just behind China, leading to revisions of the long-standing view of the Philippines as the "sick man of Asia" (e.g. Forbes 2018). Yet, this apparent achievement of the 2010–16 Benigno Aquino III presidency (Abinales 2013) had not benefited the congested slums of the big Philippines cities, where conditions remained as bleak as ever and joblessness remained pervasive (Mourdoukoutas 2019). Such conditions easily gave rise to ideas that economic advances served only a tiny elite, while most remained vulnerable to poverty, thus providing fertile ground once again for populist stirrings.

How Cross-Class Alliances and Populist Movements Are Preserving or Reordering Class Power and Wealth in Southeast Asia

In all of these cases, widespread dissatisfaction with economic and political governance—fundamentally underpinned by the consolidation of neoliberal policy sets (see Carroll, this volume)—enabled the rise of cross-class alliances between forces from below and established elite interests. Yet, contradictorily, these alliances contained those pursuing agendas of redistribution alongside those aiming to consolidate the power of oligarchy. Which agenda ultimately won out, we argue, can be explained within the approaches of what Hameiri and Jones (this volume) broadly describe as the "Murdoch School". In other words, the outcomes depended on the composition, power and strategies of the social forces involved, and wider socio-political power relations in each country context.

In Thailand, Thaksin Shinawatra became Prime Minister at the head of the TRT party following the first post-AFC election in 2001. Thaksin himself was the product of Thailand's rapid, state-led capitalist development: a police colonel, he had benefited from state contracts in the 1980s to build a new business empire in the emerging telecommunications sector, before entering politics in the 1990s to further his interests—like many businessmen before him. But it was the AFC that created his great political opportunity. With the post-crisis government in disarray and increasing resentment among rural populations, small retailers, the self-employed and construction workers, it became possible to build a political alliance between the rural and urban lower classes and elements of Thai big business seeking respite from neoliberal reform.

That the latter's interests were truly dominant was revealed in TRT's subsequent agenda, which involved pioneering a new social contract to rescue Thai business from the aftermath of the crisis (Hewison 2005: 318; Pasuk and Baker 2008: 64). Thaksin's opposition to austerity policies and deregulation did not signal fundamental hostility toward neoliberal policies but rather aimed to give time to big businesses to recapitalise themselves and prepare to re-engage with global markets (Hewison 2005). Thai banks quickly struck deals with Thaksin's supporters and the Thai Asset Management corporation began to handle some of their bad loans, keeping ailing conglomerates afloat, much as in post-crisis Indonesia (Hewison 2005: 322). Thaksin also adopted a popular, tough stance on criminals, launching a brutal "war on drugs", and on Muslim rebels in Thailand's south. Police and other state agents reportedly killed several thousand suspected criminals in this period.

Nonetheless, Thaksin's cross-class alliance also yielded real wins for subordinated social groups. Historically, Thailand's oligarchic political parties typically treated lower-class citizens as passive vote banks, courting their support at election time then ignoring them. TRT was different: a political organisation outside the established political parties surrounding the palace, it plugged directly into a large support base among the rural poor and marginalised new urban workers. Through the party, Thaksin played a role similar to the style of the traditional local boss (Pasuk and Baker 2008: 72). But he also repaid his supporters with genuine concessions, delivering on pledges of agricultural price support, farmer debt moratoriums, land for the landless, soft loans to farmers, health insurance and a universal health campaign. These policies were, naturally, widely popular with a desperate constituency, but deeply threatening to entrenched elites unused to sharing power and wealth with the lower orders.

It is therefore not surprising that the military and its political allies removed Thaksin from office in 2006 and that the same fate befell his sister Yingluck, elected as prime minister in 2011 but deposed in 2014. Their opponents within the military and politico-business elites in Bangkok argued that Thaksin's populism had descended into personalist leadership and arbitrary use of authority, accusing him of corruption, using state resources for private gain, and undermining the monarch (see Laothamatas

2006: 198). In reality, there were deeper issues at work. In one sense, this coup was hardly unusual: as Hewison (2017) points out, Thailand has seen 12 military coups since 1932. But it is important to see coups as a response to social conflict, rather than as part of a country's "political culture" or "weak institutions", as some suggest. The 2006 coup happened because Thaksin's redistributive policies and support base among the rural poor posed an existential threat to the traditional Thai ruling class. This is why the military were not satisfied with removing him from office, but set about eliminating the very constitution that enabled his rise and retreating into what is effectively a new era of authoritarian rule.

In Indonesia, the 2014 and 2019 elections saw a battle between two different populist coalitions. Jokowi's 2014 campaign raised the prospect of change and a new political era, in which politicians could emerge from outside the ranks of established state and party machines. It suggested that money politics and patronage-based parties might no longer be viable instruments for controlling and mobilising those disappointed with ineffective governments unable to provide basic services and infrastructure (see Fukuoka and Djani 2016). Jokowi's populism rested upon the appeal of efficient government to broad sections of the population frustrated with long-standing failure to share the wealth of the country and to provide education and health services and honest government. This potentially created a recipe for conflict between his elite backers and his new-found constituency.

His opponent, Prabowo Subianto, Suharto's ex-son-in-law and a former commander of Indonesian special forces accused of war crimes, mobilises a different constituency with a very different rhetoric, but nonetheless overlaps with Jokowi in significant ways. Prabowo's populist vision harks back to a world of state-managed corporatist institutions and nationalist ideals and a more centralised system of oligarchic power. This appeals to long-standing traditions of statist nationalism and ideas about "indigenous" cultural traditions, which had formed the basis for an organicist, repressive ideology under Suharto (Bourchier 2014). But, like Jokowi, it also appeals to popular frustrations with post-Suharto developments, notably failures in service delivery, entrenched corruption, and the ramshackle nature of the decentralised state, leading large parts of the urban middle classes to long for a return to "strongman" politics. Jokowi's appeals, while more rooted in market ideas, seek to address similar grievances through extending the reach of the state's welfare and health insurance systems and promising quick "fixes" to a host of debilitating bureaucratic bottlenecks (Hadiz and Robison 2017).

To further complicate matters, both respond to a seemingly resurgent Islamic-based form of populism that builds on the narrative of a marginalised "community of believers", but which has been co-opted into the mechanics of intra-oligarchic competition (Hadiz 2017). Islamism in the Indonesian context is itself a response to the socio-economic and political dislocations of capitalist development, appealing in particular to a precarious urban middle class frustrated by oligarchic corruption, and useful, too, to sections of the urban poor able to finesse Islamic identity into militias engaged in protection rackets and mobilising electoral support for oligarchic candidates (see Hadiz 2018). Islamism remained a marginal political force after 1998, but Prabowo has embraced fringe Islamic mass organisations like the Islamic Defenders Front (FPI), whose rhetoric emphasises how Muslims—the majority of Indonesians—have been marginalised since colonial times all the way to the present democratic period. It is resentful not just of foreign interests but also of the big ethnic-Chinese conglomerates that dominate the economy. This cynical alliance of convenience claimed a major scalp in the 2017 Jakarta gubernatorial elections, where Jokowi ally Basuki Tjahaja Purnama (aka Ahok) was not only ousted as governor but also jailed for blasphemy (see Rodan and Baker, and Hutchison and Wilson, this volume). Jokowi's reaction was to enlist a highly conservative cleric as his running mate in 2019 in an attempt to nullify Prabowo's appeal to those that equate piety with socio-economic marginality.

However, it is unlikely that Prabowo can harness the politics of Islamic identity in the same way as Erdogan has in Turkey or the Muslim Brotherhood did in Egypt. Indonesia has no analogue of what was a key support base for Erdogan's AKP—the Anatolian bourgeoisie, a vibrant provincial, culturally Islamic, group of big businesses, eager to displace the huge conglomerates nurtured by the secular nationalist Kemalist establishment (Tuğal 2016). Similarly, although Egypt's Muslim Brotherhood provided a model for Indonesia's once-celebrated Justice and Prosperity Party (PKS) (Hadiz 2016), the PKS was unable to replicate the networks of well-organised and -funded social welfare organisations that had underpinned the Brotherhood's success, and which had brought together Islamic populist middle-class activists and the poor (Clarke 2004). The Indonesian big bourgeoisie remains dominated by ethnic-Chinese oligarchs who have no interest in bankrolling anti-Chinese Islamist forces.

In the Philippines, Duterte's anti-elite railings have likewise mobilised a cross-class social base from the resentments and insecurities accompanying late capitalist development. President Duterte has found worldwide infamy as a foul-mouthed misogynist, a macho "Dirty Harry", "man-of-the-people" figure. He also raised some hopes domestically of a leftist turn: Duterte had once studied under Jose Maria Sison, the now long-exiled communist leader (Sabillo 2016), and he initially proposed reconciliation with the Philippines' long-running communist insurgency. However, both images were far-fetched: Duterte has too many investments in the established political order. Besides being the former mayor of the city of Davao, whose own children are now in office in an emergent mini-dynasty, Duterte is the son of a lawyer and politician whose career included a mayorship, a governorship, and a seat in one of Marcos's cabinets. He is also related to some of the country's most powerful political dynasties through both of his parents: the Duranos and Almenas of Mindanao and the Roas of the Visayas (Heydarian 2018: 210). Rather than serving as a tribune of the lower classes or as a conduit for leftist political resurgence, Duterte represents a stratum of provincial elites whose own social and political rise would be served by a movement that claimed an intent to reorganise, if not dismantle, the existing system of power.

As with other populists, Duterte did not emerge in a vacuum; he rose on the back of simmering public dissatisfaction with the post-Marcos "elite democracy", which failed to live up to its initial promise of social justice (ibid.: 237). His electoral victory—over the candidate backed by the Liberal Party of the incumbent, Benigno Aquino III—conveyed the message that political liberalism had failed to cope with the challenges of globalisation. It had also failed to address widespread corruption that helped fuel the very system of democratic electoral competition. Referencing both national pride and machismo, Duterte appealed especially to urban and rural poor populations whose lives are the most precarious, while also simultaneously attracting middle class supporters afraid of mass uprisings and in favour of a "strongman" to ensure order and stability (ibid.: 307, 440).

This broad appeal allowed Duterte to cobble together a political alliance that included the far right and far left (ibid.: 237), both of which had long been marginalised from the workings of an electoral democracy dominated by the scions of competing leading families. But a key reason for Duterte's spectacular electoral victory was "the vote in urban municipalities, with populations of 100,000 or more people, across the regions": Duterte secured 45% of all urban votes, "winning in 97 of 148 cities and securing 54% of his own votes in these cities" through "a ruthless campaign against criminal drug use prevalent in urban poor and middle class communities" (Putzel 2018). He offered a solution to ongoing fears of chaos and criminality that political liberals like Aquino III had been unable to deal with.

There is little evidence, however, that Duterte has undertaken policies that threaten, fundamentally, the oligarchic families and their corporate cronies or made headway against predatory behaviour, including in land-grabbing or the use of extra-legal coercion against opponents. While an alliance has now transpired between the Duterte, Macapagal-Arroyo and Marcos clans (Cook 2018), his links with leftists have weakened, with some now seeing him as the number one enemy of the people (Sison 2018). Unsurprisingly, we have not seen the sort of moves against him from within the elites that Thaksin had elicited in Thailand.

Conclusion: Is Southeast Asian Populism Reformist or Reactionary?

Even when in power, populist leaders cannot afford to dispense with their tenuous cross-class bases of social support. They must fulfil at least some promises. As we have seen, programmes of social welfare and health policies were at the centre of Thaksin's rule, while in Indonesia, Jokowi's universal health scheme and infrastructure projects maintain his populist credentials. In the Philippines, Duterte has increased spending on social and infrastructure projects, largely in the face of the upcoming mid-term elections in 2019.

It is clear that Duterte, Jokowi and Prabowo are all caught in a balancing act between mobilising political support on the basis of redistributional policies and sustaining the systems of oligarchy that ultimately support them. None can promise redistribution of power and wealth in the longer term. The dangers being faced are clear, as we have seen in Thailand where Thaksin—while firmly an ambitious capitalist himself—provoked a response from established politico-business interests by developing a popular base in a way that had become threatening.

Nevertheless, a nascent literature has emerged suggesting that it cannot be assumed that populist rulers will only last for a short period (Albertazzi and McDonnell 2015) and arguing that the influence of populist governments can linger on, for better or for worse, including their programmes of redistribution. For example, the World Bank estimated in 2012 that 99.5% of the Thai population was still covered by universal health coverage schemes that were promoted by the Thaksin government (World Bank 2012). Yet, it is useful to keep in mind de la Torre's (2019: 24) reminder that populism cannot be treated simply as a pathology of democracy. After all, more inclusionary forms of populism—while rare in the current global landscape—may produce democratising tendencies or legacies by opening up access to power, as Roniger (2019) argues for the neglected cases of Central America, even if their governments do not last. It has been shown, for example, that some populisms have had the effect of reducing social inequalities (Lewis et al. 2019).

This possibility is less likely in Southeast Asia if we examine the constitutive social bases and the broader contexts in which populism has evolved in the region. Here, the legacies of the Cold War are crucial. If visions of a social democratic Europe or left traditions made Syriza in Greece or Podemos in Spain still possible, in spite—or because—of the collapse of the welfare state, in Southeast Asia such traditions have long been marginalised if not decimated (see Quimpo, this volume). No cohesive and autonomous labour or other civil society-based movements exist that could steer the populist impulse away from exclusionary forms of nationalist or identity-based politics.

At the same time one should avoid viewing populism as simply a politics of irrationality, juxtaposed against the inherent rationality of liberal democracy and its accompaniment, market capitalism. Taking such a position will inhibit an understanding of the failings of the political liberalism against which democracies tend to be measured or the actual chaos and upheavals often unleashed by neoliberalising economic projects. These are the failings to which contemporary populisms are largely a response, no matter how they might be tamed.

References

Abinales, P. N. (2013). The Philippines under Aquino III, year 2: A ponderous slog continues. *Southeast Asian Affairs, 2013*, 223–239.
Albertazzi, D., & McDonnell, D. (2015). *Populists in power*. London: Routledge.
Aspinall, E. (2015). Oligarchic populism: Prabowo Subianto's challenge to Indonesian democracy. *Indonesia, 99*, 1–28.

Australian Financial Review. (2016, August 31). Populism in Q and A and parliament. *Australian Financial Review.*
Barr, R. R. (2019). Populism as a political strategy. In C. de la Torre (Ed.), *Routledge handbook of global populism* (pp. 44–56). New York: Routledge.
Berman, S. (2016, November–December). Populism is not fascism. But it could be a harbinger. *Foreign Affairs.* https://www.foreignaffairs.com/articles/united-states/2016-10-17/populism-not-fascism
Bourchier, D. (2014). *Illiberal democracy in Indonesia: The ideology of the family state.* London: Routledge.
BPS. (2018a, July 16). Profil kemiskinan di Indonesia Maret 2018 [Profile of poverty in Indonesia March 2018]. *Berita Resmi Statistik [Official News Statistics],* 57/07/Th.XXI, 1–8.
BPS. (2018b). Tingkat pengangguran terbuka menurut provinsi, 1986–2018 [Unemployment rate by province, 1986–2018]. https://www.bps.go.id/statictable/2014/09/15/981/tingkat-pengangguran-terbuka-tpt-menurut-provinsi-1986%2D%2D-2018.html. Accessed 26 Mar 2019.
Canovan, M. (1981). *Populism.* New York: Harcourt Brace Jovanovich.
Chabal, P., & Daloz, J. P. (1999). *Africa works: Disorder as political instrument.* Oxford: James Currey.
Clarke, J. A. (2004). *Islam, charity and activism.* Bloomington: Indiana University Press.
Cook, E. (2018, September 13). What does Duterte's war on Trillanes mean for the Philippines? *The Diplomat.* https://thediplomat.com/2018/09/what-does-dutertes-war-on-trillanes-mean-for-the-philippines/. Accessed 26 Mar 2019.
Crisis Group. (2018, July 17). *Philippines: Addressing Islamist militancy after the battle for Marawi. International Crisis Group.* https://www.crisisgroup.org/asia/south-east-asia/philippines/philippines-addressing-islamist-militancy-after-battle-marawi. Accessed 26 Mar 2019.
de la Torre, C. (2019). Global populism: Histories, trajectories, problems and challenges. In C. de la Torre (Ed.), *Routledge handbook of global populism* (pp. 1–37). New York: Routledge.
Forbes. (2018, October 27). The Philippines' per-capita GDP has reached an all-time high under Duterte. *Forbes.* https://www.forbes.com/sites/panosmourdoukoutas/2018/10/27/the-philippines-per-capita-gdp-has-reached-an-all-time-high-under-duterte/#308c4c7869b1. Accessed 26 Mar 2019.
Fukuoka, Y., & Djani, L. (2016). Revisiting the rise of Jokowi: The triumph of reformasi or an oligarchic adaptation of post-clientelist initiatives? *South East Asia Research, 24*(2), 204–221.
Gramsci, A. (1971). *Selections from the prison notebooks* (trans. Hoare, Q., & Smith, G. N.). London: Lawrence and Wishart.

Hadiz, V. R. (2016). *Islamic populism in Indonesia and the Middle East.* Cambridge: Cambridge University Press.

Hadiz, V. R. (2017). Indonesia's year of democratic setbacks: Towards a new phase of deepening illiberalism? *Bulletin of Indonesian Economic Studies, 53*(3), 261–278.

Hadiz, V. R. (2018). Imagine all the people? Mobilising Islamic populism for right-wing politics in Indonesia. *Journal of Contemporary Asia, 48*(4), 566–583.

Hadiz, V. R., & Robison, R. (2017). Competing populisms in post-authoritarian Indonesia. *International Political Science Review, 38*(4), 488–502.

Hawkins, K. A. (2019). The ideational approach. In C. de la Torre (Ed.), *Routledge handbook of global populism* (pp. 57–71). New York: Routledge.

Hedman, E.-L. E. (2001). The spectre of populism in Philippine politics and society: Artista, masa, eraption! *South East Asia Research, 9*(1), 5–44.

Hewison, K. (2005). Neo-liberalism and domestic capital: The political outcomes of the economic crisis in Thailand. *The Journal of Development Studies, 41*(2), 310–330.

Hewison, K. (2017). Reluctant populists: Learning populism in Thailand. *International Political Science Review, 38*(4), 426–440.

Heydarian, R. J. (2018). *The rise of Duterte: A populist revolt against elite democracy.* Singapore: Palgrave Pivot.

Huntington, S. (1968). *Political order in changing societies.* New Haven/London: Yale University Press.

Ionescu, G., & Gellner, E. (Eds.). (1969). *Populism: Its meanings and national characteristics.* New York: Macmillan.

Kazin, M. (2016, November–December). Trump and American populism: Old whine, new bottles. *Foreign Affairs.*

Keenan, J. (2013, May 7). The grim reality behind the Philippines economic growth. *The Atlantic.* https://www.theatlantic.com/international/archive/2013/05/the-grim-reality-behind-the-philippines-economic-growth/275597/. Accessed 26 Mar 2019.

Lacaba, J. F. (Ed.). (1995). *Boss: 5 case studies of local politics in the Philippines.* Pasig: Philippine Center for Investigative Journalism.

Laclau, E. (2005). *On populist reason.* London: Verso.

Laothamatas, A. (2006). *Thaksina-prachaniyom [Thaksin-style populism].* Bangkok: Matichon.

Lewis, P., Clarke, S., & Barr, C. (2019, March 8). Revealed: Populist leaders linked to reduced inequality. *The Guardian.* https://www.theguardian.com/world/2019/mar/07/revealed-populist-leaders-linked-to-reduced-inequality. Accessed 26 Mar 2019.

Mietzner, M. (2019). Movement leaders, oligarchs, technocrats and autocratic mavericks: Populists in contemporary Asia. In C. de la Torre (Ed.), *Routledge handbook of global populism* (pp. 370–384). New York: Routledge.

Mishra, P. (2016). The globalization of rage: Why today's extremism looks familiar. *Foreign Affairs, 95*(6), 46–55.

Mouffe, C. (2018, September 10). Populists are on the rise, but this can be a moment for progressives too. *The Guardian*. https://www.theguardian.com/commentisfree/2018/sep/10/populists-rise-progressives-radical-right. Accessed 26 Mar 2019.

Mourdoukoutas, P. (2019, February 10). Duterte's jobless economic boom. *Forbes*. https://www.forbes.com/sites/panosmourdoukoutas/2019/02/10/dutertes-jobless-economic-boom/#706397e43ed3. Accessed 26 Mar 2019.

Mouzelis, N. (1985). On the concept of populism: Populist and clientelist modes of incorporation in semi peripheral polities. *Politics and Society, 14*(3), 329–348.

Mudde, C. (2004). The populist zeitgeist. *Government and Opposition, 39*(4), 541–563.

Mudde, C. (2016). Europe's populist surge: A long time in the making. *Foreign Affairs, 95*(6), 25–30.

O'Donnell, G., Whitehead, L., & Schmitter, P. C. (1986). *Transitions from authoritarian rule: Tentative conclusions about uncertain democracies*. Baltimore: Johns Hopkins University Press.

OECD. (2006, October). *OECD economic surveys: Indonesia*. Paris: OECD.

Oxhorn, P. (1998). The social foundations of Latin America's recurrent populism: Problems of popular sector class formation and collective action. *Journal of Historical Sociology, 11*(2), 212–246.

Pasuk, P., & Baker, C. (2008). Thaksin's populism. *Journal of Contemporary Asia, 38*(1), 62–83.

Putzel, J. (2018, May 25). The Philippines as an extreme case in the worldwide rise of populist politics. LSE Southeast Asia Centre Blog. https://medium.com/@lseseac/the-philippines-as-an-extreme-case-in-the-worldwide-rise-of-populist-politics-6cdd248a079b. Accessed 26 Mar 2019.

Robison, R., & Hadiz, V. R. (2004). *Reorganising power in Indonesia: The politics of oligarchy in an age of markets*. London: RoutledgeCurzon.

Rodan, G., & Hewison, K. (2004). Closing the circle? Globalization, conflict and political regimes. *Critical Asian Studies, 36*(3), 383–404.

Roniger, L. (2019). The missing piece in global populism: The role populism played in Central America. In C. de la Torre (Ed.), *Routledge handbook of global populism* (pp. 451–466). New York: Routledge.

Sabillo, K. A. (2016, February 14). Joma Sison talks about former student Duterte, other candidates. *Inquirer.net*. https://newsinfo.inquirer.net/764641/joma-sison-talks-about-former-student-duterte-other-candidates?utm_expid=.XqNwTug2W6nwDVUSgFJXed.1. Accessed 26 Mar 2019.

Sison, J. M. (2018, August 28). *Duterte is no.1 enemy of his own state*. https://josemariasison.org/duterte-is-no-1-enemy-of-his-own-state/. Accessed 26 Mar 2019.

Tuğal, C. (2016). *The fall of the Turkish model: How the Arab uprisings brought down Islamic liberalism*. London/New York: Verso.
Urbinati, N. (2014). *Democracy disfigured: Opinion, truth, and the people*. Cambridge, MA: Harvard University Press.
Weyland, K. (2017). Populism: A political strategy approach. In C. R. Kaltwasser, P. Taggart, P. O. Espejo, & P. Ostiguy (Eds.), *The Oxford handbook of populism* (pp. 48–72). Oxford: Oxford University Press.
World Bank. (1991). *Managing development: The governance dimension* (Discussion paper). Washington, DC: World Bank.
World Bank. (2001). *World development report 2002: Building institutions for markets*. Washington, DC: World Bank.
World Bank. (2012, August 20). *Thailand: Sustaining health protection for all*. http://www.worldbank.org/en/news/feature/2012/08/20/thailand-sustaining-health-protection-for-all. Accessed 26 Mar 2019.
World Bank. (2016). *Indonesia's rising divide*. Washington, DC: World Bank.
Yusuf, A. A., Sumner, A., & Rum, I. A. (2013). *The long-run evolution of inequality in Indonesia, 1990–2012* (USAID-SEADI discussion paper). Washington, DC: United States Agency for International Development.

CHAPTER 7

The Internationalisation of Capital and the Transformation of Statehood in Southeast Asia

Faris Al-Fadhat

INTRODUCTION

The state has played a critical role in the development of Southeast Asia's political economy. As this volume demonstrates, this has not taken the form of so-called "developmental states", insulated from domestic social forces and autonomously directing economies. On the contrary, states and social forces interpenetrate and shape one another (Hameiri and Jones, this volume). A key relationship, especially for the purposes of this chapter, is that between the state and the capitalist class (the bourgeoisie). In the Cold War period, Southeast Asia's capitalist classes were relatively weak, depending on authoritarian regimes to repress left-wing political parties and provide favourable conditions for capitalist economies to develop (see Carroll, and Quimpo, both this volume). In practice, this led to the emergence of tight networks of business, political and economic elites, with rampant corruption, collusion and cronyism attending the emergence of

F. Al-Fadhat (✉)
Faculty of Social and Political Sciences, Universitas Muhammadiyah Yogyakarta, Bantul, Indonesia
e-mail: farisalfadh@umy.ac.id

© The Author(s) 2020
T. Carroll et al. (eds.), *The Political Economy of Southeast Asia*, Studies in the Political Economy of Public Policy,
https://doi.org/10.1007/978-3-030-28255-4_7

new capitalist classes (e.g., Hewison 1989; Robison 1986; Rodan 1989). The consolidation of national states thus went hand-in-hand with the consolidation of national capitalist classes.

However, this chapter argues that this traditional Murdoch School proposition now requires some amendment in light of Southeast Asia's deepening insertion into the global political economy. Southeast Asia's rapid economic growth was achieved only by selectively liberalising national economies to international investment, networking the region into transnational production and trade networks (see Carroll, this volume). While certain fractions of national capitalist classes remained primarily interested in protecting their domestic markets from such tendencies, other fractions have increasingly pursued international strategies for capital accumulation. This is manifested through burgeoning cross-border company mergers, acquisitions and joint ventures. According to the *ASEAN Investment Report 2015*, cross-border capitalist expansion has become one of the most significant indicators of the region's economic development in recent years (ASEAN 2015: 30–32). The total value of mergers and acquisitions rose to US$68.4bn in 2014, a 12% increase from the previous year and exceeding the figure for Japan for the first time, where mergers and acquisitions totalled US$64.7bn (Darmayana and Meryana 2015; Ito 2015). This signifies the emergence of internationalised fractions of capital based in Southeast Asian territories (Al-Fadhat 2019).

For these groups, the state institutions that once served as a cocoon now serve as fetters on their further development—a perspective shared by transnational capitalists entering the region from outside. However, previous development processes have also led to key capitalist groups being directly incorporated into various state apparatuses (see Rodan et al. 2006). This gives transnationalising capitalists significant leverage to advance and safeguard their internationally oriented accumulation strategies by promoting the transformation of states. This manifests through the reduction of interventionist, developmentalist institutions in favour of a "regulatory state", whose reach extends across borders through various regulations and negotiations aimed at facilitating the overseas expansion of big businesses. This began in the 1980s with the adoption of export-oriented industrialisation policies to facilitate the engagement of local bourgeoisies with the global economy, evolving into the removal of barriers to flows of capital, goods and labour, towards the creation of larger markets. Hence, the political dominance of a transnationalised fraction of capital is organised in and through the internationalisation of the state.

Murdoch Meets Amsterdam: The State and the Rise of the Interior Bourgeoisie

The Amsterdam School of international political economy provides valuable theoretical insights that can be incorporated into the approach of the Murdoch School to help understand these developments. Amsterdam Scholars argue that internationalised fractions of capital have become important actors in the contemporary global economy through the process of transnational class formation, which gives rise to new socio-political alliances and forms of state (Jessop and Overbeek 2019; Overbeek 2004). Thus, changes in states' strategic policies towards promoting the global expansion of business activities have been shaped by complex social and political coalitions resulting from the increasingly international orientation of large-scale capital.

This development reflects important changes in the spatial organisation of capitalism and the state. Key to understanding these changes is the recognition that capitalism is never purely "economic" but always involves key political processes. Marx and Engels (1965 [1848]) famously noted that capital always tends to expand beyond existing territorial boundaries. Yet, as Palloix (1977) argued, the expansion of capital into an internationally coordinated market is no more a purely "economic" phenomenon than was the consolidation of national markets and the reorganisation of national bourgeoisie. Early "merchant adventurers" undertook risky international transactions on their own coin, developing private mechanisms of insurance. However, the development of large-scale international trade and investment required the provision of supportive infrastructure organised by the state, whether that be the "hard" infrastructure of roads, railways and ports to connect distant markets, and the security arrangements to safeguard these, or "soft" institutional infrastructure like treaties, laws and regulations to help govern economic interactions.

Palloix (1977) further theorised the development of capitalism globally in terms of three interrelated "circuits": the productive circuit (the production of commodities); the commodity circuit (the sale of these commodities); and the money circuit (the accumulation of capital as money). Each of these requires certain supportive infrastructure: a regime that pushes people towards selling their labour, legal rules that permit and govern the production of commodities and their exchange, the institution and maintenance of money and financial systems, and so on. In pre-capitalist societies, these things existed either partially or not at all. They had to be produced through the exercise of power, and typically it was ruling elites—organised in initially rudimentary but increasingly sophisticated states—that served this function. First city governments and centralising monarchs, and later regimes dominated by emerging bourgeoisies, helped to destroy feudal social relations that impeded the emergence of wage labour, and forcibly unified local markets, regulations and weights and measures into national spaces for capital accumulation. The productive power and taxation revenue unleashed by these transformations aided the emergence of powerful nation-states, especially in Europe. These states—and later their international organisations—were subsequently central in providing the infrastructure which allowed the expansion of capitalist classes beyond national markets, initially through outright imperialism and, more recently, through the more sophisticated mechanism with which this chapter is concerned: the transnationalisation of state apparatuses.

The transformation of statehood is intimately connected to the rise of international fractions of the capitalist class. After many years of capital accumulation within the cocoon of nation-states, large-scale enterprises emerge that can no longer "continue the accumulation process within the narrow horizon of the domestic market"; they represent a growing and eventually dominant fraction of a domestically operating capital that becomes intertwined with "external" capitalist dynamics (Tsoukalas 1999: 59). Such businesses, while "producing within a nation-state, can sell on global markets and reinvest in production beyond the borders of the nation-state in which the original production process took place" (Glassman 1999: 680). Therefore, they are no longer exclusively "national" but integrated within global and regional circuits of capital, production and value creation. Poulantzas (1978: 57) developed the concept of the "interior bourgeoisie" to denote this transformation of part of the "national" bourgeoisie into one that brought international competitive dynamics to bear on national political life. While its material basis is linked to a national political structure, the interior bourgeoisie also has deep ties with global capital and production chains, forming transnational power relations (Wissel 2006: 218–219). As Carroll et al. (2019) note, these international fractions of capital emerged through the broader structural story: "the intensified formation of the world market", a process of deepening economic globalisation. In this context, both fractions of capital and the state have been pressured to adopt market-conforming behaviours, further intensifying patterns of global capitalist relations.

Crucially, the growing domination of this internationalising fraction of capital, particularly since the 1980s, does not imply that the state becomes less important, as suggested by some scholars of the "transnational capitalist class" (e.g., Robinson 2007; Sklair 2001). On the contrary, its role has become more crucial to ensure the process of internationalisation of this interior bourgeoisie (Poulantzas 1974). Capital tends to expand and move at an ever-increasing pace across national borders, and thus seems to operate at an "international" scale. Nevertheless, the production and accumulation of value must necessarily take place in territorially bounded and place-specific locations. And this requires national institutions to manage economic policies and ensure the continued maintenance of conditions favourable to capitalist accumulation (Panitch and Gindin 2004: 17). Thus, the global expansion of capital still requires the state to play a role, but a revised one: the facilitation of transnational circuits of capital, as opposed to its earlier role in facilitating national-scale accumulation strategies.

This contributes to the transformation of the state, which further shapes the nature of statehood as a locus of political struggle in the accumulation process (Bieler and Morton 2014; Glassman 1999). This transformation involves the political and economic structure of the state being adjusted to suit changes in the formations, priorities and interests of dominant social forces—namely, the capitalist class, particularly its internationalising fraction. The transformed state's role is to help (re)produce the social relationships that underpin capitalist expansion beyond territorial frontiers (Jessop 2015; Jones 1997; MacLeod and Goodwin 1999). Furthermore, such internationalisation processes have led to the broadening of the political coalitions of bourgeoisies beyond state territories through both global *and* regional capitalist networks.

The Internationalisation of Capital, the State and Crony Capitalism in Southeast Asia

The Amsterdam School has studied these transformations in developed countries, but there is now solid evidence of the emergence of an "interior bourgeoisie" in Southeast Asia, too, along with associated changes in the nature of statehood. This section provides an overview of the internationalisation of capital in the region, and how this is reshaping governance in three key cases: Indonesia, Singapore and Malaysia. In each case, the emergence of an internationalised capitalist class fraction, initially cultivated by the state, has led to the restructuring of state power to facilitate the regionalisation of capital accumulation. The character of regionalisation is heavily shaped by the state–society relations established under previous accumulation regimes.

Most of this regionalisation has occurred since the 1997–98 Asian financial crisis. The crisis struck directly at the alliances between capitalists and state apparatuses in Southeast Asia, with many leading conglomerates apparently facing bankruptcy (see Carroll, this volume). However, in retrospect, we can now observe that many were able not only to recover relatively quickly but, perhaps more importantly, to integrate their operations into transnational capitalist networks. While their domination within domestic economies remains strong, many of these business giants have expanded their reach beyond national economic frontiers—something new for many, notwithstanding their growing global engagement from the 1980s onwards.

Data on outbound foreign direct investment (OFDI) clearly shows the growing internationalisation of capital (see Fig. 7.1). In the period 2004–17,

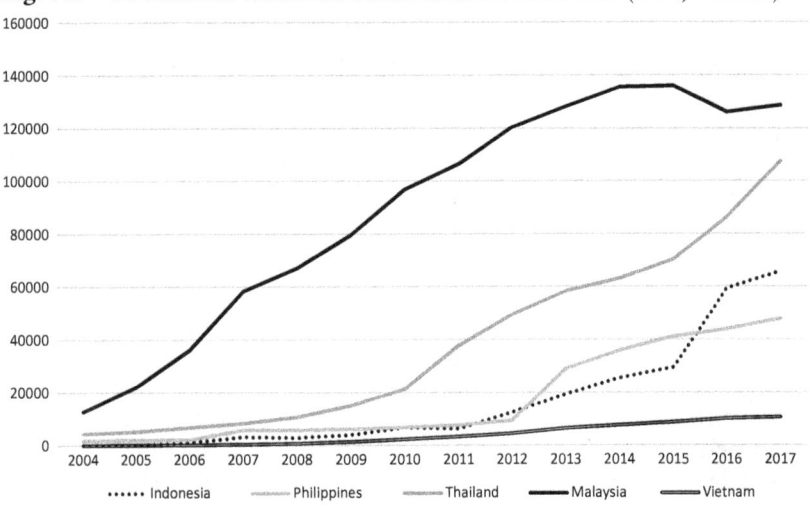

Fig. 7.1 OFDI stocks of selected Southeast Asian economies (US$, millions)

Source: UNCTAD 2018

the OFDI stock of Indonesia increased from zero to about US$65.9bn; the Philippines' OFDI increased from US$1.8bn to US$45.3bn; and Malaysian OFDI boomed, growing from US$12.8bn to US$128.5bn. The numbers would be even bigger if investments carried out by Southeast Asian companies' offshore holding companies outside of the region were included.

In this context, neoliberal agendas have been crucial in shaping the forms of governance and arrangement of economic activities that have emerged transnationally. Unilaterally, governments have restructured domestic states to facilitate the increasing flows of investment, production and trade. Governments have also increasingly sought to coordinate their regulations across national frontiers. This has given rise to informal and formal efforts to integrate markets across territorial borders, including at the regional scale (see Jones and Hameiri, this volume). Progress may be limited by contestations between fractions of capital: between internationalising fractions which stand to benefit, and residual "national" fractions that would lose out from market liberalisation; and between rival internationalising fractions emerging from different national contexts. These contestations shape the forms of state transformation and regional governance that emerge in practice. We will now turn to examine how these processes are unfolding in Southeast Asia.

The Internationalisation of Indonesian Capital

Suharto's New Order regime (1967–98) profoundly shaped the emergence of Indonesia's capitalist class. Authoritarian state-led development and patrimonialism consolidated a highly concentrated, domestically oriented capitalist class, undertaking very little international business activity, despite the export-oriented policies adopted in the 1980s (Crouch 1994; Robison 1986). However, the two decades since Suharto's fall have seen many Indonesian conglomerates venturing beyond the national economy. By developing relationships with foreign corporations to bolster their business operations, they have acquired a strong international orientation. This has been achieved through substantial investments into foreign markets; takeovers of foreign-based companies through mergers, acquisitions and joint ventures; and by playing a more significant role in regional value chains. While many large Indonesian companies continue to enjoy protection in the national market, particularly in the agricultural sector, they have also begun to advocate for further liberalisation at the regional level

(Al-Fadhat 2019). This illustrates the fact that capital is interested in making profit above all else, leading companies to support ostensibly contradictory governance arrangements insofar as these advance their interests.

Indonesian conglomerates dominate many domestic sectors, such as plantations, automobiles and mining. In the plantation sector—notably paper and oil palm—they have benefited from the conversion of vast areas of Indonesian forest for agribusiness, producing the largest plantation area of any Southeast Asian country. Unsurprisingly, the most notable business groups, such as Djarum, Sinar Mas, Gudang Garam, Salim, Rajawali, Royal Golden Eagle and Wilmar, have undertaken substantial investment in this sector. Their expansion has been supported by the conglomerates' foreign-listed management holdings and, importantly, by China's enormous investment in the region (Dewi 2013: 166). In the case of the automotive sector, business groups like Astra International and Indomobil (Salim's subsidiary) have formed joint ventures with Honda, Toyota and Suzuki to produce these brands in Indonesia for domestic and foreign consumption.

These traditional activities have been augmented by three new sectors that have expanded significantly in recent years: food and agribusiness, services (telecommunications, banking and real estate) and infrastructure. For example, conglomerates such as Royal Golden Eagle, Sinar Mas Group and Salim Group have established a strong position in the Asia-Pacific's food and agribusiness sector by acquiring companies in Singapore, Malaysia, Vietnam, China and Australia (First Pacific 2015; Golden Agri Resources 2017; RGE 2016). This regional expansion has allowed Indonesian businesses to move from their original strategy of producing goods domestically, for either domestic consumption or sometimes for export, to a vertically integrated strategy, controlling all stages of food production in value chains spread across the Asian region (Al-Fadhat 2018).

In the services sector, a similar expansion has been supported by strong economic expansion and population growth, indicating the region's large market potential (UNCTAD 2015: 41). A key example here is Lippo Group. In the real estate sector, Lippo Group consolidated its business under Lippo Karawaci—the largest property company in Indonesia—then collaborated with the Chinese state-owned China Resources Group and the Japanese company Mitsubishi Corp to expand across the region. Through mergers and acquisitions, Lippo's real estate portfolio has expanded into several Southeast Asian countries, including Singapore,

Malaysia and Vietnam, in addition to Hong Kong, China and South Korea (Lippo Karawaci 2008; Lippo Limited 2016).

Indonesian business groups have also played a role in the expansion of regional investment in the infrastructure sector. Many projects have been launched by Southeast Asian governments in recent years to address issues like the notorious traffic problems plaguing the region's capital cities, especially Manila, Jakarta and Bangkok (Koyanagi 2017). Several infrastructure projects in Metro Manila, including power generation, water supply and toll-roads, have been undertaken by Indonesia's Salim Group through Metro Pacific Investments Corporation, under its First Pacific subsidiary (First Pacific 2006).

The regional expansion of this internationally competitive section of Indonesia's bourgeoisie has led to the internationalisation of the state (Hameiri and Jones 2015). These changes were enabled and shaped by the oligarchic power relations established under Suharto, which have entrenched dominant business interests within political and bureaucratic institutions. Major post-Suharto political parties have also been led and controlled by business elites. For example, during 2009–14, Golkar was led by Aburizal Bakrie, chairman of Bakrie Group; from 2010 to 2015, the National Mandate Party was led by Hatta Rajasa, owner of Arthindo Group; and Gerindra was established in 2008 by Prabowo Subianto, Suharto's former son-in-law, who runs energy, plantation, mining and forestry businesses through Nusantara Group.

Strategic ministries key to economic policies, such as the Coordinating Ministry for Economic Affairs, the Ministry of Trade, and the Investment Coordinating Board have also been linked to big business elites or their associates. For example, since 2004, every Minister of Trade has been drawn from the business elite. Mari Elka Pangestu (minister from 2004 to 2011) and Gita Wirjawan (2011–14) are co-founders of Ancora Capital Management (Asia); Muhammad Lutfi (2014) is the co-founder of the Mahaka Group; Rachmat Gobel (2014–15) is the chairman of the Panasonic Gobel Group; Thomas Lembong (who served 2015–16, before being made chairman of the Investment Coordinating Board), is the CEO of Quvat Capital; and Enggartiasto Lukita (2016–present), despite her technocratic credentials, is a close ally of Sofjan Wanandi, chairman of Santini Group.

This strong instrumental control of state power has allowed Indonesia's interior bourgeoisie to shift government economic policy towards facilitating further capital expansion across the region and smoothing

Indonesia's integration with the global economy. For example, supporting business groups' international expansion is integral to the Indonesian government's "Masterplan for the Acceleration and Expansion of Economic Development of Indonesia 2011–2025" (known as MP3EI). One of its priorities is to enhance the interlocking of conglomerates' operations with the regional circuits of capital, especially through the neoliberal regulatory project of ASEAN economic integration (Coordinating Ministry for Economic Affairs 2011; see Jones and Hameiri, this volume). MP3EI seeks to increase capital flows across the region by implementing the ASEAN Comprehensive Investment Agreement. This agreement attempts to bolster the region's attractiveness as a single investment destination by establishing a free, open, transparent and integrated investment regime for domestic and international investors. The agreement supports the internationalisation of competitive fractions of regional capital by promoting progressive investment liberalisation across the region, establishing principles of non-discrimination and transparency, protecting investors from confiscation, and creating investor–state dispute settlement mechanisms. ASEAN member countries are thereby pushed to support corporate expansion, joint investment and regional production networks (ASEAN 2009).

The Internationalisation of Singaporean Capital

The case of Singapore illustrates how the internationalisation of capital has been facilitated by the state, and has in turn shaped the state's restructuring. The cohesion between the state and capital, supported through the formation of political institutions and government policies, has pushed economic and political governance in Singapore in a direction that is neither liberal nor democratic (see Rodan and Baker, this volume). But, most importantly, this alliance has strengthened a globalised strategy of capital accumulation through state capitalism. The internationalising fractions of Singaporean capital mainly comprised government-linked companies (GLCs), with their transnationalisation facilitated by the state from the 1980s onwards.

The roots of Singapore's state capitalism lie in the strategies of the ruling People's Action Party (PAP), which has governed Singapore since 1959. The PAP had an uneasy relationship with the city-state's domestic capitalists, doubting both their political loyalty and their capacity to industrialise Singapore. Accordingly, the PAP regime pursued post-independence development largely through developing GLCs and attracting international capital. This was reinforced after 1965 when, following Singapore's expulsion from Malaysia, the extreme limits of the city-state's domestic market—just four million people—led the PAP to embrace export-oriented industrialisation (EOI) (Boswell and Chase-Dunn 2000; Yahya 2005). The Economic Development Board (EDB), established in 1961, spearheaded the drive to attract multinational corporations (MNCs) to invest in Singapore (Okposin 1999; Yahya 2005), while state policies created the necessary physical, technical and social conditions for industrial production (Chua 1997; Tremewan 1994). As a result, foreign direct investment (FDI) increased significantly. For example, in the manufacturing sector, FDI rose from S$157m in 1965 to S$995m in 1970, then S$3.1bn by 1974. Over the same period, the value of Singapore's manufactured exports jumped from S$349m to S$1.5bn, to S$7.8bn (Rodan 2006: 143).

The GLCs form the core of Singapore's interior bourgeoisie. GLCs have proliferated through three paths: partnerships with MNCs; spin-offs from defence industries; and privatised state monopolies and public utilities (Chua 2016: 502). By the 1990s, major GLCs had begun to venture overseas, supported by Singapore's foreign economic policy, which aimed to facilitate the internationalisation of Singaporean capital across the regional market (Wong and Ng 1997: 136). This strategy was spurred by structural limits to the expansion of Singapore's manufacturing sector in the mid-1980s, as well as the global economic recession in that same period. In addition to the small size of Singapore's domestic market, GLCs' expansion at home was also constrained by the wage increases authorised by the National Wages Council in the 1970s, which decreased the competitiveness of Singaporean exports. The oil shocks and global recession of the 1970s, coupled with growing competition from manufacturing bases emerging in other Southeast Asian countries added to GLCs' problems (see Carroll, this volume). Accordingly, in the mid-1980s, the PAP government's newly formed Economic Committee launched restructuring policies to shift the economy towards high-tech industries, seeking to attract more foreign MNCs to establish operations in Singapore, and urging GLCs to invest in regional and global ventures (*Asia Times* 2002; Muller 1994; Rodan 2016). This spurred many GLCs to begin offshoring their operations to lower-wage territories, initially in the neighbouring Indonesian islands of Riau.

The internationalisation of the Singaporean state was critical in supporting the GLCs' overseas expansion. The EDB and the Trade Development Board—later renamed International Enterprise Singapore or IE Singapore (a statutory board under the Ministry of Trade and Industry)—played a significant role in facilitating overseas investment and trade (IE Singapore 2016). In addition, the government established a sovereign wealth fund, the Government of Singapore Investment Corporation (GIC) in 1981 to support GLCs' international expansion. By 1983, the GIC had extensive investment overseas totalling S$3bn and involving 58 companies (Rodan 1989: 153–154; 2006: 144). By March 2014, Singapore's largest GLC, Temasek Holdings, boasted an investment portfolio of S$223bn (Temasek Holdings 2014: 6). According to the Sovereign Wealth Fund Institute, by 2018 GIC's overseas investment had reached S$467bn, making it the eighth largest sovereign wealth fund in the world (GIC 2018; Tan 2018).

The internationalisation of Singapore's capital and state has created new spaces of capital accumulation and associated regulatory projects. One of Singapore's early symbolic initiatives was the Growth Triangle, a project which had been proposed by Singaporean government since the 1980s and which officially began in 1990. The idea was for the Malaysian state of Johor and the nearby Riau Islands of Indonesia to combine with Singapore as a coherent, trans-state economic zone of complementary specialisations (Parsonage 1992; Smith 1997). The project was essential for Singapore as it provided a spatial fix for GLCs' structural limitations at home—rising wages and the declining competitiveness of its low value-added manufacturing sectors. Offshoring labour-intensive manufacturing to lower-wage adjacent territories enabled the GLCs to recover their international competitiveness (Dent 2003; Smith 1997). Meanwhile, Singapore itself was reconfigured to host non-regional MNCs engaged in higher-value, knowledge-intensive production, thereby supporting the city-state's industrial upgrading (Smith 1997). Importantly, the realisation of Singapore's transnational economic restructuring was enabled by the complementary shift of Malaysian and Indonesian policies towards EOI since the 1980s, which sought increased investment from MNCs and allowed the liberalisation of some industries.

The Singaporean government has also been the principal architect of the ASEAN Economic Community (AEC), a regulatory project designed to integrate the entire Southeast Asian regional economy and attract more foreign capital into the region. The PAP government proposed this regional governance regime during the eighth ASEAN summit in Phnom Penh in November 2002. The creation of an integrated regional market provides an important new scale of accumulation for Singaporean capital, as Singapore drives its GLCs to become dominant regional and global players (Tsui-Auch 2006: 107). While the Growth Triangle was primarily driven by Singaporean manufacturing capital, the AEC project instead sought to bolster Singapore's new position as a regional services hub, particularly for GLCs and their foreign partners operating in business, finance, logistics and distribution, communications and information. Singapore's competitive advantage in services is underpinned by its strategic location, its advanced physical infrastructure and its minimal restrictions on the movement of goods, services and production (Chia 2005: 9). The AEC aimed to reduce barriers to the expansion of these sectors across the region.

Unsurprisingly, Singaporean conglomerates now dominate the list of ASEAN's top 50 companies, holding four of the top five spots in 2014. Singapore Telecommunications (SingTel) was first, followed by Singapore's three biggest banks: DBS Group Holdings, Oversea-Chinese Banking Corporation and United Overseas Bank (*Nikkei Asian Review* 2014). This testifies to the enormous expansion of Singaporean investment in ASEAN markets since the AEC project was initiated. When the agreement to build the AEC was signed in 2003, Singapore's total OFDI from the corporate sector amounted to S$153bn, of which S$34bn was invested in ASEAN (Department of Statistics Singapore 2009). This increased to S$783bn in 2016, just a year after the AEC was officially launched, of which direct investment in ASEAN countries comprised over S$119bn (Department of Statistics Singapore 2016).

The Internationalisation of Malaysian Capital

The important role played by the state in facilitating the internationalisation of capital is also shown in the case of Malaysia. Here, the process is rooted in the state restructuring undertaken under the New Economic Policy (NEP). The NEP was introduced in the early 1970s in response to anti-Chinese rioting among indigenous Malays (aka *bumiputera*, "sons of the soil"), who resented the long-standing ethnic-Chinese domination of the Malaysian economy. The NEP was characterised by strong state intervention by the ethnic-Malay ruling elite, led by the United Malay National Organisation (UMNO), to redistribute wealth away from the Chinese and cultivate a Malay capitalist class. Over time, this intervention established *bumiputera* enterprises with a strong interest in internationalising their activities, and the political connections required to harness the state towards this end.

The NEP established a Malay fraction of the capitalist class in a variety of ways, including the encouragement of divestment by Western companies, the facilitation of joint ventures with ethnic-Chinese-owned businesses (so-called "Ali-Baba" partnerships), and the privatisation of state assets (Gomez 2006: 121). Through privatisation, former state managers and senior bureaucrats were transferred to the private sector, and many privatised assets were sold to companies whose owners were closely connected to UMNO. The government also used its control over the banking sector to direct capital towards favoured enterprises, including the provision of loans to purchase state assets (Gomez and Jomo 1997). As a result, the equity held by *bumiputera* businesses and government-managed *bumiputera* trusts increased from 2.4% in 1970 to 20.6% in 1995 (Gomez 2006: 121). Thus, state intervention promoted the rapid rise of ethnic Malay-owned business groups with intimate ties to political and bureaucratic elites.

In the mid-1980s, under Prime Minister Mahathir Mohamad, the state began to facilitate the internationalisation of capital through an EOI strategy. This process was part of Mahathir's grand vision for Malaysia to achieve developed nation status by 2020. It was also driven by the emergence of internationally oriented Malay capitalists, organised through the Bumiputera Commercial and Industrial Community (BCIC). Mahathir promoted a "Malaysia Inc." model, based on the experience of "Japan Inc.", whereby state intervention would promote domestic industry and aid its internationalisation (Chee and Gomez 1994). The Ministry of Trade and Industry, modelled on Japan's Ministry of International Trade and Industry, was tasked with driving EOI (Gomez 2009: 357), and determined the industrial sectors that private firms should venture into (Webster 2014).

One of the internationalisation strategies that emerged was state-mediated joint ventures between local capitalists and foreign corporations. An important example is Malaysian heavy industry, especially Heavy Industries Corporation of Malaysia (HICOM). This state-owned company collaborated primarily with Japanese companies to develop a variety of industries, ranging from steel, iron and cement production to car manufacturing (Gomez 2009). In the car sector, the government led negotiations with the Japanese firm Mitsubishi to establish the joint-venture

Perusahaan Otomobil Nasional (Proton), the Malaysian national car company, with HICOM holding a controlling interest. Edaran Otomobil Nasional was established by HICOM in 1985 to handle the sales of one of Proton's products. Following arguments between the Malaysian government and Mitsubishi on the transfer of technology, another joint venture was subsequently formed with Japan's Daihatsu, and Malaysia's second national car project was introduced through another joint venture, Perusahaan Otomobil Kedua (Perodua), between Japan's Mitsui and local firm United Motor Works, which was also under state control (Gomez 2009: 358). Mahathir also encouraged conglomerates to establish joint ventures with European manufacturers to produce new models of the national car. One project involved France's PSA Peugeot Citroën and the publicly listed Diversified Resources, controlled by UMNO politician Yahaya Ahmad (Gomez 2009).

In the early 1990s, Mahathir realised the importance of Chinese capital for promoting the country's industrialisation. As China opened up its economy, Mahathir saw this as potentially lucrative for Malaysian businesses. This led to a new economic liberalisation policy that included Chinese capital in Malaysia's development plans (Gomez 2009: 361). Mahathir's strategy was to urge greater business cooperation between Chinese and Malay businesses to enhance Malaysia's industry as well as to expand into the Chinese market—something that had not happened earlier following the NEP strategy. Entering China's enormous market was thus a means to further promote the internationalisation of Malay capital (Gomez 2009: 362).

The Malaysian state has also pursued regional integration to create new spaces of capital accumulation for Malay-owned enterprises. In 1990, before the ASEAN Free Trade Area (AFTA) was established, Mahathir proposed a regional free trade block called the East Asia Economic Caucus (EAEC), to encompass ASEAN member states, Japan, China and South Korea (Akrasanee and Stifel 1992: 44). The EAEC was considered a counterweight to the emerging regional blocs in Europe and North America, and signified the desire of Malaysian firms to access a broad export market in the region. The EAEC was never officially formed, as a result of Japan's reluctance and strong opposition from the US and Australia, but the ASEAN Plus Three grouping, formed after the Asian financial crisis, was a looser form of Mahathir's vision. In the interim, Malaysia shifted its attention to AFTA. The government's policies here illustrated just how closely state practices mirrored the interests of particular fractions of capital:

where trade liberalisation would benefit Malaysian businesses, the government strongly backed AFTA measures and their implementation, but foot-dragging ensued wherever liberalisation would undermine *bumiputera* businesses, such as the automotive sector (see Athukorala 2003: 31; Nesadurai 2003: 128).

Economic restructuring following the Asian financial crisis also saw more Malaysian capitalists seek to reorganise themselves on a transnational scale, spurring further transformations in the Malaysian state, manifested in strong (although, again, uneven) support for the AEC (Lee 2014; Tan 2015; see also Jones and Hameiri, this volume). One of the key factors driving this was a concern to reduce barriers for Malaysian firms wishing to access regional markets (Alavi 2014: 231). In the banking sector, for instance, Malaysia's two largest banks, Maybank and CIMB Group, are now among the largest banks in Southeast Asia. In 2014, they were ranked in the top 25 ASEAN companies by market capitalization (Nikkei Asian Review 2014). According to Nazir Razak, chairman of CIMB Group, the opening of the regional market has enabled CIMB to strengthen its business operations in terms of intra-ASEAN trade and capital investments (Razak 2016: 37; Tan 2016).

Conclusion

A key theme in Murdoch School scholarship has always been the analysis of the process by which capitalist classes form and become important political and social forces. This chapter has developed this scholarship further by examining the changing nature of the capitalist class, through its internationalisation in the 1990s and beyond. It has advocated for a fruitful and productive engagement with the Amsterdam School of political economy, which has focused on the formation of transnational capitalist class fractions, and its impact on the forms and outcomes of political order and alliances within the state (van Apeldoorn 2004; Jessop and Overbeek 2019; Overbeek 2004). Much of this work remains highly Eurocentric, but it does not need to be: there is clearly strong evidence of similar trends in Southeast Asia. The Murdoch School tradition provides an analysis of the development of the interior bourgeoisie in the specific circumstances of Southeast Asia's political economy, which can explain the specific forms of state transformation we witness as domestically nurtured businesses internationalise.

Bringing these two traditions together, this chapter has explained the recent transformation of the capitalist class in Southeast Asia and attendant transformations in the form and functions of the state. There has clearly been a substantial shift from the consolidation of nationally oriented bourgeoisies through statist policies in the 1970s and 1980s to the emergence of new internationally oriented fractions of capital, especially after the Asian financial crisis, and states' facilitation of their transnational expansion. The nature of this "interior bourgeoisie" and its political project, however, is shaped by the legacies of previous rounds of state-led development.

References

Akrasanee, N., & Stifel, D. (1992). The political economy of the ASEAN free trade area. In P. Imada & S. Naya (Eds.), *ASEAN: The way ahead* (pp. 27–47). Singapore: Institute of Southeast Asian Studies.
Alavi, R. (2014). Malaysia's participation in the ASEAN Economic Community. In S. Basu Das & L. P. Onn (Eds.), *Malaysia's socio-economic transformation: Ideas for the next decade* (pp. 227–260). Singapore: ISEAS Publishing.
Al-Fadhat, F. (2018). Regional value chains and the internationalisation of Indonesian business. In J. D. Wilson (Ed.), *Expanding horizons: Indonesia's regional engagement in the Indo-Pacific era* (pp. 9–21). Perth: Perth USAsia Centre.
Al-Fadhat, F. (2019). *The rise of international capital: Indonesian conglomerates in ASEAN*. Singapore: Palgrave Macmillan.
ASEAN. (2009). *ASEAN comprehensive investment agreement*. Jakarta: ASEAN Secretariat.
ASEAN. (2015). *ASEAN investment report 2015: Infrastructure investment and connectivity*. Jakarta: ASEAN Secretariat and UNCTAD.
Asia Times. (2002, July 27). Singapore's regionalization challenge. *Asia Times*.
Athukorala, P. (2003). *Crisis and recovery in Malaysia: The role of capital controls*. Cheltenham: Edward Elgar.
Bieler, A., & Morton, A. D. (2014). The will-o'-the-wisp of the transnational state. *Journal of Australian Political Economy, 72*, 23–51.
Boswell, T., & Chase-Dunn, C. K. (2000). *The spiral of capitalism and socialism: Toward global democracy*. Boulder: Lynne Rienner.
Carroll, T., Gonzalez-Vicente, R., & Jarvis, D. S. L. (2019). Capital, conflict and convergence: A political understanding of neoliberalism and its relationship to capitalist transformation. *Globalizations*. https://doi.org/10.1080/14747731.2018.1560183.

Chee, P. L., & Gomez, E. T. (1994). Malaysian sogoshoshas: Superficial cloning, failed emulation. In K. S. Jomo (Ed.), *Japan and Malaysian development: In the shadow of the rising sun* (pp. 232–243). London: Routledge.

Chia, S. Y. (2005). *The Singapore model of industrial policy: Past evolution and current thinking*. Paper presented at the LAEBA second annual meeting, Buenos Aires, Argentina, 28–29 November 2005.

Chua, B. H. (1997). *Political legitimacy and housing: Stakeholding in Singapore*. Abingdon: Routledge.

Chua, B. H. (2016). State-owned enterprises, state capitalism and social distribution in Singapore. *The Pacific Review, 29*(4), 499–521.

Coordinating Ministry for Economic Affairs. (2011). *Masterplan for acceleration and expansion of Indonesia economic development*. Jakarta: Coordinating Ministry for Economic Affairs.

Crouch, H. (1994). Indonesia: An uncertain outlook. *Southeast Asian Affairs, 21*(1), 121–145.

Darmayana, H., & Meryana, E. (2015). Makin Eksis Merambah Kawasan. *Bloomberg Businessweek Indonesia*, 30 March–5 April, 20–22.

Dent, C. M. (2003). Transnational capital, the state and foreign economic policy: Singapore, South Korea and Taiwan. *Review of International Political Economy, 10*(2), 246–277.

Department of Statistics Singapore. (2009). *Singapore's investment abroad 2007*. Singapore: Department of Statistics, Ministry of Trade and Industry.

Department of Statistics Singapore. (2016). *Singapore's direct investment abroad 2016*. Singapore: Department of Statistics, Ministry of Trade and Industry.

Dewi, O. (2013). Reconciling development, conservation, and social justice in West Kalimantan. In O. Pye & J. Bhattacharya (Eds.), *The palm oil controversy in Southeast Asia: A transnational perspective* (pp. 164–178). Singapore: ISEAS Publishing.

First Pacific. (2006). *Annual report 2006*. Hong Kong: First Pacific Company Limited. http://www.firstpacific.com/wp-content/uploads/2015/08/3497_ear2006.pdf. Accessed 19 Oct 2015.

First Pacific. (2015). *Annual report 2015: Creating long-term value in Asia*. Hong Kong: First Pacific Company Limited. http://www.firstpacific.com/wp-content/uploads/2015/08/First-Pacific-2015-Annual-Report.pdf.   Accessed 15 Mar 2017.

GIC [Government of Singapore Investment Corporation]. (2018). *GIC: Report on the management of the government's portfolio for the year 2017/18*. Singapore: GIC.

Glassman, J. (1999). State power beyond the "territorial trap": The internationalization of the state. *Political Geography, 18*(6), 669–696.

Golden Agri-Resources. (2017). *Annual report 2017: Responsible growth through innovation*. Singapore: Golden Agri-Resources Ltd.

Gomez, E. T. (2006). Malaysian business groups: The state and capital development in the post-currency crisis period. In S. Chang (Ed.), *Business groups in East Asia: Financial crisis, restructuring, and new growth* (pp. 119–146). Oxford: Oxford University Press.

Gomez, E. T. (2009). The rise and fall of capital: Corporate Malaysia in historical perspective. *Journal of Contemporary Asia, 39*(3), 345–381.

Gomez, E. T., & Jomo, K. S. (1997). *Malaysia's political economy: Politics, patronage and profits*. Cambridge: Cambridge University Press.

Hameiri, S., & Jones, L. (2015). Global governance as state transformation. *Political Studies, 64*(4), 793–810.

Hewison, K. (1989). *Bankers and bureaucrats: Capital and the role of the state in Thailand*. New Haven: Yale University Press.

IE Singapore. (2016). *Annual report 2015/2016: The multiplier effect*. Singapore: International Enterprise Singapore.

Ito, M. (2015, February 2). Economic integration driving buyout boom in Southeast Asia. *Nikkei Asian Review*. https://asia.nikkei.com/Business/Trends/Economic-integration-driving-buyout-boom-in-Southeast-Asia. Accessed 28 July 2017.

Jessop, B. (2015). Crises, crisis-management and state restructuring: What future for the state? *Policy & Politics, 43*(4), 475–492.

Jessop, B., & Overbeek, H. (Eds.). (2019). *Transnational capital and class fractions: The Amsterdam School perspective reconsidered*. New York: Routledge.

Jones, M. R. (1997). Spatial selectivity of the state? The regulationist enigma and local struggles over economic governance. *Environment and Planning A, 29*(5), 831–864.

Koyanagi, K. (2017, November 22). Emerging Asian economies race to build metros amid choking congestion. *Nikkei Asian Review*. https://asia.nikkei.com/magazine/20171123/On-the-Cover/Emerging-Asian-economies-race-to-build-metros-amid-choking-congestion. Accessed 20 Mar 2018.

Lee, L. (2014, August 21). Malaysia more receptive to ASEAN Economic Community. *The Star Online*. http://www.thestar.com.my/business/business-news/2014/08/21/malaysia-more-ready-than-neighbours-for-asean-economic-community/. Accessed 19 June 2017.

Lippo Karawaci. (2008). *Annual report 2008: Towards global excellence*. Jakarta: PT Lippo Karawaci Tbk. https://www.lippokarawaci.co.id/uploads/file/Publication/AnnualReport/AnnualReport2008_EN.pdf. Accessed 22 June 2017.

Lippo Limited. (2016). *Annual report 2015/2016*. Hong Kong: Lippo Limited.

MacLeod, G., & Goodwin, M. (1999). Reconstructing an urban and regional political economy: On the state, politics, scale, and explanation. *Political Geography, 18*(6), 697–730.

Marx, K., & Engels, F. (1965 [1848]). Manifesto of the Communist Party. In K. Marx & F. Engels (Eds.), *Selected works* (pp. 35–63). New York: International Publishers.
Muller, A. L. (1994). Industrial policy in Singapore. *The South African Journal of Economics, 62*(3), 146–155.
Nesadurai, H. E. S. (2003). *Globalisation, domestic politics and regionalism: The ASEAN free trade area*. London: Routledge.
Nikkei Asian Review. (2014, November 20). The region's top companies: ASEAN 100. http://asia.nikkei.com/magazine/20141120-THE-REGION-S-TOP-COMPANIES/Cover-Story/The-regions-top-companies-ASEAN-100. Accessed 20 June 2016.
Okposin, S. B. (1999). *The extent of Singapore's investments abroad*. Aldershot: Ashgate Publishers.
Overbeek, H. (2004). Transnational class formation and concepts of control: Towards a genealogy of the Amsterdam Project in international political economy. *Journal of International Relations and Development, 7*(2), 113–141.
Palloix, C. (1977). The self-expansion of capital on a world scale. *Review of Radical Political Economics, 9*(2), 3–17.
Panitch, L., & Gindin, S. (2004). Global capitalism and American empire. In C. Leys & L. Panitch (Eds.), *Socialist register 2004: The new imperial challenge* (pp. 1–42). London: Merlin Press.
Parsonage, J. (1992). Southeast Asia's "Growth Triangle": A subregional response to global transformation. *International Journal of Urban and Regional Research, 16*(2), 307–317.
Poulantzas, N. (1974). Internationalisation of capitalist relations and the nation-state. *Economy and Society, 3*(2), 145–179.
Poulantzas, N. (1978). *State, power, socialism*. London: Verso.
Razak, N. D. S. (2016). ASEAN Economic Community in 2025. In *Asia 2025* (pp. 37–40). London: Asia House.
RGE [Royal Golden Eagle]. (2016). *Our history: From local to global*. Singapore: Royal Golden Eagle. http://www.rgei.com/about/our-history. Accessed 18 Mar 2017.
Robinson, W. (2007). The pitfalls of realist analysis of global capitalism: A critique of Ellen Meiksins Wood's Empire of Capital. *Historical Materialism, 15*(3), 71–93.
Robison, R. (1986). *Indonesia: The rise of capital*. Sydney: Allen and Unwin.
Rodan, G. (1989). *The political economy of Singapore's industrialization: National state and international capital*. Basingstoke: Macmillan.
Rodan, G. (2006). Singapore: Globalisation, the state, and politics. In G. Rodan, K. Hewison, & R. Robison (Eds.), *The political economy of South-East Asia: Markets, power, and contestation* (pp. 137–169). Melbourne: Oxford University Press.

Rodan, G. (2016). Capitalism, inequality and ideology in Singapore: New challenges for the ruling party. *Asian Studies Review, 40*(2), 211–230.

Rodan, G., Hewison, K., & Robison, R. (Eds.). (2006). *The political economy of South-East Asia: Markets, power and contestation.* Melbourne: Oxford University Press.

Sklair, L. (2001). *The transnational capitalist class.* Oxford: Blackwell.

Smith, S. L. D. (1997). The Indonesia–Malaysia–Singapore growth triangle: A political and economic equation. *Australian Journal of International Affairs, 51*(3), 369–382.

Tan, C. K. (2015, November 18). Malaysia gears up to declare regional integration. *Nikkei Asian Review.* http://asia.nikkei.com/Business/Companies/IndonesianconglomeratefacilitatingJapaneselistings. Accessed 19 June 2017.

Tan, C. K. (2016, September 1). CIMB chief calls on the private sector to move integration forward. *Nikkei Asian Review.* http://asia.nikkei.com/magazine/20160901-ASEAN-THE-GREAT-PUZZLE/On-the-Cover/CIMB-chief-calls-on-the-private-sector-to-move-integration-forward. Accessed 19 June 2017.

Tan, A. (2018, July 13). GIC 20-year returns ease to 3.4% amid challenging climate. *The Business Times.* https://www.businesstimes.com.sg/government-economy/gic-20-year-returns-ease-to-34-amid-challenging-climate. Accessed 10 Mar 2019.

Temasek Holdings. (2014). *Temasek review 2014.* Singapore: Temasek Holdings.

Tremewan, C. (1994). *The political economy of social control in Singapore.* Basingstoke: Macmillan Press.

Tsoukalas, K. (1999). Globalisation and the executive committee: Reflections on the contemporary capitalist state. In L. Panitch & C. Leys (Eds.), *Socialist register 1999: Global capitalism versus democracy* (pp. 56–75). London: Merlin Press.

Tsui-Auch, L. S. (2006). Singaporean business groups: The role of the state and capital in Singapore Inc. In S. Chang (Ed.), *Business groups in East Asia: Financial crisis, restructuring, and new growth* (pp. 94–115). New York: Oxford University Press.

UNCTAD. (2015). *World investment report 2015: Reforming international investment governance.* Geneva: United Nations Conference on Trade and Development.

UNCTAD. (2018). *UNCTADstat.* https://unctadstat.unctad.org. Accessed 16 May 2019.

van Apeldoorn, B. (2004). Theorizing the transnational: A historical materialist approach. *Journal of International Relations and Development, 7*(2), 142–176.

Webster, T. J. (2014). Malaysian economic development, leading industries and industrial clusters. *The Singapore Economic Review, 59*(5), 1–19.

Wissel, J. (2006). The transnationalization of the bourgeoisie and the new networks of power. In A. Gallas, L. Bretthauer, J. Kannankulam, & I. Stützle (Eds.), *Reading Poulantzas* (pp. 216–230). Pontypool: Merlin Press.

Wong, P. K., & Ng, C. Y. (1997). Singapore's industrial policy to the year 2000. In S. Masuyama, D. Vandenbrink, & C. S. Yue (Eds.), *Industrial policies in East Asia* (pp. 121–141). Singapore: Institute of Southeast Asian Studies; Tokyo: Nomura Research Institute.

Yahya, F. (2005). State capitalism and government linked companies. *Journal of Asia-Pacific Business, 6*(1), 3–31.

CHAPTER 8

Southeast Asian Regional Governance: Political Economy, Regulatory Regionalism and ASEAN Integration

Lee Jones and Shahar Hameiri

INTRODUCTION

Among groups of mostly developing countries, Southeast Asia is unique, having not only developed its own regional organisations but in also becoming a "hub" for wider region-building in the Asia-Pacific. The main focus has been the Association of Southeast Asian Nations (ASEAN), founded in 1967 as an anti-communist club, and expanding after the Cold War to include all Southeast Asian countries, except Timor-Leste. In response to demands for larger regional organisations to address post-Cold War security issues, ASEAN founded the ASEAN Regional Forum

L. Jones (✉)
School of Politics and International Relations, Queen Mary University of London, London, UK
e-mail: l.c.jones@qmul.ac.uk

S. Hameiri
School of Political Science and International Studies, The University of Queensland, St Lucia, QLD, Australia
e-mail: s.hameiri@uq.edu.au

(ARF) in 1993, which remains the Asia-Pacific's primary security institution. Following criticisms of the ARF's inefficacy, ASEAN co-founded the East Asia Summit (EAS) in 2005, a rotating heads-of-government meeting. ASEAN has also promoted economic integration, initiating the ASEAN Free Trade Agreement (AFTA) in 1992, and the ASEAN Economic Community (AEC) in 2007, which became one of three pillars in a wider ASEAN Community. ASEAN has also formed the ASEAN Plus Three (APT) grouping with China, Japan and South Korea, generating dialogue and cooperation on economic and security matters. There are also regional groupings not led by ASEAN, such as the Asia-Pacific Economic Cooperation (APEC) summits. Coupled with plentiful free trade agreements, this makes for a baffling array of acronyms and overlapping regional institutions, often referred to as a "noodle bowl" (see Fig. 8.1).

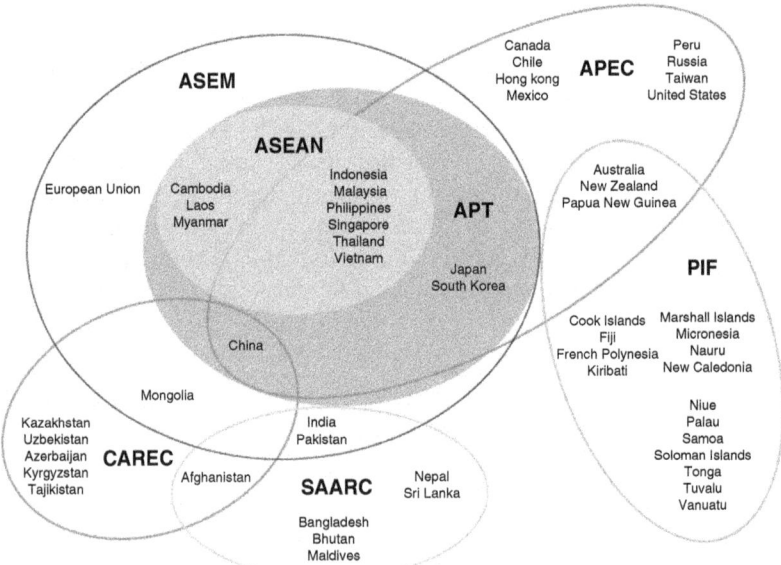

Fig. 8.1 Major Asia-Pacific Economic Cooperation Forums

Note: Non-exhaustive. APEC: Asia-Pacific Economic Cooperation, ASEM: Asia-Europe Meeting, CAREC: Central Asia Regional Economic Cooperation, PIF: Pacific Island Forum, SAARC: South Asian Association for Regional Cooperation

Notwithstanding this remarkable profusion of institutions, and the even greater explosion of publications about them, Southeast Asian regionalism is often seen as very boring, even by those who study it. As one scholar laments:

> despite the impressive volume of analysis, the discourse on Southeast Asian regionalism has not distinctly progressed. This is not surprising in view of the unchanging nature of the analytical object: ASEAN's lack of institutional evolution, and most member states' reluctance to touch upon the sensitive issue of national sovereignty, make it difficult for students of ASEAN to add any new and original findings to the debate (Dosch 2006: 164).

While this complaint is refreshingly frank, its substance is typical. Mainstream International Relations (IR) scholars may differ over which theoretical lens to use in assessing regional organisations, but they generally agree that, in Southeast Asia, these institutions are weak, because states stubbornly refuse to relinquish their sovereignty to the supranational bodies supposedly required to solve regional problems (cf. Jones 2012).

This perspective ignores evidence that Southeast Asian states have compromised their sovereignty in many important ways, such as through membership of the World Trade Organisation (WTO) or interventions by the international financial institutions (IFIs). More importantly for this chapter, it also overlooks the emergence of new modes of regional governance operating *beyond* sovereignty-usurping supranational bodies. Fundamentally, this is a product of the transformation of statehood (Al-Fadhat, this volume), underpinned by the transnationalisation of economic flows (Carroll, this volume). The fragmentation of state authority, coupled with a need to enhance and regulate transnational flows, has led to the formation of new governance networks. These are often issue-specific, with memberships that cut across established regional organisations, and are often linked to other, non-regional entities like the IFIs, helping to impose their disciplines. They operate not by establishing supranational authorities empowered to manage issues directly, but by defining rules and regulations that should be enacted in domestic governance; participating state agencies are expected to domesticate these regulations, thereby imposing international disciplines on their states and societies. This approach has been dubbed "regulatory regionalism" (Jayasuriya 2008; see also Hameiri and Jayasuriya 2011). In this mode of governance, contestation does not involve battles between proponents and opponents of "pooling" sovereignty; rather, we see struggles over the formation and (especially) implementation of regional regulations. This is because the rescaling of governance to new regional spaces, and the rules generated from this, may benefit some socio-political forces, but harm others. The resultant struggles between these groups determine how regulatory regionalism turns out in practice.

We illustrate these developments with several prominent Southeast Asian examples: monetary governance, anti-money laundering regulation, and the AEC. We focus on the AEC in considerable detail to demonstrate that regulatory regionalism is at work even in the supposedly sovereignty-bound ASEAN.

What Is Regulatory Regionalism?

Regulatory regionalism emerged out of the transformation of statehood analysed by Al-Fadhat (this volume), which is associated with the globalising trends discussed by Carroll (this volume). The fragmentation of state power enables functional ministries, regulators and other agencies to network transnationally with their counterparts to address shared problems. These actors then devise agreements at the international level, which specify the institutions, laws and/or regulations that states should develop to address a given issue. Participants are then expected to implement these measures domestically, thereby imposing regional disciplines on their states and societies. Regulatory regionalism often also involves efforts, via peer-review or external auditing, to evaluate and compare states' implementation of agreements. Hence, this mode of regional governance does not involve establishing supranational organisations that usurp state sovereignty and directly intervene to solve problems. Rather, states remain formally sovereign, but are reconfigured to pursue regionally defined objectives. This approach is not limited to regions; it is actually the dominant way in which global governance occurs today (Hameiri and Jones 2016). However, whatever the scale of governance, such reconfiguration of states is almost always contested, despite the fact that it is often depicted in a neutral, technocratic, problem-solving manner by its advocates among policy actors and scholars. This is because any change in regulations may benefit some socio-political groups, but harm others. Socio-political groups will therefore struggle to influence the framing and domestic implementation of international regulations.

This view of regionalism is underpinned by a view of state-formation and region-making as constantly evolving in response to changing political economy and social conflict dynamics, rather than a cyclical struggle between static, sovereignty-guarding states and regional organisations trying to usurp their prerogatives. Powerful social forces always seek to create modes of governance at various scales that advance their interests and agendas, whether national or regional, and accordingly changes in statehood and regional governance often evolve together (Hameiri 2013). Southeast Asia's earliest forms of regionalism expressed the efforts of embattled post-colonial national elites to consolidate control over their national territories and societies and defeat communist insurgencies. To insulate their enemies from external assistance, they made non-interference in states' internal affairs ASEAN's cornerstone—yet tolerated interference aplenty when it bolstered their position (Jones 2012). As communist insurgencies were defeated and Southeast Asia integrated into the global economy in the 1980s and 1990s, ruling elites selectively relaxed non-interference even further, producing "graduated sovereignty" (Ong 2000). As part of a shift to export-oriented industrialisation, they deregulated parts of their national territories, creating special economic zones to attract foreign investors. However, working-class populations remained subject to extensive, authoritarian regulation, to maintain existing power relations. The regional expression of this shift was the "open regionalism" of projects like AFTA and APEC, which deregulated trade and investment in competitive, export-oriented sectors. However, ruling elites were careful not to grant these institutions supranational enforcement powers, to protect non-competitive sectors, which were often closely tied to incumbent regimes (Nesadurai 2003). Jayasuriya (2003) dubbed this arrangement "embedded mercantilism". The 1997–98 Asian financial crisis (AFC) dealt this approach a terrible blow. To stabilise their economies and prevent future "contagion" of economic crises, Southeast Asian finance ministers formed the APT framework, through which they agreed to currency swaps and macroeconomic surveillance mechanisms (Rethel 2010). The APT and EAS also reflect the emergence of transnational production networks, and China's rise as a new centre of economic gravity. Thus, the overall trend is towards rescaling economic governance beyond national borders. This happens not merely at regional scales—our focus here—but globally, through participation in the World Trade Organisation, supraregional free trade agreements, and the IFIs, for example.

However, this has occurred not through the empowering of supranational bodies that directly manage economies, but rather through the networking of state apparatuses. The precursor to this development was the transformation of statehood described by Al-Fadhat (this volume). Thanks to successive reforms accompanying economic globalisation, state power is no longer concentrated in a powerful executive using "command-and-control" methods to secure desired outcomes within a hierarchically organised, Weberian state. Rather, it has been dispersed, albeit unevenly, across a wider range of public, private and hybrid actors, including functional ministries, regulators, central banks, judiciaries, etc., with the executive retreating to a regulatory function, mainly setting guidelines to steer this diverse array of agencies towards desired ends, particularly economic competitiveness (Jayasuriya 2004). Moreover, as a result of the transnationalisation of economic and social life, described by Carroll (this volume), the issues these agencies must manage are often seen to be transboundary, requiring cooperation with foreign counterparts. Accordingly, these newly empowered agencies have increasingly networked with their foreign counterparts to try to develop joint solutions, often drawing in international and non-governmental organisations, or even private sector entities (Hameiri and Jones 2015; Slaughter 2004).

These networks may start as "talk shops", but some proceed to devise "soft law" approaches to tackle a given problem, such as templates of laws, institutions and/or regulations that states should adopt. The entities involved then seek to implement these at home. In some cases, implementation necessitates substantial transformations in domestic governance arrangements, such as legal changes, new state agencies and powers or reforms to existing ones, or revised procedural arrangements between state apparatuses. Domestic implementation may also be monitored by the network and/or other agencies supporting its efforts.

This process is usually presented as neutral and technical; indeed, it may seem that tackling shared challenges is unobjectionable. But regulatory regionalism is always political. Firstly, it is often a deliberate attempt to bypass politics, which is frequently seen as an obstacle to problem-solving. Yet, the shift to technocratic cooperation does not negate the presence of power and interests; it merely grants power to the technocrats involved, while marginalising other interests and, importantly, circumventing democratic processes. This is a major criticism of the European Union, for example. Furthermore, governance institutions and rules are never neutral; they always affect different socio-political groups differently, with some gaining and others losing. Accordingly, they are often hotly contested. Because the networks producing regulatory regionalism are typically highly exclusive, groups opposed to the rules being developed may be unable to gain a hearing, unless they can lobby the actors involved, or curb the network's activities. However, regulatory regionalism must be implemented domestically to have any effect, and here there may be a greater opportunity to contest the process. Thus, precisely because regulatory regionalism is not apolitical, politics—struggles for power and resources between domestic interests—ultimately determines the extent to which it actually transforms domestic governance.

Regulatory Regionalism in Southeast Asia

In Southeast Asia, regulatory regionalism manifests through modes of governance that do not necessarily map onto regional organisations, like ASEAN, and are therefore neglected by mainstream scholars. In many cases, these modes of regional governance are linked to global governance regimes and institutions and thus reflect efforts to reinforce the embedding of their disciplines within Southeast Asian states. We discuss two particularly prominent examples: the Chiang Mai Initiative Multilateralisation (CMIM) and the Asia/Pacific Group on Money Laundering (APG). These are not unique; similar dynamics are observable with reference to many transboundary issues, including pandemic diseases and environmental degradation, for instance (see Hameiri and Jones 2015).

The Chiang Mai Initiative Multilateralisation

The Chiang Mai Initiative (CMI), was one of several regional projects to emerge following the AFC. A primary reason for the AFC's escalation was the rapid depreciation of the region's national currencies. Since many Southeast Asian banks and firms were borrowing in US dollars, they became unable to service their debts, going bankrupt and turning a financial crisis into a generalised economic downturn. The International Monetary Fund (IMF) was unwilling to provide support without recipients first signing up to domestic structural adjustment programmes, causing widespread resentment. Japan's proposed Asian Monetary Fund was scuttled by the US, but a more modest framework—the CMI—was agreed in 2000 under the APT. This reflected a broader underlying shift towards pan-regional investment, production and trade networks (see Carroll, this volume), which gave northeast Asian governments a strong interest in helping to stabilise Southeast Asia's economies.

The CMI was a set of bilateral currency swap agreements: governments agreed to establish reserves of US dollars, which fellow participants experiencing a monetary crisis could borrow using their own currencies, later repaying the dollars, plus interest (Grimes 2009: 82). In 2009, APT finance ministers agreed to multilateralise these bilateral arrangements, creating a truly regional liquidity pool, first established at US$120bn, rising to US$240bn by 2012, with China and Japan each providing 32% of the reserves. Each participating government can withdraw up to US$30bn (Pitakdumrongkit 2018).

The CMI and CMIM have both operated through regulatory regionalism by making access to dollars conditional upon adherence to economic "good governance". The risk with currency swaps is that borrowers might not repay. Accordingly, the Chinese and Japanese governments sought guarantees that funds could only be accessed by recipients whose monetary problems did not stem from economic mismanagement. However, because they struggled to agree on regional standards for evaluating countries' domestic governance, they instead adopted IMF standards (Grimes 2009: 81). Hence, despite formal claims that no conditions were attached, in reality, the CMI sought to compel APT countries to follow IMF strictures, and it established a surveillance process to monitor compliance (ibid.: 84–87). Although modified in the CMIM, two basic forms of conditionality remain. The first is the "IMF link", whereby governments can only receive 30% of requested funds before agreeing a reform package with the IMF. This "implies that [CMIM] countries need to submit to IMF guidelines, which act as a 'de facto' conditionality" (Siregar and Chabchitrchaidol 2013: 11). It further implies that CMIM acts as a regional complement to a supraregional global governor, the IMF. Second, borrowers must meet other criteria. In the CMI, these were secretive and varied from one bilateral swap agreement to another. In CMIM, preconditions and activation guidelines have been standardised (ibid.: 5). Member-states must: undergo a review of their economic and financial situation by a regional surveillance mechanism (described below); not have previously defaulted on loans; and comply with regional covenants, including submitting a periodic surveillance report and participating in the APT Economic Review and Policy Dialogue (AMRO n.d.).

CMI and CMIM have also established regional surveillance mechanisms to monitor member-states' domestic economic environment and compliance with regional undertakings. Under CMI, surveillance was provided by a network of APT finance ministers and central bankers (Grimes 2009: 88). In 2011, however, a dedicated regional body—the APT Macroeconomic Research Office (AMRO)—was established. The independent AMRO is meant to bring greater transparency, credibility and professionalism into the CMIM process. In 2017, its annual budget was US$18.5m, just below the ASEAN Secretariat's US$20m. Aside from ongoing surveillance of member-states, it is tasked with providing capacity-building and assisting with implementation. Like other forms of regulatory regionalism, however, AMRO does not manage the currency swap process directly and has no supranational powers. How far CMIM has actually managed to impose regulatory disciplines on member-states is hard to assess, as it has not yet been used. However, AMRO's objectives are certainly reinforced by governments' desire to maintain market lending credibility and attract foreign investment (see Carroll, this volume).

Asia/Pacific Group on Money Laundering

Southeast Asia is often seen to be plagued by non-traditional security (NTS) problems: non-military threats that easily traverse state borders, like environmental degradation, epidemics, terrorism and organised crime. However, most scholars lament the poverty of regional responses, blaming member-states' refusal to surrender sovereignty to ASEAN. By shifting our focus to regulatory regionalism, we can see that much more is being done than these accounts suggest.

The case of anti-money-laundering (AML) regulation is instructive. Suppressing money laundering is seen as crucial to tackling NTS threats, because it will make it harder for criminal groups to enjoy their ill-gotten gains and for terrorists to gather funds. Scholars generally lament that ASEAN does little to tackle transnational crime, drugs or terrorism—but they are looking in the wrong place. The main body tasked with managing money-laundering and terrorist financing in Southeast Asia is the Asia/Pacific Group on Money Laundering (APG)—an affiliate of the Financial Action Task Force (FATF)—whose membership encompasses 41 states, cutting across multiple regional organisations. The FATF is a small international organisation, founded by economic ministers of members of the Organisation for Economic Cooperation and Development. FATF has no supranational powers and does not manage AML directly. Rather, it has developed a set of regulations, the "40 Recommendations", for states to follow. These are highly prescriptive and intrusive, specifying legal changes, the creation of specialised institutions—notably Financial Intelligence Units (FIUs), which are tasked with coordinating AML activities—and new institutional processes. Implementation is monitored by FATF-style regional bodies (FSRBs), like the APG, which network together FIUs, coordinate peer reviews to measure each other's performance, build institutional capacity, and further develop FATF rules to reflect regional peculiarities. The IMF and World Bank also assess compliance as part of their routine surveillance of developing countries.

This regulatory form of governance has achieved remarkably widespread adherence. Despite FATF's lack of supranational powers, only Iran and North Korea decline to adopt its Recommendations. This is not due to fear of a supranational authority but rather because global financial institutions use FSRB reports to help assess investment risk, making bad reports (sometimes called "blacklisting") potentially very costly (Sharman 2011). All Southeast Asian countries are APG members, and none are currently on FATF's list of "high risk and other monitored jurisdictions". This is because every Southeast Asian state has undertaken significant domestic transformations to comply with an international regulatory regime, monitored via a regulatory regional network, a development almost entirely missed by those fixated on ASEAN. ASEAN is merely an observer at APG meetings—a marginal player in this important example of regulatory regionalism.

Despite the widespread formal adoption of FATF regulations, practical implementation is strongly contested, and shaped by dominant sociopolitical forces. Experimental research shows that it is easiest to violate FATF rules in Britain and the US (Findley et al. 2014). These countries' powerful financial sectors—which are major employers, and financially linked to leading political parties—have apparently managed to warp implementation around their established business models (Shaxson 2011). With the notable exception of Singapore, a major global tax haven, Southeast Asian countries lack highly developed financial industries, so struggles over implementation assume different forms in the region. Myanmar, for example, adopted FATF's Recommendations in the early 2000s, under a military regime, ostensibly transforming its domestic governance accordingly. However, close analysis shows that implementation has been moulded around powerful interests here, too. The AML regime is subject to strong political control, with enforcement kept deliberately weak. This allows incumbent elites to shield their clients from scrutiny, despite the fact that Myanmar's financial system was largely founded with the proceeds of drug trafficking. The only actors targeted are those who fall out with the regime (Hameiri and Jones 2015: ch. 5).

REGULATORY REGIONALISM AND THE TRANSFORMATION OF ASEAN

Although fixation with ASEAN can obscure such new modes of governance, we also argue that ASEAN itself is moving towards regulatory regionalism. This is overlooked because of scholars' obsession with measuring how much state sovereignty is ceded to ASEAN, with the norm of non-interference seen as a persistent barrier to the emergence of supranational authority. By contrast, this section shows that ASEAN technocrats have increasingly sought to circumvent this obstacle—and bypass political resistance—by pursuing regulatory regionalism, which does not empower ASEAN over member-states, but seeks to transform member-states themselves to serve regionally defined goals.[1] However, as we demonstrate by focusing on the AEC, how far this works in practice remains powerfully shaped by domestic power struggles.

ASEAN and Regulatory Regionalism

Since the end of the Cold War, ASEAN has increasingly sought to position itself at the centre of a dense web of regional governance networks and institutions. A core dimension of this has been the development of regional rules, norms and obligations that attempt to shape member-states' conduct, based on the argument that the region's challenges are often transnational.

The "ASEAN Community", formally launched in 2015, has been pivotal in this regard. The ASEAN Community institutionalises and organises the transnational cooperation that has emerged following the Southeast Asian states' transformation. In ASEAN's first few decades, regional cooperation reflected a traditional governance model, whereby foreign ministries dominated international relations. Annual "ASEAN

---

[1] As Bickerton (2012) argues, this is essentially how the EU operates. Hence, there is a stronger parallel between ASEAN and the EU than most analysts realise.

ministerial meetings" were meetings of foreign ministers, and ASEAN heads of state met only three times during the entire Cold War. The founding ASEAN Declaration (1967) was barely two pages long, and subsequent keystone documents were no more detailed. Although some functional ministries also began meeting in the late 1970s and early 1980s, cooperation was sporadic and paltry. For example, the ASEAN health ministers first met in 1980, then 1984, but did not meet again until 2000.

From the 1990s, however, with the increasing fragmentation of state power, and the perceived rise of shared transnational issues, functional ministries and agencies in many different fields began networking and developing their own regional cooperation agendas. The ASEAN Community organises these activities into three "pillars" (see Table 8.1).

However, the ASEAN Community was not merely a cosmetic rearrangement of existing dialogues; it represents a step-change in how regional governance is pursued, towards regulatory regionalism. This approach emerged sporadically over the previous decade, in preparation for the launch of the ASEAN Community, but it is now firmly entrenched across every governance domain. The ASEAN heads of government specified the broad goals of the organisation in their "ASEAN 2025" declaration, adopted in 2015 (ASEAN 2015a). Bureaucrats and policy-makers then developed an organisational "blueprint" for each pillar, specifying "strategic measures" in greater depth. These were followed by "action plans", which detail the measures that each member-state should adopt domestically. For the AEC, a long action plan covers the entire pillar. For the other pillars, issue-specific action plans have been developed, e.g. a Strategic Plan for Culture and Arts, 2016–2025, under the ASEAN Socio-Cultural Community (ASCC), setting out 44 action points. Other sectoral groups have developed regulatory standards covering issues such as forestry and agriculture. In stark contrast to the two-page statement that launched ASEAN, these documents are long, detailed and highly prescriptive (see Table 8.2).

These documents are not treaties and do not grant ASEAN supranational powers; rather, they specify various regional objectives, regulations and standards, which member-states are expected to cascade downwards to national and subnational agencies and regulators. For example, Vietnam has created a national "master plan" to implement the ASCC blueprints. Nine of its 11 national ministries developed macro-level implementation plans, followed by 54 of Vietnam's 63 cities and provincial governments (VNA 2018). Implementation is monitored at the ASEAN level by assessing member-states' progress against the blueprints and action plans,

Table 8.1 Bodies of the ASEAN Community

ASEAN grouping	Year of first meeting
ASEAN Political-Security Community (APSC)	
Ministerial Meeting (Foreign Ministers)	1967
Law Ministers Meeting	1986
Ministerial Meeting on Transnational Crime	1997
Defence Ministers Meeting	2006
Intergovernmental Commission on Human Rights	2009
Ministerial Meeting on Drug Matters	2015
ASEAN Economic Community (AEC)	
Economic Ministers Meeting	1975
Ministerial Meeting on Agriculture and Forestry	1979
Ministerial Meeting on Science and Technology	1980
AFTA Council	1992
Transport Ministers Meeting	1996
Mekong Basin Development Cooperation	1996
Finance Ministers Meeting	1997
Investment Area Council	1998
Tourism Ministers Meeting	1998
Ministers on Energy Meeting	2003
Ministerial Meeting on Minerals	2005
Telecommunications Ministers Meeting	2012
Finance Ministers' and Central Bank Governors' Meeting	2015
ASEAN Socio-Cultural Community (ASCC)	
Labour Ministers Meeting	1975
Education Ministers Meeting	1977
Ministerial Meeting on Social Welfare and Development	1979
Health Ministers Meeting	1980
Ministerial Meeting on Environment	1981
Cooperation on Civil Service Matters	1981
Ministers Responsible for Information	1989
Ministerial Meeting on Youth	1992
Ministers Meeting on Rural Development and Poverty Eradication	1998
Ministerial Meeting on Women	2002
Ministers Responsible for Culture and Arts	2003
Ministerial Meeting on Disaster Management	2004
Ministerial Meeting on Sports	2011

with regular reviews and "scorecards" issued to spur further action. For some issues, ASEAN has established regional centres to supervise progress. The region has also worked with international organisations and donors to attract funds and capacity-building assistance to implement the blueprints (Scoles 2016: 18–21; see also Table 8.3).

Table 8.2 ASEAN Community blueprints and action plans

Pillar	Blueprint		
	Length (pages)	Objectives/headings	Action points
APSC	39	52	274
AEC	43	30	232
ASCC	27	18	110

Source: ASEAN (2015b, 2016a, b)

Table 8.3 ASEAN Community-building projects, 2009–17

Pillar	Number of projects/programmes	Project/programme value (US$m)
APSC	135	138.9
AEC	261	527.2
ASCC	519	485.3
Total	975	1227.3

Source: ASEAN (2018a: 43)

A good example of the regulatory regionalism approach is the ASEAN Agreement on Disaster Management and Emergency Response (AADMER; see ASEAN 2005). AADMER does not pool sovereignty and disaster response capacities at the regional level. Rather, it primarily establishes tasks for national authorities to pursue to enhance their own resilience. It also requires member-states to identify capacities that could be deployed transnationally in emergencies; however, these would not be deployed by ASEAN, but rather by the affected member-state, using the domestic systems established by implementing AADMER. To supervise implementation, the region has created an ASEAN Coordinating Centre for Humanitarian Assistance, which receives reports from designated national "focal points". In 2017, ASEAN also asked the International Federation of Red Cross and Red Crescent Societies to evaluate AADMER's domestic implementation by comparing member-states and assessing their progress against AADMER themes and benchmarks (IFRC 2018).

The ASEAN Economic Community

The AEC is arguably the core of the ASEAN Community: it was initiated in 2007, with the other "pillars" only added later. Reflecting the intensifying regionalisation of investment and production (see Carroll, this volume), the AEC seeks to turn Southeast Asia into a single, integrated production base for transnational capital. One of its explicit goals is to

> Achieve competitive, efficient, and seamless movement of goods within the region in order to enhance ASEAN's trade and production networks, better participate in global value chains, as well as to establish a highly integrated and cohesive economy (ASEAN 2018b: 4).

Unsurprisingly, therefore, the various work-plans and action plans developed under this pillar are all designed to create a business-friendly environment by lowering barriers to investment and trade in goods and services. In short, the AEC seeks to impose neoliberal disciplines on Southeast Asia.

However, the AEC does not establish any supranational authority empowered to enact economic laws or make binding legal decisions, like the European Court of Justice, for example. Only a simple dispute settlement mechanism has been created. The AEC's objectives are instead pursued through regulatory regionalism: delineating domestic reforms that member-states must implement. This may involve the domestication of regionally developed standards, but AEC work-plans also incorporate existing international standards, reflecting its orientation towards global investment and trade (Scoles 2016: 5). The AEC thereby promotes the "deep marketisation of development" (Carroll 2012), not through traditional IFI-style conditionality, but by reconfiguring governance in ways that systematically favour international capital. This shift ultimately reflects the growing leverage of international capital and the waning of alternatives to market-led growth (Carroll, this volume).

AEC documents reflect the general pattern of regulatory regionalism, with the broad, pro-market goals of the AEC blueprint being developed into ever-more precise and intrusive regulations through sector-specific negotiations. This approach was already clear in the blueprints covering the period leading up to the AEC's supposed realisation in 2015, but has been intensified in the documents covering 2015–25. The 54-page "2015 Consolidated Strategic Action Plan" (CSAP) collates these and identifies 587 "action lines" (ASEAN 2018b). These directives are elaborated into even greater detail in 23 sector-specific plans (see Table 8.4). For example, ASEAN's Trade Facilitation Strategic Action Plan identifies seven "strategic

Table 8.4 AEC sectoral work-plans

1	AEC 2025 Strategic Action Plan for Trade in Goods
2	ASEAN 2025 Trade Facilitation Strategic Action Plan
3	Broad Direction for Customs Activities 2016–2025
4	ASEAN Standards and Conformance Strategic Plan 2016–2025
5	Strategic Action Plan for Services 2016–2025
6	2016–2025 Investment Work Programme
7	Strategic Action Plans for Financial Integration 2016–2025
8	ASEAN Competition Action Plan 2016–2025
9	ASEAN Strategic Action Plan for Consumer Protection 2016–2025
10	ASEAN Intellectual Property Rights Action Plan 2016–2025
11	ASEAN Transport Strategic Plan 2016–2025
12	ASEAN Information and Communications Technology Masterplan 2020
13	ASEAN Work Programme on Electronic Commerce 2017–2025
14	ASEAN Plan of Action on Energy Cooperation 2016–2025
15	Strategic Plan for ASEAN Cooperation in Food, Agriculture and Forestry 2016–2025
16	ASEAN Tourism Strategic Plan 2016–2025
17	Strategic Action Plan 2016–2025 for ASEAN Taxation Cooperation
18	ASEAN Minerals Cooperation Action Plan 2016–2025
19	ASEAN Plan of Action on Science, Technology and Innovation 2016–2025
20	ASEAN Strategic Action Plan for SME Development 2025
21	ASEAN Community Statistical System Strategic Plan 2016–2025
22	ASEAN Work Plan for Enhancing the Global Value Chain Agenda 2016–2025
23	ASEAN Work Plan on Good Regulatory Practice 2016–2025

objectives", drawn from the AEC action plan, generating 23 "action lines", each with specified outputs, outcomes, measurable indicators of completion, and deadlines. Beyond these sectoral plans, the Initiative for ASEAN Integration Work-plan III spells out actions to be taken to help integrate the newer, poorer ASEAN economies with their more developed neighbours, while the Masterplan on ASEAN Connectivity 2025 identifies the transregional infrastructure projects intended to physically integrate the region's markets. All of these plans promote market liberalisation through the reduction or abolition of remaining tariffs—most have been removed already to comply with competitive pressures, and WTO and AFTA rules—but also, more importantly, through the removal of non-tariff barriers (NTBs), i.e. rules and regulations that make it hard for investors, merchants and skilled workers to operate across ASEAN economies.

Implementation is assessed by the ASEAN Secretariat's Integration Monitoring Directorate, which emerged from the Macroeconomic and

Finance Surveillance unit (later renamed the ASEAN Integration Monitoring Office) established by ASEAN finance ministers in 2010. This unit produced an AEC "scorecard" to measure implementation in the run-up to the AEC's supposed realisation in 2015. Other issue-specific mechanisms provide additional scrutiny, such as the Investment Peer-Review process, whereby ASEAN states evaluate each other's policies and regulations. Independent assessments are also provided by research organisations like the Economic Research Institute for ASEAN and East Asia.

The AEC thus sets the agenda across vast swathes of internal economic policy-making, which had previously been the exclusive preserve of domestic political actors. Gone are the days of two-page declarations; the AEC specifies in minute detail what every member-state should be doing in virtually every area of economic life. Indeed, because the ASEAN economic ministers set the overall direction for "sectoral groups" through the AEC, there is virtually no area untouched by its pro-market agenda. For example, element C7 of the CSAP is healthcare. The action lines direct member-states to "continue [the] opening up" of the "healthcare market" to private investment, and to "promote Public Private Partnerships in the provision of universal healthcare". To facilitate transnational investment, the plan promotes the "further harmonisation of standards" in the training of healthcare professionals, the implementation of international standards and regional directives governing medical products and devices, and greater freedom of movement for medical professionals (ASEAN 2018b: 38–39).

However, this extraordinarily ambitious agenda encounters fierce domestic resistance, which shapes the AEC's implementation. The AEC agenda is primarily promoted by economic ministers and officials, many of whom are doubtless true believers in the neoliberal agenda. They are supported by international agents of transnational capital, like the Asian Development Bank and management consultancies, which provide policy advice and help draft AEC plans, and internationally competitive fractions of capital, including a few Southeast Asian conglomerates. For example, the Malaysian budget airline AirAsia clearly sees enormous market opportunities in the liberalisation of ASEAN's aviation markets, and has thus branded itself the "ASEAN carrier". For similar reasons, Malaysia's CIMB Bank has enthusiastically supported the AEC, establishing the CIMB ASEAN Research Institute (CARI) in 2011 to help scrutinise the implementation of its agenda.

However, these liberalising elites face a host of forces reluctant to cooperate. As noted by Carroll (this volume), and elsewhere in this volume, decades of state-led development have created deeply entrenched networks of bureaucratic, military, political and economic actors, often labelled "oligarchies", whose domination relies on the continuation of *illiberal* modes of governance. Historically, political leaders have balanced the need to attract the investment necessary for continued economic growth with protecting politically linked business interests by only *selectively* liberalising their economies. This has created relatively open, internationally competitive, export-oriented sectors, dependent on foreign investment and trade, alongside sectors dominated by state-owned or state-linked enterprises, which are dependent on continued state protection from international competition. Even some enterprises that have ventured into other Southeast Asian markets rely on these closed, clientelist arrangements to be profitable. For example, the Thai agribusiness conglomerate, Charoen Pokphand, has highly competitive, export-oriented poultry factories in Thailand, but its domestically oriented operations in Indonesia depend on import restrictions to remain profitable (Hameiri and Jones 2015: ch. 4). It is not only big business interests that stand to lose out through "deep marketisation". Some middle-class professionals fear competition from migrant workers,[2] while in some contexts the poor rely on subsidies (a form of NTB) to supplement their incomes. Front-line bureaucrats may also oppose reforms that reduce rent-seeking opportunities. These forces are generally excluded from the regional spaces where AEC plans are negotiated, but they may be able to contest the implementation of regional regulations when policy-makers and bureaucrats try to roll them out at home (Lele 2018).

This contestation accounts for the patchy implementation of AEC measures. Although the AEC was declared complete in 2015, the AEC Blueprint for 2015–2025 not only promotes even deeper marketisation, it also demands the fulfilment of the commitments made in the original round (ASEAN 2015b: 4). The formation of ASEAN's Integration Monitoring Office in 2016 reflected recognition that added pressure was needed. The ASEAN Secretariat's AEC scorecards were made secret after 2012, when widespread non-compliance was still apparent, making the

---

[2] The AEC only seeks to liberalise short-term professional labour migration to facilitate trade in services. On the more significant flows of non-professional workers, see Gerard and Bal, this volume.

Fig. 8.2 Average tariffs and number of non-tariff barriers in ASEAN

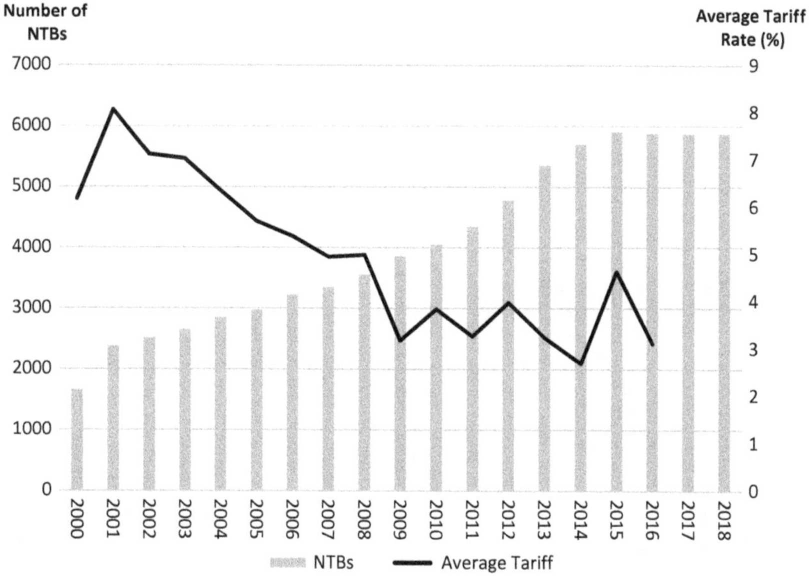

Note: These figures derive from national reporting, and hence almost certainly understate the number of NTBs
Source: World Bank 2018a; UNCTAD/ERIA 2018

AEC's realisation by 2015 effectively impossible. Independent observers like CARI (2013a: 8) found "ample evidence… that actual implementation lags significantly behind the timelines of stated objectives". Likewise, ERIA (2012) noted that NTBs remained significant; trade and investment facilitation was limited; no regional infrastructure projects were on track; and regional regulations were frequently either not being translated into domestic rules or not being properly enforced.

Indeed, rather than simply implementing the AEC's liberalising agenda, domestic power-holders can resist or even reverse liberalisation. This may be exacerbated by the fragmentation and decentralisation of state apparatuses. For example, in Indonesia, while the national government has tried to cascade AEC planning downwards, local governments have resisted, using their regulatory powers to protect local clients (Lele 2018). Resistance to liberalisation is starkly reflected in the rapid *growth* of NTBs under the AEC—the exact opposite of what was intended (see Fig. 8.2). Essentially, as tariffs have been eliminated, NTBs have replaced them, to

Table 8.5 World Bank "ease of doing business" rankings

ASEAN member	Ease of doing business rank		Trading across borders rank	
	2007	2019	2007	2019
Brunei	78[a]	55	36[a]	149
Cambodia	143	138	114	115
Indonesia	135	73	60	116
Laos	159	154	161	76
Malaysia	25	15	46	48
Myanmar	–	135	–	91
Philippines	126	124	63	104
Singapore	1	2	4	45
Thailand	18	27	103	59
Vietnam	104	69	75	100

Source: World Bank (2018b)
[a]2008

continue protecting key interests in a more targeted manner.[3] World Bank rankings also show mixed results, with some progress but also some backsliding (see Table 8.5).

A few examples can illustrate how domestic power relations and struggles shape the implementation of the AEC agenda in different sectors. First, let us consider how domestic business interests can generate contending national positions that stall ASEAN's economic integration. The aviation sector demonstrates this well. As noted, there are large-scale aviation firms interested in liberalising this sector, notably low-cost carriers like AirAsia, because they stand to increase their already-massive market share. It is no surprise, then, that Malaysia, home to AirAsia, has strongly backed this aspect of the AEC. However, Indonesia, ASEAN's largest aviation market, has fiercely resisted this liberalisation, because its domestic airlines, including flag carrier Garuda, cannot compete with foreign rivals, relying on protection to remain profitable (CARI 2013b). Consequently, Indonesia—joined by similarly-positioned member-states—has entered reservations when ratifying ASEAN "open skies" agreements, impeding liberalisation, while foreign competition on solely domestic routes remains

---

[3] Protectionism does not necessarily account for *all* NTBs. Ing et al. (2016) suggest that some stem from a desirable tightening of consumer protection regulations, with 31.3% of NTBs emerging from health ministries. Nonetheless, even "safety" regulations can easily be manipulated for protectionist purposes: see, e.g., Li and Beghin (2017).

entirely prohibited (Intal 2017: 48–49). Interests differ across sectors, generating different attitudes to AEC implementation. Malaysia is far less keen on financial integration, for example, because its politically linked banking sector—crucial for maintaining the oligarchic networks underpinning the now-defunct United Malay National Organisation regime—could not withstand international competition (Nesadurai 2012: 325). In the automotive sector, the ASEAN countries with competitive, export-oriented sectors have readily internalised international standards under the ASEAN Automotive Product Working Group's direction. However, those with uncompetitive, domestically oriented sectors, like Vietnam, have not (Scoles 2016: 8).

A second example is the energy sector, which demonstrates how the importance of protectionist measures in maintaining domestic coalitions can override liberalisation projects. The AEC envisages creating a single regional electricity market through regulatory changes and the construction of a physical ASEAN Power Grid, which proponents estimate could save $20–29bn annually (Wu et al. 2011: 4). Despite a slated completion date of 2015, the power grid project is barely half complete, and what little exists is just a series of bilateral connections. The reason for this slow progress is that integrating energy markets would require governments to terminate their subsidies to consumers, which is politically risky. In 2010, the ASEAN-5 governments alone spent US$34bn on energy subsidies, 44% of which went on electricity (Chattopadhyay and Jha 2014: 71). Some of this goes to powerful industrial interests close to incumbent regimes, such as Indonesia's petrochemicals and cement industries, and Malaysia's petroleum and automotive industries (Wu et al. 2011: 6–7). Some governments also use consumer subsidies to maintain the urban poor's quiescence. The cuts required to implement the ASEAN power grid are "socially unacceptable" from the perspective of maintaining socio-political stability (ibid.: 6–8).

A third and final example—the movement of skilled labour—shows how special interests can capture regulatory regionalism. The AEC promotes the liberalisation of services trade, to make it easier for service companies in one ASEAN state to undertake work in another. To facilitate this, the AEC seeks to reduce barriers to service firms' key workers—skilled professionals, like physicians, architects and surveyors—to work temporarily in other ASEAN states. This involves changing how member-states regulate these professions. The AEC mandates the development of Mutual Recognition Agreements (MRAs), whereby ASEAN states recognise each other's professional qualifications as equivalent, allowing someone qualified in one member-state to work freely in another. ASEAN's economic ministers delegated the drafting of MRAs to the national regulators for each profession. However, as Sumano (2013) found, these networks usually did *not* develop liberalising MRAs. National professional regulators are often dominated by the very professionals they seek to regulate, allowing them to promote regulations that benefit themselves. Where professionals had a strong mutual interest in working across ASEAN, they were able to agree on liberalising MRAs: for example, architects created an ASEAN Architect Council, which now licenses professionals to work in any ASEAN economy. However, where professionals feared foreign competition, they defended barriers such as language tests, either producing MRAs that did not actually facilitate professionals' movement, in the case of physicians, or producing no MRA at all, in the case of surveyors. Furthermore, the implementation of MRAs is shaped by local political economy relations: Lele (2018) found that while some Indonesian cities are liberalising labour rules, others are using their control over work permits to exclude ASEAN migrants, protecting their constituents from competition and violating the AEC. Unsurprisingly, the numbers of professionals mobilised under MRAs is pitiful: no physicians or dentists (as of 2017), only 55 nurses, just six engineers, and 284 ASEAN architects (Intal 2017: 51; Te et al. 2018: 962). Intal (2017: 51) concludes that "the MRAs do not contribute much to the intra-regional mobility of skilled professionals".

Conclusion

Sovereignty-jealous Southeast Asian states are widely supposed to resist any transfer of authority to regional organisations, stymieing the emergence of serious regional governance. This perception is based upon a narrow focus on regional organisations and their capacity for supranational action vis-à-vis states. As we have shown, however, regional governance in Southeast Asia increasingly operates via regulatory regionalism—the development of regional standards by networks of quasi-autonomous agencies and their attempted embedding within states. This process is closely associated with the transnationalisation of economic and social relations (Carroll, this volume), and the associated transformation of Southeast Asian states (Al-Fadhat, this volume). If we include regulatory regionalism it is clear that regional governance constitutes a significant dimension of Southeast Asian politics, but its impacts are uneven and complex, across countries and issue-areas.

The shift towards regulatory regionalism reflects attempts to get around the limitations of national sovereignty that some view as restricting the capacity to address transnational problems. However, even apparently neutral, "problem-solving" regulatory changes tend to reallocate power and resources. And because the international fora in which agreements are formed are often highly exclusive, socio-political forces that stand to lose out struggle to prevent or restrict their implementation by contesting them in domestic settings. Consequently, the contours of regional governance are increasingly shaped, not by struggles over whether sovereignty should be ceded to supranational institutions, but by conflicts within the state over the implementation of regional frameworks. The contours and future development of regional governance in Southeast Asia are thus intrinsically linked to wider struggles over power and wealth in the region.

References

AMRO. (n.d.). *Overview of the CMIM. Conditions precedent and covenants.* Singapore: ASEAN+3 Macroeconomic Research Office. https://amro-asia.org/about-amro/amro-and-the-cmim/#howitworks. Accessed 21 Jan 2019.

ASEAN [Association of Southeast Asian Nations]. (2005, July 26). *ASEAN agreement on disaster management and emergency response.* http://agreement.asean.org/media/download/20140119170000.pdf. Accessed 21 Jan 2019.

ASEAN. (2015a). ASEAN 2025 at a glance. 24 November. https://asean.org/asean-2025-at-a-glance/. Accessed 21 Jan 2019.

ASEAN. (2015b). *ASEAN Economic Community blueprint 2025.* Jakarta: ASEAN Secretariat.

ASEAN. (2016a). *ASEAN Socio-Cultural Community blueprint 2025.* Jakarta: ASEAN Secretariat.

ASEAN. (2016b). *ASEAN Political-Security Community blueprint 2025.* Jakarta: ASEAN Secretariat.

ASEAN. (2018a). *A resilient and innovative ASEAN community: Annual report 2017–2018.* Jakarta: ASEAN Secretariat.

ASEAN. (2018b). AEC 2015 consolidated strategic action plan. 14 August. http://asean.org/wp-content/uploads/2012/05/Consolidated-Strategic-Action-Plan-endorsed-060217rev.pdf. Accessed 21 Jan 2019.

Bickerton, C. (2012). *European integration: From nation-states to member-states.* Oxford: Oxford University Press.

CARI [CIMB ASEAN Research Institute]. (2013a, June). *The ASEAN Economic Community: The status of implementation, challenges and bottlenecks.* Kuala Lumpur.

CARI. (2013b, November). *Lifting-the-barriers 2013 report: Aviation.* https://www.cariasean.org/sector-analysis-report/ltb-report-2013-aviation/#.XNGS3aTTWUk. Accessed 21 Jan 2019.

Carroll, T. (2012). Working on, through and around the state: The deep marketisation of development in the Asia-Pacific. *Journal of Contemporary Asia, 42*(3), 378–404.

Chattopadhyay, D., & Jha, S. (2014). The impact of energy subsidies on the power sector in Southeast Asia. *Electricity Journal, 27*(4), 70–83.

Dosch, J. (2006). *The changing dynamics of Southeast Asian politics.* Boulder: Lynne Rienner.

ERIA [Economic Research Institute for ASEAN and East Asia]. (2012). *Mid-term review of the implementation of AEC blueprint: Executive summary.* Jakarta: ERIA.

Findley, M. G., Nielson, D. L., & Sharman, J. C. (2014). *Global shell games: Experiments in transnational relations, crime, and terrorism.* Cambridge: Cambridge University Press.

Grimes, W. W. (2009). *Currency and contest in East Asia: The great power of financial regionalism.* Ithaca/London: Cornell University Press.

Hameiri, S. (2013). Theorising regions through changes in statehood: Rethinking the theory and method of comparative regionalism. *Review of International Studies, 39*(2), 313–335.

Hameiri, S., & Jayasuriya, K. (2011). Regulatory regionalism and the dynamics of territorial politics: The case of the Asia-Pacific region. *Political Studies, 59*(1), 59–77.

Hameiri, S., & Jones, L. (2015). *Governing borderless threats: Non-traditional security and the politics of state transformation.* Cambridge: Cambridge University Press.

Hameiri, S., & Jones, L. (2016). Global governance as state transformation. *Political Studies, 64*(4), 793–810.

IFRC [International Federation of Red Cross and Red Crescent Societies]. (2018). *ASEAN disaster law mapping. Implementing AADMER: A regional stocktake.* Geneva: International Federation of Red Cross and Red Crescent Societies.

Ing, L. Y., Cadot, O., Anandhika, R., & Urara, S. (2016). Non-tariff measures in ASEAN: A simple proposal. In L. Y. Ing, S. de Cordoba, & O. Cadot (Eds.), *Non-tariff measures in ASEAN* (pp. 13–36). Jakarta: ERIA/UNCTAD.

Intal, P. (2017). Building the ASEAN economic community: Progression and progress. In P. Intal & L. Chen (Eds.), *ASEAN and member states: Transformation and integration* (pp. 34–61). Jakarta: ERIA.

Jayasuriya, K. (2003). Embedded mercantilism and open regionalism: The crisis of a regional political project. *Third World Quarterly, 24*(2), 339–355.
Jayasuriya, K. (2004). The new regulatory state and relational capacity. *Policy and Politics, 32*(4), 487–501.
Jayasuriya, K. (2008). Regionalising the state: Political topography of regulatory regionalism. *Contemporary Politics, 14*(1), 21–35.
Jones, L. (2012). *ASEAN, sovereignty and intervention in Southeast Asia*. Basingstoke: Palgrave Macmillan.
Lele, G. (2018). Compliance under fragmented governance: The case of ASEAN economic community implementation in four Indonesian city governments. *Policy Studies, 39*(6), 607–621.
Li, Y., & Beghin, J. C. (2017). Protectionism indices for non-tariff measures: An application to maximum residue levels. In J. C. Beghin (Ed.), *Nontariff measures and international trade* (pp. 167–178). Singapore: World Scientific.
Nesadurai, H. E. S. (2003). *Globalisation, domestic politics, and regionalism: The ASEAN free trade area*. London/New York: Routledge.
Nesadurai, H. E. S. (2012). Trade policy in Southeast Asia. In R. Robison (Ed.), *Routledge handbook of Southeast Asian politics* (pp. 315–329). London: Routledge.
Ong, A. (2000). Graduated sovereignty in South-East Asia. *Theory, Culture and Society, 17*(4), 55–75.
Pitakdumrongkit, K. (2018, May 5). No knight in shining armour for CMIM. *East Asia Forum*. http://www.eastasiaforum.org/2018/05/05/no-knight-in-shining-armour-for-cmim/. Accessed 19 Nov 2018.
Rethel, L. (2010). The new financial development paradigm and Asian bond markets. *New Political Economy, 15*(4), 493–517.
Scoles, S. D. (2016). *Harmonization of standards and mutual recognition agreements on conformity assessment in Indonesia, Malaysia, Thailand and Viet Nam*. ERIA research project 2015 no. 15. http://www.eria.org/RPR_FY2015_No.15.pdf. Accessed 21 Jan 2019.
Sharman, J. C. (2011). *The money laundry: Regulating criminal finance in the global economy*. Ithaca: Cornell University Press.
Shaxson, N. (2011). *Treasure islands: Tax havens and the men who stole the world*. London: Vintage Books.
Siregar, R., & Chabchitrchaidol, A. (2013). *Enhancing the effectiveness of CMIM and AMRO: Selected immediate challenges and tasks* (ADBI Working Paper No. 403). Tokyo: Asian Development Bank Institute. https://core.ac.uk/download/pdf/39418977.pdf. Accessed 21 Jan 2019.
Slaughter, A. M. (2004). *A new world order*. Princeton: Princeton University Press.
Sumano, B. (2013). *Explaining the liberalisation of professional migration in ASEAN*. PhD dissertation, School of Politics and International Relations, Queen Mary, University of London.

Te, V., Griffiths, R., Law, K., Hill, P. S., & Annear, P. L. (2018). The impact of ASEAN economic integration on health worker mobility: A scoping review of the literature. *Health Policy and Planning, 33*(8), 957–965.

UNCTAD/ERIA [United Nations Conference on Trade and Development and Economic Research Institute for ASEAN and East Asia]. (2018). *ASEAN/East Asia NTM database*. http://asean.i-tip.org. Accessed 28 Nov 2018.

VNA. (2018). Vietnam's master plan on ASEAN socio-cultural community 2025 updated. 23 July. https://en.vietnamplus.vn/vietnams-master-plan-on-asean-sociocultural-community-2025-updated/135158.vnp. Accessed 21 Jan 2019.

World Bank. (2018a). *Tariff rate, applied, weighted mean, all products (%)*. https://data.worldbank.org/indicator/TM.TAX.MRCH.WM.AR.ZS?locations=BN-KH-ID-LA-MY-MM-PH-SG-TH-VN. Accessed 28 Nov 2018.

World Bank. (2018b). *Doing business: Measuring business regulations*. http://www.doingbusiness.org. Accessed 21 Jan 2019.

Wu, Y., Shi, X., & Kimura, F. (2011). The electricity sector leads energy market integration in East Asia: Introduction. In Y. Wu, X. Shi, & F. Kimura (Eds.), *Energy market integration in East Asia: Theories, electricity sector and subsidies* (pp. 1–10). Jakarta: ERIA.

PART III

Capital, State and Society

CHAPTER 9

The Gendered Political Economy of Southeast Asian Development

Juanita Elias

INTRODUCTION

Gender inequality is rife in Southeast Asia. The region's political cultures, although variegated, are strongly patriarchal and, while a few high-profile female leaders exist, this obscures deeper political inequalities. Gender-based violence is also pervasive: for example, Southeast Asia has the highest rate of domestic violence of any world region, with an estimated 37.7% of women having been subjected to it (WHO 2013: 18). However, the experience and impact of gender inequality vary considerably across the region's states (see Table 9.1).

This chapter considers what it means to focus on gender in analysing the political economy of Southeast Asian development. A key insight of feminist political economy scholarship has been to identify the importance of gender as a lens through which we can study *any* political-economic process or phenomena. That is, *gendering* the study of the political economy of Southeast Asia is not about adding-in a specific concern with what might be understood as "women's issues" or women's activism. Rather, it

---

J. Elias (✉)
International Political Economy, University of Warwick, Coventry, UK
e-mail: Juanita.Elias@warwick.ac.uk

© The Author(s) 2020
T. Carroll et al. (eds.), *The Political Economy of Southeast Asia*, Studies in the Political Economy of Public Policy, https://doi.org/10.1007/978-3-030-28255-4_9

228 J. ELIAS

Table 9.1 Select gender inequality indicators

	UN gender inequality index		Women in parliament	Women in ministerial positions*		Maternal mortality ratio[b]	Females with at least some secondary education[c]	Female labour force participation rate[a]		Estimated income gap**
	Score	Rank/189	%	%	Rank		%	%	Ratio	Ratio
Brunei	0.236	51	9.1	0	174	23	69.1	59	0.79	0.61
Cambodia	0.473	116	18.5	9.1	142	161	15.1	80.9	0.79	0.73
Indonesia	0.453	104	19.8	25.7	46	126	44.5	50.7	0.66	0.49
Laos	0.461	109	27.5	7.4	148	197	33.6	76.9	0.78	1.04
Malaysia	0.287	62	13.1	8.3	146	40	78.9	50.8	0.66	0.67
Myanmar	0.456	106	10.2	5	162	178	28.7	51.3	0.62	0.79
Philippines	0.427	97	29.1	25	47	114	76.6	49.6	0.88	0.69
Singapore	0.067	12	23	5.3	161	10	76.1	60.5	0.96	0.7
Thailand	0.393	93	4.8	11.1	129	20	42.4	60.5	0.91	0.79
Vietnam	0.304	67	26.7	4.2	166	54	66.2	73.2	0.64	0.82

Sources: UNDP (2018), except *IPU (2017), **WEF (2018), based on UNDP methodology

Note: Ratios = value for women divided by that for men. 1 denotes total sex parity; scores below 1 indicate a gap favouring men. A score of 0.80, for example, shows women are 20% worse-off than men

[a]Ages 15 and older, ILO estimate, 2017
[b]Deaths per 100,000 live births due to pregnancy-related causes
[c]Aged 25 and older, 2010–17

is about recognising how gendered assumptions inform and construct wider structures, institutions and processes, including the processes of state and donor-led policy-making that have shaped development outcomes in the region (Waylen 2006). This chapter draws attention to the wide-ranging feminist literature on the political economy of the region—a body of research that is frequently missing in conventional and critical introductions to the politics and political economy of Southeast Asia.[1] In doing so, it highlights how a range of implicitly and explicitly gendered biases and assumptions underpin Southeast Asian developmentalism.

First, development planning that stresses the need for export-oriented industrialisation (EOI) across Southeast Asia was, and continues to be, rooted in assumptions about the availability of a reserve army of low-cost female labour. These assumptions played out in many parts of industrialising Asia in terms of widening gender pay gaps and inequalities as young women workers were channelled into manufacturing for export industries. Second, state planning for economic development across Southeast Asia has often reflected a starkly non- or even anti-welfarist orientation, which places particular burdens on female family members to undertake the work of care—burdens which are exacerbated during times of economic downturn and crisis. Third, as many development studies scholars have noted, there is a persistent "male bias" (Elson 1990) in how "the economy" and "development" are understood, such that economic activity centred in the household (paid or unpaid) is consistently undervalued relative to economic activity associated with the productive sphere. These are just some of the issues that will be explored in this chapter, which draws upon a rich body of research from across the region that points to the multifaceted ways in which gender inequalities are constructed and reproduced (as well as resisted and, occasionally, undone).

Although these gender dynamics are an integral part of the political economy of Southeast Asia's development, the production and

---

[1] For example, when gender is mentioned in textbooks that introduce students to the study of Southeast Asia's political economy, it is usually in relation to women's involvement in civil society organisations (e.g. Dragsbaek Schmidt 2010: 237), without any substantive analysis of how women's movements have, for example, worked to highlight the gender biases and impacts of regional trade and migration regimes and patterns of investment. Note also the lack of any focus on gender in a number of key Southeast Asian politics and political economy texts, including Ba and Beeson (2018), Kingsbury (2016), Robison (2012), Rasiah and Dragsbaek Schmidt (2010) and, indeed, earlier editions of *The Political Economy of Southeast Asia*.

reproduction of gender inequality occurs within the context of other forms of social inequality, most notably those of class, race and nationality, alongside rural–urban and generational divides. The emphasis on class-based social conflict found in the work of scholarship associated with the "Murdoch School" of political economy (see Hameiri and Jones, this volume) provides a potentially useful entry point. In this work, social conflict is largely understood in terms of the competition for power and resources between (elite) class factions in and around the state, alongside a broader politics of class-based struggle, through which social resistance and unrest, as well as repression, co-optation and accommodation of class interests, take place. A focus on gender, however, revises this understanding of the relationship between the state, social conflict and capitalist transformation, by examining how the reproduction of class inequalities and conflicts occur alongside and are bound up with persistent gender inequalities. Gender inequalities are themselves sustained through state policies and practices that typically fail to recognise the significant role of unpaid and underpaid feminised forms of work, often within the home. Thus, for example, efforts to increase women's labour force participation, or to increase the contribution that women make to the productive economy (e.g. through microcredit and loan schemes aimed at increasing levels of entrepreneurship), usually fail to recognise the significant responsibility that women take for what is termed "social reproduction"—labour, usually centred on the household, that is central to the reproduction of life itself and thus underpins the productive economy (Hoskyns and Rai 2007: 300; Luxton 2018). A lack of recognition for the labour of social reproduction is sustained via state ideologies that have tended to reify and naturalise women's roles as wives and mothers. This understanding of the state as acting to provide the ideological "fixing" and structuring of patterns of power relations between men and women, including how masculinities and femininities are defined within a given context, draws upon feminist work on the links between gender and nationalism (Yuval-Davis 1993) as well as Connell's (1987) concept of the "gender order", an account of how different gendered regimes of labour, intimacy and emotion are structured within a given social context.

Local gender orders that emerge from state policies and practices, which effectively police the production/social reproduction binary, are invariably sites of intensely gendered forms of contestation, which do not always overlap with the class-based social conflicts foregrounded by traditional "Murdoch School" accounts. A feminist revision to this approach, then, draws attention to how social conflicts integral to Southeast Asia's capitalist development also reflect deeply embedded tensions between production and social reproduction. In short, we need to think about more than just class; we need to understand how the material basis of gender inequality in the region emerges through conflicts around the appropriate role and position of women in society. These conflicts serve to shape an accumulation regime in which women's unpaid, barely-paid and low-paid labour has contributed to the region's economic growth and "development".

I explore these issues in two ways. First, I focus on the emergence of a highly feminised production regime in Southeast Asia as a key component of state-led development. I emphasise the links between state policies aimed at delivering economic growth via EOI and the gendered regimes of work and employment that underpinned these strategies. The chapter's second part shifts towards a broader focus on the relationship between social reproduction and gendered regimes of state power in the region. Specifically, I examine the consistent failure of Southeast Asian states to provide social welfare support that would alleviate gender inequalities. That women continue to carry the burden of the labour of social reproduction means that development policies, practices and state responses in times of crisis have been largely blind to the specific problems and issues women face. I demonstrate this through examples including the impact of the 1997 Asian financial crisis, social care policy in Singapore and Malaysia, the gendered impacts of displacement in the Philippines, and urban evictions in Indonesia.

Factory Work, Feminised Labour and State Development Projects

The gendered political economy of Southeast Asia's development is revealed most obviously in numerous studies of the rapid expansion of highly feminised, low-wage factory work that accompanied the adoption of export-led growth (for an overview see Gunawardana 2018). Women's labour played a crucial role in EOI, especially when this was centred on low value-added, labour-intensive light manufacturing industries, such as garment production, toy manufacture and consumer electronics assembly. This story is not unique. Globally, feminised employment has tended to dominate export-oriented light manufacturing. In Southeast Asia this was driven by two processes: first, the expansion of sectors of the economy in which women's labour had traditionally predominated, including garment production and some agricultural/food production; and, second, the significant increase in female employment in what had previously been male-dominated sectors (Caraway 2007: 81). The policy-makers driving EOI often did not anticipate these outcomes. In Malaysia, for example, they assumed that men—particularly ethnic Malays—would benefit from the expansion of job opportunities in the export sector (Chin 2000: 1043). The feminisation of the industrial manufacturing labour force was largely driven by multinational corporate practices, whereby women were seen as "well-suited" to assembly-line work. Nonetheless, local socio-economic conditions and cultural practices have shaped the specific mechanisms through which labour force feminisation plays out.

The link between export-led manufacturing and the rapid increase in low-cost, feminised labour is widely recognised. Seguino (2000), for example, shows how gender inequality within local labour markets was a significant competitive advantage for East Asia's newly industrialising countries (NICs) and underpinned their initially high levels of economic growth. Put simply, when production is labour-intensive, low wages are essential to suppress production costs and make goods sufficiently cheaply that they can realise a profit in global markets, where many low-wage economies may be competing. Where women's wages are below men's, their employment suppresses costs further, boosting a country's competitiveness.

Alongside gender inequality, the wage suppression necessary for EOI was also facilitated by the often brutal suppression of trade union activities and the political left more broadly (see Quimpo, this volume). But trade union suppression is also often highly gendered. For example, in Malaysia, industrial relations policies introduced from the 1980s onwards ensured that the highly export-oriented and feminised electronics sector could not be unionised (Grace 1990). State repression of mostly female garment-sector workers in Thailand and Cambodia has also been well documented (Hughes 2007; Pangsapa 2007). At the same time, trade unions in highly feminised export manufacturing sectors, such as garment production, have often completely failed to represent the needs and interests of largely feminised workforces, leaving gendered structures of low pay intact (Evans 2017).

In her study of women's factory work in Indonesia, Caraway (2007) draws attention to the "gendered discourses of work" that lead to specific forms of factory employment being almost exclusively feminised. These include claims that women are "naturally" suited to certain types of work (e.g. sewing, assembly-line work); that women do not necessarily need higher-paid work since they are unlikely to be primary "breadwinners"; and that women are less likely to cause problems on the factory floor or join/form trade unions (see also Elias 2004). These findings tally with earlier work by feminist political economists that identified a global preference for female workers in export-oriented manufacturing, with women framed as "docile", "diligent" and "nimble fingered" (Elson and Pearson 1984; Fuentes and Ehrenreich 1983; Mies 1986).

EOI in Southeast Asia, as in other regions, remains deeply feminised. Just as the export-led growth in Singapore, Malaysia, Thailand and Indonesia saw significant increases in both female employment and the feminisation of export-sector industries, we can trace similar processes in later-industrialising Southeast Asian states, notably Cambodia and Vietnam, which have witnessed a dramatic shift in female employment from agriculture to industry. For example, from 1991 to 2018, the proportion of female employees working in industry rose from 3.3% to 25.5% in Cambodia and from 7.8% to 21.2% in Vietnam, while the proportion employed in agriculture fell from 83.3% to 25.2% in Cambodia and from 75.6% to 41% in Vietnam (ILO 2018).

The feminisation of work is not simply a matter of more women taking up work that had been traditionally undertaken by men. Rather, it is also accompanied by a decline in the terms and conditions of employment, e.g. reductions in wages and lower levels of unionisation, in the sectors concerned (Standing 1989, 1999). The emergence of "feminised" work is thus a comment on the nature of the work itself—"flexible" (i.e. easy to hire and fire), feminised workforces employed in tightly controlled, intensive manufacturing work where there is little scope for resistance to these labour practices.

Although the feminisation of labour is a global trend, local socio-economic contexts shape its specific form in Southeast Asia. For example, research on women's changing economic status in Singapore during the 1970s cited "traditional religiocultural systems of Confucianism, Hinduism and Islam", which "prescribed a subordinate status to women within the household", as part of the explanation for why capitalist development had "hardly altered the sexual division of labour" (Wong 1981: 449, 451). Indeed, local socio-cultural norms and values pertaining to gender roles have been deployed by corporations themselves to secure and maintain a supply of low-cost and compliant feminised labour. A preference for young unmarried women has been a fairly consistent feature of recruitment practices into export manufacturing industries (Beresford et al. 2016; Ong 1987; Wolf 1992)—although sometimes other forms of social inequality can be equally productive of low-cost labour forces. For example, employers may benefit from employing older women with children with few other employment options (Lie and Lund 1994). More recent studies have also sought to explore how increased reliance on migrant labour forces (both documented and undocumented) has created new even more repressive forms of workplace hierarchy that are as much gendered as they are deeply racialised (Campbell 2016; Crinis 2013; Pangsapa 2015; also Gerard and Bal, this volume).

Much of the literature on women's industrial employment in Southeast Asia asks whether participation in the formal productive economy serves to "empower" women. That is, does earning a cash income undermine patriarchal structures and grant women greater levels of autonomy and/or access to significantly improved living standards? Feminists are often sceptical, highlighting the inherently exploitative nature of feminised factory employment and the new forms of managerialist discipline that shape the experience of working on the factory floor. But many studies also recognise that women often actively seek factory employment, which does offer some limited opportunities for economic autonomy. For example, Wolf's (1992) study of Javanese "factory daughters" identifies factory workers' new economic opportunities and experiences and the ways through which young women felt they were breaking and challenging traditional gender roles through everyday acts of consumption, living away from home and acquiring an identity as "workers". Critics argue that this paints an overly optimistic account, buying into a liberal-feminist myth of empowerment through the market (Eisenstein 2015). But Wolf does not suggest that factory life is not difficult, dangerous or exploitative. It is better to understand Wolf's study in terms of what feminist authors Elson and Pearson (1984) identify as the "decomposition", "recomposition" and "intensification" of gender relations within the world market factory. This recognises the inherent contradictions of gendered social transformation operating within wider capitalist transitions, including how women workers have sought to resist and transform the oppressive structures of the factory environment.

Take, for example, Ong's (1987) classic study of young, rural Malaysian women's incorporation into factory employment in the 1980s. Situated against the backdrop of the decline of small-scale cash-cropping in Malaysia, Ong shows that class struggles are completely reconstituted by industrialisation. Peasant women had to reckon with their incorporation into new modes of capitalist discipline within the factory, and with the changing nature of patriarchal gender relations outside of it, notably finding ways to respond to a moral panic over factory workers' assumed sexual promiscuity (see also Mills 2017). Because Ong focuses on how women seek to resist and undermine factory authority, this study goes some way in challenging the persistent myth of female worker docility. However, she also notes that women fought back against gendered modes of capitalist discipline by emphasising their personal religious piety, drawing on local cultural resources in ways that recomposed a gendered hierarchy.

Further challenging gendered stereotypes of "docility", women across the region have been actively involved in trade union activism, strikes and other collective forms of labour protest (McKay 2006; Pangsapa 2007; Rosa 1994). Tran's (2008) work on women's labour activism in Vietnam is especially interesting because she demonstrates how, within the specific context of the Vietnamese state, hyper-exploited female workforces have been more successful than those in other Southeast Asian states in terms of accessing labour rights and engaging in forms of labour activism and solidarity.

Beyond Production: State, Crisis and Social Welfare

Despite being the focus of many studies, export-oriented manufacturing is not the only site within which women perform important economic roles. The overwhelming focus of attention on the export sector can lead to the risk that political economists fall into a productivist bias that obscures the labour of social reproduction or fails to recognise the significance of women's labour within informal and/or subsistence economies. For example, Franck (2016) has drawn attention to the significance of informal sector employment for women through their lives. Her research from Penang, Malaysia, demonstrates that working-class women often experience short periods of employment in export manufacturing but spend the bulk of their working lives in the informal sector. Studies of women's factory employment do, of course, draw attention to the "dual burdens" of productive work and care that female workers face, and the role that perceptions of women's "secondary" income-earner status play in suppressing wages. However, to thoroughly understand the relationships between state development programmes and the reproduction of gendered inequalities, we must examine the role that assumptions about women's ability to support and maintain the household play in development planning and policy-making.

These assumptions are complex and vary across different Southeast Asian contexts. On the one hand, women are hyper-visible in development programmes focused on issues like fertility rates (Rigg 2012: 143–155; Thambiah 2010), and family policy, such as efforts by state or donor agencies to boost marriage rates, lower divorce rates, encourage "better" parenting skills, or engage in forms of "family strengthening" (Brickell 2011; Elias 2015). On the other hand, the highly gendered care and household labour undertaken mainly by women is largely unaccounted for in economic policy-making and development planning. A key technical issue here is that women's unpaid labour is not factored into things like GDP calculations, rendering social reproduction invisible to policy-makers (Hill et al. 2017: 1).

This has several significant implications. First, when policies have been established to address gender inequalities through maximising women's participation in the formal and the informal economy, there is an overwhelming failure to recognise the already significant burden of the labour of social reproduction that women shoulder (Elias 2011). Such pressures are, of course, mediated by class and nationality. Welfare systems in Southeast Asia—in both high- and low-income states—have been designed around the assumption that the family "takes care of its own", which conveniently relieves the region's capitalist states of much responsibility for social reproduction, but implicitly assigns this responsibility to women. As increasing numbers of middle-class women in higher-income Southeast Asian states have joined the labour force; this has generated demand for paid domestic labour, which transfers the care burden of middle-class women onto groups of lower-class, often migrant, female workers whose conditions of vulnerability are reproduced by state migration and labour regimes (see Gerard and Bal, this volume). Second, policy-makers fail to recognise the impacts of economic policies on women and their households. This problem is particularly acute during times of crisis, when women's unpaid labour serves to meet the additional burdens placed on households when incomes fall and state support, if it exists, is withdrawn. Third, the failure to account for social reproduction has significant detrimental material effects—what Rai et al. (2014) have termed depletion through social reproduction. "Depletion", that is the weakening of communities, households and individuals that stems from the non-recognition of social reproduction, is a highly embodied process. It encapsulates the experiences of the female factory worker who struggles to combine work and caring roles, or the migrant domestic worker who is expected to work all hours since her labour is not considered actual "work". Depletion through social reproduction calls attention to how macro-structural processes of capitalist development and state transformation are experienced in daily life and highlights how the persistent non-recognition of social reproduction has debilitating effects on communities, households and women's own health and life chances.

I illustrate these points below to demonstrate the significance of the politics and practices of social reproduction in understanding how states have pursued economic development in Southeast Asia. This blindness to women's economic roles has had negative, depletive consequences for many women. Not only must this be addressed in development policymaking; we must also ensure that it is not reproduced within mainstream and critical texts introducing students to the study of Southeast Asian politics and political economy.

The Gendered Impacts of Asia's Crisis

A major focus of political economy research on gender in Southeast Asia, especially after the 1997 Asian financial crisis (AFC; see Carroll, this volume), was the impact of the subsequent economic downturn on women. This literature has shown that the pursuit of economic transformation in Southeast Asia has rested upon assumptions that, in the context of very limited social welfare, households are essentially "shock absorbers" in times of crisis. Evaluations of the impacts of the AFC on women and their households pointed to increases in female poverty and unemployment, growing gender wage gaps, gendered health impacts, increases in women working in the sex industry, and increased levels of child labour (Aslanbeigui and Summerfield 2000). These analyses indicate how social reproduction served to ensure the survival of households in times of economic crisis, but also highlight the forms of "depletion" experienced by the poor, and poor women in particular, who undertake this vital work of care and subsistence.

After the AFC, the International Monetary Fund (IMF) imposed austerity regimes in Indonesia, South Korea and Thailand. The associated cuts in public expenditure were widely criticised because the crisis was not caused by budget deficits. Although the "real" economies in many afflicted states were relatively strong, the IMF ploughed ahead with liberalisation policies and corporate governance reform. The impact on women was striking. Across crisis-affected states, women's engagement in the informal economy increased, while their unpaid domestic work—including things like growing vegetables or meal preparation—also increased. Poor households ate less, and spent significantly less on education and healthcare, with women household members especially negatively affected; for example, women were most likely to forgo meals (Knowles et al. 1999 cited in Elson 2014; Thomas et al. 1999). In the Philippines, women's working hours increased dramatically as they took on extra work outside of the home as a crucial household survival strategy (Lim 2000). The extent to which households bore the brunt of economic recession is starkly revealed in research from Indonesia by Thomas et al. (1999), in which household size was shown to increase as urban households migrated to join extended families in rural areas where the cost of living was lower—a shift that invariably reflected increases in urban unemployment, alongside government policies that encouraged this reverse-migration to curtail rising social and political tensions in the cities (Silvey and Elmhirst 2003: 865).

Thus, as Elson (2002) has argued, post-AFC developments exemplify processes of "downloading risks to the kitchen": economic pain was "offloaded from those who took risks (mainly high income men) to women, especially low income women, who had to absorb the risks, because they could not liquidate their responsibility for their children" (Elson 2014: 193). Elson's argument shows how gendered processes, assumptions and biases are central to the operation of global finance. The financial system operates within the context of a gendered political economy that enables risk-taking or acts of extreme financial mismanagement. This gendered political economy was sustained by state policies in many "miracle" economies—in particular their role in upholding an anti-welfarist gender order that served to adversely incorporate women into the region's industrial development and left them especially vulnerable during the crisis (Truong 2000). Within this gender order, a politics of nationalism, which constructed "good" women as, first and foremost, home-makers served an important ideological purpose (Pettman 2003; Silvey 2000; Truong 2000).

Importantly, however, gender orders are not static. Economic development in Asia prior to the AFC led to shifts in popular perceptions regarding women's role and position both inside and outside the household. Silvey's (2000) work demonstrates how these shifting cultural norms fed into wider discourses concerning the gendered nature of Indonesia's crisis and the need for a reassertion of traditional (rural) values. The growth of the sex industry after the crisis, and the pressure for women internal migrants to return to rural areas, meant that women who migrated to find work were easily stigmatised. Thus "the morality of young women's autonomous mobility, and the prostitute as a symbol of the threatened social order, have emerged as defining local tropes of the post-1997 period of political and economic upheaval" (Silvey 2000: 156). Indeed, as Pettman (2003: 176) has argued, in understanding Asia's economic shifts, "the language of globalization, or Asian miracle or crisis, functions to disguise the gendered nature of these transformations and the unevenness, the inequalities, and the costs of transformation".

From Anti-welfarism to Everyday Crisis

Despite the imaginary of booming Asia, the non- or even anti-welfarist orientation of Southeast Asian states continues to shape poor women's lived experiences. Neoliberal state strategies across Southeast Asia minimise institutional support for social reproduction, seen most obviously in the emergence of a regional market for migrant domestic care labour (Elias 2018; see Gerard and Bal, this volume). Of course, it is not only the current neoliberal gender order that has marked women's care labour as "unrewarded" labour. But the anti-welfarism that has emerged as a defining feature of Southeast Asian social policy sits comfortably within a region of increasingly neoliberal states in which welfare spending, especially that targeted at the private sphere of the family, is seen as something to be reduced and/or avoided. Even the region's higher- to middle-income states have not sought to increase welfare spending in this area, leaving the work of care to female family members or, for wealthier citizens, to private care providers (Hill et al. 2017).

In high-income Singapore, notwithstanding relatively high levels of female participation in the labour force—estimated at 58.8% in 2017 (UNDP 2018)—care work is still viewed as principally a household responsibility (Lyons 2017: 55). State care services for the elderly, in particular, are virtually non-existent, being seen as a "last resort" option. The lack of investment in social welfare services to support unpaid caring needs is justified by state ideologies that have persistently clung to the view that taking care work outside the family is a form of "Westernisation" that undermines family and Asian values (Teo 2013). This rhetoric is applied rather selectively, however, and practices are heavily mediated by class.

Low-income women are most likely to give up work to take on caring roles, while skilled and high-income women's caring responsibilities are effectively "outsourced" to migrant domestic workers (Lyons 2017; Peng 2018; Yeoh and Huang 2009). Similar patterns also emerge in Malaysia, where women's relatively poor labour force participation—estimated at 44.4% in 2017 (UNDP 2018)—is seen as a major policy concern, especially with respect to educated, middle-class women who drop out of the labour market after having children. However, despite concerted government efforts to encourage women's labour force participation, this pattern stubbornly persists, with most women citing their household responsibilities as a major cause (Elias 2011). These cases illustrate how the failure to see care as a social welfare priority in Southeast Asia has produced a gendered political economy that is highly reliant on the private sector and the labour of poorer women to meet the care needs of an affluent population. Even when such systems are increasingly difficult to maintain, "maids" remain central to perceptions of having attained middle-class status (Chin 1998; Elias and Louth 2016).

For the region's poorest, however, the everyday depletive consequences of the non-recognition of social reproduction labour have been especially significant. The outsourcing of care work to "maids"—which might putatively "liberate" middle-class women in higher-income families/states—rests upon the exploitation of lower-class women from poorer families/states. The latter are often deliberately spurred to emigrate by official government "development" policies, and a lack of alternative employment opportunities and/or welfare support (Rodriguez 2010; see also Gerard and Bal, this volume), leaving behind their homes, and in some cases their children (Parreñas 2005). Migrant domestic workers are poorly paid and frequently experience abuses including the withholding of salary and passports, inadequate time off, over-work, and physical and sexual abuse. Host governments also exhibit reticence in regulating against citizens (employers) on behalf of non-citizens (foreign domestic workers). This is perhaps unsurprising given the important roles that domestic workers play in social reproduction in places such as Singapore and Malaysia. Moreover, because domestic work is not formally recognised as "work", these practices are largely shielded from workplace regulations or government intervention, with the gendered definition of the home as the "private" sphere creating opportunities for employers to act with impunity (see further Gerard and Bal, this volume). Remittances to the Philippines from migrant workers totalled a staggering US$24bn in 2013, amounting to 12.7% of GDP

(IFRC 2015), providing a vital lifeline to families and again compensating for the lack of state welfare provision. But the human cost for many women is extremely high.

Gendered effects also stem from apparently "innocent" development policies. For example, in the Philippines, a neoliberalism-compatible discourse of "resilience" has become embedded within development planning and policy-making—a legacy in large part of the country's repeated experience of catastrophic natural disasters (Eadie 2019). But resilience itself is a highly gendered discourse: the ability of citizens and communities to "bounce back" after natural disasters or conflict is often down to the unpaid labour of female household members, whose own health and access to adequate nutrition are severely constrained. In this sense, then, the deterioration in health outcomes for poor Philippine women is "among the invisible costs of sustaining a neoliberal global economy" (Tanyag 2018: 656). As Maria Tanyag's work on this topic makes clear, there has been an injurious coalescing of neoliberal and conservative values within the state that serve to naturalise and render invisible women's unpaid labour, and prevent the emergence of the kind of state interventions that would better support women experiencing displacement and disaster. Tanyag is particularly critical of the way in which an emphasis on "short-term survival" pervades both neoliberal economic thinking and conservative gender ideologies, whereby women's perceived natural "altruism" serves to stave off the worst impacts of crisis situations, "at the expense of longer term and inclusive recovery" (Tanyag 2018: 656; see also Brickell and Chant 2010).

Considering the experience of urban poor women also reveals the many ways through which development policy-making fails to recognise the essential work that women do to support their households and communities, and the detrimental consequences of this failure for poor communities more broadly. In recent years in Jakarta, for example, an urban eviction regime has had catastrophic consequences for urban poor residents who had built their lives and livelihoods around specific neighbourhoods, known as *kampungs* (see Hutchison and Wilson, and Rodan and Baker, both this volume). Urban planning has failed to recognise the gendered organisation of the household economy that underpins livelihood strategies in these *kampungs*. Research on the experiences of urban poor women has identified the persistence of gendered divisions of labour, whereby women are responsible for unpaid domestic reproductive tasks such as water and fuel collection, waste disposal, cooking, cleaning and care for children, sick and the elderly (see for example, Agarwal 1997). Urban residents are also more dependent on monetary income in a cash economy, so in addition to reproductive tasks, women often need to earn money through participation in the labour market, typically in informal, low-paid, unskilled work frequently undertaken in the home. As a result, lower-class urban women are often time-poor as well as financially deficient. For women living in informal settlements, eviction has the material impact of dispossession of property and home. Moreover, as poor urban women often undertake remunerative work in the home, eviction can also lead to disruption of economic activity and livelihood and less access to infrastructure and affordable services, such as water, sanitation and childcare. Even where ameliorative policies exist, these often fail to recognise this reality. For example, poor urban women have often been moved to high-rise public housing where they can no longer run stalls from the front of their homes or rely on trusted friends and neighbours to help with childcare or care of the elderly. These economic consequences are worsened by the fact that those who relocate to public housing are then required to pay rent and are billed for utilities. As Tilley et al. (2019) argue, these issues largely stem from deep-rooted gender ideologies embedded in the state itself, whereby the "modern" (idealised, middle-class) housewife, or "Ibu", exists within a nuclear family unit and is viewed as economically inactive (Suryakusuma 2012). These planning assumptions do not map onto the lived experiences of the urban poor, who are not easily rehoused in simple, nuclear family units, leading to significant levels of overcrowding and collapses in household income (Tilley et al. 2019).

Unsurprisingly, given the particularly gendered impacts of the eviction regime in Jakarta, women have often been at the forefront of resistance struggles. Indeed, the formation of urban poor activist networks, in which women have played a prominent role, also reflects the fact that *kampung* women had already developed community-level social infrastructure designed to support women's caring needs (e.g. communal childcare facilities), to provide financial support in the form of savings clubs, and to undertake efforts to address issues of domestic violence. This is not to say that all women involved in struggles to resist forced eviction from their home found this to be an "empowering" experience—many urban poor organisations remain highly male dominated (Eddyono 2019). But women also played highly visible roles within efforts to resist eviction, be it through involvement in court cases, taking part in protests or (re)occupying the sites from which they had been evicted (for accounts of the gender politics of resistance to *rural* evictions/land grabbing in Southeast Asia see Morgan 2017, and Park 2018).

Conclusion

What does it actually mean to "gender" the study of Southeast Asian political economy? This chapter can naturally present only a short, partial answer to this question. One potential aspect concerns the role of gender in relation to what might be termed "market deepening"—the extension of marketised social relations into the spaces of everyday life, like the household. This, for example, involves the proliferation of things like microenterprise and microfinance projects across the region (projects that tend to target women), alongside efforts to boost women's labour force participation. But such strategies do not necessarily represent a project for the "completion of the world market" (Cammack 2016). Much of what makes women's labour so cheap and exploitable stems from their positioning within the household economy, whereby the unpaid labour that they undertake at home continues to go, if not unrecognised, then certainly unrewarded. Market deepening, then, exists alongside the persistent ignoring of social reproduction. Sometimes this labour is invisible, unseen and therefore unremarkable, but at other times it is seen, yet undervalued in terms of the vital role that it plays in the feminisation of survival in crisis situations. Crisis, be it financial crisis, natural disaster, or the calamitous impact of state planning policies, hence throws into sharp relief the everyday vital work of social reproduction, alongside the depletive consequences that stem from lack of recognition.

Thus, this chapter has offered a different lens through which to view many of the big or conventional topics of political economy, and the political economy of Southeast Asia in particular. The discussion of women's factory work, for example, provides insights into the human consequences of trade and investment regimes, and the policies and practices of the developmental state, including how gender inequality is intimately tied up with trade union repression. A focus on social reproduction provides alternative understandings of work and productivity, as well as further insight into how privatised care regimes fuelled the growth of the market for migrant domestic work. These are all issues that indicate the many and varied gendered ways through which state transformation in Asia takes shape. And yet, gender remains a blind spot within a great deal of Southeast Asian political economy analysis.

References

Agarwal, B. (1997). "Bargaining" and gender relations: Within and beyond the household. *Feminist Economics, 3*(1), 1–51.

Aslanbeigui, N., & Summerfield, G. (2000). The Asian crisis: Gender and the international financial architecture. *Feminist Economics, 6*(3), 81–103.

Ba, A., & Beeson, M. (Eds.). (2018). *Contemporary Southeast Asia* (3rd ed.). London: Palgrave Macmillan.

Beresford, M., Cucco, I., & Prota, L. (2016). Child labour and gender discrimination in the garment industry of Kong Pisei, Cambodia. In V. Crinis & A. Vickers (Eds.), *Labour in the clothing industry in the Asia Pacific* (pp. 142–168). London: Routledge.

Brickell, K. (2011). The "stubborn stain" on development: Gendered meanings of housework (non-)participation in Cambodia. *Journal of Development Studies, 47*(9), 1353–1370.

Brickell, K., & Chant, S. (2010). "The Unbearable heaviness of being" reflections on female altruism in Cambodia, Philippines, The Gambia and Costa Rica. *Progress in Development Studies, 10*(2), 145–159.

Cammack, P. (2016). World market regionalism at the Asian Development Bank. *Journal of Contemporary Asia, 46*(2), 173–197.

Campbell, S. (2016). Everyday recomposition: Precarity and socialization in Thailand's migrant labour force. *American Ethnologist, 43*(2), 258–269.

Caraway, T. (2007). *Assembling women: The feminization of global manufacturing*. Ithaca: Cornell University Press.

Chin, C. B. N. (1998). *In service and servitude: Foreign female domestic workers and the Malaysian "modernity" project*. New York: Columbia University Press.

Chin, C. B. N. (2000). The state of the "state" in globalization: Social order and economic restructuring in Malaysia. *Third World Quarterly, 21*(6), 1035–1057.

Connell, R. W. (1987). *Gender and power*. Cambridge: Polity Press.

Crinis, V. (2013). Vietnamese migrant clothing workers in Malaysia: Global production, transnational labour migration and social reproduction. In J. Elias & S. Gunawardana (Eds.), *The global political economy of the household in Asia* (pp. 162–177). London: Palgrave Macmillan.

Dragsbaek Schmidt, J. (2010). Civil society and distributional conflicts in Southeast Asia. In R. Rasiah & J. Dragsbaek Schmidt (Eds.), *The new political economy of Southeast Asia* (pp. 229–256). Cheltenham: Edward Elgar.

Eadie, P. (2019). Typhoon Yolanda and post disaster resilience: Problems and challenges. *Asia Pacific Viewpoint, 60*(1), 94–107.

Eddyono, S. W. (2019). *Women's empowerment in Indonesia: A poor community in Jakarta*. London: Routledge.

Eisenstein, H. (2015, June 17). The sweatshop feminists. *Jacobin.* https://www.jacobinmag.com/2015/06/kristof-globalization-development-third-world/. Accessed 4 Mar 2019.

Elias, J. (2004). *Fashioning inequality: The multinational corporation and gendered employment in a globalizing world.* Aldershot: Ashgate.

Elias, J. (2011). The gender politics of economic competitiveness in Malaysia's transition to a knowledge-economy. *The Pacific Review, 24*(5), 529–552.

Elias, J. (2015). Civil society and the gender politics of economic competitiveness in Malaysia. *Globalizations, 12*(3), 347–364.

Elias, J. (2018). Governing domestic worker migration in Southeast Asia: Public–private partnerships, regulatory grey zones and the household. *Journal of Contemporary Asia, 48*(2), 278–300.

Elias, J., & Louth, J. (2016). Producing migrant domestic work: Exploring the everyday political economy of Malaysia's "maid shortage". *Globalizations, 13*(6), 830–845.

Elson, D. (1990). *Male bias in the development process.* Manchester: Manchester University Press.

Elson, D. (2002). The international financial architecture: The view from the kitchen. *Femina Politica, 11*(1), 26–37.

Elson, D. (2014). Economic crises from the 1980s to the 2010s. In S. M. Rai & G. Waylen (Eds.), *New frontiers in feminist political economy* (pp. 189–212). London: Routledge.

Elson, D., & Pearson, R. (1984). The subordination of women and the internationalisation of factory production. In K. Young, C. Wolkowitz, & R. McCullagh (Eds.), *Of marriage and the market: Women's subordination internationally and its lessons* (2nd ed., pp. 18–40). London: Routledge.

Evans, A. (2017). Patriarchal unions = weaker unions? Industrial relations in the Asian garment industry. *Third World Quarterly, 38*(7), 1619–1638.

Franck, A. J. (2016). From formal employment to street vending: Malaysian women's labour force participation over the life course. In J. Elias & L. Rethel (Eds.), *The everyday political economy of Southeast Asia* (pp. 159–177). Cambridge: Cambridge University Press.

Fuentes, A., & Ehrenreich, B. (1983). *Women in the global factory.* New York: Institute for Communications.

Grace, E. (1990). *Short-circuiting labour: Unionising electronic workers in Malaysia.* Petaling Jaya: Insan.

Gunawardana, S. J. (2018). Industrialization, feminization and mobilities. In J. Elias & A. Roberts (Eds.), *Handbook on the political economy of gender* (pp. 440–455). Cheltenham: Edward Elgar.

Hill, E., Ford, M., & Baird, M. (2017). Work/care regimes in the Asia-Pacific: A feminist framework. In M. Baird, M. Ford, & E. Hill (Eds.), *Women, work and care in the Asian Pacific* (pp. 1–22). London: Routledge.

Hoskyns, C., & Rai, S. M. (2007). Recasting the global political economy: Counting women's unpaid work. *New Political Economy, 12*(3), 297–317.

Hughes, C. (2007). Transnational networks, international organization and political participation in Cambodia: Human rights, labour rights and common rights. *Democratization, 14*(5), 834–852.

IFRC [International Federation of Red Cross and Red Crescent Societies]. (2015). *Statistics on labor migration within the Asia-Pacific region.* https://www.ifrc.org/Global/Documents/Asia-pacific/201505/Map_Infographic.pdf. Accessed 10 Apr 2019.

ILO [International Labour Organisation]. (2018). *ILOSTAT database data.* https://data.worldbank.org/indicator/SL.IND.EMPL.FE.ZS?view=chart. Accessed 13 Apr 2019.

IPU [Inter-Parliamentary Union]. (2017). *Women in politics, 2017.* https://www.ipu.org/resources/publications/infographics/2017-03/women-in-politics-2017. Accessed 25 Apr 2019.

Kingsbury, D. (2016). *Politics in contemporary Southeast Asia: Authority, democracy and political change.* London: Routledge.

Lie, M., & Lund, R. (1994). *Renegotiating local values: Working women and foreign industry in Malaysia.* Richmond: Curzon Press.

Lim, J. C. (2000). The effects of the Asian crisis on the employment of women and men: The Philippine case. *World Development, 38*(7), 1285–1306.

Luxton, M. (2018). The production of life itself: Gender, social reproduction and IPE. In J. Elias & A. Roberts (Eds.), *Handbook on the international political economy and gender* (pp. 37–49). Cheltenham: Edward Elgar.

Lyons, L. (2017). Singapore: Contradictions in the work/care regime. In M. Baird, M. Ford, & E. Hill (Eds.), *Women, work and care in the Asian Pacific* (pp. 55–70). London: Routledge.

McKay, S. C. (2006). *Satanic mills or silicon islands? The politics of high-tech production in the Philippines.* Ithaca: Cornell University Press.

Mies, M. (1986). *Patriarchy and accumulation on a world scale.* London: Zed.

Mills, M. B. (2017). Gendered morality tales: Discourses of gender, labour and value in globalizing Asia. *The Journal of Development Studies, 53*(3), 316–330.

Morgan, M. (2017). Women, gender and protest: Contesting oil palm plantation expansion in Indonesia. *Journal of Peasant Studies, 44*(6), 1177–1196.

Ong, A. (1987). *Spirits of resistance and capitalist discipline: Factory women in Malaysia.* Albany: SUNY Press.

Pangsapa, P. (2007). *Textures of struggle: The emergence of resistance among garment workers in Thailand.* Ithaca: Cornell University Press.

Pangsapa, P. (2015). When battlefields become market places: Migrant workers and the role of civil society in NGO activism in Thailand. *International Migration, 53*(3), 124–149.

Park, C. M. Y. (2018). "Our lands are our lives": Gendered experiences of resistance to land grabbing in rural Cambodia. *Feminist Economics*. Online first.
Parreñas, R. S. (2005). *Children of global migration: Transnational families and gendered woes.* Stanford: Stanford University Press.
Peng, I. (2018). Culture, institution and diverse approaches to care and care work in East Asia. *Current Sociology, 66*(4), 643–659.
Pettman, J. J. (2003). Gendering globalisation in Asia through miracle and crisis. *Gender, Technology and Development, 7*(2), 171–187.
Rai, S. M., Hoskyns, C., & Thomas, D. (2014). Depletion: The cost of social reproduction. *International Feminist Journal of Politics, 16*(1), 86–105.
Rasiah, R., & Dragsbaek Schmidt, J. (Eds.). (2010). *The new political economy of Southeast Asia.* Cheltenham: Edward Elgar.
Rigg, J. (2012). *Unplanned development: Tracking change in Southeast Asia.* London: Zed.
Robison, R. (Ed.). (2012). *Routledge handbook of Southeast Asian politics.* London: Routledge.
Rodriguez, R. M. (2010). *Migrants for export: How the Philippine state brokers labour to the world.* Minneapolis: University of Minnesota Press.
Rosa, K. (1994). The conditions and organisational activities of women in free trade zones: Malaysia, Philippines and Sri Lanka, 1970–1990. In S. Rowbotham & S. Mitter (Eds.), *Dignity and daily bread: New forms of economic organization among poor women in the third world and the first* (pp. 73–99). London: Routledge.
Seguino, S. (2000). Gender inequality and economic growth: A cross country analysis. *World Development, 28*(7), 1211–1230.
Silvey, R. (2000). Stigmatized spaces: Moral geographies under crisis in South Sulawesi, Indonesia. *Gender, Place and Culture, 7*(2), 143–161.
Silvey, R., & Elmhirst, R. (2003). Engendering social capital: Women workers and rural–urban networks in Indonesia's crisis. *World Development, 31*(5), 865–879.
Standing, G. (1989). Global feminization through flexible labour. *World Development, 17*(7), 1077–1095.
Standing, G. (1999). Global feminization through flexible labour: A theme revisited. *World Development, 27*(3), 583–602.
Suryakusuma, J. I. (2012, July 1). Is state Ibuism still relevant? *Inside Indonesia*. https://www.insideindonesia.org/is-state-ibuism-still-relevant-2. Accessed 4 Apr 2019.
Tanyag, M. (2018). Depleting fragile bodies: The political economy of sexual and reproductive health in crisis situations. *Review of International Studies, 44*(4), 654–671.
Teo, Y. (2013). Women hold up the anti-welfare regime: How social policies produce social differentiation in Singapore. In J. Elias & S. J. Gunawardana (Eds.),

The global political economy of the household in Asia (pp. 15–27). London: Palgrave Macmillan.

Thambiah, S. (2010). The productive and non-(re) productive women: Sites of economic growth in Malaysia. *Asian Women, 26*(2), 49–76.

Thomas, D., Frankenberg, E., Beegle, K., & Teruel, G. (1999). *Household budgets, household composition and the crisis in Indonesia: Evidence from longitudinal household survey data*. Paper presented at the Population Association America meeting, New York, 25–27 March.

Tilley, L., Elias, J., & Rethel, L. (2019). Urban evictions and public housing and the gendered rationalisation of kampung life in Jakarta. *Asia Pacific Viewpoint, 60*(1), 80–93.

Tran, A. N. (2008). Contesting flexibility: Networks of place, gender and class in Vietnamese workers' resistance. In J. Nevins & N. L. Peluso (Eds.), *Taking Southeast Asia to market* (pp. 56–72). Ithaca: Cornell University Press.

Truong, T.-D. (2000). A feminist perspective on the Asian miracle and crisis: Enlarging the conceptual map of human development. *Journal of Human Development, 1*(1), 159–164.

UNDP [United Nations Development Program]. (2018). *Human development reports*. Table 5: Gender inequality index. http://hdr.undp.org/en/composite/GII. Accessed 9 Apr 2019.

Waylen, G. (2006). You still just don't understand: Why troubled engagements continue between feminists and (critical) IPE. *Review of International Studies, 32*(1), 145–164.

WEF [World Economic Forum]. (2018). *Global gender gap report 2018*. Geneva: WEF.

WHO [World Health Organisation]. (2013). *Global and regional estimates of violence against women: Prevalence and health effects of intimate partner violence and non-partner sexual violence*. Geneva: WHO.

Wolf, D. L. (1992). *Factory daughters: Gender, household dynamics, and rural industrialization*. Berkeley: University of California Press.

Wong, A. K. (1981). Planned development. Social stratification and the sexual division of labour in Singapore. *Signs, 7*(2), 434–452.

Yeoh, B., & Huang, S. (2009). Foreign domestic workers and home based care for elders in Singapore. *Journal of Aging and Social Policy, 22*(1), 69–88.

Yuval-Davis, N. (1993). Gender and nation. *Ethnic and Racial Studies, 16*(4), 621–632.

CHAPTER 10

Labour Migration in Southeast Asia: The Political Economy of Poor and Uneven Governance

Kelly Gerard and Charanpal S. Bal

INTRODUCTION

Labour migration plays a significant role in the economic development of contemporary Southeast Asian countries. A two-tier, or "bifurcated", system allows receiving states to cherry-pick professionals from the global workforce, while leaving low-wage migrants vulnerable to precarity, exploitation, abuse and debt bondage. For receiving countries, inflows of high- and low-wage migrant workers from within and beyond the region address skill and labour shortages, while ensuring infrastructural development and competitiveness of key industrial sectors. For sending countries, high-wage migration presents a significant loss of skills and capital, while low-wage migration allows policy-makers to mitigate the effects of domestic unemployment and reduce pressures for the expansion of welfare

K. Gerard (✉) • C. S. Bal
School of Social Sciences, The University of Western Australia, Perth, WA, Australia
e-mail: kelly.gerard@uwa.edu.au

© The Author(s) 2020
T. Carroll et al. (eds.), *The Political Economy of Southeast Asia*, Studies in the Political Economy of Public Policy, https://doi.org/10.1007/978-3-030-28255-4_10

provisions. Moreover, migrant remittances have become key to stimulating growth in these economies. Despite its importance for national development and individual livelihoods, however, labour migration has been poorly and unevenly governed.

This chapter presents a political economy of labour migration in the region that explains these outcomes. It examines the specific sectoral interests that underpin migrant labour policy, as well as emergent tensions and conflicts. The first section outlines the characteristics and drivers of labour migration within and beyond Southeast Asia. The second and third sections examine the governance of low- and high-wage migration respectively.[1] Sectoral interests that drive these arrangements are identified, along with the conflicts that have emerged over these arrangements, and the outcomes of these conflicts are assessed, with an emphasis on state responses.

Labour Migration in Southeast Asia

Characteristics

Since the 1990s, the total number of immigrants and emigrants in Southeast Asia has been rising (UN 2017). About half of all migrants are female, and the vast majority are temporary, low-wage migrants, although governments are increasingly seeking to attract high-wage migrants. More recently, there has been an increase in intra-regional migration, with flows shifting from other Asian destinations and the Middle East to ASEAN countries. The United Nations estimated that of the 9.9 million migrants in Southeast Asia, approximately 6.8 million, or 69%, originated from other ASEAN states (UN 2017). Intra-ASEAN migration is highly concentrated, with Malaysia, Singapore and Thailand hosting 96% of ASEAN migrants (see Fig. 10.1 and Table 10.1). Five corridors comprise 84% of migrant stock, namely Indonesia to Malaysia, Malaysia to Singapore, and Laos PDR, Cambodia and Myanmar to Thailand (see the shaded cells in Table 10.1).

---

[1] Our focus on high- and low-wage migration, rather than the more commonly used high- and low-skilled categorisations, acknowledges two widespread phenomena: first, "skills wastage", whereby migrants' qualifications are not recognised in the destination country; and second, highly skilled migrants, such as tradespeople, taking jobs in low-wage employment.

Fig. 10.1 Intra-ASEAN migration

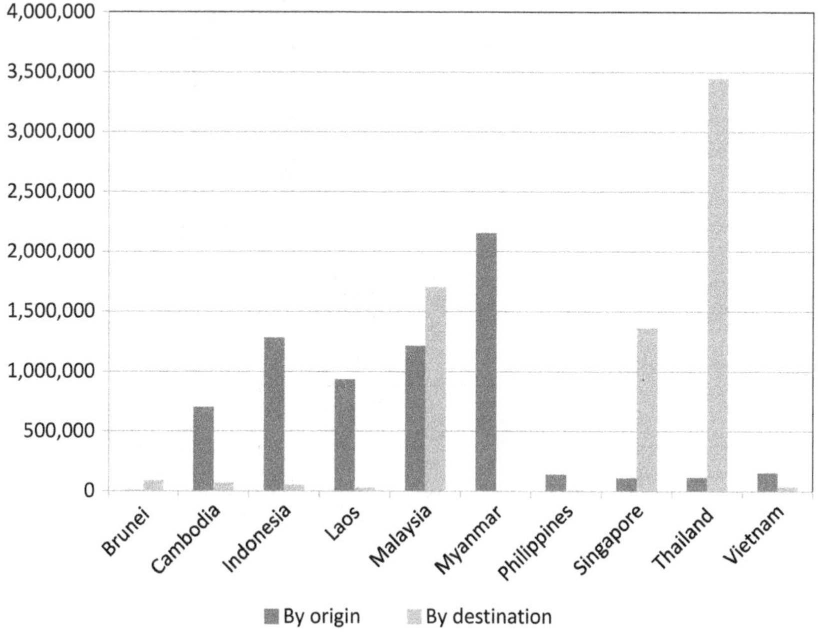

Source: Adapted from UN (2017)

Labour migration is highly gendered, with women strongly represented in domestic work, nursing and sex work, and men in construction, manufacturing, agriculture, fisheries and forestry. There are significant flows of female migrant domestic workers (MDWs) both within and beyond the region.[2] Female MDWs from the Philippines, Indonesia, Cambodia, Myanmar and Laos, and from India and Sri Lanka, find employment in households in Singapore, Malaysia and Thailand, as well as the Middle East and Northeast Asia. Low-wage male migrants from Cambodia, Laos and Myanmar are employed in large numbers in Thailand in construction, manufacturing, agriculture, fisheries and services, and female migrants in manufacturing and services. In Singapore and Malaysia, low-wage male

---

[2] Female migrant workers often face the predicament of "double discrimination"—being a woman and a migrant worker—with their vulnerability for exploitation amplified by the nature of their work, notably domestic work where they may be particularly isolated (ILO 2010: 94).

Table 10.1 Intra-ASEAN migrant stock by country of origin and destination

Country of destination	Brunei	Cambodia	Indonesia	Laos	Malaysia	Myanmar	Philippines	Singapore	Thailand	Vietnam	By destination country
Brunei	..	..	6,517	..	51,048	..	14,227	1,629	15,207	..	88,628
Cambodia	..	..	108	268	177	53	156	126	31,791	37,601	70,280
Indonesia	..	..	..	..	2,315	..	4,117	23,045	23,045	..	52,522
Laos	..	3,568	..	..	..	259	..	..	3,428	19,716	26,971
Malaysia	6,204	14,409	1,091,841	..	..	308,337	103,766	81,109	8,448	89,017	1,703,131
Myanmar	..	..	..	..	..	..	..	..	..	..	0
Philippines	84	40	3,407	296	817	434	..	845	350	425	6,698
Singapore	..	..	168,355	..	1,158,890	..	15,874	..	19,873	..	1,362,992
Thailand	..	680,686	690	923,050	1,352	1,835,106	1,349	750	..	7,255	3,450,238
Vietnam	..	1,035	8,217	7,272	133	11,695	118	1,830	12,077	..	42,377
By origin country	6,288	699,738	1,279,135	930,886	1,214,732	2,155,884	139,607	109,334	114,219	154,014	

Source: Adapted from UN (2017)

migrants from the region, and also from China and South Asia, are concentrated in construction, manufacturing, shipbuilding, agriculture, landscaping and services.

The contributions made by these migrants are huge. In destination countries, migrant workers build infrastructure, keep roads and buildings functional and clean, and produce commodities that are consumed domestically and traded abroad. MDWs and caregivers perform critical social reproductive functions, allowing local women to be drawn into the labour market (see Elias, this volume). Migrant workers do not simply make up for labour shortages; their employment keeps entire industrial sectors in operation. For example, the employment of Burmese migrant workers in factories on the Thai–Myanmar border has allowed the Thai garments industry to remain globally competitive, while almost all of Singapore's construction labour force comprises migrant workers. In sending countries, overseas employment mitigates states' inability to generate sufficient domestic employment or provide welfare. Migrant remittances are also a key source of foreign exchange earnings and a central component of economic growth. In the Philippines, for instance, a recent UN report estimated that migrant remittances are equivalent to 10.5% of GDP (UN 2017).

Drivers

Migration in the region has been driven by the significant disparities in wages and opportunities across countries. For example, the minimum wage in Thailand is 13 times higher than in Myanmar (World Bank 2014: 5). A host of complex economic and structural factors shape these differentials. High rates of population and labour force growth in sending countries relative to recipient countries drive people to migrate for work in lieu of adequate measures to generate domestic employment. Additionally, industrial transformations in the main receiving countries of Singapore, Malaysia and Thailand have generated a permanent demand for low-wage, temporary migrant labour. The absorption of women into the labour force created a demand for contract domestic labour in lieu of state-provided childcare (see Elias, this volume). Moreover, although these countries have sought to "climb the technological ladder" to higher value-added industries, labour-intensive sectors of the economy have nonetheless persisted, creating a demand for new sources of cheap and flexible labour to maintain global competitiveness, or to simply remain afloat. Further industrial restructuring, such as Singapore's transition from a high-end manufacturing centre to a global financial hub, generates a host of low-end service sector jobs—jobs that are often filled by migrants.

In addition, with neoliberal state transformation in the region and ensuing shifts in models of capital accumulation (see Carroll, this volume)—particularly the increasing commercialisation of land rights and agriculture—populations of smallholders and rural communities were left vulnerable to land dispossession (Habibi and Juliawan 2018). With industrial sectors now more exposed to global economic fluctuations, a "relative surplus labour" force has become entrenched in the countryside, with labour migration being one of an extremely limited range of livelihood options (ibid.: 664).

Beyond these factors, labour migration has been shaped by the infrastructures underpinning mobility, as highlighted by mobilities scholarship (Lin et al. 2017). Infrastructures are broadly understood as "the architecture for circulation" (Larkin 2013: 328). They include the social networks that structure migration, such as migration agents and brokers, with their connections to employers and migrants informed by existing and emergent social relationships and ethnic and religious commonalities (Lindquist 2017). Their role has expanded in the context of the recruitment industry in Southeast Asia having been commercialised, with intermediaries in both sending and recipient countries replacing public employment services (Wickramasekera 2002: 17). Community associations are another key organisational structure for labour migration, such as Singapore's Chinese clan associations that have mediated some of the tensions generated by the state's efforts to attract mainland Chinese migrants (Montsion 2012). Physical architectures are another key infrastructure, notably the growth of low-cost air carriers and the destinations they connect (Lindquist 2017). Such infrastructures play a key role in facilitating—and socially producing—labour migration across the region (Lin et al. 2017). In doing so, they affect and are affected by the ways in which governments govern labour migration.

Low-Wage Migration

Governance Frameworks in Labour-Receiving Countries

The receiving states of Singapore, Malaysia and Thailand adopt a "revolving door" policy in that low-wage migrants are considered "temporary": they come to work for a fixed term before returning home upon the completion or termination of their contracts. Such policies are meant to control the intake of migrant workers in accordance with economic conditions. However, due to the broader transformations outlined earlier, low-wage migration is a permanent feature of receiving states. In Singapore, a third of the workforce is non-resident,[3] with 90% of these comprising low-wage migrants on work permits (Bal 2017). In Malaysia and Thailand, the proportion of low-wage migrants in the labour force is estimated to be 20% and 8.5% respectively (ILO 2017; Lee and Khor 2018). While the migrant workforce in Singapore almost completely comprises documented workers who enter the country through formal channels, over half in Malaysia and Thailand are undocumented (Kaur 2010: 9). This does not necessarily mean that low-wage migration is less governed in the latter two countries. Rather, it indicates different modes of governance. While the Singapore state regulates demand and supply through bureaucratic policy instruments such as levies and restrictions on which sectors are allowed to hire migrants, the policy instruments of the Thai state often involve the opening and closing of border checkpoints as well as periodic raids on undocumented migrants in accordance with immediate economic and social agendas (Chalamwong et al. 2012). Malaysia lies in between, with periodic raids supplementing levies and industry restrictions (Kaur 2014).

Despite differences, governance frameworks in these countries share four integral features. First, they severely limit migrants' legal-political rights to a level below those of citizens. Migrant workers in Singapore and Malaysia, for instance, are not allowed to bring their families and they are prohibited from marrying citizens. Second, migrant workers are deportable: government authorities and employers retain the right to unilaterally remove both documented and undocumented workers at any time with little or no justification. Third, migrant workers are often occupationally immobile, being legally barred from changing employers or seeking jobs on the open market. Finally, migrant workers are typically cut off from trade union movements in host countries. While none of these states explicitly ban migrant workers from joining unions, they represent repressive political environments where organised labour is suppressed, tightly controlled or indifferent to the grievances of migrant workers.

Broadly speaking, these frameworks serve the interests of ruling elites and fractions of capital within specific industries. In Malaysia and Thailand, accommodative relations between political regimes and business groups, particularly builders, manufacturers and agribusinesses, underpin migrant labour policies. These segments of capital are vital in providing clientelist political support as well as the infrastructure and economic growth required

---

[3] Residents comprise citizens and permanent residents.

for ruling elites to stay in power. In Thailand, political elites have long protected the economic interests of certain fractions of domestic capital, particularly those in the agriculture, manufacturing and banking sectors, enacting policies that allowed these classes to shift from small-scale production to large-scale, globally competitive agriculture and manufacturing (Hewison 1989). For instance, allowing garment manufacturers in the Thai–Myanmar borderlands unregulated access to disempowered migrant workers enables these manufacturers to compete with lower-cost centres in China, Bangladesh and Cambodia to supply the global apparel market (Arnold and Hewison 2006). Similarly, in Malaysia, manufacturing and construction firms are overwhelmingly owned by ethnic-Chinese businessmen, whose economic interests found political representation through the Malaysian Chinese Association (MCA), a key component party of the *Barisan Nasional* (BN), which ruled from independence to 2018. These countries' migration governance regimes have given employers access to a pool of workers that can be employed well below statutory standards in order to enhance firms' global competitiveness (Crinis 2010, 2012).

This is in contrast to Singapore where domestic capital has historically been politically weak and suppressed by the party-state, while foreign capital—particularly capital-intensive manufacturing in the 1980s and 1990s—has been less reliant on low-wage migrant labour (Hing and Lee 2011). Here, employers of low-wage migrants (outside of domestic work) are largely small- and medium-sized contractors in the construction and shipbuilding industry, usually working for government bodies and government-linked companies. In this case, the benefits of a cheap and powerless labour force are indirectly accrued by the party-state, which can consistently deliver infrastructural developments in return for electoral support whilst suppressing labour grievances over poor working and employment conditions. Despite differences, all three states have systems that allow specific fractions of capital systematic access to workers saddled with recruitment debt and deprived of substantial legal-political rights.

Governance Frameworks in Labour-Sending Countries

The two largest sending countries in the region are the Philippines and Indonesia. Both have had state-driven migration policies since the 1970s, with successive political regimes seeing emigration as a solution to their inability to generate sufficient employment and a way to circumvent the need for enhanced welfare provision, as well as a lucrative source of foreign exchange earnings. The Philippines is often seen as a role model in regulating outward migration and protections, while Indonesia is found wanting. However, seen through their respective historical trajectories, both states demonstrate increasing levels of protection for migrant workers, but always constrained by a desire to expand deployment. Cambodia, Myanmar and Laos are newer sources of migrant workers. For them, out-migration has been largely irregular and dominated by private recruiters. Belated state attempts to control migration have not yet bought significant change.

Labour migration in the Philippines was initially governed by the 1974 Labour Code and, from 1982, by the Philippine Overseas Employment Administration (POEA). Further laws in the post-Marcos era strengthened the POEA's legal mandate to exert tight controls over recruitment and deployment, including the power to sanction and shut down agencies for non-compliance and to stop deployments to particular countries. These same laws also provide for on-site legal services and life and workplace injury insurance. The government is also highly active in promoting the export of Philippine labour and lobbying foreign governments for better treatment of their migrant workers. In contrast, Indonesia's first migrant labour law was introduced only in 2004, despite out-migration being a state development strategy since the late 1960s. The 2004 law sought to curb practices leading to the exploitation and abuse of Indonesian migrant workers, including by standardising procedures of recruitment and placement; weeding out corruption between ministry officials and recruiters; and establishing penalties for errant recruiters, including blacklisting and criminal sanctions.

These frameworks in the Philippines and Indonesia are underpinned by different domestic power structures, particularly variations in elite interests in relation to recruitment. The Philippines has been more successful in delivering protections because the interests of the ruling class does not intersect with those of labour recruiters. The oligarchs who dominate economic and political life have had little vested interest in the recruitment industry, which is dominated by small firms with minimal political clout (Oh 2016). Civil society, on the other hand, has played a significant role in advocating for broad reforms in the post-Marcos era. While rival oligarch clans have typically closed ranks to resist important reforms, they have been willing to reform migrant labour laws as this has not involved making costly concessions. The expansion of protections from the 1990s has also allowed oligarchs greater leeway in resisting civil society pressure for more threatening claims, such as land reform.

In contrast, since the late 1980s, Indonesian officials have worked closely with labour recruiters to facilitate the deployment of Indonesian labour overseas. The resulting licensing regime was in no way directed towards protecting migrant workers from exploitation or abuse. Rather, it embedded a set of patron–client relations between the Manpower Ministry and recruitment firms, where ministry officials worked towards enhancing the profitability of recruiters in return for a portion of the profits in the form of "consultancy fees" (Palmer 2016). When civil society groups began emerging from decades of repression to demand reforms in the post-New Order era, patron–client relations between the ministry and recruiters were already well entrenched and resistant to change. Moreover, the post-Suharto decentralisation process has allowed recruiters to ally with village- and subdistrict-level elites to prevent nascent reforms from undermining their business interests (Lindquist 2012). Hence, while civil society pressure delivered the 2004 law, central government attempts to protect migrant workers have been undermined.

Emerging Conflicts and Outcomes

As a result of governance frameworks that prioritise politico-business elites' interests over workers' well-being, migrant workers routinely suffer a litany of abuses in recruitment, employment and repatriation. These include debt-bondage from high recruitment fees, low and unpaid wages, wage theft, unreported or mismanaged work injuries, forced repatriation, and physical, psychological and sexual violence. MDWs in particular continue to be vulnerable to sexual harassment and abuse at work, insufficient food, overwork, and suicide, despite recent improvements in Indonesia and a much-lauded system in the Philippines.

Various forms of contestation have subsequently emerged, notably civil society activism. In the main sending and receiving countries, civil society activism often starts with the provision of direct services—such as legal-aid and shelter—to migrant workers in need. Organisations then document cases of abuse and exploitation to advocate for reforms to labour and immigration laws. Despite differences in circumstances both between and within sending and receiving countries, civil society demands across the region have some commonalities. These include greater access to labour justice and compensation; regulations to severely limit or ban recruitment fees; halting forced repatriations; the expansion of employment security and benefits (including minimum wage); and the recognition of MDWs as formal workers. The external reporting of migrant labour abuses to international agencies such the UN Human Rights Council and the United

States' Department of State also allows organisations to leverage international pressure for domestic reforms.

More confrontational responses from migrant workers are also evident, despite highly restrictive industrial relations regimes. In Thailand, wildcat strikes among migrant workers in the manufacturing sector have been commonplace since the 2000s (Arnold and Hewison 2006). The southern Malaysian state of Johor has seen at least two highly publicised factory riots in 2010 and 2014 involving at least 6000 workers (Fernandes 2014; Ray 2010). Meanwhile, Singapore was rocked by a bus drivers' strike involving 171 Chinese migrant workers and a riot involving 300 Indian migrant workers in the Little India district in 2012 and 2013 respectively (TODAY 2013; Wong 2013). These came in the wake of rising spontaneous protests held by construction and shipyard workers between 2008 and 2011 over salary and contractual disputes (Bal 2016: 194–195, 209).

Governments in receiving states have consequently come under pressure to enact reforms. Predictably, authorities have resorted to repressive measures to quell rising unrest through the arrest, incarceration and deportation of workers. Civil society activism has also been broadly suppressed through law enforcement agencies and the courts (Singapore) or through thugs hired by local officials or employers (Thailand). Alongside these measures, governments have pursued some legal reforms and regularisation programmes. However, while new measures in Singapore have appeared to limit overt contestation, those in Thailand and Malaysia have sparked further dissent from employers, migrant workers and activists.

In the case of Thailand, regularisation programmes began in the early 2000s and involved several amnesties, under which undocumented workers could register with the government (Chalamwong et al. 2012). A key aspect of this was a Nationality Verification process from 2006, where worker locations and histories of political activism were collected. In the context of rising mobilisations, this programme was an attempt to suppress clandestine trade union activity by monitoring and weeding-out politically active members. Following the coup of 2014, the military-led Prayuth government suddenly enacted a new migrant worker decree in 2017, spelling out harsh financial penalties and jail terms for undocumented migrants and their employers. This led to an exodus of migrant workers from the country, despite a grace period and subsequent reductions in penalties. The migrant worker decree was harshly criticised by both civil society organisations and employers: the former were outraged at the harsh penalties for undocumented workers, while the latter were abruptly stripped of access to cheap labour.

This sudden change in Thailand's policy reflected struggles within Thai society. The previously accommodative relations between employers and civilian governments—especially those dominated by the Shinawatra clan—had been disrupted by the 2014 coup. Subsequently, the military government came under considerable international pressure, particularly as it repeatedly delayed promised elections. For instance, the European Union suspended trade negotiations with Thailand, while Western governments and international NGOs also criticised the military government's record on forced labour and trafficking (The Economist 2014; US Department of State 2017). Keen to preserve markets for Thai exports, the military government made the eradication of human trafficking a "national agenda", and soon thereafter enacted the 2017 decree. Faced with international pressure and seeking to gain legitimacy for the military regime at the global level, the Prayuth government effectively cut employers off from a previously assured unregulated labour supply.

Recent developments in Malaysia have reflected similar dynamics between employers and the state. Predominantly ethnic-Chinese builders and manufacturers, long averse to paying the migrant worker levy, worked with the MCA to protest extending a new minimum wage law to migrant workers in 2012/13. While the minimum wage law stuck, migrant workers were made to pay their own levies. However, with the MCA suffering massive electoral losses in the May 2013 general elections, their influence in the ruling BN coalition waned. Sustained pressure from civil society organisations and the Malaysian Trade Union Congress then led to new rules requiring employers to pay all levies from 2018, spurring employer protests in late 2017. The 2018 general election saw the MCA decimated, winning only one of the 222 seats in the federal parliament, and the election of a new *Pakatan Harapan* government. However, while employers suffered a defeat, there are few signs that these developments might lead to better protection and rights for migrant workers. Barely two months after coming to power, and unencumbered with coalition partners clamouring for cheap migrant labour, the new government launched a massive raid on undocumented workers, deporting over a thousand workers without investigation or trial (The Daily Star 2018).

In contrast, Singapore's apparent success in mitigating contention is underpinned by the relative coherence of the party-state, particularly in relation to contractor capital and tight controls over civil society. These conditions allow the government to manage conflicts through a range of technocratic policy instruments. Limited reforms have been enacted, including outlawing kickbacks, liberalising the rules prohibiting workers from changing employers, and legislating a mandatory weekly day off for MDWs. These reforms have, however, had little to do with expanding workers' rights. Rather, they enable disputes for individual complainants to be resolved, rather than advancing rights and protections through collective mobilisation or advocacy. In a similar vein, the party-state controlled National Trades Union Congress (NTUC) set up the Migrant Workers Centre and the Centre for Domestic Employees in 2012 and 2016, respectively. These agencies provide the exact same services as civil society organisations, such as legal aid and shelter, but not independent advocacy. Moreover, the NTUC's migrant worker outreach programmes shift the agenda away from claiming better working conditions and rights towards socialising migrants to avoid workplace conflicts.

The outcomes of contestation in sending countries, similarly, reflect their societies' balance of social forces. Pressures for greater protections in the Philippines continue to be accommodated by the state, but within the scope of expanding deployments (Bal and Gerard 2018). In Indonesia, the 2004 migrant labour law saw the creation of the National Body for Placement and Protection of Overseas Indonesian Workers (the National Body) tasked with the operational role of regulating recruitment. This effectively led to a turf war over which state organ would regulate the recruitment process, with civil society organisations and recruiters aligning with different state agencies to pursue their respective agendas. Recruiters have allied with the Manpower Ministry to protect existing clientelist arrangements while civil society organisations backed the National Body to extend stringent controls over recruiters. This culminated in several legal challenges launched by the National Body against the Manpower Ministry (Dewanto 2014). The situation is further complicated by political decentralisation, which gives provincial governments significant leeway in enforcing these regulations. Regulations have consequently become contingent on the extent to which recruiters can influence implementation through clientelist relations with local political elites. While continued civil society pressure delivered a 2017 revision of the migrant labour law that seeks to expand protections, there has been no clear indication of how it will be implemented amid these bureaucratic conflicts.

Finally, the outcomes of these domestic struggles have significant impacts over the governance of low-wage migration at the regional level. Since the Cebu Declaration in 2007, in which ASEAN states committed to developing an instrument to protect and promote the rights of migrant workers, negotiations have reached an impasse. Host states, particularly Singapore and Malaysia, have steadfastly rejected any notion of a legally-binding instrument, a long-standing demand of the Philippines. When Manila abruptly backed down in late 2016, Indonesia was left isolated, blocking the ratification of a non-legally binding agreement in 2017. Host states' positions on the instrument can be attributed to the dominance of policy-makers' and employers' interests over those of civil society organisations and migrant workers (Bal and Gerard 2018). By rejecting a legally binding instrument, governments of recipient states avoid giving civil society organisations more leverage for advocacy and, in doing so, maintain a relatively free hand in managing migrant labour unrest.

High-Wage Migration

Individual governments' strategies for attracting migrants holding specific skills or capital have long shaped patterns of high-wage migration across the region. Qualified, wealthy migrants represent a windfall for recipient states, which has informed the hierarchy of entitlements that governments use to cherry-pick from the regional, and global, workforce. For sending states, high-wage migration presents the substantial challenge of "brain drain", particularly in a context where tertiary education is not widely available or accessible.

High-wage immigration is most prevalent in Singapore. The Singapore government has sought to attract high-wage migrants in response to skills shortages and economic planning agendas, notably the shift away from manufacturing to the service sector from the 1980s. Measures to attract high-wage migrants reflect concerns about an ageing population, with the proportion of the population that is elderly forecast to reach 20% by 2030 (Chia 2013). They also reflect declining fertility rates, which have been below replacement levels for over a generation (Appold 2005). The Singapore government has focused its migration efforts particularly on mainland Chinese migrants, both because of the large labour pool and also because it is presumed that these migrants will help shore up the ethnic-Chinese share of the population, which is threatened by "varying fertility rates among local groups" (Yeoh and Lin 2013).

Singapore's immigration framework is organised around attracting migrants with higher qualifications and capital through a hierarchy of entitlements granted according to migrants' monthly salary. At the top is the "EntrePass", granted to "serial entrepreneurs, high-calibre innovators or experienced investors" seeking to operate a business (Ministry of Manpower 2018). Pass-holders can bring family members and apply for annual renewals and permanent residency, subject to an increasing threshold of annual business spending and number of Singaporean employees. The

"Personalised Employment Pass" is for migrant workers earning in excess of SG$18,000 per month prior to starting work in Singapore, after which they must earn an annual salary of at least SG$144,000. This grants them the flexibility to change jobs, bring family members, and apply for permanent residency (ibid.). The lower-grade "Employment Pass" is for migrant workers earning over SG$3600 per month who possess specific qualifications or experience. They have the option to bring their families (subject to the salary of the pass-holder), and apply for permanent residency (ibid.). These benefits stand in stark contrast to the conditions attached to low-wage migration, described earlier. Since the 1990s, the government has also endorsed the reverse of this policy—namely, the temporary emigration of high-wage Singaporean citizens to Indonesia, Malaysia, Philippines, Thailand and Southern China—to service investments and support the regionalisation of Singapore's economy (Iredale 2000).

The Singapore government's strategy of importing high-wage labour is also underpinned by schemes to attract foreign students to its higher education system. This focus is driven not just by the shorter-term objective of increasing revenue; it is also part of a strategy to position Singapore as "the centre of an imagined geography of Asian opportunity", with incentives for students to first study in Singapore and then stay on for work, enabling Singaporean firms and citizens to consolidate regional networks (Collins et al. 2014: 38). This more recent focus on education extends the Singapore government's positioning of the city-state since the 1990s as the knowledge-based "gateway" between the East and West, particularly seeking to attract the brightest students from China (Montsion 2012). This emphasis on attracting foreign students "is a key plank in the state's manufacturing process", with the government increasing its investment in education by 40% from 2007 to 2012, amounting to 3.1% of its GDP (Koh and Chong 2014: 2). Moreover, it employs aggressive recruitment strategies, including scholarships granted on the condition that students work in Singapore or for a Singapore corporation for three years after graduation (Montsion 2012). Some of the targeted students are too young to leave China without supervision, which the Singapore government has accommodated through the Long-Term Visit Pass that enables mothers and grandmothers to also immigrate.[4]

---

[4] This is one case of many across the region where labour migration arrangements are highly gendered (see Elias, this volume), given the emphasis in both recruitment practices and social stereotypes on attracting young Chinese boys to study in Singapore, alongside the Singapore government's facilitation of mothers and grandmothers accompanying students (Montsion 2012).

The Singapore government's approach to importing labour has seen the city-state's population growth being driven by immigration, with the share of non-citizens increasing from 9.6% in 1970 to 36.4% in 2010 (Chia 2013). Residents' share of the labour force has declined from 82% in 1991 to 65.3% by 2010, with citizens accounting for only 58.3% (ibid.). Concerns regarding the speed and composition of the city-state's population growth have been refracted through criticisms regarding the overcrowding and overuse of public recreational spaces and public services, notably health and transportation, as well as increased housing costs (Chia 2013; Gomes 2014). Another criticism was that foreign hiring came at the cost of employing Singapore university graduates. Indeed, the Singapore government had ramped up its external hiring activities, even as domestic demand for university graduates dropped. For example, in 1997, amid the Asian financial crisis, the Ministry of Manpower established Contact Singapore, an information and resource centre aimed at recruiting "foreign talent" from North America, Australia and Europe (Appold 2005), along with the Singapore Talent Recruitment Committee in November 1998 and Manpower 21 in 1999 (Chia 2013). Contact Singapore continued its efforts by opening new offices in China and India in the early 2000s, even though economic growth had stalled and unemployment of domestic university graduates increased (Appold 2005). Conditions even spurred Singaporean graduates to pursue careers outside of the country, creating challenges for the government in retaining the country's "best and brightest".

In response to mounting criticisms, the governing People's Action Party (PAP) announced it would slow the influx of foreign workers, and subsequently increased foreign worker levies (Chia 2013). It also enacted a series of measures to distinguish citizen and non-citizen access to public services over 2009–2010, including tripling school fees for children of permanent residents, widening the gap in healthcare subsidies between citizens and permanent residents, and further tightening permanent residents' access to the government-managed public housing market (Thompson 2014). These reforms did not, however, appease critics, as reflected in historically low PAP support at the 2011 general election, as well as the Population White Paper protest on 16 September 2013, when more than 4000 people attended a rally at Hong Lim Park. The protest, one of the largest in Singapore's history, was in opposition to the government's proposed population rise of 30% by 2030, to 6.9 million, with immigrants forecast to comprise almost half of that increase. The government responded by increasing social spending, alongside establishing an extensive public consultation process, Our Singapore Conversation. This was designed to depoliticise grievances, develop a "consensus" and leave space for the PAP to design policy solutions (Rodan 2018: 114–15; also Rodan and Baker, this volume). Additional concesssions contributed to the PAP's greater success at the 2015 polls.

The Malaysian government has a similar strategy to attract high-wage labour by structuring migrants' entitlements according to wages. The Malaysian government's concerns regarding its competitiveness in terms of foreign direct investment prompted changes to its policies for attracting high-wage migrants, notably the easing of measures for recruiting expatriates, increases in their rights and freedoms, and increased access to permanent residency (Nah 2012). Like Singapore, Malaysia also seeks to attract foreign students, particularly Muslim students from China and the Middle East. This began in the late 1990s with legislation that enabled private tertiary education, opening the doors to private colleges that offered foreign university degrees through twinning programmes with British and Australian institutions (Wong and Wen 2013). In the case of Singapore, attracting foreign students and promoting their immigration and integration has been a way of drawing in foreign capital and regionalising Singaporean capital. However, for Malaysia these measures are motivated predominantly by commercial objectives. Foreign students are impeded from staying on following the completion of their course due to Malaysia's visa system, with student visas needing annual renewal and work visas difficult to acquire (ibid. 2013). This ensures that foreign students do not challenge affirmative action policies benefiting the ethnic-Malay population.

Thailand and the Philippines also incentivise high-wage migration through their investment visa schemes. In both cases, investment visas are granted to migrants investing a minimum amount in a state-backed or -endorsed investment. For example, the Thai Investment Visa was launched after the Asian financial crisis to draw capital back to the country. Applicants had to provide evidence of 3 million baht, later raised to 10 million and then 20 million, invested in some combination of: (a) a condominium unit; (b) a fixed deposit account at a Thai bank whose share capital is majority Thai owned; or (c) Thai government or Thai state enterprise bonds. Provided the visa is periodically renewed, a holder can stay for an unlimited period of time but without work rights, thereby not increasing competition in the Thai job market.

The various schemes for high-wage migration thus enable governments to attract individuals that align with specific sectoral needs and/or raise state capital. These individual government measures to attract high-wage migrants have recently been accompanied by multilateral arrangements through the ASEAN Economic Community (AEC). Entailing the "free" flow of goods and services and the "freer" flow of labour and capital, this project has ramifications for how people move throughout the region for work. To facilitate this project, regional governance has been reconfigured around a regulatory framework, where issue-specific teams negotiate regional standards and norms to be implemented domestically (see Jones and Hameiri, this volume). The outcomes of "liberalisation" have been varied, with some sectors becoming highly integrated and others remaining more nationally bound. This unevenness reflects the conflicts surrounding this attempt to reorganise the regional political economy and intervene in the associated distribution of power and resources among the region's politico-business alliances (Jones 2015; also Jones and Hameiri, this volume). Many of the region's dominant coalitions have contested integration, with their support or opposition determined by their potential to gain from this process.

This is evident in the uneven arrangements that have emerged on skills recognition to facilitate high-wage migration. Member states have negotiated Mutual Recognition Arrangements (MRAs) for six professions (engineering, architecture, nursing, medicine, dentistry and tourism). While the MRA for architects facilitates labour movement, the one for medical professionals is a protectionist arrangement that safeguards medical jobs in each country. This is because, for architects, regional labour movement builds on existing arrangements supported by national bodies, and so they have designed their MRA to facilitate labour movement. National bodies for medical professionals, however, while rhetorically supporting freer labour movement, have developed their MRA so as to protect medical jobs in each country (Sumano 2013). Hence, each government's bargaining position has been determined by whether the relevant national body has a direct interest in supporting labour migration, creating a highly uneven "integration".

Alongside agreements governing specific professions, the ASEAN Qualification Reference Framework (AQRF) was endorsed in September 2014 (ASEAN 2014). Under a task force comprising representatives from states' ministries of trade, labour and education, the framework was developed to enable the comparison of qualifications across countries so as to create more accessible career paths for migrants. However, the strong influence of private sector interests over public policy and the subsequent trajectory of the MRAs suggests the AQRF will also be designed and implemented unevenly, with outcomes determined by whether the relevant national education and professional bodies have an interest in supporting the regional recognition of qualifications.

Conclusion

By analysing how labour migration is governed in Southeast Asia, this chapter has presented three arguments. First, labour migration in the region has been profoundly shaped by historical state and industrial transformations. With respect to low-wage migration, weak welfare provisions and the commercialisation of land rights have created a large surplus labour force with limited livelihood opportunities. Simultaneously, labour-intensive industries seeking to be globally competitive, or simply to survive, generated demand for a flexible, low-wage workforce. With respect to high-wage migration, regimes have been designed to favour specific state projects and agendas, whether to raise state capital or support particular professions.

Second, given the private sector's high degree of influence over public policy across the region, which stems from historical processes of state-led development, the governance of migration has been determined by policy-makers in close consultation with employers in key economic sectors. The regulations that have emerged are both explicit, such as memorandums of understanding between individual countries, and implicit, such as sporadic crackdowns on undocumented migrant workers.

Third, these modes of governance have given rise to conflicts at both the national and regional scales, with their outcomes variegated across the region according to the confluence of social or class forces within respective societies. With respect to low-wage migration, reforms have been enacted in response to protests, strikes and civil society activism, but have largely prioritised the management of movement and the continued deployment of workers, rather than the promotion of workers' rights and welfare. With respect to high-wage migration, a highly uneven process of regional "liberalisation" has been created through the AEC, reflecting the extent to which the relevant national agencies and bodies are positioned to benefit from labour mobility.

References

Appold, S. J. (2005). The weakening position of university graduates in Singapore's labor market: Causes and consequences. *Population and Development Review, 31*(1), 85–112.

Arnold, D., & Hewison, K. (2006). Exploitation in global supply chains: Burmese migrant workers in Mae Sot, Thailand. In K. Hewison & K. Young (Eds.), *Transnational migration and work in Asia* (pp. 165–190). London/New York: Routledge.

ASEAN. (2014, October 13). *ASEAN enhances mobility of skilled labour through qualifications reference framework.* ASEAN Secretariat News. http://www.asean.org/news/item/asean-enhances-mobility-of-skilled-labour-through-qualifications-reference-framework?category_id=27

Bal, C. S. (2016). *Production politics and migrant labour regimes: Guest workers in Asia and the Gulf.* New York: Palgrave Macmillan US.

Bal, C. S. (2017). Myths about temporary migrant workers and the depoliticisation of migrant worker struggles. In K. S. Loh, P. J. Thum, & J. M.-T. Chia (Eds.), *Living with myths in Singapore* (pp. 249–262). Singapore: Ethos Books.

Bal, C. S., & Gerard, K. (2018). ASEAN's governance of migrant worker rights. *Third World Quarterly, 39*(4), 799–819.

Chalamwong, Y., Meepien, J., & Hongprayoon, K. (2012). Management of cross-border migration: Thailand as a case of net immigration. *Asian Journal of Social Science, 40*(4), 447–463.

Chia, S. Y. (2013). Foreign labor in Singapore: Rationale, policies, impacts, and issues. *Philippine Journal of Development, 38*(1–2), 105–133.

Collins, F. L., Sidhu, R., Lewis, N., & Yeoh, B. S. A. (2014). Mobility and desire: International students and Asian regionalism in aspirational Singapore. *Discourse: Studies in the Cultural Politics of Education, 35*(5), 661–676.

Crinis, V. (2010). Sweat or no sweat: Foreign workers in the garment industry in Malaysia. *Journal of Contemporary Asia, 40*(4), 589–611.

Crinis, V. (2012). Global commodity chains in crisis: The garment industry in Malaysia. *Institutions and Economies, 4*(3), 61–82.

Dewanto, P. A. (2014, December 4). The commitment to protect Indonesian migrant workers. [In Indonesian.] *KOMPAS.com.* https://nasional.kompas.com/read/2014/12/04/14000071/Komitmen.Perlindungan.TKI

Fernandes, C. (2014, August 28). Malaysia factory riots provide look at migrant workers' grievances. *The Wall Street Journal.* https://www.wsj.com/articles/malaysia-factory-riots-provide-look-at-migrant-workers-grievances-1409236485

Gomes, C. (2014). Xenophobia online: Unmasking Singaporean attitudes towards "foreign talent" migrants. *Asian Ethnicity, 15*(1), 21–40.

Habibi, M., & Juliawan, B. H. (2018). Creating surplus labour: Neo-liberal transformations and the development of relative surplus population in Indonesia. *Journal of Contemporary Asia, 48*(4), 649–670.

Hewison, K. (1989). *Bankers and bureaucrats: Capital and the role of the state in Thailand*. New Haven: Yale University Southeast Asia Studies, Yale Center for International and Area Studies.

Hing, A. Y., & Lee, K. J. (2011). Embeddedness and restructuring: Case studies from Singapore. *Journal of Contemporary Asia, 41*(3), 393–410.

ILO [International Labour Organisation]. (2010). *International labour migration. A rights-based approach*. Geneva: ILO. http://www.ilo.org/global/publications/ilo-bookstore/order-online/books/WCMS_125361/lang%2D%2Den/index.htm

ILO. (2017). *Thailand July–September 2017. TRIANGLE in ASEAN quarterly briefing note*. Bangkok: ILO. https://www.ilo.org/wcmsp5/groups/public/%2D%2D-asia/%2D%2D-ro-bangkok/documents/publication/wcms_580143.pdf

Iredale, R. (2000). Migration policies for the highly skilled in the Asia-Pacific region. *The International Migration Review, 34*(3), 882–906.

Jones, L. (2015). Explaining the failure of the ASEAN economic community: The primacy of domestic political economy. *The Pacific Review, 29*(5), 647–670.

Kaur, A. (2010). Labour migration in Southeast Asia: Migration policies, labour exploitation and regulation. *Journal of the Asia Pacific Economy, 15*(1), 6–19.

Kaur, A. (2014). Managing labour migration in Malaysia: Guest worker programs and the regularisation of irregular labour migrants as a policy instrument. *Asian Studies Review, 38*(3), 345–366.

Koh, A., & Chong, T. (2014). Education in the global city: The manufacturing of education in Singapore. *Discourse: Studies in the Cultural Politics of Education, 35*(5), 625–636.

Larkin, B. (2013). The politics and poetics of infrastructure. *Annual Review of Anthropology, 42*(1), 327–343.

Lee, H., & Khor, Y. L. (2018). *Counting migrant workers in Malaysia: A needlessly persisting conundrum* (ISEAS perspective no. 25). Singapore: ISEAS. https://www.iseas.edu.sg/articles-commentaries/iseas-perspective/item/7354-201825-counting-migrant-workers-in-malaysia-a-needlessly-persisting-conundrum

Lin, W., Lindquist, J., Xiang, B., & Yeoh, B. S. A. (2017). Migration infrastructures and the production of migrant mobilities. *Mobilities, 12*(2), 167–174.

Lindquist, J. (2012). The elementary school teacher, the thug and his grandmother: Informal brokers and transnational migration from Indonesia. *Pacific Affairs, 85*(1), 69–89.

Lindquist, J. (2017). Brokers, channels, infrastructure: Moving migrant labor in the Indonesian-Malaysian oil palm complex. *Mobilities, 12*(2), 213–226.

Ministry of Manpower. (2018). *Work passes and permits*. Singapore: Ministry of Manpower. https://www.mom.gov.sg/passes-and-permits

Montsion, J. M. (2012). When talent meets mobility: Un/desirability in Singapore's new citizenship project. *Citizenship Studies, 16*(3–4), 469–482.

Nah, A. M. (2012). Globalisation, sovereignty and immigration control: The hierarchy of rights for migrant workers in Malaysia. *Asian Journal of Social Science, 40*(4), 486–508.

Oh, Y. A. (2016). Oligarchic rule and best practice migration management: The political economy origins of labour migration regime of the Philippines. *Contemporary Politics, 22*(2), 197–214.

Palmer, W. (2016). *Indonesia's overseas labour migration programme, 1969–2010*. Leiden: Brill Academic Pub.

Ray, R. (2010, August 16). 5,000 migrants riot at Malaysian factory. *Libcom.Org*. http://libcom.org/news/5000-migrants-riot-malaysian-factory-16082010

Rodan, G. (2018). *Participation without democracy: Containing conflict in Southeast Asia*. Ithaca: Cornell University Press.

Sumano, B. (2013). *Explaining the liberalisation of professional migration in ASEAN*. PhD dissertation, School of Politics and International Relations, Queen Mary, University of London.

The Daily Star. (2018, July 5). Malaysia urged to stop crackdown. *The Daily Star (Bangladesh)*. https://www.thedailystar.net/backpage/malaysia-urged-stop-crackdown-1600204

The Economist. (2014, August 15). EU–Thai economic talks on ice. *The Economist*.

Thompson, E. C. (2014). Immigration, society and modalities of citizenship in Singapore. *Citizenship Studies, 18*(3–4), 315–331.

TODAY. (2013, December 8). Little India riot: 18 injured, 21 arrested. *TODAY*.

UN [United Nations]. (2017). *UN population division*. International migrant stock: The 2017 revision. https://www.un.org/en/development/desa/population/migration/data/estimates2/index.shtml

US Department of State. (2017). *Trafficking in persons report 2017*. Washington, DC: US Department of State. https://www.state.gov/j/tip/rls/tiprpt/2017/

Wickramasekera, P. (2002). *Asian labour migration: Issues and challenges in an era of globalisation* (Working paper). Geneva: ILO. http://www.ilo.org/asia/publications/WCMS_160632/lang%2D%2Den/index.htm

Wong, C. H. (2013, August 31). Singapore strike: The full story. *The Wall Street Journal*. https://blogs.wsj.com/indonesiarealtime/2013/08/31/singapore-strike-the-full-story/

Wong, D., & Wen, O. P. (2013). The globalisation of tertiary education and intra-Asian student mobility: Mainland Chinese student mobility to Malaysia. *Asian and Pacific Migration Journal, 22*(1), 55–76.

World Bank. (2014). *Migration and remittances: Recent developments and outlook* (Report no. 92655). Washington, DC: World Bank. http://documents.worldbank.org/curated/en/585901468326375808/Migration-and-remittances-recent-developments-and-outlook

Yeoh, B. S. A., & Lin, W. (2013). Chinese migration to Singapore: Discourses and discontents in a globalising nation-state. *Asian and Pacific Migration Journal, 22*(1), 31–54.

CHAPTER 11

Poor People's Politics in Urban Southeast Asia

Jane Hutchison and Ian D. Wilson

INTRODUCTION

"Poor people's politics" refers to poor people's struggles over poverty-making processes.[1] We conceptualise the poor in social relational terms rather than as a social category defined by measures of poverty such as income. Poverty statistics allow us to count the poor (see Carroll, this volume), but they reveal little about the underlying structures of social power and conflict which are of interest to the Murdoch School (see Hameiri and Jones, this volume). Understanding the poor in social relational terms means we view them as belonging to a class that depends upon more powerful actors to secure their everyday needs. In focusing on poor people's *politics*, we are thus less concerned with where people sit in

---

[1] The arguments in this chapter were developed with Caroline Hughes as a part of a larger project, ARC Discovery Project DP130102323.

J. Hutchison • I. D. Wilson (✉)
Asia Research Centre, College of Arts, Business, Law and Social Sciences, Murdoch University, Perth, WA, Australia
e-mail: j.hutchison@murdoch.edu.au; iwilson@murdoch.edu.au

© The Author(s) 2020
T. Carroll et al. (eds.), *The Political Economy of Southeast Asia*, Studies in the Political Economy of Public Policy,
https://doi.org/10.1007/978-3-030-28255-4_11

relation to measures of poverty than with how they are positioned within structures of power and conflict, and how this shapes their agency.

We argue that poor people's politics has distinctive attributes because it is shaped by the social relations of poverty that the poor often rely on to survive. Poor people are enmeshed in socio-economic circumstances that leave them materially deprived, but these very circumstances are also frequently the means by which they subsist, and therefore cannot easily disrupt or forgo. This is clear for urban informal settlements. Featuring often makeshift, poor-quality housing and infrastructure, overcrowded conditions, limited access to safe water and sanitation, and insecure tenure, informal settlements are a visible manifestation and further cause of poverty in urban areas (ADB 2014; Baker and Gadgil 2017). Yet, they are simultaneously "spaces of opportunity" for urban employment and livelihoods that the poor actively seek out and defend (Singh and Gadgil 2017: 63).

This chapter explains some of the distinctive attributes of poor people's politics, specifically in relation to their responses to forced evictions from informal settlements in Jakarta and Metro Manila. First, we argue that poor people's politics is generally instrumental, concerned with tangible gains in the short term, and highly opportunistic. Rarely is it ideological and transformative as, in normal circumstances, the intention of the poor is to secure what is already at hand or is discernibly within reach. Because modes of adverse socio-economic incorporation are both complex and risky, poor people are forced to hedge their bets via multiple strategies with respect to both resources and alliances. Next, we argue that poor people's politics takes different forms: *everyday*, *defensive* and *disruptive*. These differ accordingly to whether the urban poor are generally atomistic, collective or organised, and whether they operate within existing power relations or want to upset these somehow.

Finally, the chapter offers two case studies of poor people's politics. The first, from Jakarta, is of an instance of disruptive politics in which the circumstances of heightened electoral contestation in the 2017 gubernatorial election enabled networks of urban poor neighbourhoods, with the assistance of an NGO ally, to secure promises from the successful Islamist candidate. Specifically, the deepening polarisation between secular-nationalist and Islamic populisms in that election offered certain urban poor communities new possibilities for forging strategic cross-class alliances, in return for the opportunity to push issues affecting them onto the political stage (Wilson 2017). Whereas support for such candidates has been widely interpreted as religious and populist, it is shown that the urban poor's agency was far more instrumental and contingent.

In the second case study, an urban poor NGO network in Metro Manila secured an election pledge from the winning candidate in the 2010 presidential election, generating a large government programme to resettle informal settler families away from major city floodways. The NGO network pushed for minimal disruption to livelihoods through in-city relocations and for settlers to participate in their relocations as co-decision-makers with an implementing NGO. However, institutional delays combined with cost and design uncertainties to make "participatory planning" materially risky for the poor. Unable to respond in defensive or disruptive ways to their evictions, many households resorted to their everyday strategies to hedge their losses, dispensing with the participatory option their NGO allies had demanded.

Poor People's Politics

Who are the poor in "poor people's politics"? It would seem a truism that the poor live in poverty and are to be identified by the one or more measures of poverty (see Carroll, this volume). Notwithstanding important debates over the measures of poverty, these address only the material outcomes of poverty-producing processes and not the power relations that produce them (Green and Hulme 2005). By contrast, a social relational approach views poverty as an effect of "historically developed economic and political relations as opposed to 'residual' approaches which might regard poverty as the result of being marginal to these same relations" (Mosse 2010: 1157). Accordingly, for us, the poor are those undergoing processes of adverse socio-economic incorporation from which other classes, directly or indirectly, derive material and other benefits. As a class, the urban poor must struggle for a place in the city, to a greater extent than propertied and wealthier classes with greater market power and legal protections. Importantly, the urban poor are also constituted ideologically as an inferior class due to their "slum" living—regularly viewed as polluting the landscape and society, physically and morally (Pinches 1999, 2010). The urban poor are not generally among the "residual" poor, left behind by capitalist development (Rigg 2015: 8–10).[2] This is obvious

---

[2] We do not include the "destitute" who are unemployed and homeless (see Harriss-White 2005).

when attention is given less to what poor people are lacking in income and assets, and more to how they are actually getting by in the city. In Metro Manila, for example, the urban poor predominantly support themselves by working and, indeed, some 70% of them do so through wage labour (Singh and Gadgil 2017: 11). Simply put, the urban poor cannot afford unemployment; their earnings are poverty-producing, even when working full-time hours (World Bank 2016).[3] The World Bank (2016) attributes such "in-work poverty" to low educational attainment, but this fails to account for the structural predominance of informal or precarious employment and its role in producing poverty (Singh and Gadgil 2017: 28). In many instances we now need to refer to the existence of pervasive informal economic relations, rather than to a residual informal *sector* that operates in isolation from the mainstream economy (Rigg 2015: 70–80).[4] In Jakarta, circumstances are similar (Simone 2015; Suryahadi and Merlina 2018).

Thus, in their employment, the urban poor are engaged daily in poverty-producing processes that nevertheless, if relinquished, would result in their further impoverishment. Not surprisingly then, poor people's politics is generally directed at avoiding further impoverishment, *by seeking to preserve the status quo* in order to protect what they have (Wood 2003). A key source of future impoverishment of the urban poor is "displacement from established ways of living" through forced evictions (Rigg 2015: 66–69). Precisely because the urban poor are highly vulnerable to displacement, they must be especially resourceful and proactive in protecting their assets, living places and employment. Whilst this is highlighted in many studies of the ways in which poor people manage their limited resources, these "livelihood" studies often neglect the social relational dimensions of how poor people gain access to resources (Beall 2002: 83)—in other words, poor people's politics. Because the poor, "almost by definition, face more uncertainty" and "have less control over relationships and events around them" than wealthier classes, they are logically inclined to place a high value on retaining what they have at hand and what is already known to them (Wood 2003: 468).

---

[3] In the Philippines, the pervasiveness of in-work poverty means job-holders are as likely to be poor as the economically inactive and more likely to be poor than the unemployed who are more often in non-poor households (World Bank 2016: 48).

[4] The "informal" economy is that part which is not monitored, regulated or taxed by government.

Scott (1985) famously coined the term "everyday resistance" for poor people's politics in Southeast Asia. In this he aimed to distinguish between overt, organised and covert, "token" resistance to the status quo. This distinction is clearly important and is well-explained by social relational dimensions of poverty such as fear of harsh retaliation. However, Scott's concern with intention limits his focus to *oppositional* forms of politics, thereby neglecting how poor people more often need to cultivate relations with the range of more powerful actors who are capable of exerting degrees of control over their daily lives—landowners, patrons, politicians, local "bossmen", gangsters and police. Because poor people depend on such relations, they are not in a position to treat them lightly or, under normal circumstances, do much to upset them (Kerkvliet 2009; Wood 2003). Moreover, when poor people attempt more confrontational politics, it is still often to restore the status quo—as in informal settlers seeking to prevent their evictions. When they go further, into oppositional politics for change, it is frequently in association with allies with more resources and political capital, such as NGOs. In other words, as a class, the poor are not only relatively powerless, they are relatively more dependent on more powerful others to secure their basic needs.

In summary, we argue that the urban poor are always acting politically by virtue of the negotiation and struggle required of them to defend and advance their material circumstances through attention to social relations that support or threaten their livelihoods and shelter. This politics is not confined nor defined by moments of "extra-ordinary" action, mobilization and intensity, such as demonstrations, riots or elections, but permeates the experience of daily life: it is a feature of their strategies to live and work precariously in the city. This politics of the urban poor displays three key dimensions: *everyday, defensive* and *disruptive*.[5]

In *everyday* politics, the poor's survival strategies feature, in the words of Bayat (2000: 536), "quiet encroachment upon the lives and interests of the propertied and powerful in order to better their own lives": that is, "prolonged direct action by dispersed individuals and families to acquire the basic necessities of their lives (land for shelter, urban collective consumption or urban services, informal work, business opportunities, and public space) in a quiet and unassuming illegal fashion". These atomised

---

[5] Our reference to "everyday politics" is specific to poverty-producing processes and hence to a form of *class* politics and not to the everyday as a "site" within political economy analysis (see Elias and Rethel 2016: 6).

mobilisations and localised struggles constitute a form of collective action through repetition by large numbers that, by its very scale, shapes physical and political space. This is readily evident in cities throughout Southeast Asia, from the appropriation of state- or privately-owned land for livelihood generation by street vendors, to sprawling informal settlements that make use of any available empty land. In Jakarta and Metro Manila, around 30% of the population are informal residents.

Typically, quiet encroachment involves avoidance of authorities; however, once having secured their place, street vendors and informal settlers will seek degrees of protection from more powerful actors through payment of rents and or bribes to grease toleration and exclude others (Bayat 1997: 135). In Jakarta, Simone (2015) explains how encroachments into public space by the poor are "sorted out" by "unofficial authorities"—state officials acting outside their authority, and local "bossmen". The poor interact with official and unofficial authorities to "divide up turf and opportunities". Hence, to open up such opportunities, the poor need to be constantly working out "who is in alliance with whom, who is cooperating together on the surface but fighting each other behind the scenes. They try to figure out where money and resources are diverted to and through whose hands and networks those resources circle back" (Simone 2010: 293; see also Wilson 2019).

Hence, rather than a politics of protest, demand making, or intentionally defiant resistance—as Scott (1985) suggests—everyday politics is pragmatic, seeking solutions to immediate problems. Everyday politics is also without clear leadership, ideology, or structured organisation (Bayat 2000: 551). This is true also of the more *defensive* actions which the poor are subsequently drawn into to secure their previous gains, as in the case of threatened forced evictions from sidewalks and residential areas. Whereas the original encroachment was atomistic, reacting to threats to gains requires collective action, but is more often spontaneous than organised. There is little in the way of sustained collective organisation as the nature of precarious, multiple and fragmented livelihoods makes it difficult to establish the coherent grounds for this (Simone 2010).

Poor people's defensive politics can be confrontational, but still largely operates within existing power relationships, rather than disturbing or attempting to alter them. Indeed, it will often involve attempts to activate existing avenues of support, whether in the form of assistance from allies—such as NGOs—or patrons. In the former case, endeavours to mobilise collectively around shared issues and threats have occurred on different spatial scales, from the neighbourhood level to those attempting to develop city-wide or regional networks. Whilst defensive politics aims to resist threats to poor people's material circumstances, it does not constitute resistance in social relational or class terms.

In contrast to everyday and defensive politics, *disruptive* politics is when the poor start to think differently about their circumstances and seek to somehow alter existing power relationships rather than manoeuvre within them. Importantly, this is not necessarily through acts of disruption, such as violent protest, but can simply entail a consequential shift in allegiances. Disruptive politics is often the result of critical junctures presented by either a fresh opportunity (such as a new populist leader or movement) or existential threats to survival (as in a major development or infrastructure project). It is, however, frequently galvanised by other political actors, including by middle-class allies; further, if poor people's disruptive politics is organised it is generally also because other actors are involved, such as a specific NGO ally.

Across these three dimensions of poor people's politics, we argue this politics is distinctive in being instrumental and opportunistic. Generally, it is not ideological and transformative as the objectives are usually short-term and immediate. Finally, because surviving under conditions of adverse socio-economic incorporation is both complex and risky, poor people pursue multiple strategies with respect to both resources and relationships and alliances, displaying contingent loyalties—much to the annoyance, bewilderment and/or displeasure of authorities, patrons and allies alike.

Instrumental Populism in Jakarta

Indonesian politics is increasingly characterised by competition between secular-nationalist and Islamic populisms (Hadiz and Robison 2017). Robison and Hadiz (this volume) argue that populism is a cross-class form of politics in which rival socio-economic interests are obscured in order to forge broad alliances. However, in relation to Islamic populism a burning question is the extent to which electoral support is based on religious adherence. Other scholars tend to assume it is. They have used voter surveys to assert that religion and identity politics were indeed key factors in the 2017 Jakarta gubernatorial election, overriding voter assessments of the incumbent's track record in office (Mietzner and Muhtadi 2017; Setijadi 2017). By contrast, we argue that urban poor support for the main

Islamic candidate in that election was less based on issues of identity and religion than it was on their distinctive politics.

The New Order of President Suharto had seen repeated waves of mass evictions and dislocations of poor and informal settlements. Towards the end of the New Order, several organisations emerged that sought to organise the urban poor. One of the most significant of these was the Urban Poor Consortium (UPC), established in 1997. It sought to build upon existing self-organising practices in Jakarta's *kampung* ("villages"), establishing a network of 58 neighbourhoods throughout the city as well as organisations for informal sector workers, such as *becak* (pedicab) drivers. As with many NGOs, key UPC organisers have middle-class backgrounds, but UPC practices nevertheless focus upon mentoring urban poor activists to self-organise in their own settlements. Aside from UPC, a host of new organisations arose post-New Order that claimed to represent the poor but were enmeshed in patterns of local patronage and coercion. Many of these, such as the ethnic militia the Betawi Brotherhood Forum (*Forum Betawi Rempug* or FBR) combined particularist benefits for their largely urban poor membership with forms of racketeering and extortion, and political brokerage for Jakarta's political elites (Wilson 2014).

The reintroduction of competitive direct elections for district, provincial and national government in the late 1990s saw new opportunities for negotiations and bargaining, for both elites, urban poor groups and NGOs. In Jakarta, UPC focused its energies away from protest actions and towards formulating alternate urban development models and policy, in the hope that greater access to formal power could enable policy influence.

When Joko Widodo (aka Jokowi) emerged on the Jakarta political scene in 2011, he was viewed as a new breed of regional politician without close political ties to the New Order or the strong support of a political party machinery. Jokowi appealed directly to voters with promises to fix Jakarta's social and infrastructural problems, together with his relaxed and relatable style. He came with a widely publicised record of modest governance reform successes and participatory urban renewal programmes as mayor of Solo, a mid-sized city in Central Java. Urban poor groups, including UPC, began discussions with Jokowi and his campaign team, seeing possibilities for substantive, participatory social and political reforms. A broad set of demands were formulated into a political contract signed between an alliance of urban poor groups and Jokowi that committed to involve the urban poor in spatial planning and budget allocation processes, recognise *kampung* dwellers' right to tenure and disavow evictions, and acknowledge the importance of the informal street economy.

In Indonesia, political parties do not have grassroots social bases and are not clearly differentiated on ideological lines. As a result, electoral politics has focused upon candidates, which has served to entrench patterns of localised personalist regimes and patronage. In their everyday politics, the poor have often been short-term beneficiaries of this, with campaign periods seen as a 'harvest time' during which candidates offer a variety of particularistic material or social benefits, often at the expense of coherent programmes or policy. In this context, political contracts (*kontrak politik*) have been viewed as a means to obtain specific commitments from candidates if elected (Gibbings et al. 2017; Savirani and Aspinall 2017). Conversely, candidates have also embraced contracts as a means of allaying distrust and garnering votes (Savirani and Aspinall 2017).

The contract with Jokowi was widely distributed among poor neighbourhoods, generating enthusiasm not just for his candidacy but for the election itself, with increased levels of participation by the poor. UPC saw this as a substantive shift: the poor thinking of elections beyond an immediate material gain, and more in terms of concrete claim-making leading to substantive changes in the status quo. As one UPC activist explained "this was not politics as usual. We, the poor, were entrusting this candidate to work with us in achieving the goals we'd set together".[6]

On winning the elections, Jokowi's administration initially conformed to some elements of the contract. There was a successful in-city relocation from flood areas and a slum upgrading pilot; but the promise to confer legal tenure in informal neighbourhoods was abandoned from the outset. Evictions continued, mostly without adequate alternative housing.[7] Aside from difficulties in negotiating the legal and political complexities of land ownership in Indonesia's capital, the broad principles of the contract clashed with the expectations and interests of Jokowi's other constituencies, in particular the middle class. Many perceived in him a leader who could deliver the amenities and lifestyle of Singapore or Seoul, which in turn required a disciplining hand towards the poor. Powerful developers also lobbied to scupper reforms that would be a major hindrance to their interests. With diminished lines of communication between Jokowi and

---

[6] UPC activist, interview with Ian Wilson, Jakarta, April 2017.
[7] Director of the Jakarta Residents' Forum (FAKTA), interview with Ian Wilson, Jakarta, December 2014.

urban poor groups the political contract was, just 12 months on, largely in tatters.

Jokowi's ascendancy to the presidency in 2014 saw his deputy, Basuki Purnama Tjahaja, aka Ahok, assume the governorship. From the outset his relationship with urban poor groups was tense, lacking Jokowi's skills of rapport. As he consolidated his power, Ahok distanced himself further from urban poor groups while becoming more rhetorically hostile, such as publicly admonishing the poor who protested evictions as ungrateful and suggestive of communism. Ahok's administration intensified the building of low-rent social housing apartments, but on low-value, government-owned land in largely peripheral parts of the city and not at a sufficient rate to accommodate the thousands made homeless (Savirani and Wilson 2018). For urban poor activists, "Ahok was hell".[8] At the same time, Ahok's straight-talking approach to governmental corruption and bureaucratic inefficiency had wide appeal to the middle class, as did what many perceived as his "firm" enforcement of the rule of law in the case of urban poor evictions, invoked via discourses of the poor as undisciplined and a source of disorder. This led to the fraying of alliances between urban poor groups and some middle-class liberal sympathisers.

However, allegations made by Islamist groups that Ahok had blasphemed against Islam when he suggested rivals were wrongly using a Quranic verse to block his re-election bid fundamentally changed the contours of what otherwise appeared an easy election win (Mietzner et al. 2018). His elite political rivals pumped resources into what had been a largely fringe movement opposed to him on religious grounds. During the campaign, mass sectarian demonstrations weaponized religious identity against Ahok. On the other hand, his status as an ethnic-Chinese Christian made him, almost by default, the embodiment of liberal constructions of identity pluralism, which consolidated the support of socially liberal middle classes.

The resulting populist polarisation nonetheless delivered important strategic advantages for the poor and urban poor groups. While by no means the defining issue of the election, evictions and treatment of the poor came to occupy a more central place in political debate, as did populist rhetoric regarding inequality. What remained of neighbourhoods that had borne the brunt of Ahok's evictions regime became literal campaign stages for an array of politicians, activists, religious preachers, mass

[8] Urban poor activist, interview with Ian Wilson, Jakarta, July 2016.

organisations, celebrities and assorted political brokers now 'outraged' at the injustice the poor had suffered, all offering material logistical assistance and access to new networks. However, this meant the poor also faced dilemmas.

After the blasphemy issue first emerged, the residents of a poor neighbourhood in North Jakarta debated at length over whether to allow an Islamist group linked to opposition political parties to establish a visible presence in the neighbourhood as a strong deterrent to threatened evictions. The group had previously provided logistical support to the neighbourhood in times of crisis, such as severe flooding, and so were seen favourably. However, some residents worried that being perceived as a stronghold for the group could needlessly antagonise the city administration at a time when a negotiated settlement was still considered a possibility, albeit remotely. Also, the group's reputation for sectarian rhetoric and aggressive confrontation was understood to be potentially alienating to middle-class NGO allies, the latter considered vital mediators with government and interpreters of the complex and confusing legal system. As one resident summarised: "there are many who want to help us; the problem is, one kind of help can prevent other kinds of help or can even create new sets of problems".[9] In this instance, the community kept both options open, accepting assistance from the Islamist group (who temporarily hoisted a flag) while continuing to work with existing NGO allies, aided by these groups not crossing paths in the community.

While not aligning itself to any political candidate or party during the actual campaign, UPC adopted the position that, due to his regime of evictions, Ahok needed to be removed from office. After the first round of voting ensured a run-off between the incumbent and the former minister for education, Anies Baswedan, key allies of UPC helped to facilitate contact with Anies's campaign team. As Savirani and Aspinall (2017) document, a detailed strategy was developed. Learning from the experiences of 2012, UPC outlined a set of specific demands, formulated via a complex, iterative process that involved grassroots teams in 41 neighbourhoods. Through consultations, the grassroots teams documented and conveyed the aspirations of the poor to an "expert team" consisting of academics, lawyers and urban planners. Unlike the contract with Jokowi, the result was detailed, specific and rigorously checked against existing regulatory frameworks and the executive authority of the governor. This was in return

[9] Interview with Ian Wilson, Jakarta, July 2016.

for securing electoral victory in 41 neighbourhoods, representatives of whom were contract signatories.

The alliance generated significant hostility from some middle-class, liberal activists. For them, the election had become a zero-sum game between the defence of pluralism, embodied by Ahok and his double-minority status as Christian and ethnic Chinese, and the forces of the xenophobic religious right, who had used race, religion and the blasphemy laws to take down an otherwise popular politician. This was overlaid with the appeal of Ahok's technocratic efficiency versus the nepotistic corruption that the coalition supporting Anies was believed to represent. For urban poor groups, however, these were peripheral issues; what the middle-class liberal activists saw as a betrayal was in fact consistent with the opportunism of poor people's disruptive politics.

Permanent conditions of insecurity mean that poor people need to keep their options open and will often pursue multiple avenues in order to hedge risk rather than pursue a coherent ideology (Simone 2015). Commonly, poor communities have relationships, alliances and clientelist arrangements with an array of groups and interests ranging from liberal NGOs, civil society and religious organisations, to militias, gangsters, political parties and a plethora of brokers and entrepreneurs, each offering sets of opportunities, the challenge being one of juggling the contrasting expectations and risks that each entail (Wilson 2019). In doing this they can, in some instances, "quietly encroach" on and alter organisational purposes and ideologies.[10] However, this has become more fraught within the context of populist polarisation, where apparent affiliation with one 'side' can close doors to others. Anies winning the election comfortably has amplified this as both sides look to the implications for the next presidential election (Mietzner et al. 2018; Setijadi 2017).

In putting their support behind an Islamist-backed candidate in the Jakarta election, the urban poor not only substantially switched sides for tactical, instrumental reasons, they did so in the face of significant criticism from middle-class liberal activists. The fact that the electoral support was in this instance secured through a negotiated contract, quite detailed and

---

[10] Notably, within the Islamic Defenders Front (*Front Pembela Islam*, FPI), tensions exist between urban poor's instrumental concerns to gain strategic advantage in street and protection economies, on the one hand, and the ostensible political goals of its leadership and ideological and religious drives of middle-class members, on the other. FPI's critics label this "hypocrisy", but it reflects the divergent interests and concerns driving different social classes within it (Wilson 2014).

technical in its content, should not obscure the underlying elements of poor people's politics that are daily constrained—by their treatment by others, and by their lack of power and resources, but especially by their internalisation of poverty's effects, in the form of irrational, irresponsible behaviours (Mosse 2010: 1170).

Everyday Participation in Metro Manila

As in Indonesia, major political parties in the Philippines are not easily differentiated on programmatic lines, so elections potentially offer fresh opportunities for alliance-building with candidates. Key elections for Metro Manila's urban poor are those for local mayors—there is no city governor—and for the president. Local governments have substantial powers and incentives in relation to urban development but are also required by legislation to follow humane guidelines in evictions and identify land suitable for social housing within their jurisdictions. The president has oversight of major infrastructure programmes, but also has executive power to dispose of national government land in favour of informal occupants. Since the early 1990s, this authority has been a periodic target of urban poor disruptive politics, when and where it could apply. Whereas communities have generally lacked the alliances to confront local mayors' intentions, NGO advocacy networks have made more headway pursing institutional reforms on the national political stage (Hutchison 2007; Hutchison et al. 2014: 99–101).

Against this background, during the 2010 presidential election campaign, the Urban Poor Alliance (UP-ALL), formed in 2005, successfully negotiated a 10-point "covenant" with the winning candidate, Benigno Aquino III. A good number of the UP-ALL's NGO members had decades-long histories in grassroots organising and national advocacy and had helped to drive various pro-urban poor policy and institutional reforms since the fall of the Marcos dictatorship in the late 1980s (Carroll 1998; Karaos and Porio 2015). The 2010 election covenant included a moratorium on informal settler evictions and the provision of social housing through participatory in-city relocations. Some months after the election, the covenant was operationalised in a large, five-year, PHP50 billion (over US$1bn) government-funded programme to resettle about 104,000 informal settler households from major floodways in Metro Manila. Called *Oplan Likas: Lipat Para Iwas Kalamidad at Sakit* (Operational Plan: Evacuation to Prevent Calamity and Sickness), the programme also constituted the new administration's response to a previous Supreme Court decision ordering the demolition of all informal structures and dwellings along the riverbanks and waterways entering Manila Bay, on environmental grounds.

Consistent with UP-ALL's demands—and international best practice in relation to resettlement—Oplan Likas was to fund relocations in-city, "within the vicinity of... livelihoods, leaving off-city relocation as a last resort" (World Bank 2017: 3). In addition, programme guidelines advocated the use of "people's plans" to ensure affected communities' direct participation in decision-making over land acquisition, site development and building construction, with NGOs the implementing partners for specific neighbourhoods.

For UP-ALL activists, Oplan Likas represented "a dream come true" in the opportunities it promised for large-scale participatory development.[11] However, from the start the programme was burdened with competing logics (Galuszka 2018). In particular, the "people's plans" were much harder to implement than the plan of the National Housing Authority (NHA), which intended to transfer the urban poor to newly-constructed, semi-detached housing at specific locations on the city's edges. First, private land was generally too expensive, while public and institutionally held land was difficult to secure without the backing of a mayor and/or the relevant land-owning agency; moreover, when land was apparently available there were still lengthy delays, sometimes exceeding a year, to obtain necessary approvals. Second, the imperative that budgeted funds be dispersed annually greatly favoured the NHA's standard approach. This agency had long-held interests in dispensing building contracts to private firms and no experience in partnering with NGOs or communities of informal settlers—nor any interest in doing so. As a result, about 70% of total allocated funds went to the NHA, and a much smaller proportion to the government agencies associated with the financing of the "people's plans" (ibid.: 5–6). As in the past, urban poor advocacy proved to have less political force in relation to the implementation of a reform than in its introduction (Hutchison 2007; Shatkin 2000).

How did informal settlers respond to the evictions?[12] Displacement severely threatens the strategies and processes through which poor people

---

[11] NGO organiser, interview with Jane Hutchison, Metro Manila, August 2014.

[12] The research for this case study covered seven sites in 2014–2016: four in-city sites where participatory planning was underway and three distant relocation sites.

are already getting by. Thus, despite several major flooding episodes in previous years, most of the floodway households preferred to stay where they were or move within the vicinity. However, their ability to react in defensive or disruptive ways was very limited in this instance. All levels of government were on board with the resettlement programme one way or another, as were the urban poor's usual allies, the NGOs. At some sites, for their own ideological reasons, other leftist organisations were encouraging collective resistance by the informal settlers, but this never amounted to much; overwhelmingly, evictions were understood to be a given.

There were some collective elements to informal settlers' decision-making as neighbourhoods were to be transferred generally as a group, but predominantly the choice between options was a matter for the household. Once informed of their imminent evictions, some households resorted immediately to everyday strategies of "quiet encroachment" and moved themselves to a location in the city, reportedly on the basis of their social and familial networks. When affected communities had no connections with an NGO, the information they received about the resettlement programme came exclusively from authorities who made no mention of the "people's plan" option and stated the window of opportunity for NHA housing would be very short. The households concerned risked homelessness and, despite knowing the income losses they risked in relocating to a peri-urban area with limited employment and long commutes to their existing jobs, in the NHA option they saw at least an opportunity to retain or acquire a major tangible asset: a semi-detached house and accompanying small plot, initially mortgaged but with the prospect of future ownership or sale to others. Understandably, many signed up.

Yet signing up did not necessarily mean that households relocated as a unit. In some cases, the pattern was that men remained in-city to keep their jobs, returning on weekends (or less frequently) to their wives and young children at the off-city relocation site. Some families left their older children behind with relatives to be able to complete their schooling. In other cases, within 12 months of moving, a significant number of households had either sold up or were renting out their new dwelling in order to return in-city to be closer to their employment or other livelihood sources. At one NHA site, after one year this applied to over 30% of dwellings, while another 10–15% were empty—possibly abandoned—or had only one or two family members remaining as caretakers.[13]

---

[13] Relocated households, interviews with Jane Hutchison, Bulacan, July 2015.

In contrast to the speed with which the NHA constructed new housing for the programme, participatory planning processes involved in the "people's plan" were drawn-out and frequently have yet to deliver concrete outcomes, even well into the designated five years. Consequently, the implementing NGOs had ongoing difficulties in recruiting enough households for their construction plans to be viable. One NGO had identified 1200 eligible households initially, but some 18 months later the number participating had dropped to 320; more than double that number was still needed. Another year later, the same NGO had engaged 463 households but expected to lose up to 20% of these in coming months.[14]

The problem lay in the participatory processes going hand-in-hand with *preparing* for a future housing outcome that was uncertain in its dimensions and fulfilment. Along the way, implementing NGOs could not guarantee construction would in fact be completed, let alone that it would be acceptable to participating households in cost or liveability terms. Affordability was a major issue for participating poor households, yet NGOs could not predict prices with certainty, given the contingencies in building projects for which there were no precedents. In-city construction had to be medium-rise and was thus anticipated to be more expensive than NHA-built semi-detached housing; however, taking the off-city option would entail significant income losses and additional expenses, especially transport-related. The point is that, for all households, the cost implications remained undetermined, moreover there was always the risk a "people's plan" might deliver nothing, whereas NHA dwellings were immediately available. Finally, for many households a unit in a medium-rise was less flexible than semi-detached housing: it could not be extended to accommodate more family, renters or a small shop and there were to be restrictions on keeping dogs and poultry. Dropout rates from the "people's plans" tended to peak after households received the offer of an NHA relocation in association with the imminent demolition of their neighbourhood.

Joshi and Moore (2000: 25) reiterate the wide international acceptance that, in order to respond to the needs of the poor, the development programmes targeting them "should have significant collective and mobilising dimensions". Moreover, they argue, besides endeavouring to organise the poor, allies also need to foster poor people's own active participation; this is done by addressing the facets of the programme that can discourage

---

[14] NGO organiser, interview with Jane Hutchison, Metro Manila, August 2016.

such participation. These facets include whether, for beneficiaries, the programme is *predictable* or not, and as well the degree to which programme implementers are considered *credible* and trustworthy (ibid.: 30).

With respect to the former, in relation to Oplan Likas, informal settlers expected to be evicted and an official offer of alternative housing only confirmed this. Other aspects of the programme were less certain. The risks of impoverishment through displacement were broadly known, but the complexities entailed made calculations of actual risks very difficult. Participatory planning processes were advocated precisely to find the ways to address these risks, yet they were unable to cater for the urban poor's pressing need to preserve what they have at hand—or at least find an immediate substitute—and not forgo relative certainty for an indeterminate outcome in the future. Many households withdrew from their "people's plans" because they were not sufficiently predictable to make their engagement worthwhile. With respect to the *credibility* of the programme implementers, NGOs tended to fare better in terms of their commitment to being on the side of the poor; however, this commitment was no real substitute for their capacity to deliver results in a timely fashion. In other words, NGOs were generally considered to be trustworthy in their motivations, but in terms of actually resolving informal settlers' problems, they again fell short.

Oplan Likas was the product of urban poor NGO advocacy in the context of an election. Formally, it adhered to pro-poor principles, but from the beginning, the logics of a government-funded infrastructure programme clashed with those of a participatory planning process which aimed to transform the status quo. Not only did implementing NGOs face predictable opposition to acquiring land for in-city resettlements—and then lengthy approval delays—they were not able to provide, via their participatory planning approach, for the shelter needs of a number of the communities facing certain eviction. As a result, many households took the opportunity to secure an NHA dwelling as a tangible asset, even when they did not consider it an immediate shelter solution. Subsequently, they thus continued to address their shelter needs informally, by way of the everyday politics of "quiet encroachment" back in the city—the outcome NGOs had sought to improve upon through their original election covenant.

Conclusion

As a direct consequence of "the social relations which produce poverty effects" (Green and Hulme 2005: 874), poor people's basic needs are not guaranteed and protected, whether by law, money or naked power, in the same way that they are for propertied and wealthier classes. The states of uncertainty and deprivation poor people live in, as a consequence, constrain and shape their agency and politics vis-à-vis resource acquisition and utilisation and the social relations through which this occurs. Accordingly, we argue that there is a distinctive short-termism to poor people's politics, coupled with marked propensities to endeavour to keep various options open via multiple courses of action. Whereas normally, in everyday and defensive forms, poor people's politics does not seek to upset or challenge prevailing power relations (indeed, the converse is true: it is concerned mostly with availing themselves of what is present), in instances of disruptive politics, the poor can seize opportunities to make a more concerted stand to unsettle prior relations.

Thus, the urban poor's recent electoral stance in Jakarta is best explained, not by their susceptibility to ideological and/or religious manipulation by populist figures, but rather in terms of the particular class agency that is required to secure resources, living places and livelihoods under conditions of adverse socio-economic incorporation. In Metro Manila, disruptive politics in the context of an election created a rare opportunity for NGOs to handle forced relocations differently, to minimise the affected informal settlers' losses. However, the NGOs' participatory approach was too materially risky for many poor households who instead resorted to everyday strategies of encroachment to secure their resources, living places and livelihoods, thwarting the best intentions of their allies in the process.

References

ADB [Asian Development Bank]. (2014). *Urban poverty in Asia*. Mandaluyong City: Asian Development Bank.

Baker, J. L., & Gadgil, G. U. (Eds.). (2017). *East Asia and Pacific cities: Expanding opportunities for the urban poor*. Washington, DC: World Bank.

Bayat, A. (1997). *Street politics: Poor people's movements in Iran*. New York: Columbia University Press.

Bayat, A. (2000). From "dangerous classes" to "quiet rebels": Politics of the urban subaltern in the global south. *International Sociology*, 15(3), 533–557.
Beall, J. (2002). Living in the present, investing in the future – Household security among the poor. In C. Rakodi & T. Lloyd-Jones (Eds.), *Urban livelihoods: A people-centred approach to reducing poverty* (pp. 71–87). London: Earthscan Publications.
Carroll, J. J. (1998). Philippine NGOs confront urban poverty. In G. S. Silliman & L. G. Noble (Eds.), *Organizing for democracy: NGOs, civil society, and the Philippine state* (pp. 113–137). Quezon City: Ateneo de Manila University Press.
Elias, J., & Rethel, L. (2016). Southeast Asia and everyday political economy. In J. Elias & L. Rethel (Eds.), *The everyday political economy of Southeast Asia* (pp. 3–24). Cambridge: Cambridge University Press.
Galuszka, J. (2018). *Civil society and public sector cooperation: Case of Oplan LIKAS*. Policy Notes, 2018–10 (October). Quezon City: Philippine Institute for Development Studies.
Gibbings, S. L., Lazuardi, E., & Prawirosusanto, K. M. (2017). Mobilizing the masses: Street vendors, political contracts, and the role of mediators in Yogyakarta, Indonesia. *Bijdragen tot de taal-, land- en volkenkunde*, 173(2–3), 242–272.
Green, M., & Hulme, D. (2005). From correlates and characteristics to causes: Thinking about poverty from a chronic poverty perspective. *World Development*, 33(6), 867–879.
Hadiz, V., & Robison, R. (2017). Competing populisms in post-authoritarian Indonesia. *International Political Science Review*, 38(4), 488–502.
Harriss-White, B. (2005). Destitution and the poverty of its politics, with special reference to South Asia. *World Development*, 33(6), 881–891.
Hutchison, J. (2007). The disallowed political participation of Manila's urban poor. *Democratization*, 14(5), 853–872.
Hutchison, J., Hout, W., Hughes, C., & Robison, R. (2014). *Political economy and the aid industry in Asia*. Basingstoke: Palgrave Macmillan.
Joshi, A., & Moore, M. (2000). Enabling environments: Do anti-poverty programmes mobilise the poor? *Journal of Development Studies*, 37(1), 25–56.
Karaos, A. M., & Porio, E. (2015). Transforming the housing process in the Philippines: The role of local–global networks by the urban poor. In P. Herrle, A. Ley, & J. Fokdal (Eds.), *From local action to global networks: Housing the urban poor* (pp. 107–121). Farnham: Ashgate.
Kerkvliet, B. (2009). Everyday politics in peasant societies (and ours). *Journal of Peasant Studies*, 36(1), 227–243.
Mietzner, M., & Muhtadi, B. (2017, May 5). Ahok's satisfied non-voters: An anatomy. *New Mandala*. https://www.newmandala.org/ahoks-satisfied-non-voters-anatomy/

Mietzner, M., Muhtadi, B., & Halida, R. (2018). Entrepreneurs of grievance. *Bijdragen tot de taal-, land- en volkenkunde, 174*(2–3), 159–187.

Mosse, D. (2010). A relational approach to durable poverty, inequality and power. *The Journal of Development Studies, 46*(7), 1156–1178.

Pinches, M. (1999). Cultural relations, class and the new rich of Asia. In M. Pinches (Ed.), *Culture and privilege in capitalist Asia* (pp. 1–55). London/New York: Routledge.

Pinches, M. (2010). The making of middle class civil society in the Philippines. In Y. Kasuya & N. G. Quimpo (Eds.), *The politics of change in the Philippines* (pp. 284–312). Pasig City: Anvil Publishing.

Rigg, J. (2015). *Challenging Southeast Asian development: The shadows of success*. London: Routledge.

Savirani, A., & Aspinall, E. (2017). Adversarial linkages: The urban poor and electoral politics in Jakarta. *Journal of Current Southeast Asian Affairs, 36*(3), 3–34.

Savirani, A., & Wilson, I. D. (2018). Distance matters: Social housing for the poor in Jakarta. *Inside Indonesia*, 132. https://www.insideindonesia.org/distance-matters-social-housing-for-the-poor

Scott, J. (1985). *Weapons of the weak: Everyday forms of resistance*. New Haven: Yale University Press.

Setijadi, C. (2017). *Ahok's downfall and the rise of Islamist populism in Indonesia* (ISEAS perspective, 38). Singapore: ISEAS-Yusof Ishak Institute.

Shatkin, G. (2000). Obstacles to empowerment: Local politics and civil society in Metropolitan Manila, the Philippines. *Urban Studies, 37*(12), 2357–2375.

Simone, A. (2010). On intersections, anticipations, and provisional politics: Remaking district life in Jakarta. *Urban Geography, 31*(3), 285–308.

Simone, A. (2015). The urban poor and their ambivalent exceptionalities: Some notes from Jakarta. *Current Anthropology, 56*(S11), S15–S23.

Singh, G., & Gadgil, G. (2017). *Navigating informality: Perils and prospects in Metro Manila's slums*. Washington, DC: World Bank.

Suryahadi, A., & Merlina, C. (2018). *Understanding metropolitan poverty: The profile of poverty in Jabodetabek area* (SMERU working paper). Jakarta: SMERU Research Institute.

Wilson, I. D. (2014). Morality racketeering: Vigilantism and populist Islamic militancy in Indonesia. In K. Boo Teik, V. Hadiz, & Y. Nakanishi (Eds.), *Between dissent and power: The transformations of Islamic politics in the Middle East and Asia* (pp. 248–274). New York: Palgrave Macmillan.

Wilson, I. D. (2017, April 19). Jakarta: Inequality and the poverty of elite pluralism. *New Mandala*. https://www.newmandala.org/jakarta-inequality-poverty-elite-pluralism/

Wilson, I. D. (2019). Urban poor activism and political agency in post-new order Jakarta. In T. Dibley & M. Ford (Eds.), *Activists in transition: Contentious politics in the new Indonesia* (pp. 173–203). Ithaca: Cornell University Press.

Wood, G. (2003). Staying secure, staying poor: The "Faustian bargain". *World Development, 31*(3), 455–471.
World Bank. (2016). *Republic of the Philippines labor market review: Employment and poverty*. Washington, DC: World Bank.
World Bank. (2017). *Project Information Document (PID) appraisal stage* (Report no. PIDA72805). Washington, DC: The World Bank. http://documents.worldbank.org/curated/en/569821495531675047/text/PID-Appraisal-Print-P153814-05-23-2017-1495531642159.txt

CHAPTER 12

The Changing Aid Landscape and the Political Economy of Development in Southeast Asia

Andrew Rosser

INTRODUCTION

The aid landscape in Southeast Asia has changed dramatically in recent decades. Most importantly, "emerging" donors—particularly China—have become increasingly active as providers of aid to the region, challenging the dominant position of "traditional" donors. Accompanying this change have been important shifts in the geographical distribution of aid within the region and the types of aid provided to recipient countries. This chapter maps these changes in the regional aid landscape and assesses their impact on the political economy of development in the region. Using a Murdoch School approach, it assesses how these changes have affected the balance of power between competing political and social actors in Southeast Asian countries and the implications this has had for the nature of development policies and institutions in these countries.

A. Rosser (✉)
Asia Institute, University of Melbourne, Melbourne, VIC, Australia
e-mail: andrew.rosser@unimelb.edu.au

© The Author(s) 2020
T. Carroll et al. (eds.), *The Political Economy of Southeast Asia*, Studies in the Political Economy of Public Policy, https://doi.org/10.1007/978-3-030-28255-4_12

Much analysis has suggested that the growing role of China as a donor in Southeast Asia has empowered predatory, populist and authoritarian elites within the region and, in so doing, undermined efforts by traditional donors and their allies to promote neoliberal and liberal-democratic reform. Echoing claims that China is a "rogue" donor (Naim 2007), this analysis has suggested that Chinese aid has contributed to "human-rights abuses, endemic corruption, home seizures, arrests, murders of dissidents, [and] many other problems" in Southeast Asian countries (Brinkley n.d.; see also Landingin 2013; Walker and Cook 2010). More generally, the claim is that Chinese aid is shifting the region's developmental trajectory away from progress towards liberal markets and democracy and back towards statism and authoritarianism.

In this chapter, I argue that the situation is more nuanced than this analysis suggests. On the one hand, political and social actors committed to neoliberal and liberal-democratic reform, including traditional donors, have never been particularly strong in political terms in Southeast Asian countries, meaning that the apparent hope of the region making an easy transition to liberal markets and democracy aided by traditional donors is misplaced. On the other hand, the changed regional aid landscape has had less of an impact on power relations in the region than the rogue donor thesis implies. There is certainly evidence to suggest that the changed regional aid landscape has empowered predatory, populist and authoritarian elites in Southeast Asian countries by creating greater scope for them to forgo aid from traditional donors in favour of Chinese aid with fewer policy or institution-related conditions attached or that otherwise better fits with their political priorities. However, this effect has been mitigated by two factors. These are: concerns about the impact of Chinese aid on government foreign debt levels, something that has made Southeast Asian governments cautious about shifting completely away from traditional donors' aid towards Chinese aid; and the fact that China—perhaps contrary to expectations—has backed some liberal policy and institutional reform initiatives, meaning that in certain areas its agenda has been more or less the same as traditional donors.

In presenting this argument, I begin by examining in greater detail the changes in the regional aid landscape identified above. I then explore how these changes, and especially the growing role of China as a donor, have impacted on the political economy of development in the region, first by examining the agendas of traditional and emerging donors with regard to the nature of development policy and institutions in recipient countries and, second, by assessing how the changed aid landscape has affected power relations in Southeast Asia and the implications this has had for development policies and institutions in the region.

Before beginning with this analysis, however, it is necessary to briefly define some key terms as they are used in this chapter:

- *Traditional donors* are the countries that make up the membership of the Organisation for Economic Cooperation and Development's (OECD) Development Assistance Committee (DAC) and the multilateral institutions over which they exercise great influence. They include the United States, Japan, the United Kingdom, Germany, France, the Netherlands and Australia, and multilateral institutions such as the European Union (EU), the International Monetary Fund (IMF), the World Bank, and the Asian Development Bank (ADB).
- *Emerging donors* are countries that "have become substantial donors in the last 20 years; are not part of the [OECD DAC] or have only joined it [recently]; and received aid and/or other development assistance themselves in the recent past (and may still be doing so)" (Callan et al. 2013). They include China, Saudi Arabia, Kuwait, the United Arab Emirates, South Korea, India, Brazil, Mexico, South Africa and a small number of Southeast Asian countries, namely, Thailand, Indonesia and Singapore. They also include multilateral institutions established at these countries' initiative such as the Asian Infrastructure Investment Bank (AIIB), which was the result of a Chinese proposal, and the New Development Bank (NDB), which was jointly founded by Brazil, Russia, India, China and South Africa.
- *Aid* is defined as the sum of "official development assistance" (ODA) and "other official flows" (OOF), as those terms are employed by the OECD DAC. To count as ODA, financial flows must be to countries and territories on the DAC list of ODA recipients or multilateral institutions, be provided by official agencies, be aimed at promoting economic development and welfare objectives, and be concessional in character, conveying a grant element of at least 25% (OECD n.d.-a). OOF are official flows that do not meet the definition of ODA (OECD n.d.-b). There are complications in using the notions of ODA and OOF to discuss aid flows from emerging donors because the latter typically do not report their aid flows using these terms, if they report them at all. Nevertheless, I define aid as ODA+OOF in this chapter because it combines the OECD DAC's preferred definition of aid (ODA) with the form of aid that appears to be dominant within the aid programmes of emerging donors (especially China),

namely, OOF.[1] At the same time, some recent innovations in aid research—most notably the creation of the AidData database—have gone some way towards addressing data gaps for emerging donors, at least in relation to Chinese aid. This database tracks China's global aid flows using open source materials, distinguishing between flows that are "ODA-like" and those that are "OOF-like".[2]

The Changing Aid Landscape in Southeast Asia

During the Cold War, traditional donors pumped massive amounts of aid into Southeast Asia in an attempt to stem the expansion of communist influence in the region. Since the end of the Cold War, however, they have re-focused their aid on other parts of the world, particularly the Middle East and sub-Saharan Africa. Global international development initiatives such as the United Nation's Millennium Development Goals (MDGs), which were announced in 2000, and the Sustainable Development Goals (SDGs), which were adopted by the UN in 2015, have shone a light on the plight of poor countries in sub-Saharan Africa, encouraging traditional donors to allocate more of their aid to these countries. At the same time, Southeast Asian countries have become increasingly prosperous, making it difficult for traditional donors to justify large amounts of aid to these countries on poverty-related grounds; fiscal difficulties in traditional donor countries in the wake of the global financial crisis in 2008 have led in some cases to cuts in aid budgets, and efforts by donors to focus their aid on priority countries; and some Southeast Asian countries have sought to reduce their dependence on aid from traditional donors and limit these donors' influence over their policies. Finally, and most importantly, since the terrorist attack by Al Qaeda in New York in 2001, traditional donors have allocated vastly increased amounts of aid to Afghanistan and Iraq as part of the US-led "War on Terror".

Traditional donors have continued to provide substantial and growing amounts of aid to countries in Southeast Asia in real terms despite these developments (see Fig. 12.1). However, as Fig. 12.2 shows, traditional donors' aid to the region has fallen markedly as a share of their total aid flows to developing countries.

---

[1] On the relative proportions of ODA and OOF in China's aid programme, see the following section.

[2] It also reports on flows that do not fall clearly into either the ODA-like or OOF-like categories, labelling these "vague".

Fig. 12.1 Traditional donor aid to Southeast Asian countries (commitments, US$ millions at constant prices)

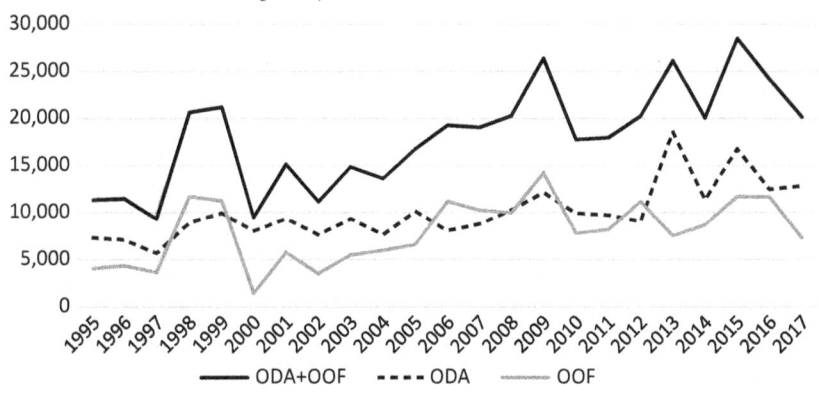

Note: Traditional donors include OECD DAC member countries, EU institutions, the IMF, World Bank and the ADB

Source: OECD 2019a

Fig. 12.2 Percentage of traditional donor aid devoted to Southeast Asian countries (commitments, US$ millions at constant prices)

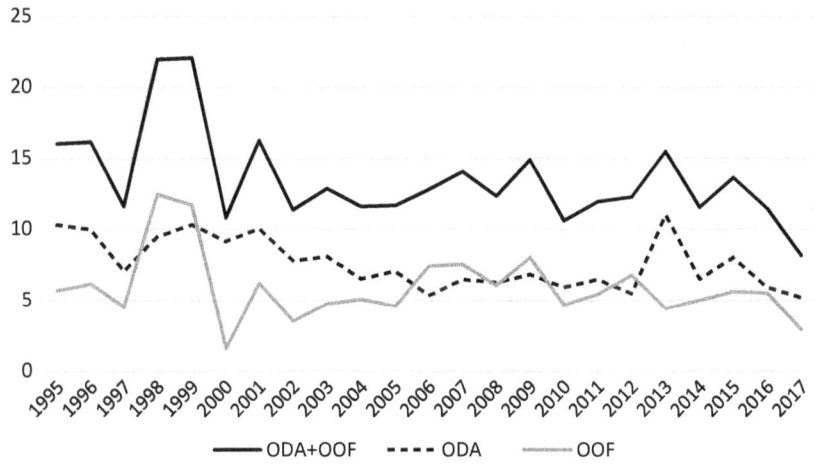

Note: Traditional donors include OECD DAC member countries, EU institutions, the IMF, World Bank and the ADB

Source: OECD 2019a

At the same time, in allocating aid to the region, traditional donors have given increased priority to Cambodia, Laos, Myanmar and Vietnam (the CLMV countries) (see Fig. 12.3). This shift has reflected a number of factors including the relative poverty of these countries compared to most of their Southeast Asian neighbours; in Cambodia's case, the end of a long-running civil war in 1991 and subsequent transition to formally democratic rule; in Vietnam and Laos, transition away from a reliance on Soviet aid following the collapse of the Soviet Union in the early 1990s; and in Myanmar's case, transition to more democratic rule from 2011 onwards. The emerging capitalist economies of the region—Indonesia, Thailand, the Philippines and Malaysia—have correspondingly experienced a sharp decline in their respective share of total traditional donor aid flows to the region. As Fig. 12.3 shows, they experienced a significant increase in aid from traditional donors during and after the Asian financial crisis in the late 1990s and early 2000s as they sought international assistance to help weather the economic and social effects of this crisis. After that time, however, such flows declined sharply until 2007 when they began to pick up again at a level broadly commensurate with aid flows to the CLMV countries. The wealthier countries of the region—Singapore

Fig. 12.3 Traditional donor aid to CLMV and emerging capitalist economies (commitments, US$ millions at constant prices)

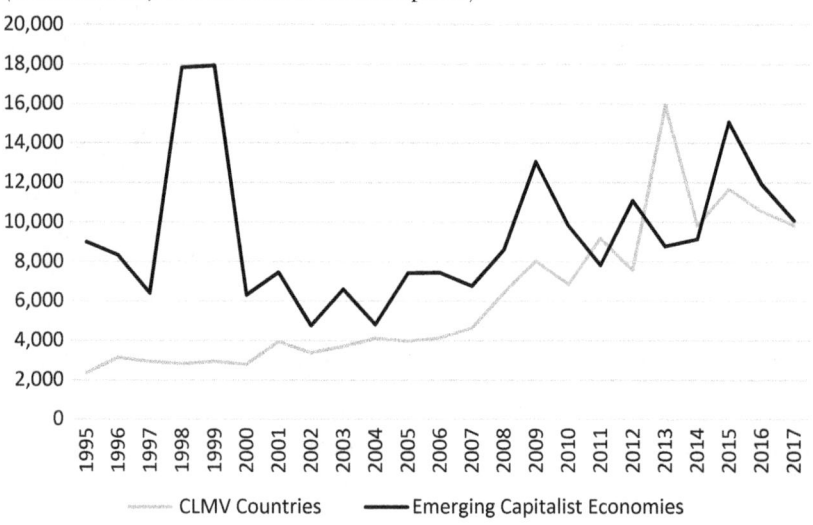

Note: Traditional donors include OECD DAC member countries, EU institutions, the IMF, World Bank and the ADB

Source: OECD 2019a

and Brunei—which were only minor recipients of traditional donor aid during the Cold War despite being broadly aligned with the US and its allies, have received virtually no aid at all from these donors during the post-Cold War period.

Combined with strong economic growth in Southeast Asia in the post-Cold War era, the effect of these shifts in aid allocation has been to dramatically reduce the dependence of Southeast Asian countries on aid from traditional donors. This is true even for the CLMV countries and Timor Leste. At the same time, it is important to note that private flows such as foreign direct investment and portfolio investment from OECD DAC countries have grown enormously in recent decades. As Table 12.1 shows, net private flows from OECD DAC countries to Southeast Asian countries increased sharply as a share of total resource flows between 1980 and 2017, interrupted only by the disruptive effects of the Asian financial crisis in the late 1990s. In 2017, they exceeded net official flows (ODA+OOF) by a factor of 13 to 1.

Alongside these developments, emerging donors have become increasingly active as aid providers within the region as they have sought to expand their influence in that part of the world and pursue commercial objectives. In China's case, in particular, key motivating factors have been a desire to secure support for China's position on the status of Taiwan, a territory over which it claims sovereignty, to gain access to natural resources, and to facilitate Chinese firms' expansion abroad. Reliable data on emerging donors' aid activities are scarce for the reasons mentioned earlier: few such donors publicly report their aid flows and, if they do, typically do not use ODA and OOF as the basis of measurement. Nevertheless, numerous studies have suggested that emerging donors have become increasingly important aid providers at both the global level and within Southeast Asia specifically. In a comprehensive survey of the relevant lit-

Table 12.1 Total net resource flows from OECD DAC countries to Southeast Asia (US$ millions at current prices)

	1980		1990		2000		2010		2017	
	$	%	$	%	$	%	$	%	$	%
Total net official flows	2961	65	5080	43	3324	92	6462	23	1860	7
Total net private flows	1615	35	6798	57	286	8	21,461	77	24,751	93

Source: OECD (2019b)

erature that is sensitive to the measurement problems involved, Walz and Ramachandran (2011) found that estimates of emerging donors' annual aid flows to all countries ranged from US$11bn to US$41.7bn, or 8–31% of global gross ODA, depending on the definition and measure of aid used. Within Southeast Asia, China has loomed as the most significant emerging donor, in terms of the size of its aid programme as well as in terms of its geopolitical and geo-economic importance. For instance, Oh (2016) has estimated that China is now the second-largest provider of ODA to the region behind Japan, with particularly large aid programmes in the Philippines, Cambodia, Malaysia, Laos and Indonesia, although other sources suggest that the CLMV countries have been the principal focus of China's aid programme (Tan-Mullins 2017). Tan-Mullins also notes that recent years have seen a significant increase in Chinese OOF to the region.

The growing role of emerging donors—and specifically China—within Southeast Asia has also led to important changes in the types of aid on offer to countries within the region. Traditional donors' aid programmes have tended to involve ODA, fund stand-alone projects and, at least in the case of bilateral donors, provide grants rather than concessionary loans, although Japan has been a notable exception in this respect. They have also had a strong orientation towards the MDGs and SDGs, reflecting the fact that since the end of the Cold War they have generally had poverty reduction as their official objective. In sectoral terms, they have funded activities in a range of areas including education, health, governance, private sector development, capacity-building and civil society strengthening (van der Eng 2017) but given relatively little attention to infrastructure. As Fig. 12.1 shows, OOF grew sharply in importance as a form of traditional donor aid to the region between 2000 and 2009 but by 2017 ODA still accounted for about 60% of total aid flows from these donors. ODA has been far and away the dominant form of traditional donor aid to the CLMV countries, accounting for almost 80% of such aid in 2017. ODA has declined in importance relative to OOF for emerging capitalist economies within the region but still accounted for around half of total traditional donor aid to these countries.

By contrast, emerging donors—and China in particular—have tended to provide aid in the form of OOF rather than ODA. They have focused overwhelmingly on infrastructure and economic growth rather than the social sectors, governance, capacity-building and civil society strengthening; tended to provide concessional loans or other forms of finance rather than grants; and often provided aid as part of larger economic packages that have included a multiplicity of financing instruments as well as trade agreements, rather than as stand-alone projects (AidData n.d.; Kilby 2012: 1005–1008; Mawdsley 2012: 84). In the case of China in particular, aid has often been linked to infrastructure projects that form part of the Chinese government's Belt and Road Initiative (BRI) (Kilby 2017: 2–3). The BRI is a vast programme of infrastructure development centred on China's immediate region. While many commentators have seen the BRI as a way for China to exercise influence over its neighbours, it has also been motivated by domestic economic concerns such as the underdevelopment of China's hinterland and rustbelt and its chronic excess industrial capacity (Cai 2017: 1).

In the next two sections, I present my analysis of the impact of these changes on the political economy of development in the region. I begin by examining the agendas of traditional donors and emerging donors with regard to the nature of development policies and institutions in aid-recipient countries.

Donors and Their Development Agendas

To the extent that traditional and emerging donors have used aid to promote development-related objectives and, in particular, to shape the nature of development policies and institutions in aid-recipient countries—as indicated above, foreign policy, security and commercial objectives have also been key drivers of donors' aid programmes—they have taken distinctive approaches. Traditional donors have pursued an approach that has been heavily informed by neoliberalism, the ideological framework that has dominated economic and social policy-making in the West since the late 1970s. In policy terms, neoliberalism has involved a commitment to the so-called "Washington consensus" (WC), a set of economic policies that include fiscal discipline, tax reform, trade liberalisation, foreign direct investment liberalisation, deregulation, interest rate liberalisation, privatisation, exchange rate liberalisation, and secure property rights (Williamson 1990). Since the mid-1990s, it has entailed a commitment to an augmented version of this approach known as the "post-Washington consensus" (PWC) which blends WC policies with a concern to promote "good governance" and ensure social conditions conducive to market-oriented economic reform and economic growth. In practical terms, this has meant funding projects and programmes seeking to improve the efficiency and effectiveness of public management, enhance state accountability, promote the rule of law, increase information and transparency in the public sector, and provide social protection through the use of social safety nets (Jayasuriya and Rosser 2001; Moore 1993). Some scholars have suggested that neoliberalism has since entered a third phase characterised by a continued commitment to the PWC accompanied by efforts to promote "enabling environments" via benchmarking exercises, facilitate "access to finance" for the poor, and allocate resources directly to the private sector. They have referred to this phase as "deep marketisation" (Carroll 2017). At the same time, traditional donors' approach has also been informed by liberal notions of democracy and human rights, if perhaps less so than neoliberalism, reflecting the fact that the international financial institutions (IFIs) have been required by their respective charters to avoid engaging in political affairs and some bilateral donors, most notably Japan, have shown limited commitment to human rights (Katsumata 2006).

In promoting the adoption and implementation of policy and institutional reform in aid-recipient countries, traditional donors have made extensive use of both conditionality and selectivity, with an apparent shift in favour of the latter over time. Conditionality refers to the imposition of requirements on aid-recipient countries to adopt reforms as part of grant or loan agreements while selectivity refers to the channelling of aid to countries that meet specified criteria indicating a commitment to reform (Hout 2004).

By contrast, emerging donors have been much less normatively committed to neoliberal and liberal-democratic notions of good governance, reflecting the fact that few could be accurately described as liberal democracies or market-based economies themselves. They have accordingly been much less active in promoting the adoption and implementation of governance-related reforms in aid-recipient countries.[3] As Paczynska (2016: 2) has noted, in contrast to traditional donors, emerging donors have expressed a strong commitment "to the principle of non-interference in internal affairs of other states"; eschewed the use of conditionalities in the provision of aid; "avoid[ed] using the terminology of assistance" in favour of "South–South cooperation";

---

[3] See Gu and Kitano (2018) and Shiga (2018) on India as a possible exception in this respect.

emphasised the principle of mutual benefit for all participants involved in aid relationships; "frame[d] their assistance in language that prioritizes solidarity, sharing of development experiences, and mutual support"; and described themselves as partners rather than donors. Consistent with this broad model of aid-giving, emerging donors have accordingly provided aid with fewer strings attached in terms of changes to recipient countries' policies and institutions, even if they have imposed other sorts of conditionalities. Broadly, they have viewed governance conditionalities "as unnecessary and an unwelcome interference in domestic policies" (ibid.: 8).

This approach to promoting development in aid-recipient countries is apparent in China's model of aid-giving specifically. As Tan-Mullins (2017: 149) has noted, the principle of "non-interference" has been "the cornerstone of Chinese overseas aid policy" for many decades, leading to a marginalisation of "the bigger issues of transparency and good governance, especially in terms of volume and allocation in receiving countries". Initially proclaimed by Premier Zhou Enlai in 1964 as the second of eight principles of foreign aid, it was reaffirmed in the Chinese government's 2011 and 2014 aid White Papers (Reilly 2012: 75). The latter, for instance, states:

> When providing foreign assistance, China adheres to the principles of not imposing any political conditions, not interfering in the internal affairs of the recipient countries and fully respecting their right to independently choosing (*sic*) their own paths and models of development. The basic principles China upholds in providing foreign assistance are mutual respect, equality, keeping promise[s], mutual benefits and win-win (State Council of the People's Republic of China 2014).

China accordingly allocates aid between partner countries without considering governance-related criteria (Dreher et al. 2018) and does not impose conditions related to the deregulation of recipient countries' economic policies, privatisation of their state-owned assets, and/or adherence to orthodox norms of "good governance"—let alone democracy and human rights—when it provides aid. Nevertheless, as several analysts have noted, it has imposed conditions related to support for China's position on the status of Taiwan, access to recipient countries' natural resources, and the employment of Chinese companies and workers on aid-funded projects

(Kilby 2012; see also Kilby 2017; Mawdsley 2012).[4] China's decision to endorse the international aid agreement produced at the 2011 High Level Forum on Aid Effectiveness in Busan, South Korea, after initially indicating that it would not do so, suggests that it and other emerging donors may increasingly adhere to international aid policy norms. But it is notable that China only signed up to the agreement after wording was inserted making its compliance voluntary, so the extent of its commitment to these norms remains to be seen (O'Keefe 2011; Tran 2011).

As noted earlier, this approach to promoting development has led to concern among some commentators that China's aid is undermining efforts by traditional donors to promote political and economic reform in these countries (e.g. Naim 2007). At the same time, however, it is clear that China varies its model of aid-giving, including in relation to policy and institutional matters, depending on the country context in which it is operating, possibly reflecting division and contestation within the Chinese state about how its aid programme should evolve in relation to international aid norms (Breslin 2013; Varrall 2016). For instance, studies by Tan-Mullins and collaborators found that Chinese aid projects were "more transparent and ha[d] better governance mechanisms in Ghana compared to Angola due to the more democratic nature of Ghana and the strong presence of NGOs in the country" (Tan-Mullins 2017: 149). Likewise, China has supported some governance-reform initiatives that have been sponsored by traditional donors. The Extractive Industries Transparency Initiative (EITI), an initiative aimed at improving the transparency of revenue flows from extractive firms to national governments and in so doing reducing corruption, is a case in point. In a recent report, the EITI International Secretariat (2016) found that Chinese extractive firms, many of which are state-owned enterprises, have participated in the EITI to the same extent as companies from other countries.

---

[4] While accepting that China's aid is not typically used to promote particular forms of governance in a direct way, Mattlin and Nojonen (2015) suggest that it can influence the nature of aid recipients' policies and institutions indirectly through what they call "lock-in" effects. The notion of lock-in "denotes circumstances where the recipient country becomes restricted in its ability to make autonomous decisions on how to develop or control its economy, or certain segments of it" because of the "cumulative weight of Chinese driven development projects and associated institutional arrangements" (ibid.: 718)—in other words, because of path dependence created by the initial choice to accept Chinese aid and investment.

What, then, has been the impact of the changing regional aid landscape—and, in particular, the rise of China as donor—on the balance of power between competing political and social forces in Southeast Asia? And what have been the consequences of this impact for the nature of development policies and institutions in Southeast Asian countries? I address these questions in the following section.

POWER RELATIONS AND THE IMPACT OF THE CHANGING AID LANDSCAPE

The countries of Southeast Asia, especially those that have been aid recipients, have been dominated in recent decades by predatory, populist and authoritarian elites who have had a vested interest in illiberal modes of governance—in particular, state-led economic systems that have generated rents for senior state officials and well-connected business groups, and authoritarian or semi-democratic political systems that have limited the scope for political oppositions to challenge their rule. The exact composition of these elites has varied from country to country and, within countries, from period to period, reflecting specific histories, social and economic structures, and changes in governing coalitions. Whatever the precise configuration of the different elements in individual countries, these elites have generally given little support to the neoliberal and liberal-democratic agenda promoted by traditional donors, except where this has opened up new opportunities for specific sections of the elite—as has been the case in some instances with the privatisation of state-owned enterprises or the deregulation of economic sectors. Instead, they have sought to defend the illiberal modes of governance from which they have benefited and which have underpinned their rule (Hewison et al. 1993; Hughes 2006; Rosser 2002; also Robison and Hadiz, this volume).

In some countries, these elites have encountered a degree of opposition from technocratic officials in the state apparatus, who have been concerned about the general economic effects of predatory, populist and nationalist economic policies, and sections of capital that have stood to benefit from market-oriented policy and institutional reform. They have also encountered opposition from liberal and progressive elements in civil society and opposition politicians who have argued against authoritarian controls on political activity and abuses of human rights, at least in more democratic countries where such elements have been able to exist and operate. Traditional donors have offered some support to both these groups in the form of complementary policy advice and grants and loans with related conditions attached, albeit in a manner constrained by geopolitical imperatives to secure alliances, maintain stability and security, and promote their commercial interests. But, on the whole, these groups have been relatively weak compared to powerful elites in Southeast Asia, limiting their ability to effect neoliberal and liberal-democratic reform (Robison and Hadiz 2004; Rodan and Hughes 2014; also Hughes, this volume). This is notwithstanding broader changes in the global political economy that have seen capital mobility increase significantly and with that structural pressure on states to adopt neoliberal economic reforms to attract the investment resources required to promote economic growth (see Carroll, this volume). These groups have exercised decisive influence only during periods of economic or political crisis when the balance of power has momentarily tilted in their favour, although they have often found their successes during these periods unravelled over time as power relations have normalised.

The result of this situation has been the emergence of a set of political regimes within the aid-recipient countries of the region that are either authoritarian or semi-democratic in nature—few Southeast Asian countries have been rated "free" in Freedom House's (2018) "Freedom in the World" assessments since the mid-1970s[5]—and a set of economic regimes characterised by substantial state control, strategic and/or predatory forms of protection, widespread cronyism, and limited state bureaucratic capacity in key areas of administration.

The changing regional aid landscape—and, in particular, the emergence of China as a major donor—has exacerbated this power imbalance and its implications for the region's political and economic regimes by creating greater scope for predatory, populist and authoritarian elites to reduce aid from traditional donors in favour of aid from emerging donors that has imposed fewer constraints or better fits with their political priorities. Perhaps the clearest illustration of this is provided by events in Cambodia during 2017 and 2018. In September 2017, the Hun Sen government arrested the country's main opposition leader and dissolved his party in the lead-up to national elections in 2018, moves that were widely condemned in the US and Western Europe. In response, the US and the

---

[5] The exceptions, all temporary, have been: Thailand, 1976, 1989–1990, 1998–2005; the Philippines, 1987–1989, 1996–2005; and Indonesia, 2006–2013.

EU announced that they would wind back their aid programmes to the country including support for the forthcoming elections. Russia and China then stepped into the breach created by the US and EU's withdrawal of aid with the former providing election monitors and the latter election ballot boxes and booths—assistance the Cambodian government gratefully accepted. Supporters of the detained opposition leader and his dissolved political party protested these moves and tried to put pressure on other traditional donors, most notably Japan, which had opted to continue its support for the elections. They also called on the Cambodian people to boycott the elections. But with Russia and China effectively backing Hun Sen's moves to silence the political opposition and traditional donors divided in their response to the situation, the Cambodian government remained unmoved. The elections were held in July 2018, producing a resounding win for Hun Sen's Cambodian People's Party (Elmer 2018; Irish 2018; Thul 2018; Touch 2018).

A second illustration relates to the EU's aid programme in the Philippines. Soon after being elected president in 2016, Rodrigo Duterte launched a nationwide anti-drug campaign that resulted in thousands of extrajudicial killings of suspected drug users and traffickers, generating widespread criticism of his government for human rights abuses, especially in the US and Europe. At the same time, he began negotiating new aid and infrastructure deals with China worth billions of dollars and more generally cosying up to China in diplomatic terms. In May 2017, news broke that the Duterte government had decided to reject EU aid grants with human rights conditions attached on the grounds that they constituted interference in the country's affairs. This clash was eventually resolved when the EU agreed to amend the standard wording in its development financing agreements with the Philippines to remove conditions related to human rights. The EU's Director-General for International Cooperation defended this move on the grounds that the conditions were already contained in its underlying Partnership and Cooperation Agreement with the Philippines and did not need to be repeated in lower-level agreements (Elemia 2018; Ravelo 2018). But the move was interpreted in human rights circles as a watering down of the EU's commitment to human rights (Trade Justice Pilipinas n.d.).

A third and final illustration relates to the Indonesian government's budget. In 2003–04, the Indonesian government adopted legislation that limited foreign aid to a maximum of 3% of its annual budget and in 2007 it dissolved the Consultative Group on Indonesia, the body comprising the country's main donors that had previously coordinated foreign aid flows to the country, in both cases in order to reduce the country's dependence on aid from traditional donors and rein in foreign debt. However, in 2015 and 2016, Indonesia's concessionary interest rate foreign debt levels increased after declining for several years due to an increase in concessionary loans from emerging donors, especially China (van der Eng 2017). According to van der Eng (ibid.), the Indonesian government has opted to shift away from traditional sources of aid to Chinese aid because of the latter's greater orientation towards infrastructure projects, a key development priority of the Widodo government elected in 2014.

While the changing regional aid landscape has served to empower predatory, populist and authoritarian elites in Southeast Asia in this way, however, the extent to which it has done so has been mitigated by a number of factors. Foremost among these has been widespread concern about the impact of Chinese-backed infrastructure projects on government foreign debt levels even when funded in part through ODA-like or OOF-like mechanisms. Such concern has enabled a range of individuals including government technocrats, liberal and progressive elements in civil society, senior figures in traditional donor countries, and representatives of IFIs to call on governments to exercise restraint in signing up to Chinese-funded infrastructure projects (Lindberg and Lahiri 2018). Together with security-related anxieties about China's intentions in the region (particularly its activities in the South China Sea) and popular resentment about China's growing economic involvement in the region (including the presence of Chinese workers), this push has triggered a wave of moves by Southeast Asian governments to suspend, cancel, or downgrade Chinese-backed infrastructure projects, particularly after the Sri Lankan government was forced in 2017 to hand back control over a strategic port built by Chinese companies because it was unable to repay the debts incurred to finance the project (Nitta and Htway 2018).

In mid-2018, for instance, the newly elected Mahathir government in Malaysia announced that it would cancel a set of Chinese-funded infrastructure projects approved by the preceding Najib government, including two major rail projects and two gas pipelines, claiming that they had caused Malaysia's foreign debt to balloon and that the country could not afford them (Azhar 2018; Erikson 2018; Reuters 2018). In at least one case (a planned high-speed rail link connecting Singapore and Kuala Lumpur), Mahathir was forced to settle for a delayed start to the project rather than cancellation after Singapore, whose companies were also involved in the projects, protested (Sukumaran 2018). Malaysian officials have been negotiating to continue the projects on more favourable financial terms. But the Malaysian government's disquiet about the impact of the financing arrangements has been clear. In a similar move, in August 2018, the Myanmar government dramatically reduced the scale of a major Chinese-funded port project over concerns it was "too expensive and could ultimately fall under Beijing's control if Myanmar were to default on its debt" (Bhattacharjee 2018). The AidData database lists a series of other Chinese-backed infrastructure projects across Southeast Asia funded through ODA-like and OOF-like mechanisms that have been suspended or cancelled in recent years, suggesting that similar concerns have arisen in other countries.

A further mitigating factor has been that in Southeast Asia, as in other parts of the world, China has backed some liberal governance-reform initiatives supported by traditional donors, reducing scope for predatory, populist and authoritarian elites to shop around for a better deal. In the case of Cambodia, for instance, Reilly (2012: 81) has observed that:

> while the bulk of China's aid to Cambodia supports projects that advance China's broader diplomatic, economic, and strategic interests, there are signs that a process of nascent socialization [to international aid norms] is emerging. Chinese collaboration with international consortia, greater transparency, and diversity in aid projects all cohere more closely with international norms and practices on development assistance than with China's traditional approach to ODA.

Reilly notes that the same pattern is occurring in Laos but not Myanmar and attributes the difference to the "thickness of the institutional environment" (ibid.: 71) in which Chinese aid is delivered, especially the degree to which there is a wider international aid presence in a country.

This inclination to adhere to international norms appears to extend to China's involvement in the AIIB, a new multilateral institution that was established at China's initiative. The AIIB funds infrastructure projects in sectors such as transport, energy, water, ports, and information and communications technology in an effort to address Asia's growing demand for infrastructure and large infrastructure financing gap (Australia's Department of Foreign Affairs and Trade n.d.). Despite being in its infancy, the AIIB has already approved or is considering major infrastructure projects in Indonesia, Myanmar and the Philippines worth more than

$US650m according to Strawson (2017: 37, 46). With 26.6% of the AIIB's vote share, China has veto power within the AIIB over decisions requiring a super-majority, although it does not have veto power over operational matters (Hameiri and Jones 2018). Importantly for our purposes here, the AIIB has co-funded most of its projects with other multilateral development banks rather than going it alone, meaning that it has to operate according to these institutions' rules (ibid.: 575). Wilson (2018) argues that the AIIB "has a well-defined and transparent set of governance policies, which ensures international best practices are maintained and evaluated for all funded projects".

In this context, and because Southeast Asian governments—including those with relatively poor democratic and human rights records such as those in the CLMV countries and the Duterte government in the Philippines—have continued to deal with traditional donors, these governments remain subject to pressure from traditional donors and their domestic political allies for neoliberal and liberal-democratic reform. However, such pressure is arguably weaker than it was before the recent changes in the regional aid landscape. This will help to make continued predatory, populist and authoritarian/semi-democratic rule in the region a much more likely scenario for the future than transition towards liberal markets and democracy.

References

AidData. (n.d.). *By the numbers: China's global development footprint.* https://www.aiddata.org/china-official-finance. Accessed 15 Mar 2019.

Australia's Department of Foreign Affairs and Trade. (n.d.). *Asian Infrastructure Investment Bank.* https://dfat.gov.au/international-relations/international-organisations/multilateral-development-banks/Pages/asian-infrastructure-investment-bank.aspx. Accessed 22 Dec 2018.

Azhar, K. (2018, June 14). Minus HSR, whither Bandar Malaysia? *The Edge Weekly.* http://www.theedgemarkets.com/article/minus-hsr-whither-bandar-malaysia. Accessed 17 Nov 2018.

Bhattacharjee, G. (2018, October 20). Trap of the century. *The Straits Times.* https://www.straitstimes.com/asia/east-asia/chinas-belt-and-road-initiative-debt-trap-or-hope. Accessed 29 Dec 2018.

Breslin, S. (2013). China and the south: Objectives, actors and interactions. *Development and Change, 44*(6), 1273–1294.

Brinkley, J. (n.d.). *China's aid to Cambodia ignores rights abuses.* http://www.worldaffairsjournal.org/article/china%E2%80%99s-aid-cambodia-ignores-rights-abuses. Accessed 22 Dec 2018.

Cai, P. (2017). *Understanding China's belt and road initiative.* Sydney: Lowy Institute.

Callan P., Blak, J., & Thomas, A. (2013). *Emerging voices: Callan, Blak, and Thomas on the landscape of emerging aid donors.* http://blogs.cfr.org/development-channel/2013/04/02/emerging-voices-callan-blak-and-thomas-on-the-landscape-of-emerging-aid-donors/. Accessed 24 July 2015.

Carroll, T. (2017). Neoliberalism and multilateral development organizations in Southeast Asia. In A. McGregor, L. Law, & F. Miller (Eds.), *Routledge handbook of southeast Asian development* (pp. 69–84). London: Routledge.

Dreher, A., Fuchs, A., Parks, B., Strange, A., & Tierney, M. (2018). Apples and dragon fruits: The determinants of aid and other forms of state financing from China to Africa. *International Studies Quarterly, 61*(1), 182–194.

EITI International Secretariat. (2016). *Brief: Chinese companies reporting in EITI countries. Review of the engagement of Chinese firms in countries implementing the EITI.* Oslo: EITI International Secretariat.

Elemia, C. (2018, March 2). After Duterte tirades, EU won't repeat human rights clause in PH deals. *Rappler.* https://www.rappler.com/nation/197268-eu-human-rights-financial-agreements-philippines. Accessed 30 Dec 2018.

Elmer, K. (2018, June 19). China pledges more military aid as Cambodia prepares for controversial election. *South China Morning Post.* https://www.scmp.com/news/china/diplomacy-defence/article/2151495/chinas-pledges-more-military-aid-cambodia-prepares Accessed 9 Feb 2018.

Erikson, A. (2018, August 21). Malaysia cancels two big Chinese projects, fearing they will bankrupt the country. *The Washington Post.* https://www.washingtonpost.com/world/asia_pacific/malaysia-cancels-two-massive-chinese-projects-fearing-they-will-bankrupt-the-country/2018/08/21/2bd150e0-a515-11e8-b76b-d513a40042f6_story.html?utm_term=.26db9925fc64. Accessed 17 Nov 2018.

Freedom House. (2018). *Freedom in the World.* https://freedomhouse.org/report-types/freedom-world. Accessed 16 May 2019.

Gu, J., & Kitano, N. (2018). Introduction: Beyond aid—The future of development cooperation. *IDS Bulletin, 49*(3), 1–12.

Hameiri, S., & Jones, L. (2018). China challenges global governance? Chinese international development finance and the AIIB. *International Affairs, 94*(3), 573–593.

Hewison, K., Robison, R., & Rodan, G. (Eds.). (1993). *Southeast Asia in the 1990s: Authoritarianism, democracy and capitalism.* Sydney: Allen and Unwin.

Hout, W. (2004). Political regimes and development assistance: The political economy of aid selectivity. *Critical Asian Studies, 36*(4), 591–613.

Hughes, C. (2006). Cambodia. *IDS Bulletin, 37*(2), 67–78.

Irish, J. (2018, July 20). Boycott sham Cambodian elections, says opponent Rainsy. *Reuters.* https://www.yahoo.com/news/boycott-sham-cambodian-elections-says-opponent-rainsy-172141027.html. Accessed 13 Dec 2018.

Jayasuriya, K., & Rosser, A. (2001). Economic orthodoxy and the Asian economic crisis. *Third World Quarterly, 22*(3), 381–396.

Katsumata, H. (2006). Why does Japan downplay human rights in Southeast Asia? *International Relations of the Asia-Pacific, 6*(2), 249–267.

Kilby, P. (2012). The changing development landscape in the first decade of the 21st century and its implications for development studies. *Third World Quarterly, 33*(6), 1001–1017.

Kilby, P. (2017). *China and the United States as donors: Past and future trajectories.* Honolulu, HI: East West Center.

Landingin, R. (2013). Chinese foreign aid goes offtrack in the Philippines. In Reality of Aid Management Committee (Ed.), *The reality of aid. South–south cooperation: A challenge to the aid system?* (pp. 87–94). Quezon City: IBON Books.

Lindberg, K., & Lahiri, T. (2018, December 28). From Asia to Africa, China's "debt trap diplomacy" was under siege in 2018. *Quartz.* https://qz.com/1497584/how-chinas-debt-trap-diplomacy-came-under-siege-in-2018/. Accessed 9 Feb 2019.

Mattlin, M., & Nojonen, M. (2015). Conditionality and path dependence in Chinese lending. *Journal of Contemporary China, 24*(94), 701–720.

Mawdsley, E. (2012). *From recipients to donors: Emerging powers and the changing development landscape.* London: Zed Books.

Moore, M. (1993). Declining to learn from the east: The World Bank on "governance and development". *IDS Bulletin, 24*(1), 39–50.

Naim, M. (2007). Rogue aid. *Foreign Policy, 159,* 95–96.

Nitta, Y., & Htway, T. (2018, July 4). Myanmar will ask China to downsize project, minister says. *Nikkei Asian Review.* https://asia.nikkei.com/Politics/Myanmar-will-ask-China-to-downsize-project-minister-says. Accessed 9 Feb 2019.

O'Keefe, A. (2011, December 9). Busan: A good result for Australia. *Lowy Interpreter.* http://www.lowyinterpreter.org/post/2011/12/09/Busan-A-good-result-for-Australia.aspx. Accessed 17 Nov 2013.

OECD. (2019a). *Creditor reporting system.* https://stats.oecd.org/Index.aspx?DataSetCode=crs1. Accessed 1 Feb 2019.

OECD. (2019b). *Geobook: Geographical flows to developing countries.* https://stats.oecd.org/Index.aspx?DataSetCode=DACGEO. Accessed 1 Feb 2019.

OECD. (n.d.-a). *Official development assistance: Definition and coverage.* http://www.oecd.org/dac/stats/officialdevelopmentassistancedefinitionandcoverage.htm. Accessed 22 Dec 2018.

OECD. (n.d.-b). *Other Official Flows (OOF).* https://data.oecd.org/drf/other-official-flows-oof.htm. Accessed 22 Dec 2018.

Oh, Y. (2016). *China's development finance to Asia: Characteristics and implications* (KIEP working paper no. 16–12). Sejong-si: Korea Institute for International Economic Policy.

Paczynska, A. (2016). *Emerging and traditional donors and conflict-affected states: The new politics of reconstruction* (Policy brief no. 1). Washington, DC: George Mason University/Stimson Center. https://www.stimson.org/sites/default/files/file-attachments/Changing%20Landscape%20of%20Assistance%20to%20Conflict-Affected%20States-%20Emerging%20and%20Traditional%20Donors%20and%20Opportunities%20for%20Collaboration%20Policy%20Brief%20%2311.pdf. Accessed 9 Feb 2019.

Ravelo, J. (2018). After a tumultuous year, EU aid to continue in the Philippines. *Devex*. https://www.devex.com/news/after-a-tumultuous-year-eu-aid-to-continue-in-the-philippines-92247. Accessed 30 Dec 2018.

Reilly, J. (2012). A norm taker or a norm maker: Chinese aid in Southeast Asia. *Journal of Contemporary China, 21*(73), 71–91.

Reuters. (2018). Malaysia's Mahathir cancels China-backed rail, pipeline projects. *Reuters*. https://www.reuters.com/article/us-china-malaysia/malaysias-mahathir-cancels-china-backed-rail-pipeline-projects-idUSKCN1L60DQ. Accessed 17 Nov 2018.

Robison, R., & Hadiz, V. (2004). *Reorganising power in Indonesia: The politics of oligarchy in an age of markets*. London: Routledge.

Rodan, G., & Hughes, C. (2014). *The politics of accountability in Southeast Asia: The dominance of moral ideologies*. Oxford: Oxford University Press.

Rosser, A. (2002). *The politics of economic liberalisation in Indonesia: State, market and power*. Richmond: Curzon.

Shiga, H. (2018). India's role as a facilitator of constitutional democracy. *IDS Bulletin, 49*(3), 93–110.

State Council of the People's Republic of China. (2014). *China's foreign aid*. http://english.gov.cn/archive/white_paper/2014/08/23/content_281474982986592.htm. Accessed 9 Feb 2019.

Strawson, T. (2017). *Financing the sustainable development goals in ASEAN: Strengthening integrated national financing frameworks to deliver the 2030 agenda*. Bangkok: UNDP.

Sukumaran, B. (2018, September 5). Not cancelled: Malaysia–Singapore high-speed rail delayed in Mahathir u-turn. *South China Morning Post*. https://www.scmp.com/week-asia/geopolitics/article/2162841/malaysia-singapore-high-speed-rail-delayed-mahathir-u-turn. Accessed 17 Nov 2018.

Tan-Mullins, M. (2017). Implications of non-OECD aid in Southeast Asia: The Chinese example. In A. McGregor, L. Law, & F. Miller (Eds.), *Routledge handbook of southeast Asian development* (pp. 142–152). London: Routledge.

Thul, P. (2018, February 28). Cambodia "shocked" by "disrespectful" U.S. aid cut, says democracy intact. *Reuters*. https://www.reuters.com/article/us-cambodia-politics-usa/cambodia-shocled-by-disrepesctful-s-s-aid-cut-say-democracy-intact-iduskcn1gc0x0. Accessed 21 Nov 2018.

Touch, D. (2018, July 13). Why Japan is supporting Cambodia's elections. *The Interpreter*. https://www.lowyinstitute.org/the-interpreter/why-japan-supporting-cambodias-election. Accessed 21 Nov 2018.

Trade Justice Pilipinas. (n.d.). *Human rights should be central to EU–Philippines partnership*. https://focusweb.org/content/human-rights-should-be-central-eu-philippines-partnership. Accessed 9 Feb 2019.

Tran, M. (2011, December 11). China and India to join aid partnership on new terms. *The Guardian*. http://www.theguardian.com/global-development/2011/dec/01/china-india-aid-partnership. Accessed 17 Nov 2013.

van der Eng, P. (2017). *Why does Indonesia seem to prefer foreign aid from China?* http://www.eastasiaforum.org/2017/12/02/why-does-indonesia-seem-to-prefer-foreign-aid-from-china/. Accessed 11 Dec 2018.

Varrall, M. (2016). Domestic actors and agendas in Chinese aid policy. *Pacific Review, 29*(1), 21–44.

Walker, C., & Cook, S. (2010, March 24). The dark side of China aid. *New York Times*. https://www.nytimes.com/2010/03/25/opinion/25iht-edwalker.html. Accessed 23 Dec 2018.

Walz, J., & Ramachandran, V. (2011). *Brave new world: A literature review of emerging donors and the changing nature of foreign assistance* (CGD working paper no. 273). Washington, DC: Center for Global Development.

Williamson, J. (Ed.). (1990). *Latin American adjustment: How much has happened?* Washington, DC: Institute for International Economics.

Wilson, J. (2018). The AIIB and Australian participation in Chinese infrastructure initiatives. *Devpolicy*. http://www.devpolicy.org/the-aiib-and-australian-participation-in-chinese-infrastructure-initiatives-20180814/?print=print. Accessed 9 Feb 2019.

PART IV

Capital, State and Nature

CHAPTER 13

The Political Economy of Southeast Asia's Extractive Industries: Governance, Power Struggles and Development Outcomes

Pascale Hatcher

INTRODUCTION

Southeast Asia is exceptionally rich in extractive resources (oil, gas and minerals), with resource abundance having played a central role in the history of numerous countries in the region.[1] The role of extractive resources began significantly with the arrival in Southeast Asia of colonial powers, many of which were drawn by the lure of the region's mineral riches. This said, the role and impact of resources vary considerably from one country to the next. Building on insights from the Murdoch School, this

---

[1] While there are good reasons to expand the definition of extractive industries to include all extractive-linked activities (such as fisheries, logging or mono-cropping), given space limitations this chapter will exclusively focus on oil, gas and minerals. For a thorough analysis of land and environmental issues, see the chapters by Hirsch and Gellert, respectively, in this volume.

P. Hatcher (✉)
Department of Political Science and International Relations, University of Canterbury, Christchurch, New Zealand
e-mail: pascale.hatcher@canterbury.ac.nz

© The Author(s) 2020
T. Carroll et al. (eds.), *The Political Economy of Southeast Asia*,
Studies in the Political Economy of Public Policy,
https://doi.org/10.1007/978-3-030-28255-4_13

chapter provides an overarching analysis of the political economy of extractive industries in the region, emphasising how multi-scalar politics have profoundly shaped modes of governance in the sector, and in turn, regional development outcomes.

The chapter is divided into four sections. The first section details the theoretical framing of the topic. The second section provides a broad overview of Southeast Asia's extractive industries production and explores how domestic and international power struggles have shaped modes of governance in the sector and generated specific developmental outcomes. The third section provides an analysis of the socio-environmental ramifications that derive from the modes of governance of the region's extractive industries. In the final section, the analysis turns to the significance of nascent platforms of dissent dedicated to the contestation of the neoliberal norms forged by pro-extractive industry interests.

Framing the Political Economy of Extractive Industries in Southeast Asia

In this chapter, the concept of "modes of governance" is used to refer to "the sum of the forms of regulation for each of the related dimensions (economic, social, political and environmental), which determines, in any given period, the conditions of exploitation of mining resources" (Campbell 2013: 5). This is broader than the concept of "governance", which has often been limited in the literature on extractive industries to technocratic approaches focused on institutions and their ability, given the right (insulated) bureaucratic environment, to harness the sector for economic development. By contrast, and in accordance with Murdoch School positions, the concept of modes of governance is useful here not only to highlight the interaction between different forms of regulation and institutional arrangements, but also to stress the structural relations of power and influence that shape and govern extractive industries. These struggles for power and control over resources take many forms at multiple levels, leading to a wide range of political outcomes across Southeast Asia's resource-rich countries.

While at the national level extractive industries have been—and continue to be—bound up with the interests of local elites, they also remain inherently embedded in and shaped by global processes of capitalist transformation and wider geopolitical power relations (Hameiri and Jones, this volume). Well beyond the state, a plurality of actors—including multinational corporations, the governments of the home countries of extractive industry companies, bilateral donors, international financial institutions (IFIs), non-governmental organisations and activists—are involved in shaping, promoting and challenging the modes of governance that oversee extractive industries. This plurality of actors, as well as the multiple levels at which the sector's modes of governance are being shaped, requires that a clear distinction be maintained between the instruments of a given mining regime—that is, its formal rules and decision-making procedures—and the more permanent aspects of the regime, including definitive norms and principles. Gagné-Ouellet (2012) insists on this distinction as it highlights that while the rules and decision-making procedures in regulatory regimes may often change, for example, when a country adopts a new mining code, the norms and principles attending a particular regulatory regime seldom change. Focusing upon modes of governance in any given country is thus useful in terms of avoiding "false developmentalist hopes" whereby those within policy circles and academics are quick to celebrate formal changes in rules and decision-making procedures while ignoring, for example, the persistence of socio-political impediments to the operation of these formal changes, and vast structural inequalities solidly rooted in the world capitalist system (Gellert 2010: 29). Modes of governance in extractive industries reflect a combination of domestic politics extending well beyond formal institutions and the manner in which these combine with global capitalist processes (such as particular patterns of growth and the attendant demand for commodities) and wider geopolitical power relations (see Hameiri and Jones, this volume).

The following section presents a brief overview of extractive industries in Southeast Asia, followed by an explanation of how the sector's modes of governance have been shaped over the course of the past decades by evolving struggles for power and resources both locally and within the wider global political economy.

INTERNATIONAL CAPITAL, NATIONAL DEVELOPMENT AND REGIME CONSOLIDATION

In 2014, the Asia-Pacific region accounted for more than half of the world's total production of metal ore and metals. The region produced 97% of the world's mercury, 89% of its tin, 89% of its tungsten, 78% of its lead, 69% of the alumina and iron ore, 67% of the bauxite, 64% of the zinc (metal), 58% of the nickel,[2] 53% of the copper (refined and primary), 41% of the manganese, and 29% of the world production of gold (USGS 2017: 1.7). Value-added production remains minimal but the region nonetheless accounted for 78% of the world's lead production, 75% of its pig iron, 65% of its crude steel, and 56% of its aluminium (metal) (ibid.). Together, the Association of Southeast Asian Nations (ASEAN) countries' production of major minerals in 2012, namely gold, copper, nickel, tin, iron, bauxite, zinc, coal and gemstones, was worth a staggering US$53.5bn (ASEAN 2016: 1).

Among the region's producers, Indonesia stands out. As of 2014, it was the world's top producer of nickel, second-largest producer of tin, fourth of bauxite and twelfth of gold (EITI 2018). Mining has expanded rapidly, with total mineral exports more than tripling in value between 2001 and 2013, from US$3bn to US$11.2bn (ibid.). However, other countries are also important world producers. Malaysia ranked third in terms of bauxite in 2015 (USGS 2018a: 18.1), while the Philippines mined 24% of the world's nickel and 3% of its cobalt (USGS 2018b: 24.1). In Thailand, 7% of the world's feldspar[3] is being produced, and 5% of the gypsum[4] (USGS 2018d: 29.1). In 2015, Vietnam produced almost a fifth of the world's total output of bismuth,[5] 6.3% of the tungsten and 2% of the tin (USGS 2018e: 29.1). Table 13.1 provides a summary of Southeast Asia's main production of non-fuel mineral commodities.

Importantly, mineral production in Southeast Asia is expected to increase in the 2020s. ASEAN (2016: 1) estimates that mineral trade in the region will gradually emerge as one of the main growth drivers in Asia's economy, with intra-ASEAN trade having already increased from US$14bn in 2004 to US$44bn in 2013. Currently, significant mineral prospecting is underway, notably in Cambodia (copper and gold), Indonesia (gold and silver) and the Philippines (gold) (USGS 2017: 1.7). While this chapter focuses on large-scale extractive industries, it is also important to note that artisanal and small-scale mining activities (ASM) are taking place across the region. The Philippines has the largest estimated

---

[2] By nickel content of mine output or 45% of the metal/refined nickel.
[3] Used mainly in glass-making and ceramics.
[4] Used mainly as a fertilizer and as the main constituent in forms of plaster, blackboard chalk and wallboard.
[5] Mixed with other metals, it is used mainly to form low-melting alloys.

Table 13.1 Production of selected mineral commodities in Southeast Asia, 2014

	Indonesia	Laos	Malaysia	Myanmar	Philippines	Thailand	Vietnam
Bauxite	2555	–	3258	–	–	–	150
Copper: Mine output, cu content	406	71	–	33	92	–	16
Gold (k)	69,100	5265	4038	900	18,423	4576	NA
Iron ore	–	1149	9615	–	827	348	4355
Lead: Pb content (t)	–	–	–	18,000	–	–	6000
Manganese	38	–	NA	97	3	7	–
Mercury (t)	–	–	–	–	–	–	–
Nickel: Ni content	55	–	–	21	523	–	–
Tin: Mine output (t)	38,545	866	3777	35,000	–	156	5400
Tin: Metal, primary (t)	58,233	–	35,018	30	–	16,929	4000
Tungsten (t)	–	–	–	143	–	100	–
Zinc: Mine output (t)	–	–	–	6100	–	39,140	20,000
Zinc: Metal (t)	–	–	–	–	–	65,694	18,000

Source: USGS (2016)
Notes: Measured in thousands of metric tonnes except: k (kilograms), t (tonnes). Brunei, Cambodia, Timor-Leste and Singapore have no significant production of mineral commodities (metals); Cambodia produces iron ore although data are unavailable

number of artisanal miners (325,000), followed by Indonesia with 180,000; ASM also occurs in countries such as Myanmar (50,000), Vietnam (55,000), Thailand (20,000), Laos (10,000), Malaysia (5000) (IGF 2017: 80) and Cambodia.[6]

In terms of mineral fuels, despite the fact that the region's share of natural gas and crude petroleum production remains relatively low—respectively 10% and 12% of world production—in 2014 it accounted for 82% of the world's production of anthracite coal and 69% of bituminous coal (USGS 2017: 1.7). Table 13.2 provides an overview of the region's production and reserves of natural gas, crude oil and coal. Again, Indonesia

[6] Data for Cambodia are unavailable, but ASM of gold and rubies is taking place.

Table 13.2 Mineral fuels: Production and recoverable reserves in Southeast Asia

	Brunei	Indonesia	Malaysia	Myanmar	Philippines	Timor-Leste	Thailand	Vietnam
Natural gas production[a]	11,400	67,500	61,400	7600	3330	–	35,800	9630
Natural gas reserves[a]	248,000	2,560,000	1,050,000	475,000	88,700	79,200	198,000	555,000
Crude oil production[b]	6	40	31.9	0.8	1	4	17.2	17.4
Crude oil reserves[b]	150	498	471	3	15	59	49.2	595
Coal production[b]	–	274.4	–	–	–	–	10.605	29.06274
Coal reserves[b]	–	19,611.9	–	–	–	–	867.3	105

Source: World Energy Council (2016)
[a]Million tonnes of oil equivalent
[b]Million tonnes per year

stands out. It is the world's fifth-largest coal producer[7] and the tenth-largest natural gas producer (World Energy Council 2016). Brunei, Malaysia, Myanmar, Thailand and Vietnam also possess important reserves of mineral fuels. This abundance of mineral resources has played a central part in the history and development outcomes of a handful of Southeast Asian countries.

Gellert (2010: 28) proposes the concept of an "extractive regime" to highlight a given country's "reliance on extraction of multiple natural resources in the formation of an economic and political order that is also supported by global and regional forces". These regimes build on claims that extraction benefits the public good while providing important state revenues, but "without the burden of building… [a] large meritocratic and effective state capacity" (ibid.: 33). In Southeast Asia, such regimes have seen extractive industry revenues feed into government coffers, allowing state managers to pursue ambitious development goals. Figures 13.1 and 13.2 show the region's significant rent intake from natural resources in selected countries over time.[8] They also clearly highlight the unreliability of revenues from the sector, especially given the highly volatile nature of international commodity prices, as exemplified by the end of the most recent commodity boom in 2012. Note that while no yearly data are available for Timor-Leste, the 2018 US Geological Survey points out that since the country's independence, the petroleum sector had accounted for almost 90% of government revenues (USGS 2018c).

In several instances, political elites in the region have also diverted extractive industry revenues towards the task of consolidating authoritarian or illiberal regimes. In Indonesia, extractive industries have played—and continue to play—a key part in the country's development trajectory. By the late 1950s, while the strongholds of foreign capital established during colonial rule were being expropriated, new production-sharing schemes emerged, notably in the petroleum and mining sectors, where the Indonesian government had realised that, given the highly capital-intensive and technologically intricate nature of the sectors, foreign corporate participation was essential (Robison 2009: 79–80). The lucrative oil sector, particularly following the rise of international prices in the late

---

[7] This is mainly low-rank thermal coal exported to China and India for use in power stations.

[8] Natural resource rents have never exceeded 1% of GDP in Singapore and 5% in the Philippines and Thailand, so they are excluded.

Fig. 13.1 Total natural resources rents (percentage of GDP), 1981–2015: Brunei, Indonesia and Malaysia

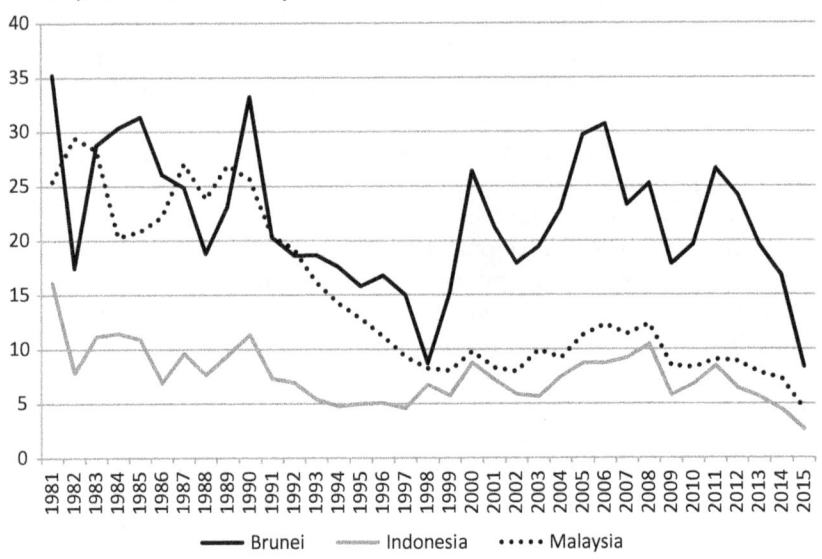

Source: World Bank 2019b

Fig. 13.2 Total natural resources rents (percentage of GDP), 1981–2015, CLMV countries

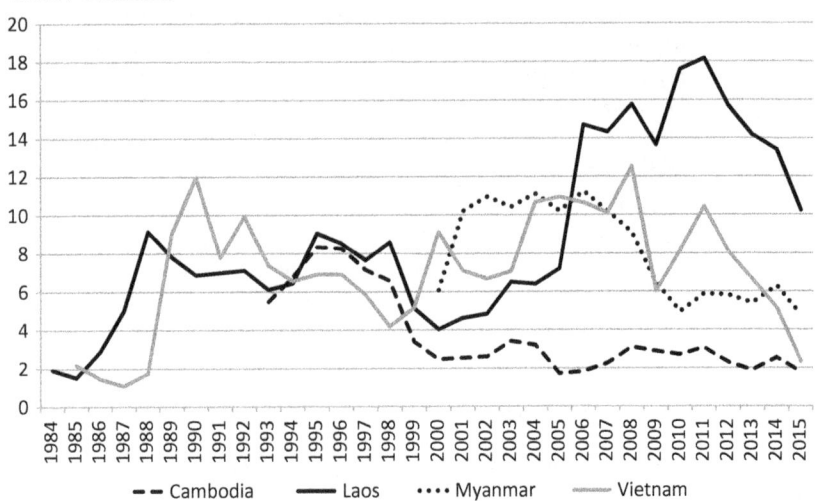

Source: World Bank 2019b

1970s (see Carroll, this volume), had become a key source of revenues for the Indonesian state, and therefore, for the consolidation of the Suharto regime (1967–98).[9] In the Philippines, the mining sector was strictly controlled by the Marcos regime throughout the period of the dictatorship (1965–86) (Bello et al. 2004: 225). Marcos himself had direct interests in the mining industry, including the Marcopper mine, half of which he owned through a number of cover companies (Nettleton et al. 2004: 7). As with Indonesia under Suharto, extractive industries in the Philippines were an important lubricant for the complex system of "bountiful patronage" that prevailed under Marcos.[10] In Brunei Darussalam (Brunei), where revenues from extractive industries have bequeathed the country the highest per capita income in the Asia-Pacific region, mineral fuel rents continue to ensure the government's hold on power, and with it, the serious human rights abuses against its population (Human Rights Watch 2016).

While the history of the institutional arrangements governing the sector has greatly varied from one country to the next, the mid-1990s brought a wave of changes across the region. Fed by continuous economic growth, Asia's appetite for mineral imports appeared infinite (USGS 1996: 1). Asia's "tigers"—Hong Kong, Japan, the Republic of Korea, Singapore and Taiwan—all lacked mineral resources. Their rapid growth was pivotal in propelling demand, although China was also quickly becoming a key importer during this period (second in the region after Japan). Japan, Indonesia, Malaysia and Thailand's manufacturing activity also underpinned high demand for metals (USGS 1997: A3). However, by the end of the 1990s, with the exception of Indonesia, rich in copper, nickel, coal, gold and tin which was increasing its exports (USGS 1996), most of the countries in the region had relatively low levels of mineral exports. Nevertheless, while Myanmar, Cambodia, Laos, Thailand and Vietnam all exhibited underdeveloped extractive sectors, all were deemed to have "significant mineral potential" (ibid.).[11]

---

[9] State corporations, including Pertamina (oil), Timah (tin mining), Aneka Tambang (mining) and Inhutani (forestry), were "essentially the terminals through which the state establishes production and work sharing agreements with the foreign companies which make the bulk of investments and carry out production" (Robison 2009: 217).

[10] For example, Leith (2002) documents how the Freeport copper mine was a lucrative source of patronage for President Suharto. Also see Robison (2009).

[11] The Philippines was once one of the world's top exporters of copper and gold but by the turn of the twenty-first century, its production had declined significantly.

The 1997–98 Asian financial crisis opened the door for IFIs to step in with sizeable reforms (see Carroll, this volume). For several developing countries in the region, this meant important regulatory reforms of their mining sectors, given protectionist and bureaucratic "restrictive regulations" (USGS 1997: A1). Naito et al. (1998: 77) noted:

> Exploration investment in Asia lags [behind] that in most other regions, and while expenditures have increased in the 1990s, the rate of increase lags [behind] that of Australia, South America and Africa. Political, legal, and fiscal uncertainties or barriers, in some cases, effectively make private exploration and mining investment difficult.

Crucially, by the end of the 1990s, under the guidance of IFIs (mostly the World Bank and the Asian Development Bank—ADB), resource-rich countries began reforming their mining sectors, a process that embedded new competitive pressures within global extractive sectors, setting country against country, and compelling further patterns of liberalisation (Campbell 2009; Hatcher 2014). According to the Extractive Industries Review (EIR 2003: 10), in the 1990s, no fewer than 100 countries underwent reforms in line with the World Bank's advice. Out of the 1097 changes in national foreign direct investments (FDI) laws adopted between 1992 and 2000 alone, 94% created a more favourable investment climate (MIGA 2010, cited in Hatcher 2014).

These reforms were spearheaded by a discourse that championed—and legitimised—a development model driven by resource extraction. As such, they prioritised attracting foreign investors by emphasising the privatisation and liberalisation of the sector, enhanced transferability of mineral rights, closer links between exploration and mining rights, and the provision of generous taxation regimes for mining corporations (Naito et al. 1998: 77). Such incentives were deemed necessary to attract foreign investors given the uniquely high-risk environment which characterises extractive industries, especially given the long lead times and capital-intensive nature of the sector, not to mention the high volatility of commodity prices and the uncertainties of geological exploration and reserve depletion rates. In light of such risks, and given constrained developmental options in the post-Cold War period (see Carroll, this volume), resource-rich countries were encouraged to prioritise high profits for investors in the sector (see for instance World Bank 2005). Multilateral pressures for reform were heightened in the case of Southeast Asia: the region's most resource-rich countries have historically been highly aid dependent and therefore more exposed to donor pressures to develop neoliberal policy templates for the sector (see Rosser, this volume).

In short, by the end of the 1990s, all the major mineral-rich countries in Southeast Asia had entered a race for reforms which would bring them to compete against each other for the most deregulated and liberalised mining regime. Amongst countries in the region that embarked upon reform during this period were Cambodia (1994), Laos (1997), Malaysia (1994), Myanmar (1994), Thailand (1991), the Philippines (1995) and Vietnam (1996). Indonesia was one of the region's key exceptions, already boasting Southeast Asia's "most attractive" policies for foreign investment in mining (USGS 1997: A1).

These reforms, which continued throughout the 2000s, took different forms but were united in embedding neoliberal norms into the modes of governance relating to the sector. These included:

- Priority given to the private sector for mining development
- Priority given to mining over other types of territorial use
- Priority given to exportable resources over other mineral resources
- Priority given to the industrial sector over artisanal and small mines
- Guarantees protecting mining rights (Gagné-Ouellet 2012).

The case of the Philippines is illustrative of such reform processes. By the mid-1990s, the country was struggling to tap into its vast mineral reserves at a meaningful scale. With a sizeable external debt,[12] the World Bank consistently noted that the Philippines lagged behind its regional neighbours in terms of FDI (IBRD and IFC 1999). In 1995, under the auspices of then Senator (later President) Gloria Macapagal-Arroyo, the country adopted the 1995 Philippine Mining Act (Republic Act 7942). This occurred in a context where lacklustre economic growth and rising poverty that stretched back five decades were plaguing the country, earning it a reputation as the "sick man of Asia" (ADB 2007: 2). Closely moulded by the World Bank and the ADB, the provisions of the new mining code clearly spoke to foreign investors (Doyle et al. 2006; Hatcher 2014; Holden 2005). Despite the constitutional maximum limit on foreign ownership being set at 40%, the 1995 Mining Act allowed mining con-

---

[12] In 1993, the Philippines' total debt servicing cost was just under 9% of its gross national income (World Bank Data 2019a).

tractors with investments of at least US$50m to apply for a Financial or Technical Assistance Agreement that would enable the company to secure 100% foreign ownership. The new mining law was quickly singled out as "the most foreign-friendly mining policy" from among 70 countries that had reformed their mining sectors (SAPRIN 2001: 5). Although the Act was highly successful in attracting foreign investors to the country, the liberalisation of the mining regime also had severe socio-environmental ramifications (Hatcher 2014).

Crucially, the main thrust of the reforms across the region was to isolate the state institutions governing the sector from political "interference". In other words, the reforms sought to adopt institutions and legal/juridical mechanisms that permanently "locked in" neoliberal norms (Gill 1995; Hameiri and Jones, this volume). This reflected IFI orthodoxy that, once neoliberal norms were solidly anchored in a country's regulatory mining regime, local institutions would be able to provide the "right" business environment needed by foreign investors: predictability, efficient institutions, transparent laws and advantageous tax codes (Cornish and Vivoda 2016: 1076). This pressure for states to attract foreign capital to the sector has only increased, with the "Ease of Doing Business" series—which scores countries on their attractiveness to international capital—indicative of the proliferation of instruments to internationally benchmark the provision of market-friendly institutions in specific countries (see Carroll, this volume). Regulatory regionalism has also played a key role in imposing neoliberal discipline in the region's extractive industries.[13] For instance, by the end of the 1990s both the Asia-Pacific Economic Cooperation forum and ASEAN were decisively committed to bolstering mining in the region for the following decades, using neoliberal modalities (Kemp and Owen 2017).

The liberalisation of the region's mining regimes, combined with rising demand from Asia's largest economies—China, India and Japan—as well as the commodity boom of 2002–12, triggered a wave of investments in the region.[14] In this climate, resource-poor economic giants across Asia have been competitively deploying capital to secure access to natural

[13] See, e.g. ASEAN (2016). For a discussion on regulatory regionalism, see Jones and Hameiri, this volume.

[14] The race for Asia's resources was also fed by the depletion of mineral reserves in other regions of the world, which raised commodity prices in the first decade of the 2000s, and by new technologies that allowed investors to venture further into previously untapped markets.

resources.[15] By 2010, approximately US$750m was being channelled to mineral exploration in Southeast Asia and the Pacific (excluding Australia) (USGS 2012: 1.3). In 2014, Indonesia and the Philippines, alongside Papua New Guinea, accounted for a staggering 82% of the total mineral exploration budget for the region (USGS 2017: 1.2).[16] Notably, all of the world's largest mining companies currently have projects in the Asia-Pacific region (Kemp and Owen 2017: 131).[17]

Socio-Political and Environmental Conflict

The reform of extractive industries around neoliberal norms championed across the Global South, here exemplified by Southeast Asia, has been spearheaded by a discourse emphasising the merits of an extractive-led development model. However, these specific norms, which now permeate the modes of governance of mining regimes in countries across the region and beyond, have had profound, and often highly negative, socio-environmental ramifications.

It is well established that large-scale mining is one of the world's most environmentally destructive activities (Bebbington et al. 2008), with long-lasting impacts including the destruction of natural habitats, soil degradation and acid mine drainage, riverbed pollution, soil contamination, air emissions, the use of scarce water and energy resources, and the different risks associated with exposure to toxic substances (Belem 2009: 121; see also Gellert, this volume). Southeast Asia has long been at the centre of some of the world's worst environmental disasters resulting from large-scale mining activities. In 1996, a spillage at the Marcopper mine in the Philippines released between 1.5 and 3 million cubic metres of toxic mining slurries and tailings into local rivers, "effectively killing the small island of Marinduque's ecosystem and livelihood" (Bello et al. 2004: 224). In West Papua, the world's largest gold mine, Grasberg, operated by the US mining giant Freeport (BIC et al. 2006: 4) discharges an estimated 230,000 tons of tailings (waste rock) into the Aghawagon River every day (Taylor 2011). With the company's contract due to expire in 2021, the Indonesian government estimates that Freeport has caused environmental

---

[15] For an analysis of resource politics in Asia-Pacific, see Wilson (2017).
[16] 2014 is the most recent year for which USGS data are available.
[17] These include Rio Tinto, Barrick Gold, BHP Billiton, MMG, Glencore Xstrata, Gold Fields, Newmont, Newcrest, Anglo American and Vale.

damage worth US$13.25bn (Munthe and Jensen 2018). Also in Indonesia, there are allegations that Newmont's Minahasa Raya mine has had devastating impacts on the health of villagers living nearby (Kemp and Owen 2017: 131). Additionally, extractive industries have been repeatedly associated with severe socio-economic ramifications for the communities living in the vicinity of large-scale mining projects, most notably conflict over land access and resources (see Hirsch, this volume).

In light of the sector's record, by the late 1990s, most of the new-generations of mining laws adopted across the Global South had far tighter socio-environmental safeguards. Mining corporations, investment banks and local elites were keen to back a discourse suggesting that, with the "right" institutions in place, extractive industries could spearhead economic growth and poverty reduction while also managing the socio-environmental impacts of mining activities (World Bank 2012, 2013). However, this has proven a difficult task. After all, as emphasised by the Murdoch School, institutions remain tied up with socio-political conflict and power relations and, therefore, reflect and serve to entrench existing distributions of power among social groups (see Hameiri and Jones, this volume). Unsurprisingly, political elites have continued to shape institutions that benefit their domestic clients above all else. For example, despite the fall of the Suharto regime, the Indonesian economy has remained dominated by a small number of massive conglomerates established under Suharto's patronage regime (see Robison 2009). Likewise in the case of Myanmar, amidst the political transition and despite substantial regulatory reforms sponsored by IFIs and foreign investors,[18] the military junta, which has ruled over the country's extractive industries (notably the infamous jade industry) for over half a century, continues to operate in an opaque system plagued with human rights abuses.[19] As Cornish and Vivoda (2016: 1075) have noted, "As long as corruption and crony culture remain modus operandi, the regulatory process will remain captured".

Campbell (2004, 2009, 2013) argues that the core issue is that the neoliberal reforms adopted over the course of the past three decades in the

---

[18] Myanmar embarked on legal and regulatory reform of its extractive industries in 2011.

[19] Well beyond Southeast Asia, human rights reports are bleak for extractive industries. Global Witness highlights that in 2017 alone, 197 environmental activists were murdered, four times the number estimated for 2002 (cited in Watts 2018). Crucially, the non-profit organisation reports that extractive industries were one of the top drivers of such violence (ibid.).

Global South have profoundly contributed to the weakening of states' institutional capacity to enforce regulations essential for the protection of the environment and local communities. This has led to what Szablowski (2007) refers to as the "strategically absent" state, whereby neoliberal norms have pushed the state to gradually retreat from its formal monitoring role in the sector, while simultaneously delegating its regulating, mediating and monitoring functions to the private sector. Given this reality, isolated communities have increasingly been left with the burden of negotiating with mining corporations, international investors and local authorities looking for windfalls (Hatcher 2014).

The management of the mining sector's socio-environmental impacts has also become increasingly complex, now involving a plurality of actors well beyond the state. IFIs, mining corporations, international governmental organisations, and a wide range of non-governmental actors have all begun to champion various market-friendly schemes to standardise the management of extractive industries (see Dashwood 2013). In this regard, the Extractive Industries Transparency Initiative (EITI) has brought some much-needed transparency to the industry.[20] On the corporate side, cognisant of reputational risks, international mining companies have been at the forefront of a narrative linking the sector to sustainable development— the very thing that such companies have historically been criticised for undermining. While all global companies now undertake corporate social responsibility initiatives, there are also collective corporate initiatives taking place. A clear example is the International Council on Mining and Metals, comprising some of the world's largest mining and metals companies. Collectively, these companies have committed to principles which serve as a best-practice framework for sustainable development in the industry (ICMM 2017). International organisations have also developed intricate guidelines and safeguards for the sector, including the Guidelines for Multinational Enterprises of the Organisation for Economic Co-operation and Development, or the United Nations' Global Compact and the Voluntary Principles on Security and Human Rights. Crucially, however, the newly revised Performance Standards on Environmental and Social Sustainability of the International Finance Corporation (IFC) (the World Bank Group's private sector arm) are probably the most respected and stringent in the mining industry. Introduced in 2006, and revised in

---

[20] In Southeast Asia, the following countries have joined the EITI: Indonesia (in 2010), Myanmar (in 2014), the Philippines (in 2013) and Timor-Leste (in 2008).

2012, the latter detail the IFC's commitments, roles and responsibilities in relation to environmental and social sustainability.[21]

However, if such global normative activities have highlighted the need for better socio-environmental management in extractive industries, these mechanisms have done little to tackle the neoliberal norms embedded in countries' modes of governance, which continue to be shaped by interests favouring the industry at the local, national and international levels. Critics emphasise that these norms have weakened the state and have forced local communities to seek redress in supranational arenas separate from formal domestic representative bodies. Emblematic of this is the Compliance Advisor Ombudsman (CAO), the independent accountability mechanism for projects funded by the IFC and the Multilateral Investment Guarantee Agency. In Southeast Asia, local communities seeking redress have lodged several complaints relating to extractive industries with the CAO. In the Philippines, complaints have been filed in relation to Mindoro Resources Ltd., a junior mining company headquartered in Canada, and its plans to build an exploration and mining company (for nickel, copper and gold) in the Northern Mindanao Island, as well as two hydroelectric power plants (Ambuklao-Binga Hydroelectric). In Indonesia, complaints were lodged against a nickel and cobalt mine and a hydrometallurgical processing plant project in eastern Indonesia (PT Weda Bay Nickel project), the Rajamandala hydropower project near Bandung, and the palm oil related activities of the agribusiness conglomerate Wilmar Group. All of these cases are now closed. In a recent in-depth report on CAO-related complaints, including the cases of Wilmar and PT Weba Bay Nickel, Balaton-Chrimes and Macdonald (2016: 8) conclude that "the CAO ultimately made little tangible difference to human rights outcomes". In fact, while these international platforms are crucial as last-resort arenas for local communities to file complaints in a context where political spaces are increasingly narrowing, they remain problematic as they mostly rely on sanctioning mechanisms provided by informal law, which include dialogue, shaming, community pressure and, ultimately, the "threat of expulsion from the regime and the forfeiture of the reputation or other benefits provided by participation" (Szablowski 2007: 63).

---

[21] The implementation of these standards is required for any project in which the IFC invests. However, the standards have since been adopted by several public and private companies on a voluntary basis and are now considered the *de facto* global standard (see Dashwood 2013).

More broadly, and as emphasised by Campbell and Laforce (2016), a key question remains: are the institutional mechanisms intended to secure compliance with global voluntary norms equipped to respond to the very socio-environmental crisis brought forth by the industry in the first place? On this count, Coumans (2011: 120) argues that:

> far less is said by the industry and by the international financial institutions about the various mechanisms—including confidential contracts and stability agreements, mining Acts, and trade agreements—through which mining companies secure lengthy tax holidays, keep tax and royalty levels to a minimum, and secure protection from potential costs associated with future environmental or social legislation aimed at protecting communities from negative impacts from mining... Additionally, little is said by the industry about the various means by which taxes are avoided and revenues related to resource extraction are removed from host countries through accounting mechanisms such as transfer pricing and the use of tax havens such as the Cayman Islands.

Winds of Change?

While pro-industry interests have sought to address the socio-environmental legacy of the extractive industry by attempting to forge the "right" institutions for the management of the sector, the results have been limited at best. As discussed above, cases across Southeast Asia show that the management of socio-environmental struggles linked to extractive projects has increasingly shifted away from local representative arenas to transnational forums in which mediation "is cast as a technical concern" for beneficiaries who are acknowledged to now possess "needs", rather than "rights" (Szablowski 2007: 304–305). This has had important ramifications in terms of the role and legitimacy of the main stakeholders involved in extractive industries, particularly the state.

Crucially, however, these institutional arrangements and market reforms have failed to change the deeply political nature of the policies engineered to aggressively expand the extractive frontier in the region. While there are clear attempts to assign technocratic roles to actors seeking redress or to challenge the legitimacy of an extractive-led development model, cases across Southeast Asia expose the deep contradictions embedded in the neoliberal norms forged by pro-industry interests. As such, the contraction of political space at the local level is often proving temporary, with the re-emergence of multiple platforms of dissent, including parliaments, local government and civil society (see Carroll 2010; Hatcher 2014; Jayasuriya 2003). For instance, in the Philippines, a coalition of civil society groups has repeatedly, and at times successfully, challenged the country's mining regime, including via the court system. There are also illustrative cases where local government units have challenged international and national pro-mining interests by banning mining activities (Hatcher 2014; Holden 2005).

More broadly, amidst the rise of commodity prices, some governments have sought to challenge some of the established neoliberal norms in the sector, notably by increasing taxes or by claiming larger stakes in a mining project. For example, in the Philippines, President Duterte recently announced that he would impose a royalty tax equivalent to 5% of the market value of mineral products extracted or produced. In Indonesia, the very day after he announced his candidacy for the 2019 presidential election, President Widodo proclaimed that the country's stakes in the oil, gas and mining industries should be used for the people (Venzon 2018). Moreover, by 2014, Indonesia had passed a law that prohibited exports of unprocessed ores. While critics have been quick to label such attempts as displays of "resource nationalism", "populism" and or new attempts at cronyism, these policy changes are symptoms of the increasing dilemma forced upon states attempting to reconcile pro-mining interests with rising discontent on the ground, especially during election times (Hatcher 2016; see also Robison and Hadiz, this volume).

Crucially, it is the heightened presence of China and its increasing levels of investment in this sector across the region that may further disturb the international and domestic power relations that profit from the mediated neoliberal agenda. Importantly, both the Asian Infrastructure Investment Bank and the Belt and Road Initiative are now providing alternative sources of investment for the region's extractive industries.

Conclusion

Southeast Asia is extremely rich in natural resources, including oil, gas and minerals. Despite the wide range of experiences across countries, this chapter has sought to tease out common themes that inform the political economy of extractive industries in the region. Drawing upon Murdoch School positions regarding power and the form and function of institutions, the chapter has emphasised that a complex array of international and local actors have sought to benefit from the neoliberalisation of the sector, with international capital and local elites prominent—though not always harmonious—protagonists. However, the modes of governance embedded within extractive regimes have intrinsically shifted relations between communities, companies and the state, with frequently devastating ramifications for local stakeholders seeking redress. Amidst the rise of social conflicts across the region and a changing context which has seen the rise—and more recently, the fall—of commodity prices, as well as increased investment flows from non-traditional sources (mainly China), neoliberal modes of governance embedded in mining regimes continue to be challenged. However, mining rent remains highly malleable and will continue to permeate predatory practices across a region characterised by a lack of alternative development prospects within capitalism.

References

ADB [Asian Development Bank]. (2007). *Philippines: Critical development constraints*. Manila: Asian Development Bank.

ASEAN. (2016). *ASEAN Minerals Cooperation Action Plan 2016–2025 (AMCAP-III): Phase (2016–2020)*. Jakarta: ASEAN Secretariat.

Balaton-Chrimes, S., & Macdonald, K. (2016). *The compliance advisor ombudsman for the IFC/MIGA: Evaluating potential for human rights remedy* (Non-judicial redress mechanisms report series 17). http://corporateaccountabilityresearch.net/njm-report-xvii-cao. Accessed 7 Feb 2019.

Bebbington, A., Hinojosa, J., Bebbington, D., Burneo, M. L., & Warnaars, X. (2008). Contention and ambiguity: Mining and the possibilities of development. *Development and Change, 39*(6), 887–914.

Belem, G. (2009). Mining, poverty reduction, the protection of the environment and the role of the World Bank Group in Mali. In B. Campbell (Ed.), *Mining in Africa: Regulation and development* (pp. 119–149). New York: Pluto Press.

Bello, W., Docena, H., de Guzman, M., & Maliq, M. L. (2004). *The anti-development state: The political economy of permanent crisis in the Philippines*. London: Zed Books.

BIC [Bank Information Centre], Bretton Woods Project, Earthworks, Oxfam International, & Campagna per la Riform della Banca Mondiale. (2006). *The World Bank Group's gold mining operations*. Tarnished gold: Mining and the unmet promise of development. www.bicusa.org/proxy/Document.9518.aspx. Accessed 7 Feb 2019.

Campbell, B. (Ed.). (2004). *Regulating mining in Africa: For whose benefit?* (Discussion paper no. 26). Uppsala: Nordiska Afrikainstitutet.

Campbell, B. (Ed.). (2009). *Mining in Africa. Regulation and development*. London/Ottawa/Uppsala: Pluto/IDRC/Nordiska Afrikainstitutet.

Campbell, B. (Ed.). (2013). *Modes of governance and revenue flows in African mining*. Basingstoke: Palgrave Macmillan.

Campbell, B., & Laforce, M. (2016). *La responsabilité sociale des entreprises dans le secteur minier [Corporate social responsibility in the mining sector]*. Montreal: Presses de l'Universite du Quebec.

Carroll, T. (2010). *Delusions of development: The World Bank and the post-Washington consensus in Southeast Asia*. Basingstoke: Palgrave Macmillan.

Cornish, G., & Vivoda, V. (2016). Myanmar's extractive industries: An institutional and regulatory assessment. *The Extractive Industries and Society, 3*, 1075–1083.

Coumans, C. (2011). Whose development? Mining, local resistance, and development agendas. In J. Sagebien & N. M. Lindsay (Eds.), *Governance ecosystems: CSR in the Latin American mining sector* (pp. 114–132). New York: Palgrave Macmillan.

Dashwood, H. S. (2013). Sustainable development and industry self-regulation. *Business & Society, 53*(4), 551–582.

Doyle, C., Wicks, C., & Nally, F. (2006). *Mining in the Philippines: Concerns and conflicts. Report of a fact-finding trip to the Philippines*. Knowle: Society of St. Columban.

EIR [Extractive Industries Review]. (2003). *Striking a better balance. Vol 1: The World Bank and the extractive industries. The final report of the extractive industries review*. Washington, DC: World Bank Group.

EITI [Extractive Industries Transparency Initiative]. (2018). *Indonesia. Extractive industries transparency initiative*. https://eiti.org/indonesia. Accessed 7 Feb 2019.

Gagné-Ouellet, S. (2012). Regulatory framework revision and mining regime reform in Mali: Degrees of rupture and continuity. In B. Campbell (Ed.), *Modes of governance and revenue flows in African mining* (pp. 47–100). London: Palgrave Macmillan.

Gellert, P. K. (2010). Extractive regimes: Toward a better understanding of Indonesian development. *Rural Sociology, 75*(1), 28–57.

Gill, S. (1995). Globalisation, market civilisation, and disciplinary neoliberalism. *Millennium: Journal of International Studies, 24*(3), 399–423.

Hatcher, P. (2014). *Regimes of risk: The World Bank and the transformation of mining in Asia*. Basingstoke: Palgrave Macmillan.

Hatcher, P. (2016). Le boom minier de la Mongolie et la montée du nationalisme des ressources: Tensions politiques, promesses électorales et normes néolibérales [The Mongolian mining boom and the rise of resource nationalism: Political tensions, electoral promises and neoliberal norms]. *Canadian Journal of Development Studies, 37*(4), 466–483.

Holden, W. N. (2005). Civil society opposition to nonferrous metals mining in the Philippines. *Voluntas: International Journal of Voluntary and Nonprofit Organizations, 16*(3), 223–249.

Human Rights Watch. (2016, February 10). *Human rights shouldn't be sidelined at ASEAN summit.* https://www.hrw.org/news/2016/02/10/human-rights-shouldnt-be-sidelined-asean-summit. Accessed 7 Feb 2019.

IBRD, & IFC [International Bank of Reconstruction and Development & International Finance Corporation]. (1999). *Philippines: Country assistance strategy.* Washington, DC: World Bank.

ICMM. (2017). *ICMM 10 principles.* International council on mining and metals. https://www.icmm.com/en-gb/about-us/member-commitments/icmm-10-principles. Accessed 7 Feb 2019.

IGF. (2017). *Global trends in artisanal and small-scale mining (ASM): A review of key numbers and issues. Intergovernmental forum on mining, minerals, metals and sustainable development.* Winnipeg: IISD.

Jayasuriya, K. (2003). *Civil society, regulatory state and the new anti-politics.* Murdoch: Asia Research Centre, Murdoch University.

Kemp, D., & Owen, R. (2017). Grievance handling at a foreign-owned mine in Southeast Asia. *The Extractive Industries and Society, 4*(1), 131–139.

Leith, D. (2002). Freeport and the Suharto regime, 1965–1998. *The Contemporary Pacific, 14*(1), 69–100.

Munthe, B. C., & Jensen, F. (2018, May 24). Distraction or disaster? Freeport's giant Indonesian mine haunted by audit report. *Reuters.* https://www.reuters.com/article/us-indonesia-freeport-environment-analys/distraction-or-disaster-freeports-giant-indonesian-mine-haunted-by-audit-report-idUSKCN1IP1H5. Accessed 7 Feb 2019.

Naito, K., Otto, J., & Eggert, R. G. (1998) Mineral investment risk and opportunities in Asia. *Resources Policy, 24*(2), 77–78.

Nettleton, G., Whitmore, A., & Glennie, J. (2004). *Breaking promises, making profits: Mining in the Philippines.* London: Christian Aid and Philippine Indigenous Peoples Links.

Robison, R. (2009). *Indonesia: The rise of capital.* Reprint. Singapore: Equinox Publishing.

SAPRIN. (2001). *The impact of investment liberalization and the Mining Act of 1995 on indigenous peoples, upland communities and the rural poor, and on the environment: A summary report.* Manila: Structural Adjustment Participatory Review International Network.

Szablowski, D. (2007). *Transnational law and local struggles: Mining, communities and the World Bank.* Oxford: Hart Publishing.

Taylor, N. A. J. (2011, October 19). West Papua: A history of exploitation. *Al Jazeera.* https://www.aljazeera.com/indepth/opinion/2011/08/201182814172453998.html. Accessed 14 Mar 2019.

USGS [United States Geological Survey]. (1996). *The mineral industries of Asia and the Pacific*. Washington, DC: U.S. Department of the Interior, Geological Survey-Minerals Information.
USGS. (1997). *The mineral industries of Asia and the Pacific*. Washington, DC: U.S. Department of the Interior, Geological Survey-Minerals Information.
USGS. (2012). *2010 minerals yearbook: Asia and the Pacific*. Washington, DC: U.S. Department of the Interior, Geological Survey-Minerals Information. https://minerals.usgs.gov/minerals/pubs/country/asia.html. Accessed 7 Feb 2019.
USGS. (2016). *2013 minerals yearbook: Asia and the Pacific*. Washington, DC: U.S. Department of the Interior, Geological Survey-Minerals Information.
USGS. (2017). *2014 minerals yearbook: Asia and the Pacific*. Washington, DC: U.S. Department of the Interior, Geological Survey-Minerals Information.
USGS. (2018a). *2015 minerals yearbook: Philippines (advance release)*. Washington, DC: U.S. Department of the Interior, Geological Survey-Minerals Information.
USGS. (2018b). *2015 minerals yearbook: Malaysia (advance release)*. Washington, DC: U.S. Department of the Interior, Geological Survey-Minerals Information.
USGS. (2018c). *2015 minerals yearbook: Timor-Leste (advance release)*. Washington, DC: U.S. Department of the Interior, Geological Survey-Minerals Information.
USGS. (2018d). *2015 minerals yearbook: Thailand (advance release)*. Washington, DC: U.S. Department of the Interior, Geological Survey-Minerals Information.
USGS. (2018e). *2015 minerals yearbook: Vietnam (advance release)*. Washington, DC: U.S. Department of the Interior, Geological Survey-Minerals Information.
Venzon, C. (2018, August 25). Flare-up of resource nationalism burns miners across Asia. *Nikkei Asian Review*. https://asia.nikkei.com/Business/Markets/Commodities/Flare-up-of-resource-nationalism-burns-miners-across-Asia. Accessed 7 Feb 2019.
Watts, J. (2018, February 2). Almost four environmental defenders a week killed in 2017. *The Guardian*. https://www.theguardian.com/environment/2018/feb/02/almost-four-environmental-defenders-a-week-killed-in-2017. Accessed 7 Feb 2019.
Wilson, J. D. (2017). *International resource politics in the Asia-Pacific: The political economy of conflict and cooperation*. Cheltenham: Edward Elgar.
World Bank. (2005). *Extractive industries and sustainable development: An evaluation of World Bank Group experience*. Washington, DC: World Bank.
World Bank. (2012). *The World Bank Group in extractive industries: 2012 annual review*. Washington, DC: World Bank.
World Bank. (2013). *Mining: Sector results profile*. http://www.worldbank.org/en/results/2013/04/14/mining-results-profile. Accessed 7 Feb 2019.

World Bank Data. (2019a). *The Philippines: Total debt service (% of GNI)*. https://data.worldbank.org/indicator/DT.TDS.DECT.GN.ZS?locations=PH. Accessed 7 Feb 2019.

World Bank Data. (2019b). *Total natural resources rents (% of GDP)*. https://data.worldbank.org/topic/energy-and-mining?contextual=region&end=2016&locations=4E&start=1975. Accessed 7 Feb 2019.

World Energy Council. (2016). *Southeast Asia and the Pacific*. https://www.worldenergy.org/data/resources/region/southeast-asia-pacific/oil/. Accessed 7 Feb 2019.

CHAPTER 14

The Political Economy of Land and Agrarian Relations in Southeast Asia

Philip Hirsch

INTRODUCTION

This chapter examines how Southeast Asia's wider, post-colonial political economy has shaped agrarian relations within particular national contexts. Class relations and conflicts surrounding agriculture have fundamentally changed in this region over the past 50 years, through a shift from a peasant rural economy to a neoliberal era defined by globalisation, marketisation, livelihood diversification and precarity, including growing exclusions and enclosures that alienate people from their land. The end of the Cold War and the 2008 global financial crisis (GFC) were especially significant turning points. The rise of neoliberal property rights regimes, along with the growth of national and transnational agribusiness, have helped to radically reshape rural social relations. Certain forms rooted in the region's peasant past remain superficially tenacious, notably smallholder

P. Hirsch (✉)
School of Geosciences, The University of Sydney, Sydney, NSW, Australia
e-mail: philip.hirsch@sydney.edu.au

farming,[1] but these belie fundamental changes (Rigg et al. 2018). Capitalist development has led to dramatic changes in land usage, transforming agricultural production from a labour- to a more capital-intensive process. In almost all key agricultural commodities, production growth has outstripped growth in harvested area, showing sharp productivity increases (FAO 2019). The expansion of mechanised, large-scale plantation agriculture—along with the construction of hydropower dams, and the expansion of forestry and mining—has displaced smallholders from their land (see Hatcher, and Gellert, both this volume). This has bred growing resentment, and collective and individual resistance. In some cases, rural grievances have helped to fuel the rise of populist politics.

This chapter begins by setting out agrarian relations during the Cold War, when land was a key focus of struggles between capitalist and socialist forces. Collectivisation and land reform designed to reduce peasant disaffection limited marketisation, but this was underway by the late 1980s. The second section details the impact of marketisation after the Cold War, while the third explores the politics of this neoliberal era, which are now less concerned with left-right struggles and more with civil society and, occasionally, populist mobilisation.

Agrarian Political Economy, the Cold War and Post-Socialism

In the early post-colonial period, rural areas in Southeast Asia were predominantly marked by peasant-based farming, undergoing early stages of capitalist social transformation and associated processes of accumulation and dispossession. During the Cold War, rural unrest intensified throughout the region, as agricultural and land issues were prominent in the competing strategies of pro- and anti-communist forces fighting for territorial control and the "hearts and minds" of rural populations.

In socialist-inspired rural movements, land redistribution from wealthy landlords to peasant farmers was an important rallying cry. Landlordism had grown rapidly during the colonial period as local elites were co-opted by colonial authorities and as rising levels of debt defaults during the depression of the 1930s led creditors to seize land from indebted

---

[1] Smallholdings are small farms, typically supporting a single family, often involving a mixture of subsistence farming (food production for domestic consumption) and the production of crops for sale (cash crops).

smallholders (Boomgaard and Brown 2000; Scott 1976). This spurred many peasant farmers to support radical social movements (see Quimpo, this volume). Following the defeat of the French and the division of Vietnam, rapid land reform occurred in North Vietnam, often involving the violent dispossession of local landlords, followed by the collectivisation of agriculture. In Burma, all land was nationalised, which precluded large-scale accumulation, except by the military.

In the non-socialist countries, land reform was pursued to undercut peasant support for revolts against anti-communist regimes. In Nguyen Van Thieu's land reform in South Vietnam, Marcos's land reform in the Philippines, and the work of Thailand's Agricultural Land Reform Office from the mid-1970s, the reallocation of land to peasant farmers was intended to reduce rural unrest. Elsewhere, the pressure-valve of landlessness or land poverty was addressed through schemes to resettle the rural poor into newly developed areas and assist them to develop cash cropping. Examples included Malaysia's Federal Land Development Authority programme and Indonesia's Transmigration scheme.

Other prescribed solutions to rural poverty introduced new tensions. In core rice-growing areas of the Philippines, Indonesia, Malaysia, Thailand and South Vietnam, a predominant concern was the effect of new technologies based on input-dependent,[2] high-yielding varieties of rice, supported by the US-based Rockefeller Foundation, Ford Foundation, and the US Agency for International Development (USAID). In 1968, the USAID director coined the term "Green Revolution" as a direct alternative to the "red revolution" against which the US was then engaged openly or covertly in most Southeast Asian countries (Patel 2013). The aim was to build a buffer against communism through prosperity generated by intensifying small-scale farming (Dayley 2011: 351). This slogan caught on and was institutionalised through a network of rice research centres in most US-allied Southeast Asian countries.

However, the programme's benefits largely mirrored the relative power of key social forces. Cleaver (1972: 180) argued that the Green Revolution sought to provide opportunities for American agribusiness to sell inputs and dominate trading networks, though the profits anticipated had largely failed to materialise. The more pernicious results were the emergence of capitalist production relations in the countryside benefiting landlords and

[2] Agricultural inputs include consumables, e.g., seeds, fertilisers, feed, packing materials, pesticides, veterinary medicines, and capital goods, e.g. threshers, tools, tractors, etc.

other elites at the expense of the rural poor (Feder 1976). Because of the high costs of hybrid seeds, fertilisers, pesticides and agricultural machinery, intensified agriculture favoured those with easier access to credit—namely landlords and wealthier peasants—and was thus associated with growing class inequality (Hart et al. 1989; White 1989). It also promoted monocropping, which had negative environmental consequences, including reduced biodiversity and growing dependence on chemical fertilisers and pesticides, and socio-nutritional consequences, with farmers increasingly reliant on purchased foods (Glaeser 1987).

Southeast Asia's agrarian political economy bifurcated after 1975 with the establishment of communist regimes across Indochina. Hanoi extended its collectivisation programme to the South after Vietnam's reunification, while Laos also began a more limited and ill-fated collectivisation of agriculture. In Cambodia, the Khmer Rouge's ultra-Maoist collectivisation programme caused widespread suffering. In the subsequent Vietnamese occupation of the 1980s, Cambodian farmers were grouped into smaller "solidarity groups" (*krom saamakhi*) that precluded individual land accumulation.

Meanwhile in the non-socialist states, rural class struggle intensified as governments deployed coercive, anti-communist programmes couched in the language of development (Hirsch 1990). These programmes sought to fight ongoing insurgencies, in Thailand and the Philippines, and to consolidate anti-communist regimes' social control, in Malaysia and Indonesia (Hart et al. 1989). In Indonesia, agrarian policy also favoured oligarchic interests, with programmes such as the "nucleus–plasma" outgrowing scheme,[3] which gave corporations favourable leases and access to the labour of surrounding smallholders (Peluso 2017: 851). State patronage of a proto-capitalist class of rural entrepreneurial traders and agricultural suppliers and other local elites also sought to allow national elites to secure political and economic control of the countryside (Hart 1989).

During this period, much of the increase in rice production in the Philippines and Indonesia was aimed at achieving national self-sufficiency, while Thailand entrenched its position as the staple's leading global

---

[3] In such arrangements, smallholder producers ("plasma") are contractually tied to a corporate actor ("nucleus"). The "nucleus" may be a plantation, surrounded by smaller "plasma" farms, or it may even grow nothing; its key role is as a "middle man", selling inputs (often at inflated prices) to, and buying outputs (often at low, fixed prices) from "plasma" farms.

exporter. However, the production of other export-oriented crops rapidly grew as commercial agriculture expanded into frontier areas of Thailand, Indonesia and the Philippines, producing sugar for the international market and maize, cassava and other products to supply the intensive livestock industries of European and Northeast Asian economies. Nonetheless, at this stage, agricultural production remained largely smallholder-based throughout the region. The progressive marketisation of agriculture mainly involved smallholders selling to middlemen, and borrowing from multiple sources, including informal local moneylenders, who often doubled as traders and input suppliers, as well as from state-initiated agricultural cooperatives and banks at more favourable interest rates.

The late 1980s and early 1990s marked the start of the "post-socialist" period, which increasingly brought Cambodia, Laos, Myanmar and Vietnam (the CLMV countries) into the currents of marketisation (see Carroll, and Hughes, both this volume). Post-socialist transitions involved a dramatic transformation of property relations. In the countryside, land ownership was de-collectivised, with ownership shifting to individuals. Land could now be bought and sold, turning it into a commodity and permitting the emergence of large-scale plantations on land claimed by the state but leased out to large investors. This convergence with agrarian structures and related class processes elsewhere in the region led to rapid growth in the production of agricultural commodities, albeit usually from a very low base, especially by comparison with Southeast Asia's more established market economies (see Fig. 14.1, Table 14.1). Meanwhile, de-collectivisation often sparked social dislocation, as larger farmers or non-local investors—often in cahoots with local officials—seized opportunities to buy up land from impoverished smallholders, generating rural tensions and increasing land poverty (Lund 2011; Sikor et al. 2012; see also Hughes, this volume).

The 1980s also saw a growth spurt in the more marketised Southeast Asian economies as Northeast Asian investment spurred industrialisation and accelerated urbanisation, with attendant increases in migration from the countryside (Carroll, this volume). A global boom in land prices also affected the region, intensified by the growing commodification of land, and saw many farmers selling their plots to neighbours and outsiders. These sales were partly a response to new opportunities, including investment in children's education, housing, vehicles and machinery, and partly due to distress, as debt mounted amid the increased use of inputs, unstable commodity prices, growing household consumption, and weak or

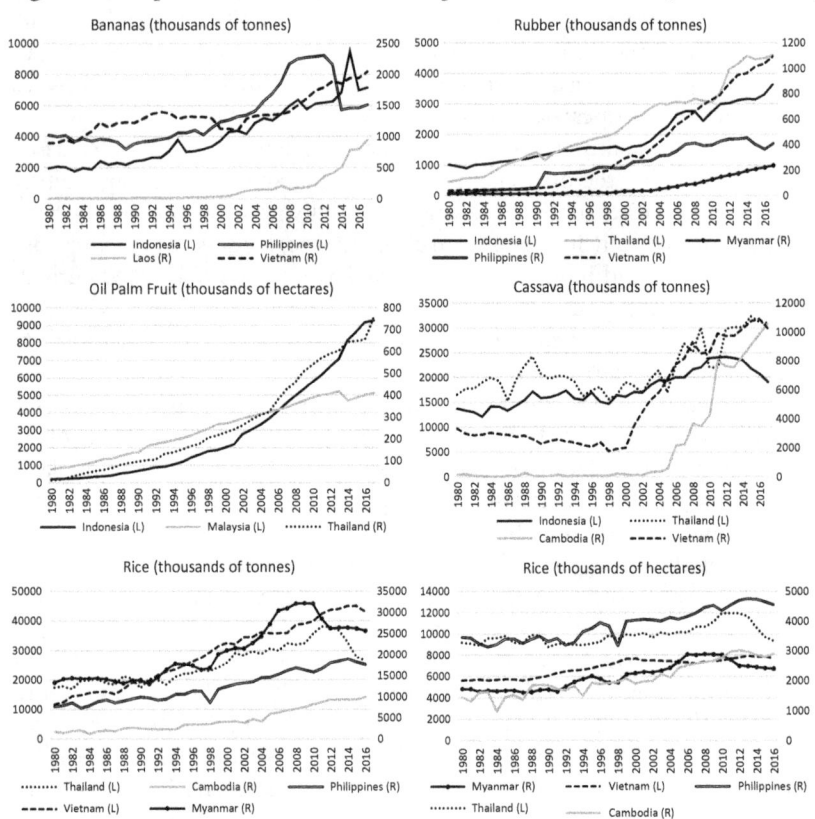

Fig. 14.1 Expansion of selected boom crops in selected countries, 1990–2017

Note: Countries marked (L) should be read on the left-hand y-axis, (R) on the right-hand y-axis
Source: FAO 2019

non-existent welfare systems. In Indonesia, for example, the withdrawal of government subsidies on inputs in the 1990s undermined "nucleus–plasma" arrangements in the pivotal palm oil sector, which had hitherto allocated 70% of land and half of the profits to smallholders. Subsequently, many farmers had to sell their land to larger estates, while the surviving smallholders became dependent on "nucleus" companies' credit to purchase overpriced farming inputs, squeezing their profitability. As a result, and following the sector's massive growth in the 2000s, plasma farms now control only 30% of land and receive just 20% of profits (Hameiri and Jones 2015: 103).

Table 14.1 Expansion of selected crops in CLMV economies (tonnes)

	1990	2017	Increase (1990–2017) Raw	Percentage (%)		1990	2017	Increase (1990–2017) Raw	Percentage (%)
Cambodia					*Laos*				
Beans, dry	12,000	83,167	71,167	593	Bananas	14,000	946,820	932,820	6663
Cassava	60,000	10,577,812	10,517,812	17,530	Cassava	65,000	2,277,050	2,212,050	3403
Maize	88,000	750,000	662,000	752	Coffee	5204	150,795	145,591	2798
Pulses	12,000	83,167	71,167	593	Maize	66,566	1,192,525	1,125,959	1691
Soybeans	22,000	168,000	146,000	664	Sugar cane	96,360	1,764,390	1,668,030	1731
Sugar cane	258,000	686,505	428,505	166	Watermelons	3500	128,850	125,350	3581
Myanmar					*Vietnam*				
Beans, dry	263,500	5,466,166	5,202,666	1974	Nuts[c]	495,700	2,191,882	1,696,182	342
Maize	187,024	1,909,334	1,722,310	921	Cassava	2,275,800	10,267,568	7,991,768	351
Pulses	427,410	7,053,336	6,625,926	1550	Coffee	92,000	1,542,398	1,450,398	1577
Sugar cane	1,930,700	10,370,042	8,439,342	437	Maize	671,000	5,109,766	4,438,766	662
Seeds and nuts[a]	786,809	2,754,397	1,967,588	250	Rubber	57,939	1,094,519	1,036,580	1789
Peas[b]	163,665	1,586,208	1,422,543	869	Sugar cane	5,405,600	18,356,398	12,950,798	240

Source: FAO (2019)
[a]Areca nuts, ground nuts (with shell), sesame seed, sunflower seed
[b]Peas, dry, and pigeon peas
[c]Cashew nuts (with shell), groundnuts (with shell), treenuts

Capitalist development has gradually transformed social life in the countryside. Rural livelihoods have shifted away from dependence on farming, while social and geographical boundaries between cities and countryside have broken down (Rigg 1998, 2000). The rural labour force has become partially proletarianised, through the emergence of agribusiness plantations and the pull of paid employment in the cities. Increasingly, young people—initially men but then especially women as they were drawn into export-oriented industry from the 1980s onwards (see Elias, this volume)—moved to urban areas, either permanently or for part of the year, sometimes returning to family farms at harvest time. This rural influx has swelled the ranks of informal settlements in Southeast Asia's cities (see Hutchison and Wilson, this volume), but it has also spilled over national boundaries, as poor farmers move overseas in search of work (see Gerard and Bal, this volume).

The Political Economy of Land and Agriculture in the Neoliberal Era

The neoliberal era, which intensified in Southeast Asia after the end of the Cold War, has seen a progressive deepening of market logics in the shaping of land control, agricultural production and labour processes in Southeast Asia, albeit to different degrees and in different ways between and within countries. This section explores these developments.

Neoliberalism has increasingly reshaped land and agrarian relations through several routes. First, international institutions, such as the World Bank and Asian Development Bank (ADB), have sought to marketise land and land-based natural resources as a means to bring capital into otherwise low-productivity areas of economic activity and to reap the advantages of regional and global economic integration. The ADB's Greater Mekong Subregion, for example, advances a model for infrastructure development largely based on privatisation and public–private partnerships. The World Bank's private sector arm, the International Finance Corporation (IFC), has also supported large-scale plantations, including oil palm in Indonesia, where the World Bank played a key role in transforming "nucleus–plasma" relations (Hameiri and Jones 2015: 103); the IFC has also backed hydropower development in Laos and Myanmar.

Second, governments have harnessed neoliberal market logics, alongside "modernisation" ideologies, to marginalise peasant-based farming, which they see as backward and unproductive. This has paved the way for large land concessions, as well as policies for farm consolidation, such as in Vietnam and Thailand, heavily benefiting the oligarchic business interests surrounding Southeast Asian regimes. Ultimately, land itself has not only become a means of producing agricultural commodities, but a commodity in its own right.

Third, a "perfect storm" of events around 2008 drove marketisation even further. There was a global spike in food and commodity prices, with the cost of staples increasing by 100–200% due to combined weather events, oil (and therefore fertiliser) price rises, and demand competition from biofuels. This sparked what has become known as the "global land-grab", as concerns over food shortages and a dearth of investment in agriculture prompted the World Bank and many governments to promote large-scale land deals (Wolford et al. 2013). This occurred alongside growing unemployment associated with the GFC. Unlike in previous downturns, however, farming no longer provided a "shock absorber" in many economies, because there was no farmland for urban-dwellers to return to, or because younger unemployed workers had little experience of farming (cf. Li 2014).

As a whole, this period intensified the shift away from peasant agriculture towards neoliberal agribusiness, with class relations increasingly shaped by processes of alienation and exclusion and the rural labour force's growing proletarianisation. Below, I examine several important, interrelated trends in turn.

Globalisation and Regionalisation

The neoliberalisation of agriculture worldwide is closely associated with the global land-grab, as transnational investors gain long-term access to land for commodities that supply global markets. In Southeast Asia, investment is dominated by regional and national players, based on the stark differences in endowments of land (and other natural resources), capital and labour between national economies, and the emergence of agribusiness conglomerates in some countries, notably Thailand, Indonesia, the Philippines and, more recently, Vietnam. Furthermore, China, a significant player in global land and resource deals, doubles as a regional investor and the most significant export market. As of 2012, Chinese companies had invested in over 3 million hectares in Southeast Asia (Hofman and Ho 2012: 17), a figure that excludes many smaller cross-border investments in Myanmar and Laos (Friis 2015; Mills 2018). Agricultural exports from the region to China increased from US$7.1bn in 2007 (10.7% of the total) to US$21.1bn (15%) by 2017 (UN Comtrade 2017).

Agribusiness in Southeast Asia has grown through the expansion of domestic firms and partnerships with global corporations. US firms like Dole made early inroads into pineapple cultivation in the Philippines and Thailand, for example, but they have increasingly been eclipsed by local agribusiness giants, which have grown through supplying and processing agricultural products and diversification into non-agricultural activity. In Thailand, for example, the Charoen Pokhaphand (CP) conglomerate grew from a seed supplier for animal feed crops, to producing seed and other inputs, to involvement in intensive livestock production, to retail brands for the finished products. CP maize is now an important crop in Myanmar (Woods 2015), and CP supplies the shrimp industry in Thailand, Vietnam and elsewhere in the region. CP also makes motorcycles in China, and owns the telecommunications giant True and the 7–11 store franchise in Thailand. Similarly, Thailand's Mitr Phol Group began as a sugar supplier before working its way upstream through sugar milling to ownership of sugar plantations in Laos, Cambodia, Australia and elsewhere.

The regional investment boom has been led by several crops, most notably palm oil and rubber, though cassava, maize, sugar and even the traditional staple, rice, are also highly significant (see Fig. 14.1). Cassava and maize are largely geared toward producing feed for European, Japanese and Chinese livestock industries, while the boom in rubber has overwhelmingly been led by industrial—mainly automotive—demand from China. Palm oil is a truly global commodity, demand for which is driven by cooking oil and biofuel industries in Europe, China and South Asia, while cassava and sugar prices have also been elevated by biofuel demand. Bananas have rapidly replaced staple food production in lowland and upland rice-growing areas of northern Laos, northern Thailand and northern Myanmar, while coffee has expanded into previously forested lands in upland parts of Vietnam and Laos and shrimp farming into coastal areas of Thailand, the Philippines, Malaysia, Vietnam and Indonesia. Vietnam has also joined Thailand to become a globally significant exporter of rice, earning US$2.15bn from rice exports in 2016, while Thailand exported US$4.3bn worth (UN Comtrade 2017). From 1980 to 2016, Vietnam's rice production quadrupled despite only modest increases in the harvested area, indicating vastly improved productivity (Fig. 14.1). Myanmar and Cambodia have also become significant rice exporters, earning US$438.9 m and US$305.8 m in 2016 (UN Comtrade 2017).

Land-Grabbing and Agribusiness

The establishment of large-scale agricultural concessions can frequently only occur through the exclusion of previous land occupiers and users. This results in peasant farmers' displacement or subordination as workers to large-scale landowners and/or agribusiness companies, leading some to identify a "reverse land reform" (Byerlee 2014; GRAIN 2014).

Two basic models of capitalist engagement with agriculture exist, each with exclusionary implications that shape rural class structures and urban–rural relations. The first is the establishment of large-scale plantations under direct control of a single agribusiness, often financed by regional investors. In Indonesia and Malaysia, these are overwhelmingly oil palm plantations (Cramb and McCarthy 2016). Over two-thirds of Indonesia's oil palm investment comes from Singapore and Malaysia (Varkkey 2012). In Cambodia and Laos, concessions are largely based on investments from, and joint ventures with, neighbouring countries' agribusiness (Schönweger et al. 2012; Socheth 2012). In Myanmar, they have been associated with military land-grabs and crony capitalism, but also involve Thai and Chinese investors (Woods 2014).

The second model is contract farming, whereby local farmers maintain nominal control over land and its management, but are contractually bound to grow and supply particular crops to large agribusiness interests (Delforge 2007; Simmons et al. 2005; Woods 2015). This binds farmers into agreements to purchase seeds, fertilisers and pesticides, and to sell their crops to companies at fixed prices (Delforge 2007). These contracts are often extremely one-sided, reflecting the overwhelming power imbalance between smallholders and large agribusiness interests. Contract farming helps to keep companies more flexible, allowing them to shift production to places where labour and other production costs are lowest, and to change crops in response to global price shifts. Furthermore, their profit margins in upstream and downstream activities, such as the sale of inputs to farmers, are often greater than in the riskier farming operation. However, the contract farming model also reflects the fact that smallholders in Southeast Asia have sought to retain nominal control of their land, which complicates the establishment of large-scale plantations under company control.

The emergence of large-scale agricultural concessions has been particularly notable in the three countries portrayed in policy narratives as "land-rich but capital-poor"—Cambodia, Laos and Myanmar—though Vietnam and the Indonesian islands of Sumatra and Kalimantan have also seen major agribusiness investments. Many of these concessions are for boom crop plantations (Hall 2011), notably rubber and oil palm, but rice, cassava, bananas, sugar, coffee and other commodities are also produced for regional and global markets, including shrimp farming and other forms of aquaculture. Figure 14.1 and Table 14.1 show this dramatic expansion for selected crops and countries.

These developments have been hugely beneficial for Southeast Asian elites able to control investors' access to land. In many cases, land-grabbing and agribusiness development are tied to crony capitalism and neopatrimonialism (see Hughes, this volume). In Cambodia, for example, associates of Prime Minister Hun Sen have received large swathes of land as economic land concessions. In Myanmar, partnerships between military officials, crony capitalists and Chinese investors have involved large-scale land-grabbing for agribusiness, as well as mining and hydropower development. A similar situation obtains in northern Laos, though Chinese investments tend to take the shape of "control-grabbing" rather than direct land alienation (Friis and Nielsen 2016). In Indonesia, land allocation is hugely corrupt, with logging companies tied to the Suharto regime transitioning into plantation agriculture, especially oil palm, and their owners becoming some of the country's richest elites. Post-Suharto decentralisation has multiplied the opportunities for patronage in agricultural concessions, fuelling widespread land-grabbing, deforestation, and the burning of degraded forests to clear them for agriculture—producing the annual "haze" crisis (see Gellert, this volume). Land concessions have also provided an outlet for capital accumulated through real estate and other investments by large corporate players. Vietnam's Hoang Anh Gia Lai grew exponentially on the back of real estate investments in Ho Chi Minh City (Kenney-Lazar 2012: 1025), and later became the largest investor in rubber and other plantation crops in north-eastern Cambodia and south-eastern Laos (Dwyer 2015: 26). Thailand's Mitr Phol Sugar has investments covering tens of thousands of hectares in western Cambodia and southern Laos (Equitable Cambodia and Inclusive Development International 2013: 35).

These developments are facilitated and legitimised by modernisation ideologies that cast existing practices as backward and hence requiring replacement by larger-scale and technologically superior enterprises. Most concessions have been granted in the region's upland resource frontiers, at the expense of smallholders as well as forest communities, particularly ethnic minorities practising shifting cultivation.[4] The gazetting of large areas as "wastelands"—and thus open to agribusiness—has historical antecedents (Ferguson 2014), but this is a wider phenomenon specific to the post-GFC era, also linked to the new forms of transnational capital involved in the region's agriculture. Shifting cultivation comes under particular pressure, because it leaves significant areas fallow and hence, in the absence of legally recognised customary land rights, seemingly "abandoned" (Cramb 2007). Legislation has entrenched this approach, nowhere more starkly than in Myanmar's 2012 Vacant, Fallow and Virgin Land Act. This identified large swathes of the country's territory, including areas outside the central government's actual control, as available for development by concessionaires on the basis that it is unused and unowned (Chao 2013: 143). In September 2018, all users of land that falls under the Act had to register their claims within six months or face fines, imprisonment and appropriation, with the expectation that any unclaimed land would be leased to crony investors.

De-agrarianisation and Displacement

The result of the increasingly marketised development of Southeast Asian agriculture—combined with other transformations in land usage—is the continued shrinking of the rural population as a proportion of the total. Southeast Asia continues to be one of the world's most rural and agrarian regions, if measured by the percentage of the population living in the countryside and employed in agriculture. However, agriculture's contribution to gross domestic product (GDP) is proportionately much lower than the rural labour force in most countries (see Fig. 14.2).

There are several factors behind this apparent paradox. First, the imbalance between agricultural and non-agricultural GDP stems from the greater productivity and profitability of the industrial and services sectors, which are increasingly drawing people off the land and into the cities. Second, the mismatch between the rural population and the proportion of people working in farming reflects changes in the nature of agricultural production. As land is consolidated and agricultural production increasingly uses machinery, fertilisers and other advanced inputs, it becomes

---

[4] Also known as "swidden" or "slash-and-burn" agriculture, this involves developing land for farming for a short period, then moving onto a new area, leaving the previous area to recover its fertility (fallow), and possibly later rotating back to it.

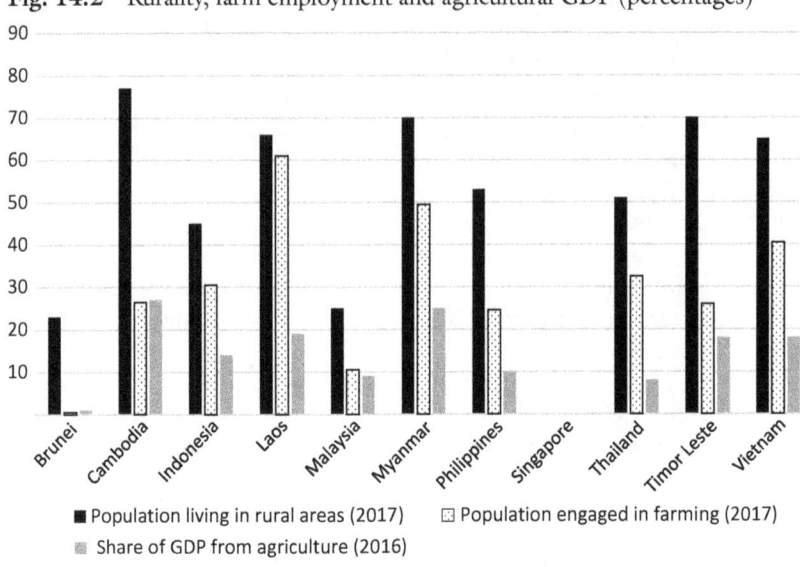

Fig. 14.2 Rurality, farm employment and agricultural GDP (percentages)

- Population living in rural areas (2017)
- Population engaged in farming (2017)
- Share of GDP from agriculture (2016)

Sources: Carroll, this volume, Tables 2.3 and 2.4; World Bank (2017)

more productive, requiring less land and labour per unit of output. The vastly improved productivity of Vietnam's rice sector, for instance, is noted above (and see Fig. 14.1). Other examples include important export crops like bananas: in Indonesia, the area of land given over to bananas fell by 10% from 1990 to 2017, yet output increased by 197% (FAO 2019). Furthermore, as production becomes increasingly capital-intensive, rather than labour-intensive, a "surplus" population emerges in the countryside. This also has particularly gendered effects: historically, when men have left rural communities to work in the cities, left-behind female family members have tended the farms; but agriculture's mechanisation often involves the displacement of female by male workers.

Third, there are many non-agrarian demands on land hitherto used by smallholders for food and cash crop cultivation. These include resource extraction in the form of mining concessions, and hydropower dams, whose reservoirs flood fertile valley lands (see Hatcher, and Gellert, both this volume). They also include service-sector investments in tourism and associated infrastructure, and the expansion of urban areas into rural land. This partly collapses the divide between real estate and farming as means of land-based accumulation, and brings the relevant actors into direct conflict—particularly where such development is achieved through compulsory dispossession, as in Vietnam and Cambodia (Labbe and Musil 2013; Nguyen 2009). Finally, large areas are increasingly set off-limits to farming through proclamation of conservation zones (Hall et al. 2011: ch. 3).

Neoliberalism has accelerated non-agrarian displacements through a combination of economic policy that prioritises large-scale resource projects funded by transnational capital, and transformations in rights of access that have resulted in smallholders losing their land to non-agricultural enterprises. In most countries' uplands and peripheral areas, this has occurred through the enforcement of state claims over land hitherto farmed under various customary or usufruct arrangements,[5] leading to dispossession. In more established agricultural areas, it has often occurred more incrementally through market power, but ultimately with similar results.

Neoliberal-inspired displacement is exemplified by public–private projects such as the World Bank's flagship Nam Theun 2 hydropower dam project in Laos. The World Bank's main role was to provide sovereign risk guarantees to make the investment safe for the private sector, while also supporting the Laotian state's minority share in the Nam Theun Power Corporation, whose majority shareholders are from France and Thailand. The dam flooded 45,000 hectares of farmland and forest, displacing more than 6000 people, and more than 100,000 downstream farmers and fishers have been adversely affected by altered river flows (Shoemaker and Robichaud 2018). Given the political constraints in Laos, resistance to the project was largely articulated in transnational arenas and among international players in-country (Hirsch 2002), and it has served as a model for privatised infrastructure development including dozens of hydropower investments in Laos since its completion in 2008.

Neoliberalised Property Relations

Not all the neoliberal governance measures in the region involve large-scale farming and resource projects. In many ways, the more significant reforms have been in property rights through various national land-titling programmes, targeting smallholders. The World Bank and the Australian

---

[5] Usufruct denotes an individual or collective right to use others' or public land without an associated property claim and without damaging it.

Agency for International Development (AusAID) have been key players in these reforms, as has the Australian company Land Equity International (Hall et al. 2011: ch. 2).

Land-titling programmes are closely associated with Hernando de Soto (2000), whose *Mystery of capital* saw the key to poverty alleviation in the unlocking of "dead capital" through the creation of individual, transferable property rights. For the capital-poor smallholder, the ability to mortgage, buy and sell land was supposed to provide the pathway to becoming a full market citizen. The World Bank–AusAID land-titling programme in Thailand, initiated in 1984, has been promoted as a global model for improving land administration and providing the springboard for broad-based growth (Feder et al. 1988; Rattanabirabongse et al. 1998). It inspired similar projects in Laos, the Philippines, Indonesia and Cambodia.

Critics have highlighted the exclusionary dimensions of land-titling programmes (Bachriadi 2009), and in all Southeast Asian countries there are geographical limits to the areas that have been deemed suitable for titling. On the one hand, these programmes provide security of tenure for those able to register land previously held under non-transferable or less clearly demarcated status. They also provide collateral for agricultural and other loans. On the other, the security offered to those acquiring title has not mitigated against grabbing and other means of land accumulation by the wealthy (Hirsch 2011). Land-titling has played a crucial part in embedding market-based social relations, but it has produced less obvious resistance and social struggles than the more blatant land-grabs.

The Politics of Land and Agriculture in a Neoliberal Age

Agrarian transformations in Southeast Asia have been both a response to, and an influence upon, the region's politics. Land has long been at the centre of popular resistance in Southeast Asia, be it in the form of rebellions provoked by colonial and capitalist infringements on peasants' "moral economy" (Scott 1976), everyday resistance in response to agrarian differentiation (Scott and Kerkvliet 1986), or the evasion of state territorialisation at the margins (Scott 2009). As we have seen, communist movements also took peasant grievances as a rallying point, under Maoist influence (see Quimpo, this volume). Resistance in the neoliberal era is in many ways more complex, partly because land-titling, market engagement and flight from agriculture are embraced enthusiastically by significant numbers of rural people, particularly by younger generations. Yet egregious land-grabbing and other injustices continue, and some farmers continue to resist, through civil society activism and, less frequently, electoral politics.

The contemporary foregrounding of civil society activism over political contestation is a legacy of Cold War authoritarian rule, which destroyed the left and related organisations that once represented poor people's interests (see Quimpo, this volume). Today's civil society organisations are quite diverse, and are less clearly framed around class than previously. Environmentalists have tended to take up the mantle, framing issues that are fundamentally about land in terms of ecology, culture and livelihoods (Lohmann 1991). The most strident actions have been associated with the global *Via Campesina* movement in support of peasant rights and livelihoods, especially in Indonesia (Transnational Institute 2013). Thailand's Assembly of the Poor, and more recently the People's Movement for a Just Society, are also part of this movement (Missingham 2003), which retains a peasant-oriented discourse and involves a coalition of locally based land activists. These networks tend to respond to agribusiness encroachments, but also dams, mines and other instances of land-grabbing and environmental injustice.

The space for civil society resistance varies across the region and over time. In the extreme case of Laos, no civil society advocacy is tolerated, with enforced disappearances used to suppress dissidence (Alston 2019). In Cambodia and the Philippines, active resistance has been tempered, but not eliminated, through a climate of violence and threat. Thailand was once a haven for civil society activism on land and related issues on behalf of the rural poor, but authoritarian rule after the 2014 coup precludes mass action. Myanmar has seen a relative opening up of space since the formal transition from military rule in 2011, but after decades of authoritarianism, farmers remain weakly organised, and protests against land-grabs are often still brutally repressed. The forces nurtured under Myanmar's old regime dominate the new democracy: major agribusiness owners, for example, helped steer two highly regressive land acts through parliament in 2012.

Yet, there remains space for resistance even under the more authoritarian regimes. Land-related mobilisation is the most common form of civil unrest in Vietnam and is closely associated with compulsory land acquisition. Petitions and other modes of expression of discontent have led to moratoria on the granting of land concessions in Cambodia and even

Laos, as ruling elites became concerned over their legitimacy. This has particular political resonance in the two remaining one-party communist states, whose revolutionary credentials were built on issues of land justice (see Hughes, this volume).

Resistance is also shaped in part by new opportunities, as well as impositions, engendered by globalisation and associated networks. Voluntary global guidelines have been negotiated and established to resist land-grabbing (FAO 2012). Sustainability certification schemes, driven mainly by European consumers, have reacted against some of agribusinesses' more egregious social and environmental practices. For example, a so-called "blood sugar" campaign targeted Tate and Lyle, Coca Cola, Pepsi and other companies that buy sugar grown on land grabbed from smallholders in western Cambodia (Pred and Vuthy 2016). The Roundtable on Sustainable Palm Oil has 4000 members from across the global supply chain and related interest groups, and seeks to address issues like deforestation—albeit with little success, as the exponential growth in planted area shows (Fig. 14.1). Certification schemes, corporate accountability, region-wide programmes oriented toward smallholder security,[6] regional alliances, and nimble counter-responses such as "follow the money" actions (Dwyer 2015), all demonstrate creative responses that are fundamentally and necessarily different to the peasant resistance movements of the past. But they are up against the forces of authoritarianism and repression that have enabled the more egregious expressions of neoliberalism in dispossessing smallholders.

Land conflicts have also become part of formal, electoral politics. Given that more than half of the region's population continues to reside in non-urban areas (see Fig. 14.2), this is unsurprising. In Cambodia, for example, the rural electoral support base of the Cambodian People's Party regime has been substantially eroded in recent years by the growing impact of land-grabbing on rural livelihoods (see Hughes, this volume).

Rural grievances have also been part of populist mobilisations in the region. The rise of Duterte in the Philippines, and especially the enduring popularity of Thaksin in Thailand, stem in part from strong support from rural voters. However, as Robison and Hadiz (this volume) note, populist mobilisation does not necessarily imply a counter-movement against

[6] For example, Mekong Region Land Governance: see www.mrlg.org.

neoliberal marketisation, or even any real redistribution of power and wealth. Thaksin's platform, for example, was strongly pro-business and pro-market. He promoted CEO-style provincial administration and proposed weakening restrictions on land plots allocated through land reform so that they would be fully alienable, along the principles of de Soto-inspired land-titling (Pasuk and Baker 2009: 116–117). And, although Thaksin extended low-cost welfare programmes to rural areas, his main development policy, "one *tambon* [sub-district], one product", was entirely market-oriented: it encouraged rural communities to specialise in particular products, with infrastructure development to connect them to domestic and international markets.

In Thailand, the term "populism" (*prachaniyom*) is used pejoratively against politicians like Thaksin who are said to cynically garner support from "ignorant" rural masses through electoral "bribes". Indeed, Thaksin's sister, Yingluck Shinawatra (prime minister 2011–14), was found guilty of dereliction of duty by a Thai court in 2017 over a failed "rice pledging" scheme run from 2011 to 2013. Her government was said to have bought millions of tonnes of rice from farmers at double the market value to gain political support, ultimately filling up government warehouses with overpriced crops that could not be sold on (Cochrane 2017). Yet Thaksin and Yingluck are hardly alone in courting farmers in this way. Electorally oriented crop price support schemes have a long history in Thailand. Other forms of populist appeals to rural constituencies include NGOs associated with the "community culture" movement promoting neo-populist alternatives to earlier leftist opposition to the dominant capitalist and modernist development paradigm. Royal populism, associated with King Bhumiphol's "sufficiency economy" discourse, appeals to conservative notions of limited consumption and moral living. The post-2014 junta has also mounted essentially populist programmes, including the tripartite *Pracharath* (civic–state) programme, which seeks to bring business, government and communities together for local initiatives that are dominated by some of Thailand's largest agribusiness corporations. The *Palang Pracharath* (Civic–State Power) political party, which effectively seeks the extension of military-bureaucratic rule, also revived the proposal to grant fully alienable property rights to land reform plots, similar to the Thaksin government's 2002 proposal. Another programme, *Thai-niyom* (literally, Thai-ness), mimics many of Thaksin's village-level projects.

Conclusion

Agrarian political economy is clearly part of the wider political economy at global, regional and national levels. During the Cold War, land and rural populations were often intensely politicised as part of a wider, global struggle over the social, political and economic orders. Leftists experimented with collectivisation, while rightists promoted land reform to undercut peasant support for revolutionary movements. Since the 1980s, however, with the demise of left movements and socialist regimes, marketisation and neoliberalism have increasingly defined the contours of rural life. The political economy of land, and agrarian relations more generally, is more complex in today's Southeast Asia. The protagonists are more diverse. The old certainties and ideological associations no longer hold. The players are more mobile and multi-occupational, and rural–urban relations and distinctions are not as clear-cut. States have opened up to the rural populace in ways previously unseen, but they have also transformed social relations through marketisation, property rights reforms and land expropriation, opening channels for national and transnational capital to control land and farming. Resistance to impositions on rural smallholders' livelihoods is shaped less obviously by class-based discourse and more by agendas framed in environmental, localist, ethnic and other categories. Yet class, power and social conflict remain fundamental concerns of agrarian political economy. Control over land, labour and capital remains a basic determinant of agrarian structures and processes. Superimposed on these fundamental political-economic structures and processes are forces of globalisation, its regional expression of economic integration, and evolving political forms to which rural people respond but also help shape.

References

Alston, P. (2019, March 18–28). *Statement by Professor Philip Alston, United Nations Special Rapporteur on extreme poverty and human rights on his visit to Lao PDR*. Vientiane: Office of the UN High Commissioner for Human Rights. https://www.ohchr.org/en/NewsEvents/Pages/DisplayNews.aspx?NewsID=24417&LangID=E

Bachriadi, D. (2009). *Australian overseas development assistance and the rural poor: AusAID and the formation of land markets in Asia-Pacific*. Amsterdam: Transnational Institute. https://www.tni.org/files/download/landpolicy7.pdf

Boomgaard, P., & Brown, I. (2000). *Weathering the storm: The economies of Southeast Asia in the 1930s depression*. Singapore: Institute for Southeast Asian Studies.

Byerlee, D. (2014). The fall and rise again of plantations in tropical Asia: History repeated? *Land, 3*(3), 574–597.

Chao, S. (2013). National updates on agribusiness large-scale land acquisitions in Southeast Asia. Brief #8 of 8: Union of Burma. In S. Chao (Ed.), *Agribusiness large-scale land acquisitions and human rights in Southeast Asia: Updates from Indonesia, Thailand, Philippines, Malaysia, Cambodia, Timor-Leste and Burma* (pp. 140–157). Moreton-in-Marsh: Forest Peoples Programme. http://www.forestpeoples.org/region/burma/publication/2013/agribusiness-large-scale-land-acquisitions-and-human-rights-southeast

Cleaver, H. M., Jr. (1972). The contradictions of the green revolution. *American Economic Review, 62*(1/2), 177–186.

Cochrane, L. (2017, September 27). Thai ex-PM Yingluck Shinawatra found guilty over rice subsidy scheme. *Australian Broadcast Corporation*. https://www.abc.net.au/news/2017-09-27/ex-thai-prime-minister-yingluck-sentenced-to-five-years/8992908. Accessed 30 Apr 2019.

Cramb, R. (2007). *Land and longhouse: Agrarian transformation in the uplands of Sarawak*. Honolulu: University of Hawaii Press.

Cramb, R., & McCarthy, J. (Eds.). (2016). *The oil palm complex: Smallholders, agribusiness and the state in Indonesia and Malaysia*. Singapore: National University of Singapore Press.

Dayley, R. (2011). Thailand's agrarian myth and its proponents. *Journal of Asian and African Studies, 46*(4), 342–360.

de Soto, H. (2000). *The mystery of capital: Why capitalism triumphs in the west and fails everywhere else*. New York: Basic Books.

Delforge, I. (2007). *Contract farming in Thailand: A view from the farm* (Occasional paper no. 2). Bangkok: Focus on the Global South.

Dwyer, M. B. (2015). *Trying to follow the money: Possibilities and limits of investor transparency in Southeast Asia's rush for "available" land* (CIFOR working paper no. 177). Bogor: CIFOR. http://www.cifor.org/publications/pdf_files/WPapers/WP177Dwyer.pdf

Equitable Cambodia, & Inclusive Development International. (2013). *Bittersweet harvest: A human rights impact assessment of the European Union's everything but arms initiative in Cambodia*. https://www.tni.org/files/download/bittersweet_harvest_web_version.pdf

FAO [Food and Agriculture Organization]. (2012). *Voluntary guidelines on the responsible governance of tenure of land, fisheries and forests in the context of national food security*. Rome: Food and Agriculture Organization. http://www.fao.org/docrep/016/i2801e/i2801e.pdf

FAO. (2019). *FAOStat*. Rome: Food and Agriculture Organization. http://www.fao.org/faostat. Accessed 24 Apr 2019.

Feder, E. (1976). McNamara's little green revolution: World Bank scheme for self-liquidation of third world peasantry. *Economic and Political Weekly, 11*(14), 532–541.

Feder, G., Onchan, T., & Chalamwong, Y. (1988). Land policies and farm performance in Thailand's forest reserve areas. *Economic Development and Cultural Change, 36*(3), 483–501.

Ferguson, J. M. (2014). The scramble for the waste lands: Tracking colonial legacies, counterinsurgency and international investment through the lens of land laws in Burma/Myanmar. *Singapore Journal of Tropical Geography, 35*(3), 295–311.

Friis, C. (2015). Small-scale land acquisitions, large-scale implications: The case of Chinese banana investments in northern Laos. In *Land grabbing, conflict and agrarian-environmental transformations: Perspectives from East and Southeast Asia*. Chiang Mai: Land Deals Politics Initiative.

Friis, C., & Nielsen, J. O. (2016). Small-scale land acquisitions, large-scale implications: Exploring the case of Chinese banana investments in northern Laos. *Land Use Policy, 57*, 117–129.

Glaeser, B. (Ed.). (1987). *The green revolution revisited: Critique and alternatives*. London: Allen and Unwin.

GRAIN. (2014). *Hungry for land: Small farmers feed the world with less than a quarter of all farmland*. Barcelona: GRAIN. https://www.grain.org/article/entries/4929-hungry-for-land-small-farmers-feed-the-world-with-less-than-a-quarter-of-all-farmland

Hall, D. (2011). Land grabs, land control, and Southeast Asian crop booms. *Journal of Peasant Studies, 38*(4), 837–857.

Hall, D., Hirsch, P., & Li, T. (2011). *Powers of exclusion: Land dilemmas in Southeast Asia*. Singapore: Singapore University Press.

Hameiri, S., & Jones, L. (2015). *Governing borderless threats: Non-traditional security and the politics of state transformation*. Cambridge: Cambridge University Press.

Hart, G. (1989). Agrarian transformations in the context of state patronage. In G. Hart, A. Turton, B. White, B. Fegan, & L. T. Ghee (Eds.), *Agrarian transformations: Local processes and the state in Southeast Asia* (pp. 31–49). Berkeley: University of California Press.

Hart, G. P., Turton, A., White, B. N. F., Fegan, B., & Ghee, L. T. (Eds.). (1989). *Agrarian transformations. Local processes and the state in Southeast Asia*. Berkeley: University of California Press.

Hirsch, P. (1990). *Development dilemmas in rural Thailand*. Singapore: Oxford University Press.

Hirsch, P. (2002). Global norms, local compliance and the human rights–environment nexus: A case study of the Nam Theun II Dam in Laos. In L. Zarsky (Ed.), *Human rights and the environment: Conflicts and norms in a globalizing world* (pp. 147–171). London: Earthscan.

Hirsch, P. (2011, April 6–8). *Titling against grabbing? Critiques and conundrums around land formalisation in Southeast Asia*. Paper presented at the LDPI conference Global Land Grabbing. http://www.iss.nl/fileadmin/ASSETS/iss/Documents/Conference_papers/LDPI/34_Philip_Hirsch.pdf

Hofman, I., & Ho, P. (2012). China's "developmental outsourcing": A critical examination of Chinese global "land grabs" discourse. *Journal of Peasant Studies, 39*(1), 1–48.

Kenney-Lazar, M. (2012). Plantation rubber, land grabbing and social-property transformation in southern Laos. *Journal of Peasant Studies, 39*(3–4), 1017–1037.

Labbe, D., & Musil, C. (2013). Periurban land redevelopment in Vietnam under market socialism. *Urban Studies, 51*(6), 1146–1161.

Li, T. (2014). *Land's end: Capitalist relations on an indigenous frontier*. Durham: Duke University Press.

Lohmann, L. (1991). Peasants, plantations and pulp: The politics of eucalyptus in Thailand. *Bulletin of Concerned Asian Scholars, 24*(4), 3–17.

Lund, C. (2011). Fragmented sovereignty: Land reform and dispossession in Laos. *Journal of Peasant Studies, 38*(4), 885–905.

Mills, E. N. (2018). Framing China's role in global land deal trends: Why Southeast Asia is key. *Globalizations, 15*(1), 168–177.

Missingham, B. (2003). *The assembly of the poor: From local struggles to national protest movement*. Chiang Mai: Silkworm Books.

Nguyen, V. S. (2009). Agricultural land conversion and its effects on farmers in contemporary Vietnam. *Focaal: European Journal of Anthropology, 2009*(54), 106–113.

Pasuk, P., & Baker, C. (2009). *Thaksin*. Chiang Mai: Silkworm Books.

Patel, R. (2013). The long green revolution. *Journal of Peasant Studies, 40*(1), 1–63.

Peluso, N. L. (2017). Plantations and mines: Resource frontiers and the politics of the smallholder slot. *The Journal of Peasant Studies, 44*(4), 834–869.

Pred, D., & Vuthy, E. (2016, June 22). The sugar industry has been catastrophic for Cambodia's poor, so why are companies being honoured? *Thompson Reuters*. http://news.trust.org/item/20160622152147-nz9qj

Rattanabirabongse, V., Eddington, R. A., Burns, A. F., & Nettle, K. G. (1998). The Thailand land titling project: Thirteen years of experience. *Land Use Policy, 15*(1), 3–23.

Rigg, J. (1998). Rural–urban interactions, agriculture and wealth: A Southeast Asian perspective. *Progress in Human Geography, 22*, 497–522.

Rigg, J. (2000). *More than the soil: Rural changes in Southeast Asia*. Toronto: Pearson Education.
Rigg, J., Salamanca, A., Phongsiri, M., & Sripun, M. (2018). More farmers, less farming? Understanding the truncated agrarian transition in Thailand. *World Development, 107*, 327–337.
Schönweger, O., Heinimann, A., Epprecht, M., Lu, J., & Thalongsengchanh, P. (2012). *Concessions and leases in the Lao PDR: Taking stock of land investments*. Bern: Centre for Development and Environment, University of Bern.
Scott, J. C. (1976). *The moral economy of the peasant*. New Haven: Yale University Press.
Scott, J. C. (2009). *The art of not being governed: An anarchist history of upland Southeast Asia*. New Haven: Yale University Press.
Scott, J. C., & Kerkvliet, B. J. T. (Eds.). (1986). *Everyday forms of peasant resistance in Southeast Asia*. London: Frank Cass.
Shoemaker, B., & Robichaud, W. (2018). *Dead in the water: Global lessons from the World Bank's model hydropower project in Laos*. Madison: University of Wisconsin Press.
Sikor, T., Sidel, M., & Tai, H.-T. H. (2012). Property, state and society in Vietnam. *The Asia-Pacific Journal: Japan Focus, 10*(10). https://apjjf.org/2012/10/10/Thomas-Sikor/3710/article.html
Simmons, P., Winters, P., & Patrick, I. (2005). An analysis of contract farming in East Java, Bali, and Lombok, Indonesia. *Agricultural Economics, 33*(3), 513–525.
Socheth, H. (2012). *Foreign investment in agriculture in Cambodia. A survey of recent trends*. Manitoba: IISD. http://www.iisd.org/tkn/pdf/foreign_investment_ag_cambodia.pdf
Transnational Institute. (2013). *The global land grab. A primer*. Amsterdam: Transnational Institute.
UN Comtrade. (2017). *UN Comtrade database*. https://comtrade.un.org. Accessed 30 Apr 2019.
Varkkey, H. (2012). Patronage politics as a driver of economic regionalisation: The Indonesian oil palm sector and transboundary haze. *Asia Pacific Viewpoint, 53*(3), 314–329.
White, B. (1989). Problems in the empirical analysis of agrarian differentiation. In G. Hart, A. Turton, B. White, B. Fegan, & L. T. Ghee (Eds.), *Agrarian transformations: Local processes and the state in Southeast Asia* (pp. 15–30). Berkeley: University of California Press.
Wolford, W., Borras, S. M., Jr., Hall, R., Scoones, I., & White, B. (2013). Governing global land deals: The role of the state in the rush for land. *Development and Change, 44*(2), 189–210.
Woods, K. (2014, March 3). A political anatomy of land grabs. *Myanmar Times*. http://www.mmtimes.com/index.php/national-news/9740-a-political-anatomy-of-land-grabs.html

Woods, K. (2015). *CP maize contract farming in Shan State, Myanmar: A regional case of a place-based corporate agro-feed system* (BICAS working paper no. 14). BRICS Initiative for Critical Agrarian Studies. https://www.tni.org/files/download/bicas_working_paper_14_woods.pdf

World Bank. (2017). *World Bank open data.* https://data.worldbank.org. Accessed 24 Apr 2019.

CHAPTER 15

The Political Economy of Environmental Degradation and Climate Disaster in Southeast Asia

Paul K. Gellert

INTRODUCTION

This chapter examines environmental degradation and climate change as inseparable parts of the political economy of Southeast Asia's development. It rejects the mainstream view of the environment as an "issue" or "sector" impacted by the form of capitalist "development", and the notion that, given population growth, all humans are equally responsible for environmental change. Certainly, humans and nature have co-produced Southeast Asian and global environments for millennia. Yet, it is capitalist development—including an extractive approach to nature, a disregard for environmental costs as "externalities", and burgeoning demands for resources and energy—that has deeply damaged the ecology of the region and the planet. Thus, rather than merely human–nature relations, *capital–nature* relations are key to understanding the dynamics of exploitation and

P. K. Gellert (✉)
University of Tennessee, Knoxville, TN, USA
e-mail: pgellert@utk.edu

© The Author(s) 2020
T. Carroll et al. (eds.), *The Political Economy of Southeast Asia*,
Studies in the Political Economy of Public Policy,
https://doi.org/10.1007/978-3-030-28255-4_15

degradation that shape Southeast Asia's environment, and the dwindling prospects for human well-being.

In adding an ecological dimension to the Murdoch School of political economy, this chapter thus begins from two premises. First, political economy is inseparable from political ecology. This premise rejects the assumed "trade-off" between environmental protection and development, which occurs whenever development is defined narrowly as growth, rather than in wider terms of human flourishing (Burton and Somerville 2019; see also Carroll, this volume). Second, nation-states are just one site of, and are themselves fundamentally shaped by, broader socio-political and environmental conflict. Accordingly, mainstream "good governance" projects, which assume that well-designed state or market institutions can solve environmental problems, are misguided, because they ignore—and thus fail to transform—the social power relations that underpin environmental degradation. In particular, they neglect the domination of interests supporting ever-expanding commodity production, particularly among entrenched alliances of oligarchic, politico-bureaucratic interests, which inevitably shape governance outcomes (see also Jones and Hameiri, this volume).

The chapter's first section reviews environmental indicators for Southeast Asia, illustrating the dire state of regional ecosystems. The second section explains this situation with reference to the patterns of regional and political development surveyed earlier in this book (see Carroll, this volume). The third section addresses the limitations of good governance and market-based solutions to environmental problems, leading to the conclusion that social conflicts related to the overall direction and socio-ecological characteristics of the region's development are paramount.

Environmental Degradation in Southeast Asia

The empirical evidence of environmental degradation of air, water and land in Southeast Asia is overwhelming. While each alone is alarming, combined, this degradation is driving biodiversity loss, species extinction and climate change.

Air

Of all the world's regions, South and Southeast Asia[1] has one the highest ambient air pollution levels, averaging over five times safe limits (WHO

---

[1] Unfortunately, the World Health Organization defines "Southeast Asia" to include South Asia and does not provide national-level data.

2018). The World Health Organisation (WHO) estimates that, of the 7 million annual deaths worldwide from combined outdoor and household air pollution, over 2 million occur in this region. Key Southeast Asian cities are well above WHO guidelines of 10 μg/m^3 annual mean particulate matter of 2.5 microns or less (PM$_{2.5}$) (WHO 2016). PM$_{2.5}$ includes pollutants such as sulphates, nitrates and black carbon, which penetrate deep into the lungs and cardiovascular system, posing the greatest risks to human health. In 2016, Yangon registered 26 μg/m^3 on an annual mean basis; Phnom Penh, 26–35; Bangkok, 28; Manila, 34; Hanoi, 48; Jakarta, 45; and Mandalay, 78. These figures are not as severe as cities in India (Delhi, 143) or China (Beijing, 93). However, Southeast Asia is one of just three regions—along with the Eastern Mediterranean and low- and medium-income Western Pacific—where air pollution increased more than 5% from 2008 to 2013 (WHO 2016).

Water

Southeast Asia is dominated by water: rivers in the mainland, and seas on the periphery. Industrial pollution and poor sanitation are rife. One in seven main rivers suffer from high levels of organic pollution, and both organic and faecal coliform pollution have increased precipitously in the last two decades, as only 14% of wastewater is treated in Southeast Asia, second only to South Asia's 7% (UNEP 2016). The region's rivers and coastlines suffer from pollution, deforestation (e.g., of coastal mangroves and peat swamp forests), damaging fishing practices (e.g., using cyanide and explosives), and climate change. Indonesia, the Philippines and Vietnam are among the world's top five emitters of plastic waste, together contributing 20% of the world's annual 8 million tonnes (Jambeck et al. 2015). By 2000, 88% of coral reefs in Southeast Asia were threatened by overfishing, destructive fishing practices, and sedimentation and pollution (Burke et al. 2002). These threats are exacerbated by climate change. As CO_2 levels exceed 320 parts per million (ppm) and oceanic temperatures rise, mass coral bleaching has ensued. Scientists worry that reefs will become functionally extinct at 450 ppm. Current levels are over 400 ppm (Veron et al. 2009).

Land

Deforestation is the most important dynamic affecting the terrestrial ecologies of Southeast Asia. It has been driven by logging, land-clearance for

Table 15.1 Forest cover and deforestation in Southeast Asia, 1988–2017

	Forest cover %, 1988–90[a]	Forest cover, %, 2010[b]	Planted forest as proportion of total forest area[b]	Tree cover %, >30% canopy, 2010[c]	Tree cover loss, 2001–2017[c] Millions of ha	Tree cover loss, 2001–2017[c] % loss	Deforestation rate, % change[d] 2000	Deforestation rate, % change[d] 2015
Brunei	–	–	–	74	0.26	4.8	0.40	–
Cambodia	41	57	0.7	32[e]	2.06	23.0	1.20	1.33
Indonesia	56	52	3.8	60[e]	24.4	15.0	1.89	0.75
Laos	47	68	1.4	63	2.71	14.0	0.67	−1.02
Malaysia	56	62	8.8	51[e]	7.90	25.0	0.36	−0.06
Myanmar	47	48	3.1	50	3.10	7.2	1.23	1.85
Philippines	21.5	26	4.6	50	1.09	5.9	−0.68	−3.08
Singapore	28	–	–	24	–	–	–	–
Thailand	NA	37	21	30	1.79	9.0	−1.80	−0.18
Vietnam	28	42	25.5	40	2.42	15.0	−2.06	−0.88
Southeast Asia	–	49	6.8	–	–	–	–	–

Sources: [a]Potter (1993: Table 5.2), different years depending on country; [b]FAO (2011: Table 2.1 and 2.2); [c]Global Forest Watch (2019); [d]FAO data in ADB (2018)

Notes: Most sources do not aggregate beyond the national level. Deforestation rate in the last columns refers to percentage change over previous year. A negative value indicates that deforestation is decreasing (i.e., reforestation); [e]"Natural forest cover" (excluding plantations of 340,000 ha in Cambodia, 15.1 m ha in Indonesia, and 6.33 m ha in Malaysia)

timber and agricultural plantations (see Hirsch, this volume), fire, mineral extraction and hydropower development (Cramb and McCarthy 2016; Hirsch 2017; Potter 1993; Seymour and Busch 2016). Measuring deforestation is plagued by definitional problems: varying canopy cover of 70, 40, 20 and 10% are all defined as "forest" by the United Nation's Food and Agriculture Organisation, FAO (FAO 2011: 10). By this extremely loose definition, Southeast Asia's forest area declined by 1% annually from 1990 to 2000; 0.3% over 2000–05; and 0.5% from 2005–10 (ibid.: 5). The total loss for 1990–2010 was 42 million hectares, about 8% of the region's land area, and greater than Vietnam's total territory (ibid.: 9). However, other data sources differ (see Table 15.1). Relying on satellite data, Global Forest Watch (2019) identifies forest loss at 23, 25 and 17% in Cambodia, Malaysia and Indonesia respectively over 2001–17. The FAO's definitions may account for the recorded reversal of deforestation in the Philippines and Vietnam: while some of this could stem from reforestation programmes, most satellite-based estimates cannot distinguish between old-growth forests, with their vastly superior biodiversity, and human-made plantations of tree crops, including fast-growing acacia trees for pulp and paper and oil palm trees for palm oil production, whose lack of biodiversity seriously impinges on long-term ecological health and the livelihoods of forest-dwellers (Colchester et al. 2006). Recent studies attempt to distinguish tree cover loss that may eventually result in forest regeneration, such as forest management, shifting (swidden) cultivation and forest fires, from permanent and commodity-driven deforestation. Southeast Asia leads the world with 78% of forest loss attributed to the latter causes (Curtis et al. 2018).[2]

Biodiversity and Climate Change

All of these depredations on the air, water and especially the forests of Southeast Asia are contributing to biodiversity loss and climate change.

Biodiversity loss is increasingly recognised as a serious threat, with the UN warning of "unprecedented" and "accelerating" species loss and 1 million of the planet's 8 million species threatened with extinction by humans (IPBES 2019). Some worry that a "sixth (mass) extinction" could end our epoch, which many now call the Anthropocene.[3] Biodiversity is higher in tropical regions like Southeast Asia, especially in the rainforests; the Mekong region currently leads the world in species discovery, with hundreds of new ones identified annually (Hughes 2017). However, due to the loss of suitable habitat, including perhaps almost all unprotected forest in the region within a decade, millennia-old diversity—from Sumatran tigers and orangutans to less-famous species—is threatened (Hughes 2018).

Southeast Asia is also a growing contributor to global climate change, creating a direct threat to coastal populations in particular. The United Nations' Intergovernmental Panel on Climate Change (IPCC) has revised its earlier estimates of likely sea level change by 2100 from under 1 meter

---

[2] The FAO's definition of forests takes into account designated land uses and is based on various data-gathering methods, including national forest inventories. Global Forest Watch's definition is purely biophysical (height, canopy cover and extent of trees). Global Forest Watch continues to improve its data collection but also cautions against direct comparison of different years as a result of changing techniques. For a useful discussion of the complex and potentially complementary measures, see Harris et al. (2016).

[3] Anthropocene refers to humans changing the geology and climate of the earth, but others dub it the Capitalocene due to capitalism's impact (see Moore 2016).

to as much as 3–5 metres (IPCC 2013). With a 1-meter rise, 74,000 km^2 of land in 12 Asian countries, including Brunei, Cambodia, Indonesia, Malaysia, Myanmar, Philippines, Thailand and Vietnam, would risk permanent inundation, displacing 37 million people (Dasgupta et al. 2007). Indonesia is most vulnerable; 13,800km^2 would be inundated and 2.8 million people displaced. Low-lying areas of the Mekong delta are also vulnerable, affecting over 10% of Vietnam's population. Climate change is also expected to produce more violent storms and tidal surges, exacerbated by losses of mangrove forests. One study anticipates over 40% of the impact of storm surges on lives, property and infrastructure in developing countries falling on three cities: Manila (Philippines), Karachi (Pakistan) and Jakarta (Indonesia) (Brecht et al. 2012).

The IPCC's October 2018 report expresses more urgency than ever about the need for action to address human-caused climate change and limit warming to 1.5 degrees centigrade *within 12 years* to avoid catastrophic outcomes for humans (IPCC 2018; see also The Guardian 2018). At the current level of governmental commitments (and even the Paris Accord is in serious doubt), however, the world is on course for 3 degrees of warming, threatening droughts, flooding, risks to ocean food-web structures, and negative impacts on agricultural production. The IPCC advocates the complete phasing-out of fossil fuels, specifically declaring that coal-fired electricity must end by 2050, and warns that deforestation is turning potential carbon "sinks" into further sources of emissions.

Nowhere is this risk clearer than in Indonesia, where forest clearing for oil palm and pulpwood plantations relies heavily on burning as the cheapest method. In October 2015, the country and its neighbours faced a forest fire and "haze" crisis, exacerbated by a long dry season caused by the El Niño effect—a more extreme repetition of early fire episodes in 1983 and 1998 (Gellert 1998). George Monbiot (2015) declared it "almost certainly the greatest environmental disaster of the 21st century—so far". According to the Indonesian government, 2.6 million hectares of land burned between June and October 2015, an area 23 times the size of Hong Kong (Purnomo et al. 2017). On many days in October the daily greenhouse gas (GHG) emissions from fires were estimated to be larger than emissions from the United States (roughly 15 million tonnes CO_2 per day). A total of 380 Tg C (teragrams of carbon) were emitted. This figure translates to 1.5 billion metric tons CO_2 equivalent which is "in between the 2013 annual fossil fuel CO_2 emissions of Japan and India" (Field et al. 2016: 9208). Indonesia leads Southeast Asia and is currently

13th in the world in CO_2 from fossil fuel combustion, including for electricity (UCS 2018). Conservationists (e.g., Seymour and Busch 2016) focus on emissions from forests, which contributed 16% of GHG emissions from 1970 to 2000. That figure declined to 11% from 2000 to 2011 whereas fossil fuel and industrial processes, by contrast, increased from 59% to 65% of total GHG emissions across the two periods (IPCC 2014: Figure SPM.2).

Health scientists estimated over 100,000 "premature deaths" (of adults alone) from the "haze" that blanketed much of Borneo, closing schools and airports there as well as in parts of Sumatra and Papua, while also drifting over peninsular Malaysia and Singapore (Marlier et al. 2015). While local NGOs joined the critique, raised public awareness, and blamed oil palm companies and their national and international backers (Conway 2015), health ministers and other politicians in Indonesia, Malaysia and Singapore rejected the scientific analysis, arguing it was not "reflective of the actual situation" (The Guardian 2016). The World Bank (2016: 1) estimated the economic losses at US$16.1bn and noted that "a few hundred businesses and a few thousand farmers profit from land and plantation speculation practices, while tens of millions of Indonesians suffer health costs and economic disruptions". Ironically, the Bank played a key role in shaping Indonesia's political economy, including the palm oil sector (see Hirsch, this volume; Hameiri and Jones 2015: 103). Thus, I now turn to examine the intertwining of Southeast Asia's social and environmental woes.

Accumulation, Hyperglobalisation and Hyperdegradation

Southeast Asia's extreme environmental degradation stands in vivid contrast to the region's touted economic "success" (see Carroll, this volume). The region's environmental degradation is causally linked to the mode of development adopted from colonialism, through post-independence national industrialisation efforts, to the current period of hyperglobalisation. Rather than unfortunate or ill-managed externalities of otherwise successful development, degradation has been inherent in Southeast Asia's mode of capitalist development.

In the colonial period, natural resource extraction and coerced forms of labour created a large wealth "drain" to Europe. After independence, under US hegemony and in Japan's "embrace", most Southeast Asian countries opened their trade and imported capital goods to extract natural resources and produce low value-added manufactured goods while putting their economies into debt (Hatch and Yamamura 1996). Deforestation was legitimated by a modernist ideology of state control over territory and spread to feed the "insatiable appetite" of the US and Japan (Tucker 2007).

In the era of flexible accumulation, while urban manufacturing grew via offshoring to benefit from Southeast Asia's cheap labour, the extraction of value from forest and land resources remained important. Though macroeconomic data show a decline in the agricultural sector's share of the economy to less than 20%, except in Cambodia and Myanmar (see Hirsch, this volume), extraction broadly construed continues to underpin the region's economies. In the Philippines, mining companies have relied for a century on both expansive land appropriations and cheap labour exploitation (Camba 2016). In Malaysia, raw natural resource exports account for 11% of GDP but manufacturing, "mainly of said natural resources", accounts for another 40% (Varkkey 2014: 195). In Indonesia, resource-based exports, including minimal processing, have accounted for roughly 40% of total exports for the past two decades (Gellert 2019). In the post-socialist states, such as Cambodia and Myanmar, the state has struggled to control the forests, via both violent and legal methods of oppression and exclusion of indigenous populations, to support lucrative earnings (Hughes, this volume).

The contradictions of economic growth and environmental degradation seem only to have sharpened in the hyperglobalisation era, when the pattern of accumulation via limited manufacturing and intensive resource extraction has produced what might be termed hyper-degradation. One key difference from the earlier period of flexible accumulation is the role of China as importer and investor. The commodity price boom (ca. 2000–2013) was led especially by Chinese (and also Indian) demand and spurred export earnings, especially in palm oil and coal, but also in rubber, cacao, coffee and mineral commodities.

In 2014, palm oil contributed US$12bn of export earnings in Malaysia and US$17.5bn (second only to coal) in Indonesia. Indonesian coal saw export growth of 15% per year from 2003 to 2013, peaking at US$26bn in 2012 (Gellert 2019). This boom in mining low-quality thermal coal (including lignite grade) made Indonesia the world's number two exporter of coal after Australia. In 2016, Indonesia produced 350 million tonnes coal equivalent (Mtce), of which 290 Mtce was exported, mostly to India, China and other Asian destinations (IEA 2017). Vietnam ranks second in regional coal production, with 30 Mtce of high-quality anthracite coal, three-quarters of which is exported to China.

Both commodities have serious environmental effects and have provoked widespread social conflict. By 2017, unstoppable growth of oil palm plantations had gobbled up huge swathes of land, with 70% of Malaysian agricultural land devoted to the crop, increasing social conflicts over local and indigenous rights to land (McCarthy and Robinson 2016). Although data are (again) uncertain, Indonesian land devoted to oil palm plantations skyrocketed from less than 4 million hectares in 2000 to over 12 million by 2014 (see Fig. 14.1 in Hirsch, this volume), relying on conversion of forests often previously logged over. NGOs continue to document myriad land conflicts and advocate for those losing land (Colchester and Chao 2018). The NGO *Konsorsium Pembaruan Agraria*, for example, found 410 conflicts on over 800,000 ha in 2018 with one-third of cases related to plantations. Although not as vast as plantations, coal mining is land-extensive and, if the labour conditions of extraction are not precarious enough, mining leaves behind dangerous and contaminated pits.

Yet, palm oil and coal provide opportunities for domestic accumulation, and they have continued to grow even after the boom subsided. The growth spurred by the commodities boom has created vast wealth among well-connected oligarchs. Southeast Asian corporations with legal domiciles in Indonesia, Malaysia and Singapore (and holding companies in the British Virgin Islands) dominate control of land and basic palm oil processing (Pye 2018; Teoh 2012). As a so-called "flex crop", palm oil allows producers to respond to global market prices and adjust end products between food, feed, biofuel and other commercial products. Coal is able to move from export to domestic sales and back again as global demand and price have recovered from 2016 lows, leaving policy-makers with the question of how to balance rising domestic electricity demand with exports that are more lucrative to the coal companies (Reuters 2018). In the lead-up to Indonesia's 2019 election, the government capped the price on coal sold to the national electricity company at US$70 per tonne as part of the 25% domestic market obligation. Domestic coal producing firms have been able to dominate particularly after a wave of resource nationalism that was more pervasive in a sector that has fewer downstream products and dominant transnational buyers than palm oil (Warburton 2017). Not surprisingly, politicians on both sides of the 2019 presidential election own significant stakes in the coal sector (Greenpeace et al. 2018).

Although much resource extraction is focused on export markets, the region continues to experience high economic growth rates supported by domestic consumption. Since the Asian financial crisis, manufacturing had been slow to return to the region and developmentalist ambitions to "capture the gains" from high-tech and other high value-added manufacturing industries have not come to fruition. The growth of mega-urban regions with millions relying on low-wage jobs under precarious sub-contracting arrangements persists, however (Jones 2014; Kalleberg and Hewison 2012). Underlying it all is a powerful development-as-growth ideology that ignores the environmental side of the growth equation. Reliance on cars by those who can afford them is widespread and, until recent Chinese-backed projects, investment in public transport infrastructures was limited. Although industry leads energy demand, transport is the fastest growing sector. Supported by consumer credit, the region's passenger vehicle stock more than doubled to 36 million from 2006 to 2016, and analysts see room for growth adding to urban traffic congestion. The growth in cars is accompanied by a lack of emissions standards, leading to projections that fuel economy will be 20% below global averages by 2040, further exacerbating air quality concerns (IEA 2017: 21).

Efforts to expand the electricity supply, a core aspect of the region's growth and extraction model, have increasingly relied on hydropower and coal (see Hatcher, this volume). Hydropower dominates on mainland Southeast Asia, especially in Cambodia and Myanmar, where it accounts for 50% and 60% of electricity, respectively (IEA 2017: 25). Ignoring decades of criticism of dams' negative impacts on local economies and biodiversity, more dams are planned in Southeast Asia than any other region, with over 100 projected to be built (Hirsch 2016; Hughes 2017: 12). While the World Bank is reportedly cautious, it provided "deal-making" support to the Nam Theun 2 (NT2) hydropower project in Laos (Baird and Quastel 2015). The Asian Development Bank and Chinese policy banks have provided increasing support. Dams have direct impacts on biodiversity decline, as well as climate change due to methane from decomposition in inundated areas. Diverse livelihoods of local people that have relied on land are often marginalised in the process.

Coal-fired electrical plants have also continued to grow in the region (see Hatcher, this volume). Regionally, coal-fired plants are supported by Japan. Japan's Bank for International Cooperation plans to provide up to US$5.2bn in financing for six coal-fired power plants in Asia, including in Vietnam and Indonesia (Sugiura and Okutsu 2018). As Table 15.2 shows,

Table 15.2 Coal-fired electrical power in Southeast Asia, China and India

	Existing plants MW	Rank	Coal MW/1000 people[a]	New coal plants (>35 MW) built 2006–18 MW	Rank	Announced + pre-permit + permitted plants MW	Rank	Under construction MW	Rank
Cambodia	505	60	0.03	505	35	3190	18	0	–
Indonesia	28,472	10	0.11	20,372	4	21,069	5	12,842	3
Laos	1878	43	0.28	1878	22	0	–	0	–
Malaysia	11,008	18	0.35	7098	9	0	–	2600	11
Philippines	8123	23	0.08	4366	13	9428	8	3040	10
Thailand	5607	25	0.08	2365	20	3506	16	600	24
Vietnam	16,171	15	0.17	14,776	6	35,890	4	9435	4
China	957,280	1	0.69	715,406	1	76,325	1	126,339	1
India	219,015	3	0.17	156,969	2	63,331	2	39,368	2
World	2,002,620	–	0.27	1,027,015	–	365,049	–	236,919	–
Less China and India	826,325	–	0.17	154,640	–	225,393	–	71,212	–
Of which Southeast Asia	71,764	–	0.11	51,360	–	73,083	–	28,517	–

Source: End Coal (2018)

Note: [a]Figures per 1000 people calculated using Carroll, this volume, Table 2.1

Indonesia leads the region in existing coal-fired electrical power plants. Malaysia and Laos lead electricity production capacity, but Laos's 1878 MW are all exported to Thailand (Lao PDR 2018). Indonesia and Vietnam rank fourth and sixth in the world in terms of recent coal plant construction. Leaving China and India—the two giants of coal-fired electricity production—out of the equation, the Southeast Asian total accounts for almost half of the world's remaining 155,000 MW. Even Singapore opened its first coal-fired electrical plant in 2013 to supply petrochemical industries. Coal accounts for around 40% of Southeast Asia's primary energy production, underpins the region's role as a net energy exporter, and fulfils a growing portion of domestic industrial energy needs, which now exceed residential and commercial building use (IEA 2017).

Limits of Environmental Governance

In seeking to alter the pattern of extractivism and growth-led accumulation that has only expanded under hyperglobalisation, multilateral policy-makers, mainstream scholars and NGOs have turned to "governance"—establishing clear policies, rule of law and strong environmental management. Governance approaches assume that states can rationally "manage" their sovereign territories' resources. Yet, as social and political relations in Southeast Asia, and hence the very nature of state power, have been fundamentally shaped by the extractivist mode of accumulation I describe, such approaches are severely limited. I demonstrate this below via several brief examples: national climate change commitments, trans-national support for efforts to reduce deforestation (via REDD+), and addressing forest fires and unsustainable palm oil via private voluntary industrial (RSPO) standards.

In addressing the climate crisis, international negotiations for the Paris Agreement in 2015 adopted nationally determined contributions (NDCs). The voluntary NDCs of Southeast Asian countries are modest departures from business-as-usual and do not address the basic contradiction of accumulation based heavily on over-exploitation of natural resources. For example, Malaysia promotes mandatory use of a 5% blend of palm biodiesel, thereby expanding the demand for palm oil (UNFCCC 2015). The Philippines' targets are pitched to achieve the goal of staying within the Copenhagen 2 degrees of global warming (not Paris's aspirational 1.5 degrees), but even that is unlikely if planned expansion of coal-fired power plant capacity goes ahead (Climate Action Tracker 2019). Indonesia commits to increasing its renewable energy share to 30%, but given the powerful interests profiting from the sector and the push to provide electricity to its large population, it has not shelved plans to double coal-fired electricity production. Moreover, while fighting the EU's phase-out of palm oil biofuel in 2019, the Indonesian government extended a domestically mandated 20% blend of biodiesel to non-public transportation, which will create a 2.5 million tonne increase in palm oil demand (USDA 2018).

Because land and forests are arguably as important as energy in addressing the climate crisis, much of the region's efforts are focused on REDD+ (Reduced Emissions from Deforestation and forest Degradation plus conservation, sustainable management of forests and enhancement of forest carbon stocks). Developed under the United Nations Framework Convention on Climate Change (UNFCCC), REDD+ aims eventually to create a carbon market and allow rich countries to purchase REDD+ credits to offset their own emissions. For now, it adds "results-based finance" to conservation initiatives by linking payments from wealthier countries to proven results in reducing deforestation (Seymour and Busch 2016). The basic premise is that because deforestation of carbon-rich tropical forests is such an important contributor to global warming, averting it deserves international financial support in the form of payments to the government, provided deforestation can be reduced. The implementation of REDD+ relies on local and indigenous people to resist incentives and pressures to clear forests for commercial use, but also to abandon forest clearing for their own subsistence needs, effectively losing control of forest areas they have claimed for generations.

Indonesia and Brazil were the first to enter bilateral agreements with Norway for performance payments. In 2010, Norway committed to providing US$1bn to Indonesia, based on institutional and legal reforms to the forestry sector and a commitment to reduce emissions by at least 29% by 2030 compared to business-as-usual, and up to 41% with international support. By 2014 only 4.5% of the amount had been released for the preparatory efforts (Maxton-Lee 2018). Some international advocates celebrated the first release of a results-based payment in 2019 and encouraged further international support (Seymour 2019).

The outcomes are sobering, however. Because of the huge role of plantations (and mining) in deforestation, REDD+ was accompanied by a moratorium on new permits for forest clearance. The so-called "One

Map" effort ensued to create a clear picture of the multiple forestry, mining and plantation permits and their overlap with conservation and other uses of land. Indigenous rights to the forest were not recognised despite a 2013 Constitutional Court ruling acknowledging them. The moratorium has been flouted, however, in the context of political decentralisation, by companies and local government officials who have had their permits and clearing activities "legalised" at the national level (Gellert and Andiko 2015). Greenpeace (2015: 6) concluded that one-fifth of deforestation from 2011 to 2013 (the moratorium's first two years) occurred "within areas mapped as covered by the moratorium" (see also Maxton-Lee 2018).

In other words, what seems like a technical exercise is fraught with social and political conflicts. The One Map effort has gone through multiple iterations, revisions and alterations to get it right, and the 2015 version of the map still had 1.5 million hectares *within* existing concession areas. Even in December 2018, when President Joko Widodo at last launched the One Map reference database in order "to prevent any overlap, to give certainty, to give clarity, and to have consistency in building this nation", he simultaneously noted that there were 40,000 km^2 of overlap among the 85 "reconciled" maps and that 12,000 km^2 of indigenous lands, already formally recognised at local levels, were excluded (Jong 2018).

Some maintain faith that international funding for REDD+ has merely been too low, slow and constrained, adding that most indigenous groups have "cautiously embraced" REDD+ as a way to value their forests and strengthen their rights (Seymour and Busch 2016: 21). Yet indigenous forests and lands are recognised in this process either for their market value or for not being used by indigenous people at all. Given the continuing commodification and land conversion, others argue that the future for indigenous and precarious populations "lies not in expanding markets but in better sharing the wealth we already have" (Fletcher et al. 2017: 723).

While the effectiveness of REDD+ relies on government power limiting private accumulation, from which officials often benefit, the expansion of private authority in the global economy is illustrated by the establishment of the Roundtable on Sustainable Palm Oil (RSPO) in 2004 in response to consumer pressure after the 1997–98 forest fires (Gellert 1998; Pye 2018). RSPO is a voluntary industry effort to promote legal and sustainable palm oil products. It establishes environmental and social criteria, including provision of fair working conditions, recognition of local people's land and rights, and no clearing of primary forest. Companies must comply with these criteria (verified by independent certifiers) in order to produce Certified Sustainable Palm Oil (CSPO). Member companies account for half the world's production and 19% of palm oil is certified. The goal is to increase that figure, so that "we don't need to cut down trees to produce palm oil" (RSPO 2019a). Member companies purportedly benefit from the market access that the RSPO label confers, with CSPO now accounting for 21% of global markets. This market-based mechanism relies on consumers who are willing to pay more for CSPO, but the partially sensitive markets of Europe trail the non-sensitive, leading importing countries of China and India. RSPO reports that only half of the CSPO produced is sold, due to the complexities of supply flow logistics and the fact that many consumers are industries (e.g., cosmetics, animal feed) which are not willing to pay the US$30 per tonne premium (Raghu 2019).

Moreover, the RSPO framework's effectiveness in reining in bad behaviour by oil palm plantation companies, including violations of its sustainability criteria, is limited. In February 2019, for example, the Rainforest Action Network (RAN) finally succeeded, after more than two years of formal complaints, in removing Indonesian company PT London Sumatra's sustainability certificate (RAN 2016; RSPO 2019b). The Indonesian producers' association, GAPKI, has effectively withdrawn from the RSPO by setting up a less stringent mandatory certification body, ISPO. Given that Indonesia and Malaysia together dominate over 80% of the market and 90% of CSPO, this is a significant move. The increased importance of palm oil money to decentralised electoral politics in Indonesia further abets the sector (Gecko Project and Mongabay 2018). One analyst summarises the reliance on market certification and legal designations of CSPO as part of a "fetishisation" of certification with "no impact" on the regional dynamic of plantation expansion and the land acquisition and exploitative labour practices that undergird expansion (Pye 2018: 3).

Conclusion

This chapter has argued that the environment is not an issue area that can be separated from the overall thrust of the region's political economy. The region's litany of environmental problems, including the ongoing disasters of biodiversity loss and climate change, cannot be simply ameliorated through improved governance, international payments to cooperative states, or voluntary market mechanisms. These problems are rooted in deeply embedded patterns of accumulation and attendant social and political relations, with their roots in the colonial era, which serve to enrich a small class of oligarchs benefiting from the status quo. The rapacious extraction of value from natural resources as commodities and from cheap and precarious labour in manufacturing also bolsters the increasingly urban and consumer-based growth that congests and pollutes Southeast Asia's mega urban centres. The scale and permanence of the ecological destruction accompanying growth and "development" have only increased this century.

Against commonly held neo-Malthusian assumptions of population growth translating almost automatically into environmental degradation, it is important to recognise the problem as one of *capital*-nature relations. Political support for the region's environmentally destructive mode of accumulation has been dominated by global capital, international financial institutions, and allied elements of domestic states, working in conjunction with the domestic oligarchs. Opposition from NGOs, activists, indigenous groups, and fragmented and nascent social movements is important but has not gained sufficient ground to alter the overall path of *development as growth* in Southeast Asia, notwithstanding the opening up of political space following democratisation in some regional states. Disturbingly, an increasing turn to right-wing populist authoritarianism has taken place in the region that bodes ill for attempts to contest the environmentally destructive pathway of capitalist development (Robison and Hadiz, this volume).

References

ADB [Asian Development Bank]. (2018). *Key indicators for Asia and the Pacific 2018*. Asian Development Bank. www.adb.org/statistics. Accessed 6 May 2019.

Baird, I. G., & Quastel, N. (2015). Rescaling and reordering nature–society relations: The Nam Theun 2 hydropower dam and Laos–Thailand electricity networks. *Annals of the Association of American Geographers, 105*(6), 1221–1239.

Brecht, H., Dasgupta, S., Laplante, B., Murray, S., & Wheeler, D. (2012). Sea-level rise and storm surges: High stakes for a small number of developing countries. *The Journal of Environment & Development, 21*(1), 120–138.

Burke, L., Selig, E., & Spalding, M. (2002). *Reefs at risk in Southeast Asia*. Washington, DC: World Resources Institute. https://www.wri.org/publication/reefs-risk-southeast-asia. Accessed: 24 Apr 2019.

Burton, M., & Somerville, P. (2019). De-growth: A defence. *New Left Review, 115*(Jan–Feb), 95–104.

Camba, A. A. (2016). Philippine mining capitalism: The changing terrains of struggle in the neoliberal mining regime. *ASEAS – Austrian Journal of South-East Asian Studies, 9*(1), 69–86.

Climate Action Tracker. (2019). https://climateactiontracker.org/. Accessed 30 Apr 2019.

Colchester, M., & Chao, S. (Eds.). (2018). *Conflict or consent? The oil palm sector at a crossroads*. Moreton-in-Marsh: Forest Peoples Programme, Sawit Watch and TUK INDONESIA.

Colchester, M., Jiwan, N., Andiko, Sirait, M., Firdaus, A. Y., Surambo, A., & Pane, H. (2006). *Promised land. Palm oil and land acquisition in Indonesia: Implications for local communities and indigenous peoples*. Moreton-in-Marsh/Bogor: Forest Peoples Programme/Perkumpulan Sawit Watch.

Conway, J. (2015). *Indonesia's palm oil fires: Interview with Friends of the Earth Indonesia*. https://medium.com/economic-policy/indonesia-s-palm-oil-fires-interview-with-friends-of-the-earth-indonesia-eed27e2518cf. Accessed 25 Apr 2019.

Cramb, R., & McCarthy, J. (Eds.). (2016). *The oil palm complex: Smallholders, agribusiness and the state in Indonesia and Malaysia*. Singapore: National University of Singapore Press.

Curtis, P. G., Slay, C. M., Harris, N. L., Tyukavina, A., & Hansen, M. C. (2018). Classifying drivers of global forest loss. *Science, 361*(6407), 1108–1111.

Dasgupta, S., Laplante, B., Meisner, C., Wheeler, D., & Yan, J. (2007). *The impact of sea level rise on developing countries: A comparative analysis* (Research working paper no. WPS 4136). Washington, DC: World Bank. http://documents.worldbank.org/curated/en/156401468136816684/The-impact-of-sea-level-rise-on-developing-countries-a-comparative-analysis. Accessed 25 Apr 2019.

End Coal. (2018). *Summary statistics*. https://endcoal.org/global-coal-plant-tracker/summary-statistics/. Accessed 10 Dec 2018.

FAO [Food and Agriculture Organization]. (2011). *Southeast Asian forests and forestry to 2020: Sub-regional report of the second Asia-Pacific forestry sector outlook study*. Bangkok: FAO. www.fao.org/3/i1964e/i1964e00.htm. Accessed 31 Mar 2019.

Field, R. D., van der Werf, G. R., Fanin, T., Fetzer, E. J., Fuller, R., et al. (2016). Indonesian fire activity and smoke pollution in 2015 show persistent nonlinear sensitivity to El Niño-induced drought. *Proceedings of the National Academy of Sciences, 113*(33), 9204–9209.

Fletcher, R., Dressler, W., Büscher, B., & Anderson, Z. R. (2017). Debating REDD+ and its implications: Reply to Angelsen et al. *Conservation Biology, 31*(3), 721–723.

Gecko Project & Mongabay. (2018, April 18) Ghosts in the machine: The land deals behind the downfall of Indonesia's top judge. *Mongabay Series: Indonesia for Sale*. https://news.mongabay.com/2018/04/ghosts-in-the-machine-the-land-deals-behind-the-downfall-of-indonesias-top-judge/. Accessed 20 Apr 2018.

Gellert, P. K. (1998). A brief history and analysis of Indonesia's forest fire crisis. *Indonesia, 65*, 63–85.

Gellert, P. K. (2019). Neoliberalism and altered state developmentalism in the twenty-first century extractive regime of Indonesia. *Globalizations, 16*(3), 894–918.

Gellert, P. K., & Andiko. (2015). The quest for legal certainty and the reorganization of power: Struggles over forest law, permits, and rights in Indonesia. *The Journal of Asian Studies, 74*(03), 639–666.

Global Forest Watch. (2019). *Tree cover loss.* https://data.globalforestwatch.org/datasets/63f9425c45404c36a23495ed7bef1314. Accessed 8 May 2019.

Greenpeace. (2015). *Indonesia's forests under fire.* Amsterdam: Greenpeace International. https://www.greenpeace.org/archive-international/en/publications/Campaign-reports/Forests-Reports/Under-Fire/. Accessed 16 Feb 2018.

Greenpeace, JATAM, ICW, & Auriga. (2018). *Coalruption: Elite politik dalam pusaran disnis batu bara* [*Coalruption: Elite politics in the whirlpool of coal business*]. http://m.greenpeace.org/seasia/id/PageFiles/110812/COALRUPTION_INDONESIA_WEB.pdf. Accessed 24 Dec 2018.

The Guardian. (2016, September 21). Indonesia dismisses study showing forest fire haze killed more than 100,000 people. *The Guardian.* https://www.theguardian.com/environment/2016/sep/21/indonesia-dismisses-study-showing-forest-fire-haze-killed-more-than-100000-people. Accessed 25 Apr 2019.

The Guardian. (2018, October 8). We have 12 years to limit climate change catastrophe, warns UN. *The Guardian.* https://www.theguardian.com/environment/2018/oct/08/global-warming-must-not-exceed-15c-warns-landmark-un-report. Accessed 12 Dec 2018.

Hameiri, S., & Jones, L. (2015). *Governing borderless threats: Non-traditional security and the politics of state transformation.* Cambridge: Cambridge University Press.

Harris, N., Petersen, R., Davis, C., & Payne, O. (2016). *Global forest watch and the forest resources assessment, explained in 5 graphics.* World Resources Institute. https://www.wri.org/blog/2016/08/insider-global-forest-watch-and-forest-resources-assessment-explained-5-graphics. Accessed 14 May 2019.

Hatch, W., & Yamamura, K. (1996). *Asia in Japan's embrace: Building a regional production alliance.* New York: Cambridge University Press.

Hirsch, P. (2016). The shifting regional geopolitics of Mekong dams. *Political Geography, 51*, 63–74.

Hirsch, P. (2017). Introduction: The environment in Southeast Asia's past, present, and future. In P. Hirsch (Ed.), *Routledge handbook of the environment in Southeast Asia* (pp. 3–13). New York: Routledge.

Hughes, A. C. (2017). Understanding the drivers of Southeast Asian biodiversity loss. *Ecosphere, 8*(1), e01624.

Hughes, A. C. (2018). Have Indo-Malaysian forests reached the end of the road? *Biological Conservation, 223*, 129–137.

IEA. (2017, November 14). *World energy outlook 2017.* International Energy Agency.

IPBES [Intergovernmental Science-Policy Platform on Biodiversity and Ecosystem Services]. (2019, May 6). *Media release: Nature's dangerous decline "unprecedented"; Species extinction rates "accelerating".* IPBES. https://www.ipbes.net/news/Media-Release-Global-Assessment. Accessed 7 May 2019.

IPCC [Intergovernmental Panel on Climate Change]. (2013). *Climate change 2013: The physical science basis.* New York: Cambridge University Press. https://www.ipcc.ch/report/ar5/wg1/. Accessed 25 Apr 2019.

IPCC. (2014). *Climate change 2014: Synthesis report. Contributions of working groups I, II, and III to the fifth assessment report of the Intergovernmental Panel on Climate Change.* Geneva: IPCC. www.ipcc.ch/report/ar5/syr/. Accessed 31 Mar 2019.

IPCC (2018). *Global warming of 1.5°C. An IPCC special report on the impacts of global warming of 1.5°C above pre-industrial levels and related global greenhouse gas emission pathways, in the context of strengthening the global response to the threat of climate change, sustainable development, and efforts to eradicate poverty.* Geneva: IPCC.

Jambeck, J. R., Geyer, R., Wilcox, C., Siegler, T. R., Perryman, M., et al. (2015). Plastic waste inputs from land into the ocean. *Science, 347*(6223), 768–771.

Jones, G. W. (2014). Urbanisation and development in South-east Asia. *Malaysian Journal of Economic Studies, 51*(1), 103–120.

Jong, H. N. (2018, August 10). *Indonesia's "one-map" database blasted for excluding indigenous lands.* https://news.mongabay.com/2018/08/indonesias-one-map-database-blasted-for-excluding-indigenous-lands/. Accessed 15 Mar 2019.

Kalleberg, A. L., & Hewison, K. (2012). Precarious work and flexibilization in South and Southeast Asia. *American Behavioral Scientist, 57*(4), 395–402.

Lao PDR. (2018). *Lao PDR energy statistics 2018.* Jakarta: Economic Research Institute for ASEAN and East Asia. http://www.eria.org/uploads/media/0_Lao_PDR_Energy_Statistics_2018_complete_book.pdf. Accessed 7 May 2019.

Marlier, M. E., DeFries, R. S., Kim, P. S., Koplitz, S. N., Jacob, D. J., et al. (2015). Fire emissions and regional air quality impacts from fires in oil palm, timber, and logging concessions in Indonesia. *Environmental Research Letters, 10*(8), 085005.

Maxton-Lee, B. (2018). *"Common sense" versus good sense: A critical analysis of forest conservation and deforestation in Indonesia.* PhD dissertation, Hong Kong University.

McCarthy, J. F., & Robinson, K. (2016). *Land and development in Indonesia: Searching for the people's sovereignty.* Singapore: ISEAS-Yusof Ishak Institute.

Monbiot, G. (2015, October 30). Indonesia is burning so why is the world turning away? *The Guardian.* https://www.theguardian.com/commentisfree/2015/oct/30/indonesia-fires-disaster-21st-century-world-media. Accessed 12 Dec 2018.

Moore, J. W. (Ed.). (2016). *Anthropocene or capitalocene? Nature, history, and the crisis of capitalism.* Oakland: PM Press.

Potter, L. (1993). The onslaught on the forests in South-East Asia. In H. Brookfield & Y. Byron (Eds.), *South-East Asia's environmental future: The search for sustainability* (pp. 103–123). New York: United Nations University Press.

Purnomo, H., Shantiko, B., Sitorus, S., Gunawan, H., Achdiawan, R., et al. (2017). Fire economy and actor network of forest and land fires in Indonesia. *Forest Policy and Economics, 78*, 21–31.

Pye, O. (2018). Commodifying sustainability: Development, nature and politics in the palm oil industry. *World Development.* https://doi.org/10.1016/j.worlddev.2018.02.014.

Raghu, A. (2019, January 13). The world has loads of sustainable palm oil… But no one wants it. *Bloomberg.* https://www.bloomberg.com/news/articles/2019-01-13/world-has-loads-of-sustainable-palm-oil-just-no-one-wants-it. Accessed 9 May 2019.

RAN. (2016). *The human cost of conflict palm oil: Indofood, Pepsico's hidden link to worker exploitation in Indonesia.* Rainforest Action Network, Oppuk and ILRF. https://d3n8a8pro7vhmx.cloudfront.net/rainforestactionnetwork/pages/15889/attachments/original/1467043668/The_Human_Cost_of_Conflict_Palm_Oil_RAN.pdf?1467043668. Accessed 12 Aug 2017.

Reuters. (2018, March 8). Indonesia caps domestic coal price for power stations, could hit miners. *Reuters.* https://www.reuters.com/article/us-indonesia-coal/indonesia-caps-domestic-coal-price-for-power-stations-could-hit-miners-idUSKCN1GL0F7?rpc=401&. Accessed 28 Apr 2019.

RSPO [Roundtable on Sustainable Palm Oil]. (2019a). *Roundtable on Sustainable Palm Oil.* www.rspo.org. Accessed 8 May 2019.

RSPO. (2019b). *Final decision on complaint against PT. PP London Sumatra Indonesia Tbk.* Roundtable on Sustainable Palm Oil. https://askrspo.force.com/Complaint/s/case/50090000028ErzBAAS/detail. Accessed 12 Mar 2019.

Seymour, F. (2019, February 21). *Indonesia reduces deforestation, Norway to pay up.* Global Forest Watch blog. https://blog.globalforestwatch.org/climate/indonesia-reduces-deforestation-norway-to-pay-up. Accessed 17 Apr 2019.

Seymour, F., & Busch, J. (2016). *Why forests? Why now? The science, economics, and politics of tropical forests and climate change.* Washington, DC: Center for Global Development.

Sugiura, E., & Okutsu, A. (2018, November 21). Why Japan finds coal hard to quit. *Nikkei Asian Review.* https://asia.nikkei.com/Spotlight/Cover-Story/Why-Japan-finds-coal-hard-to-quit. Accessed 4 Feb 2019.

Teoh, C. H. (2012). Malaysian corporations as strategic players in Southeast Asia's palm oil industry. In O. Pye & J. Bhattacharya (Eds.), *The palm oil controversy in Southeast Asia: A transnational perspective* (pp. 19–47). Singapore: ISEAS.

Tucker, R. P. (2007). *Insatiable appetite: The United States and the ecological degradation of the tropical world*. Lanham: Rowman & Littlefield Publishers.

UCS [Union of Concerned Scientists]. (2018). *Each country's share of CO2 emissions*. Union of Concerned Scientists. https://www.ucsusa.org/global-warming/science-and-impacts/science/each-countrys-share-of-co2.html. Accessed 8 May 2019.

UNEP [United Nations Environment Program]. (2016). *Snapshot of the world's water quality*. Nairobi: United Nations Environment Programme. https://uneplive.unep.org/media/docs/assessments/unep_wwqa_report_web.pdf. Accessed 8 May 2019.

UNFCCC [United Nations Framework Convention on Climate Change]. (2015). *Intended nationally determined contribution (various governments)*. https://www4.unfccc.int. Accessed 2 Dec 2018.

USDA [United States Department of Agriculture]. (2018). *Indonesia expands biodiesel mandate*. GAIN reports, Foreign Agricultural Service. https://gain.fas.usda.gov. Accessed 2 Dec 2018.

Varkkey, H. (2014). Natural resource extraction and political dependency: Malaysia as a rentier state. In M. L. Weiss (Ed.), *Routledge handbook of contemporary Malaysia* (pp. 189–199). New York: Routledge.

Veron, J. E. N., Hoegh-Guldberg, O., Lenton, T. M., Lough, J. M., Obura, D. O., et al. (2009). The coral reef crisis: The critical importance of <350ppm CO2. *Marine Pollution Bulletin, 58*(10), 1428–1436.

Warburton, E. (2017). Resource nationalism in Indonesia: Ownership structures and sectoral variation in mining and palm oil. *Journal of East Asian Studies, 17*(3), 285–312.

WHO [World Health Organization]. (2016). *Ambient air pollution: A global assessment of exposure and burden of disease*. Geneva: World Health Organization. https://www.who.int/phe/publications/air-pollution-global-assessment/en/. Accessed 4 Apr 2019.

WHO. (2018, May 2). 9 out of 10 people worldwide breathe polluted air, but more countries are taking action. *World Health Organization News*. https://www.who.int/news-room/detail/02-05-2018-9-out-of-10-people-worldwide-breathe-polluted-air-but-more-countries-are-taking-action. Accessed 18 Feb 2019.

World Bank. (2016). *The cost of fire: An economic analysis of Indonesia's 2015 fire crisis*. Washington, DC: World Bank. http://documents.worldbank.org/curated/en/776101467990969768/pdf/103668-BRI-Cost-of-Fires-Knowledge-Note-PUBLIC-ADD-NEW-SERIES-Indonesia-Sustainable-Landscapes-Knowledge-Note.pdf

Index

A
Acid mine drainage, 329
Advanced Micro Devices, 68–69
Agency, 13–14
　historical institutionalism, 12, 13
　poor people, 272, 273, 288
Agribusiness, 341
　contract farming, 351
　crony capitalism, 352
　globalisation, 349–350
　Indonesia, 184
　land-grabbing, 351, 352
　Myanmar, 116
　Thailand, 359
Agriculture and agrarian relations, 341, 349, 360
　class relations, 341
　Cold War, 342–343
　collectivisation programmes, 344
　communist regimes, 344
　contract farming, 351
　de-agrarianisation, 353–355
　displacements, 354–355
　gross domestic product, contribution to, 354
　industrialisation, impact of, 345
　neoliberalism, 348; international institutions, 348; modernisation ideologies, 348, 352
　non-agrarian demands, 354
　non-plantation agriculture, 120
　non-socialist countries, 344; land reform, 343
　plantation agriculture, 120
　plantations, 120, 351
　production growth, 342
　regional investment; cash crops, 350
　self-sufficiency, 344
　socialist countries; collectivisation programmes, 344; land reform, 342
　war, impact on, 122
Aid, *see* International aid
Air pollution, 329, 368–369
　public health, 373

Amsterdam School, 179, 192
  accumulation, 179–181
  Eurocentric nature, 192
  internationalisation of capital;
    Indonesia, 183–186; Malaysia,
    189–192; Singapore, 186–189
  production of commodities, 179
  sale of commodities, 179
  transformation of statehood, 180
Anti-money-laundering (AML)
    regulation
  Asia/Pacific Group on Money
    Laundering, 205, 207–209
Anti-welfare policies, 229
  women, 239–243
APT Macroeconomic Research Office
    (AMRO), 207
ASEAN Agreement on Disaster
    Management and Emergency
    Response (AADMER), 212
ASEAN Community, 210
ASEAN Comprehensive Investment
    Agreement, 186
ASEAN Economic Community
    (AEC), 28, 188, 200
  automotive sector, 219
  aviation sector, 218
  blueprints and action plans, 213
  dispute settlement mechanism, 213
  domestic power relations, 218
  energy sector, 219
  goals, 212–213
  implementation, 214–218
  international standards, 213
  movement of skilled labour, 219
ASEAN Free Trade Agreement
    (AFTA), 200
  open regionalism, 203
ASEAN Free Trade Area (AFTA), 191
ASEAN Qualification Reference
    Framework (AQRF), 266
ASEAN Regional Forum (ARF), 200
Asian Development Bank (ADB), 27

environmental protection, 376
extractive industries, reform of, 326
international aid, 295
land use policies, 348
marketisation, promotion of, 27
Asian financial crisis (1997-98), 53–54
  embedded mercantilism, 203
  IMF assistance, 24, 237
  impact, 55, 298
  Indonesia, 25, 54–55
  Malaysia, 24, 54–55; economic
    restructuring, 192
  reform of extractive industries, 326
  regionalisation of capital
    accumulation, 182
  rise of populism, 162–163
  Thailand, 24
  women, impact on, 237–238;
    engagement in the informal
    economy, 238;
    unpaid domestic work, 238
Asian Infrastructure Investment Bank
    (AIIB), 334
  China, 309
  environmental protection, 376
  international aid, 295
Asia-Pacific Economic Cooperation
    (APEC), 200
  extractive industries, 328
  open regionalism, 203
Asia/Pacific Group on Money
    Laundering
  anti-money-laundering regulation,
    205, 207–209
  Financial Action Task Force, 207
  regulatory regionalism, 207–209
Association of Southeast Asian
    Nations (ASEAN),
    24, 26, 199
  ASEAN Agreement on Disaster
    Management and Emergency
    Response, 212 (*see also* ASEAN
    Economic Community (AEC))

ASEAN Plus Three, 28, 200, 203
  expanding membership, 56
  extractive industries, 328
  regulatory regionalism, 209;
    ASEAN Community, 209–212
  Third Indochina War, 142
August Revolution (1945), 135, 136
Australia
  international aid, 295, 309, 355
  Murdoch School, 14
Australian Agency for International
    Development (AusAID), 355
Authoritarianism, 12, 23, 92, 112,
    294, 306, 382
  authoritarian developmentalism,
    22–23, 134
  bureaucratic-military
    authoritarianism, 114, 115
  capitalism and, 89
  competitive authoritarianism, 13
  electoral authoritarianism, 13
  elite authoritarianism, 118–120, 305
  quasi-authoritarianism, 14–28
  technocratic authoritarianism,
    95–96, 160
Autocracy, 157, 158
  populism, 156
Automotive sector
  ASEAN Economic Community, 219
  Indonesia, 184; internationalisation
    of capital, 184
  subsidies, 219
Autonomy of women, 234
Aviation sector
  ASEAN Economic Community, 218
  liberalisation of markets, 215

B
Bamboo Curtain, 135
Bandung Conference (1955), 136
Bangladesh
  garment production, 37, 256

Belt and Road Initiative, 28, 69, 115,
    125, 334
Borneo
  air pollution, 373
  insurgencies, 138, 143
Brazil
  international aid, 295
  New Development Bank, 295
  populism, 155
Bribery, 47, 119, 276, 359
  See also Corruption
Brunei, 37, 138
  extractive industries, 325
  international aid, 299
  mineral resources, 323
  oil industry, 49
Buddhism
  Myanmar, 112, 128; ethnic
    insurgencies, 125
Bureaucratic capacity, 7–9, 306
Burma
  conflict, 51
  land nationalisation, 343
  leftist movements and parties,
    137–138, 143
  state socialism, 44, 53, 111,
    135, 142
  See also Myanmar

C
Cambodia, 18, 25, 70
  asset-stripping of natural
    resources, 114
  bureaucratic-military
    authoritarianism; asset-stripping
    of natural resources,
    114; business elites,
    support from, 115
  capitalist development, 92
  Chinese investors, 115
  collectivisation programmes, 344
  communism, 44, 114

Cambodia (cont.)
  economic liberalisation, 112
  economic ranking, 63
  female employment, 233
  hydropower, 376
  industrial discontent, 123
  industrialisation, 27
  international aid, 298, 306, 309
  land conflicts, 122
  land-grabs, 352
  land-titling programmes, 356
  Maoism, 140–141
  post-socialist transformation of property relations, 345
  pro-market reforms, 53, 56, 112
  state-building interventions, 26
  state-business relationships, 114–115
  state socialism, 111
  transition to market economies, 114–115
Cambodian People's Party (CPP), 112
Capital accumulation, 28, 62, 181
  Amsterdam School, 179–181
  Indonesia, 101, 106
  land acquisition, 101, 254
  Malaysia, 191
  regionalisation, 182
  Singapore, 99, 186–189
  state capitalism, 186
  transnationalism, 178
Capitalist development
  former socialist countries, 92
  Indonesia, 91
  institutionalised conflict, 90–91
  Murdoch School, 90–91
  Philippines, 91
  political institutions, 93
Cash crops, 120, 350
  capitalist development, 16, 120
  competition with other land uses, 354

Cebu Declaration on the Protection and Promotion of the Rights of Migrant Workers, 2007, 261
Chiang Mai Initiative Multilateralisation (CMIM)
  IMF standards, 206
  monitoring and surveillance mechanisms, 207
  origins, 205
  regulatory regionalism; good governance condition, 206
China, 18
  ASEAN Plus Three, 200
  automotive sector, 68
  Belt and Road Initiative, 28, 69, 115, 125, 334
  communism, 45
  'factory to the world', 37, 59
  foreign direct investment, 58, 70–71
  industrialisation, 27
  international aid, 295, 302–305; Cambodia, 306–307, 309; Indonesia, 307; Malaysia, 308; Myanmar, 309; Philippines, 307
  low-cost manufacturing, 60
  New Development Bank, 295
  World Trade Organization, 56
Chinese Cultural Revolution (1966-76), 134, 139, 141, 143
Civil society activism, 149, 258, 267, 356–358
Civil unrest, 51–52
  economic impact, 52–53 (see also Ethnic insurgencies; Rural unrest)
  solidarity movements, 51–52
  See also Civil society activism
Class relations, 6, 14, 17
  agriculture, 341, 349
  economic development, impact of, 5
  See also Middle classes; Peasant farmers; Urban poor

Climate change, 126, 367
  air pollution, 368–369
  biodiversity loss, 371–373, 381
  deforestation, 369 (*see also*
    Environmental degradation)
  nationally determined
    contributions, 378
  water pollution, 369
Coal industry, 321
  environmental degradation,
    374–375
  See also Extractive industries
Cold War, 23, 44
  agriculture and agrarian relations,
    342–343
  globalisation, onset of, 20
  international aid, 296
  political legacy, 92, 152, 171, 357
  Southeast Asian conflicts, impact on,
    20, 41, 48, 88, 122, 133,
    135, 139
  strategic commodities, 44
Collectivisation programmes
  agriculture and agrarian
    relations, 344
  Cambodia, 344
  land ownership, 344
  Laos, 344
  Vietnam, 344
Colonialism, impact of, 23, 41, 42, 44
  environmental degradation, 382
  imbalances of social and political
    power, 22–23
  independence, 41
  land and land ownership, 342, 356
  productive capacity, 42
  resistance movements, 46, 95,
    133, 143
  resource extraction, 373
  World War II, 41
Commercial, technological, and
  organizational innovation, 48–51

Commodities boom, 44, 61, 62, 112,
  114, 127, 328, 375
Communism, 44–45
  See also Leftist movements and
    parties
Communist Party of Burma (CPB),
  137, 139, 143
Communist Party of Malaysia
  (MCP), 143
Communist Party of Thailand
  (CPT), 144
Communist Party of the Philippines
  (CPP), 144, 148–149
Company mergers, acquisitions and
  joint ventures, 184
  transnationalism, 178, 184
Competition, 36
  China's emergence, impact of,
    26–27
Competitiveness, 48–57, 204,
  253, 256
Conceptualising institutions
  historical institutionalism, 5
  Murdoch School approach, 6
  Weberian approach, 5
Confucianism, 233
Consultative representation, 93
  Singapore, 97–99
Consumer electronics
  female labour, 231
Consumption
  Fordism, 43
  Murdoch School, 17
Contract farming, 351
Corporate accountability, 358
Corporate social responsibility, 331
Corruption, 294
  bribery, 47
  crony capitalism, 117, 177, 330
  land allocation, 352
  patronage, 117, 119
  See also Patronage systems

Crony capitalism, 116
  agribusiness, 351, 352
  corruption, 116, 117, 177, 330
Cross-border capitalist expansion
  company mergers, acquisitions and joint ventures, 178, 183
Cross-class alliances, 165, 170
  Indonesia, 166–168, 277–283
  Philippines, 168–170, 283–287
  Thailand, 165–167

D

Data transmission improvements, 50
Debt (private debt), 49, 61, 70
  debt bondage; low-wage migrants, 249, 256, 258
  farmer debt moratoriums, 166 (*see also* Foreign debt)
  smallholders, 343, 345
Decentralisation, 217
  Indonesia, 24, 92, 101, 167, 258, 261, 352, 381
  See also Fragmentation of state power
Defective democracies, 13, 25
Deforestation, 369–371, 374
  climate change, 372
  REDD+, 378, 379
  river and coastline degradation, 369
Democratic representation, 93
Democratisation, 12, 101, 382
Developmental state model
  Fordist development, 45
  historical institutionalism, 13
  Murdoch School approach, 18–20
  Singapore, 20–22
  Weberian approach, 8–11
Deviant democracies, 13
Discursive institutionalism, 11
Displacement
  development of agricultural land, 354–355
  peasant farmers, 351
  Philippines, 231
  urban evictions, 100, 102–103, 231, 277–278, 283–287; women, 241–243
Doi moi, *see* Pro-market reforms; Vietnam
Domestic violence, 227, 242
Donor countries
  emerging donors, 293
  traditional donors, 294
Duterte, Rodrigo, 157, 158, 160, 164, 169–170

E

East Asia Economic Caucus (EAEC), 191
East Asia Summit (EAS), 200, 203
East Timor
  annexation, 143
  Maoist rebellions, 142
  Revolutionary Front for an Independent East Timor, 143
  See also Timor-Leste
Economic globalisation
  reforms, impact of, 204
Economic liberalisation, 57, 112, 178
Economic rankings, 37, 62–63
  exports, 37
  growth, 37
  market capitalisation, 66–68
  poverty and deprivation, 37
Economic reform, 26, 57, 117, 301, 304, 306
Economy
  class structure, impact on, 5
  political conflict, impact of, 3–5
Efficiency and effectiveness of public management, 302

Electoral politics, 381
  Communist Party of the Philippines, 148, 149
  land conflicts, 357, 358
  Maoist groups, 148
  populist appeals to rural constituencies, 359
Elites
  bureaucratic elites, 18, 22, 23, 102, 190
  business elites, 23, 25, 43, 47, 53, 101, 115, 185
  military elites, 23, 55, 112, 116, 124, 125
  political elites, 20, 23, 72, 93, 122, 256, 261, 278, 323, 330
  politico-business elites, 24, 25, 166, 258
  ruling elites, 9, 113, 119, 120, 141, 159, 180, 189, 203, 255, 256, 358
Empowerment
  women, 234
Energy sector
  ASEAN Economic Community, 219
Energy subsidies, 219
Environmental degradation, 207, 329, 367
  air, 368–369
  biodiversity loss, 371; hydropower projects, 376
  capitalist development; colonial period, 373; growth of urban manufacturing, 374
  capital–nature relations, 367 (*see also* Climate change)
  commodities boom, 374
  domestic accumulation, 373–374
  economic growth dichotomy, 373–378
  extractive industries, impact of, 329, 373–378

human–nature relations, 367
hydropower, 376
land; deforestation, 369–371
palm oil, 374–375
regulation, 123
water, 369
Environmental governance
  bilateral agreements for performance payments, 379
  limitations; One Map effort, 380; REDD+, 379
  nationally determined contributions, 378
  private voluntary industrial (RSPO) standards, 378
  United Nations Framework Convention on Climate Change, 379
Epidemics, 207
Erdogan, Recep Tayyip, 155, 157, 168
Ethnic insurgencies
  Burma/Myanmar, 116, 121, 124–125, 138, 144
European Union (EU)
  international aid, 295, 307
  populism, 155, 161
  technocrats, 204
Evictions, *see* Displacement; Urban evictions
Export-oriented foreign direct investment, 52, 54, 123
Export-oriented industrialisation (EOI), 56, 113, 178, 187, 190
  deregulation, 203
  female labour, 229
  feminised production regime, 231
  gender inequality, 231–232
  low-wage factory work, 231
  trade unions, 232
  wage suppression, 232

Extractive industries, 318
  control by elites, 323
  corporate social responsibility, 331
  environmental impact, 329
  governance norms and
    principles, 319
  investment, 329
  land use; deforestation, 369; priority
    to exportable resources, 327;
    priority to mining, 327;
    private sector mining
    development, 327
  modes of governance, 318,
    334–335
  producers, 320
  production statistics, 319
  redress for communities, 332
  regulatory reforms, 325–329
  socio-environmental impacts,
    330, 331
  taxation, 334
Extractive Industries Transparency
  Initiative (EITI), 304, 331

F
Farm consolidation, 349, 353–355
Feminisation of work, 231–234
Financial Action Task Force (FATF)
  Asia/Pacific Group on Money
    Laundering, 207
  practical implementation of
    recommendations, 208
  recommendations; monitoring, 208;
    non-compliance, 208
Financial Intelligence Units (FIUs)
  coordination of AML activities, 208
First Indochina War (1946–54), 136
Flexible accumulation, 36, 49–51, 67,
  72, 374
Foreign debt, 121, 205, 294,
  307–308, 327, 374

Foreign direct investment (FDI),
  187, 299
  dependency on, 57
  internationalisation of capital, 182
  Japan, 49–51
  Malaysia, 46
  national security concerns, 123–124
  Singapore, 47
Foreign students
  Malaysia, 265
  Singapore, 263, 265
Fragmentation of state power, 201,
  202, 210, 217
  transnationalisation of economic and
    social life, 204 (*see also*
    Decentralisation)
France
  First Indochina War, 136
  international aid, 295
Free trade agreements, 200
  See also ASEAN Free Trade
    Agreement (AFTA)
Frontier capitalism, 12

G
Garment industry
  female labour, 231
  industrial discontent, 123
Gendered social transformation,
  234–235
Gender inequality, 227
  anti-welfare policies, 229
  export-oriented industrialisation, 229
  low-paid work, 231
  male bias in concept of economic
    development, 229
  Murdoch School, 230
  state policies and practices, 230
  See also Women
Germany
  international aid, 295

Global economic slowdown (1970s), 48–49
Global financial crisis (2008), 59, 341, 349
Globalisation, 20, 181
Good governance, 26, 70, 158
  environmental concerns, 368
  international aid, 301–304
  regulatory regionalism, 206
Greater Mekong Subregion
  transnational alliances, 112

H
Heavy Industries Corporation of Malaysia (HICOM), 190
High-wage migration, 262–267
  ASEAN Economic Community, 266
  ASEAN Qualification Reference Framework, 266
  Malaysia, 264–265
  Mutual Recognition Arrangements, 266
  Philippines, 265
  Singapore, 262–265
  Thailand, 265
Hinduism, 233
Historical institutionalism, 5, 11–12, 90
  incrementalist institutionalism, 14
  local institutional variegation, 27
  path-dependent institutions, 11–14
  See also Path-dependent institutionalism
Human rights
  extractive industries, 330
  human rights abuses, 24, 294, 307, 325, 330
  international aid, 302
Hybrid regime theory, 13, 89–90, 105
  Murdoch School approach compared, 22, 25, 93
  third-wave transitions, 90

Hydropower, 348
  Cambodia, 376
  Laos, 119, 376
  Myanmar, 116, 376
Hyperglobalisation, 36, 58
  productivity challenges, 66–67

I
Import-substitution industrialisation (ISI), 52
  post-independence economies, 42
Incomes per capita, 37, 42, 46, 61, 325
Independence
  economic situation of countries, impact on, 42
India
  international aid, 295
  movement populism, 157
  New Development Bank, 295
  populism, 155
Indonesia
  Asian financial crisis, 23–25, 237
  authoritarian developmentalism, 134
  authoritarianism, 101
  automotive sector, 68
  business elites, 185
  capitalist development, 91
  Coordinating Ministry for Economic Affairs, 185
  decentralisation, 24, 92, 101, 167, 258, 261, 352, 381
  deforestation, 372
  democratisation, 101
  direct elections, 278
  economic ranking, 63
  electoral politics, 151
  extractive industries, 323
  foreign direct investment, 51
  gubernatorial elections; religion and identity politics, 277, 280–281
  IMF assistance, 49
  industrialisation, 27

Indonesia (*cont.*)
  inequality/inequalities, 37, 61–62, 101–102; neighbourhood displacements, 102–103, 241–243
  international aid, 295, 307–308
  internationalisation of capital, 183–186
  Investment Coordinating Board, 185
  Islamic populism, 104, 106, 158, 168, 272, 277
  Islamism, 168
  land acquisition, 101; state-owned enterprises, 101
  land allocation; corruption, 352
  land-titling programmes, 356
  leftist movements and parties, 135–137
  low-paid work, 232
  low-wage migration, 257–258
  Maoist rebellions, 142
  Ministry of Trade, 185
  neighbourhood associations; bottom up representation, 100; elections, 99
  neighbourhood displacements, 100, 102–103; women, 241–243
  neighbourhood representation, 106, 272, 278–279; growing political importance, 103–105; neighbourhood displacements, 103–104
  oil industry, 49
  oligarchic capitalism, 12, 22–25, 53, 61–62, 91, 101, 157
  populism, 155, 158, 162; cross-class alliances, 166–168, 277; drivers of, 162–164
  post-WWII commodity boom, 44, 61–62
  post-WWII political and economic instability, 45–46
  pro-market reforms, 53
  property development; social conflict, 100
  service sector, 184
  state-building interventions, 26
  technocratic populism, 157, 160, 162
  urban evictions, 231, 272
  Urban Poor Consortium, 278, 279, 281
  women; factory work, 232; urban eviction policies, 241–243
Indonesian Communist Party (PKI), 45
  decline, 142
Indonesian Democratic Party of Struggle (PDI-P), 151
Industrialisation
  agrarian relations, impact on, 345
  class struggles, 235 (*see also* Export-oriented industrialisation (EOI); Import-substitution industrialisation (ISI))
Industrial-related resistance
  foreign investment, protests against, 124
  young workers, 123–124
Inequalities, 37, 61
  Indonesia, 37, 61–62, 101–102
  Malaysia, 37
  Singapore, 37, 96–98, 105
  See also Gender inequality; Social inequality
Inequality-trapped capitalism, 12
Informal employment
  women, 235–236
Infrastructure sector
  internationalisation of capital, 185
  populist investment, 170
  transnational alliances, 112, 214, 217, 308, 309
  See also Belt and Road Initiative

Institutional fundamentalism, 10–11
International aid, 44–45
  aid defined, 295
  emerging donors, 295; China, 293, 299–305; good governance condition, 302; growing role, 300; infrastructure and economic growth, 300 (*see also* Foreign direct investment (FDI); International donors)
  non-interference principle, 302; China, 302–304
  official development assistance, 295 (*see also* Official development assistance (ODA))
  other official flows, 295, 308
  Philippines, 310
  political priorities, 294
  post-Cold War; foreign direct investment, 299
  recipient countries, 306; conditionality, 302; elite authoritarianism, 305; political oppositions, 305–306; selectivity, 302
  traditional donors, 294–296; conditionality and selectivity, 302; priority countries, 298–299
International Council on Mining and Metals, 331
International donors
  emerging donors, 295; China, 293, 299–305; good governance condition, 302; growing role, 300; infrastructure and economic growth, 300; non-interference principle, 302
  traditional donors, 294–296; Cold War, 296; conditionality and selectivity, 302; priority countries, 298–299
International Finance Corporation (IFC)
  land use policies, 348
  Performance Standards on Environmental and Social Sustainability, 331
International financial institutions, 6, 52, 116, 201, 203, 302, 333, 382
  extractive industries, 319, 326, 330, 331
  See also Asian Development Bank (ADB); World Bank
Internationalisation of capital, 53, 181–183
  government-linked companies (Singapore); partnerships with multinational corporations, 187; privatised state monopolies and public utilities, 187; spin-offs from defence industries, 187
  Government of Singapore Investment Corporation (GIC), 188
  Indonesia; agribusiness, 184; automotive sector, 184; food sector, 184; infrastructure sector, 185; mining operations, 184; origins, 183; plantations, 184; services, 184
  Malaysia; "Ali-Baba" partnerships, 190; Asian financial crisis, 192; automotive sector, 190; export-oriented industrialisation, 190; heavy industry, 190; importance of Chinese capital, 191; New Economic Policy (NEP), 189; origins, 189–190; privatisation of state assets, 190; state-mediated joint ventures, 190
  Singapore; capital accumulation, 188; government-linked companies, 186–188; Growth Triangle, 188; origins, 186–187; overseas expansion, 188; regulatory projects, 188–189

International Monetary Fund
    (IMF), 48
  anti-money-laundering
    compliance, 208
  Asian financial crisis, 24
  bail-outs, 24, 55
  Chiang Mai Initiative
    Multilateralisation
    (CMIM), 205
  international aid, 295
Islam, 233
Islamic populism, 104, 106, 158, 168,
    272, 277

J
Japan, 20
  ASEAN Plus Three, 200
  automotive sector, 68
  defeat in the Pacific war, 135
  foreign direct investment, 49,
    51, 376
  international aid, 295
Jokowi, 104, 278
  cross-class alliances, 167, 168
  populism, 157, 158, 160, 170, 278
  urban poor, 278, 279

K
Korean War (1950–53), 44, 51, 135
Kuwait
  international aid, 295

L
Labour migration, 249–250
  ASEAN Economic Community, 219
  drivers; commercialisation of
    recruitment, 254; industrial
    restructuring, 253; wages, 253
  governance, 267; labour-receiving
    countries, 254–256; labour-
    sending countries, 256–258

high-wage migration, 262–267 (*see
    also* High-wage migration)
  liberalisation, 265–267
  low-wage migration, 267; conflicts,
    258–262; governance reforms,
    267; labour-receiving countries,
    254–256; labour-sending
    countries, 256–258 (*see also*
    Low-wage migration)
  movement of skilled labour, 219
  Mutual Recognition
    Agreements, 219
  statistics, 250–254
Land conflicts
  Cambodia, 122
  deforestation, 122
  plantation agriculture, 121
  reclassification of rural land, 122
  Vietnam, 122
Land expropriation, 101–102, 116,
    122, 127, 159, 284, 357,
    360, 381
Land-grabbing, 352
  agribusiness, 351, 352
  voluntary global guidelines, 358
Land ownership
  collectivisation programmes, 344
  de-collectivisation, 345
Land redistribution, 342
Land reform, 257, 342
  non-socialist countries, 343
  socialist countries, 342
  See also Collectivisation programmes
Land-titling programmes,
    355–356, 359
  criticisms, 356
Laos, 70
  capitalist development, 92
  collectivisation programmes, 344
  communism, 44
  corruption, 119
  de-collectivisation of agriculture, 118
  economic liberalisation, 112
  economic ranking, 63

elite authoritarianism, 118–120
frontier capitalism, 12
hydropower, 348
international aid, 298
land-grabs, 352
land-titling programmes, 356
marginalisation of subordinate groups, 119
natural resource sector, 118
post-socialist transformation of property relations, 345
pro-market reforms, 53, 112
state socialism, 111
transition to market economies, 118–120
Lee Kuan, Yew, 47, 95
Leftist movements and parties, 152
  China, influence of, 151
  decline, 133–135; Burma, 137–138; Indonesia, 135–137; Latin America compared, 146–148; Malaya, 137–138; Maoism as a cause of, 134; Philippines, 136–137; reasons for, 145–147; Singapore, 138–139
  reorientation; Third Indochina War, 142
  role, 133
  upturn; Vietnam, 139–140
Legitimacy, 4, 260, 358
  legitimacy crisis, 112, 121, 126–128
  populism, 156
Liberalisation, 7, 22, 23, 28, 53, 62, 267, 326
  ASEAN way, 26
  aviation markets, 215
  economic liberalisation, 57, 113
  Indonesia, 183, 186
  Malaysia, 191, 192
  market liberalisation, 163, 183
  mining regimes, 328
  Singapore, 188

trade liberalisation, 56, 192
Washington consensus, 301
Logistics and production efficiency, 50
Low-cost manufacturing, 59–60
  value-added ladder, 60, 67–68
Low-wage migration, 267
  governance reforms, 267
  labour-receiving countries; deportation, 255; governance frameworks, 254–256; limited legal-political rights, 255; occupational immobility, 255; temporary/fixed term nature of work, 254–256; trade union membership, 255

M
Mahathir, Mohamad, 308
Malaya
  leftist movements and parties, 137–138
  post-WWII commodity boom, 44
  See also Malaysia
Malaysia, 24
  Advanced Micro Devices, 68
  Asian financial crisis, 24
  authoritarian developmentalism, 134
  automotive sector, 68
  Democratic Action Party (DAP), 145
  economic ranking, 63, 66
  electoral success, 150
  export-oriented development, 43
  Federal Industry Development Authority, 43
  foreign direct investment, 51
  foreign students, 265
  hybrid regime, 89
  industrialisation, 27
  inequality, 37
  international aid, 308

Malaysia (*cont.*)
  internationalisation of capital, 189–192
  land reform, 343
  leftist movements and parties; decline, 143
  migrant workers; high-wage migration, 264–265; low-wage migration, 255; minimum wage law, 260
  mineral resources, 323
  oil industry, 49; declining oil revenues, 66
  post-war political and economic instability, 45–46
  social care policy, 231
  state subsidies for export industries, 43
  women; employment, 232, 234, 235; informal employment, 235
Malaysia's Democratic Action Party (DAP), 145
  electoral success, 150
Maoism, 134, 145–146, 151
  Burma, 143
  Cambodia, 141
  East Timor, 142
  Indonesia, 142
  Malaysia, 143
  Philippines, 144, 148
  Thailand, 144
  Vietnam, 140
Marcos, Ferdinand, 52, 145, 164
  end of rule, 149, 283
  land reform, 343
  martial law, 144
  mining sector, 325
Market-oriented governance, 36, 305
Marxism, 8, 15
Masterplan for the Acceleration and Expansion of Economic Development of Indonesia (2011–2025), 186
Mexico
  international aid, 295

Middle classes, 5, 16, 22, 23, 87, 167
  disruptive politics, 277
  immigration, fear of, 216
  neoliberalism, 159
  populism, 23, 160, 165, 168, 169, 279, 280
  social reproduction, 240
  See also Class relations
Middle income trap, 62
Migrant domestic workers, 251
  abuse at work, 258
  destination countries, 253
  importance, 253 (*see also* Migrant workers)
  sexual harassment, 258
Migrant workers
  abuses in recruitment, employment and repatriation, 258; protection of workers, 258–262
  low-wage migration; labour-receiving countries, 254–256; labour-sending countries, 256–258 (*see also* Migrant domestic workers)
  minimum wages, 260
  protection of workers; civil society activism, 258
  protests by, 259
  regularisation programmes, 259
  rights restrictions, 255; Malaysia, 255; Singapore, 256; Thailand, 255
  statistics, 255
Millennium Development Goals (MDGs), 296, 300
Mineral fuels, 321, 323, 325
  See also Extractive industries
Mineral fuels and resources, 321
  Laos, 119
Mineral production
  demand, 325 (*see also* Extractive industries)
  growth, 320
Mining operations, 113
  Extractive Industries Transparency Initiative (EITI), 304

Indonesia; internationalisation of
    capital, 184
  Laos, 119
  Myanmar, 116
  See also Extractive industries
Mining rights, 326
  protection of, 327
  See also Extractive industries
Modernisation theory
  early theorists, 89
  "third wave" of democratisation, 89
Modes of governance
  concept explained, 318
  extractive industries, 318
Modes of Participation (MOP)
    framework, 88, 93
  ideologies of representation;
    consultative ideologies, 93;
    democratic ideologies, 93;
    particularist ideologies, 93;
    populist ideologies, 93
Modi, Narendra, 157
Movement of skilled labour
  ASEAN Economic Community,
    219, 266 (*see also* High-wage
    migration)
Multinational corporations
    (MNCs), 39
  agribusiness, 350
  capitalist development, 16
  extractive industries, 318
  feminisation of industrial
    manufacturing, 232
  OECD Guidelines, 331
  partnerships with, 187
  Vietnam, 113
Murdoch School, 14–15
  Amsterdam School compared,
    179–181
  Amsterdam School,
    importance of, 192
  development of national
    economies, 17

failure of Western donor projects, 26
foundational assumptions;
  globalisation, 16; socio-political
  conflict, 15–16
gender inequality, 230
hybrid regimes, 22, 25
institutional forms, 18–19, 90, 105;
  strategic selectivity, 19
international state-building
  interventions, 26
methodological nationalism, 17
Modes of Participation framework
  (*see* Modes of Participation
  (MOP) framework)
poor people's politics, 271
practical application of framework,
  17–18
procurement rules, 17–18
social classes; capitalism, impact of,
  15–17
social conflict, 6
state/market relationship, 6
state transformation, 17
struggles over power and
  resources, 25
Mutual Recognition Agreements
    (MRAs)
  high-wage migration, 219, 266
Myanmar, 25, 56, 70
  bureaucratic-military
    authoritarianism, 116
  capitalist development, 92
  ceasefire capitalism, 116
  Chinese investment, 116
  crony capitalism, 116
  economic ranking, 63
  economic sanctions, 26
  ethnic insurgencies, 116, 121,
    124–125
  exploitation of natural
    resources, 116
  hydropower, 348, 376
  international aid, 298, 309

Myanmar (*cont.*)
  land-grabs, 352
  military dictatorship, 115
  mineral resources, 323
  post-socialist transformation of property relations, 345
  pro-market reforms, 112
  state-business relationships, 115–117
  state socialism, 111
  transition to market economies, 115–117
  See also Burma

N

National Congress for Timorese Reconstruction (CNRT), 151
National Democratic Party (NasDem) (Indonesia), 151
National Housing Authority (NHA) (Philippines), 284–287
Nationalism, 45, 52, 72, 112, 121, 128, 161, 238
Neoliberalism, 6–8, 150, 159, 183
  agrarian transformations; civil society activism, 356–359; popular resistance, 356
  enabling environments, promotion of, 302
  international aid, 301–302
  populism, rise of, 159
  post-Washington consensus, 301
  Washington consensus, 301
Neopatrimonialism, 352
Netherlands
  international aid, 295
Network for Social Democracy in Asia (SocDem Asia), 150, 151
New Development Bank (NDB)
  international aid, 295
New Order (Indonesia), 45, 46, 52, 55, 101, 163, 183, 278

Non-Aligned Movement, 136
Non-government organisations, emergence of, 149
Non-traditional security (NTS) problems, 207
North Atlantic Treaty Organisation (NATO), 135

O

Official development assistance (ODA), 36, 308
  See also International aid
Offshore manufacturing, 50–51
  China, 57
  Japan, 49–50
Oil and gas extraction, 321, 334
  oil-importing countries, 49
  oil-producing countries, 49, 51; declining oil revenues, 66
  See also Extractive industries
Oligarchic capitalism, 12, 72, 91
  Indonesia, 22–25, 53, 61–62, 101
  populism, 156, 162
  Thailand, 53
Open-led state capitalism, 12
Order Baru (Indonesia), 45, 46, 52, 55, 101, 163, 183, 278
Organisation for Economic Co-operation and Development (OECD)
  Development Assistance Committee (DAC), 295
  extractive industries, 331
Organised crime, 207
Our Singapore Conversation (OSC), 95, 97–98

P

Palm oil
  domestic accumulation, 375
  environmental governance, 378–379

INDEX 405

environmental impact, 62, 332, 358, 374
government subsidies, 346
palm oil biofuel, 378–379
regional investment, 350
Roundtable on Sustainable Palm Oil (RSPO), 358, 380; voluntary industrial standards, 378
Partial democracies, 13
Participation, *see* Modes of Participation (MOP) framework
Participatory planning, 273, 286, 287
Particularist representation, 93
Path-dependent institutionalism
  patterns of development; coordinated market economies, 12; liberal market economies, 12
  political regime dynamics, 12–13
  weaknesses; agency, lack of, 13–14; institutions given primary causal status, 13; methodological nationalism, 13–14; non explanatory, 13
Patronage systems, 23, 92, 135, 149, 152, 156
  Cambodia, 70, 114, 123, 125
  East Timor, 150
  Indonesia, 25, 46, 54, 61, 92, 167, 278, 279, 330, 344, 352
  Laos, 119
  Malaysia, 46, 66
  Philippines, 164, 325
  Vietnam, 117, 118
Peasant farmers, 16, 122, 348
  capitalist development, 16
  displacement, 351
  land redistribution, 342
  land reform, 343
  militarisation post-WWII, impact of, 122
  social activism, 343
People's Action Party (PAP) (Singapore), 21, 47, 138, 186, 264

People's Democratic Party (PRD) (Indonesia), 149
Philippines
  authoritarian populism, 157
  Board of Investment, 43
  capitalist development, 91
  conflict, 51
  disaster resilience policies, 240–241
  displacement, 231
  economic ranking, 63
  electoral politics, 150
  export-oriented development, 43
  extractive industries, 325; regulatory reform, 327–328
  foreign direct investment, 51
  high-wage immigration, 265
  hybrid regime, 89
  IMF assistance, 49
  inequality-trapped capitalism, 12
  international aid, 307
  land reform, 343
  land-titling programmes, 356
  leftist movements and parties, 136–137
  low-wage migration, 256–257
  Maoism, 144
  oligarchic capitalism, 91
  populism, 155, 158, 162; cross-class alliances, 168–170; drivers of, 163–165
  post-WWII economy, 44
  protectionism, 46–47
  urban evictions, 272, 273
  women; resilience policies, 241
Plantation agriculture, 342, 351
  agribusiness plantations, 348
  deforestation, 369
  Indonesia, 352; internationalisation of capital, 184
  land conflicts, 121
  palm oil, 375
  peasants, impact on, 122
Plaza Accord (1985), 20, 50

Political conflict, 72, 97, 99, 158, 330, 380
  economy, impact on, 3–5
Political economy
  economics distinguished, 3
  politics and international relations distinguished, 4
Pollution, *see* Environmental degradation
Poor people's politics, 288
  concept defined, 271–272
  defensive politics, 276–277
  disruptive politics, 276–277, 282, 283, 288
  everyday politics, 275–276, 279, 287
  urban poor, 273–274
Populism, 155–156
  analysis of, 157–159
  authoritarian populism, 157
  authority, 156
  concept, 156
  cross-class alliances, 277 (*see also* Cross-class alliances)
  drivers of populism; Indonesia, 162–164; Philippines, 163–165; Thailand, 162–163
  globalisation, 159
  global rise of, 157–158
  Islamic populism, 104, 106, 158, 168, 272, 277
  legitimacy, 156
  movement populism, 157
  neoliberalism, 159
  oligarchic populism, 157, 162
  political economy analysis of, 160–161
  populist leaders, 160
  reformulation of power among elites, 161
  technocratic populism, 157
Populist representation, 93
Post-independence economies
  export-oriented development, 43
  governments' roles, 42–44
  import-substitution industrialisation, 42
Post-state capitalism, 12
Post-Washington consensus (PWC), 301
  good governance, 301
Post-WWII economies, 43, 71–72
  Cold War, impact of, 44
  commodities boom, 44
  communism, 44–45
  leftist movements and parties; Cold War, impact of, 135; domestic roots, 135
Poverty and deprivation, 37, 61, 120
  Asian financial crisis; IMF imposed austerity regimes, 237
  women, 237–239 (*see also* Women)
Prabowo, 157, 167
Precarity, 249, 274
  displaced workers, 159, 169, 276, 380
  extraction industries, 375
  urban middle class, 168
  urban poor, 169, 376, 382
Privatisation, 53, 112, 116, 159, 163, 190, 301, 303, 305, 326, 348
Productivity challenges, 66
Progressive Alliance (PA), 150
Pro-market reforms
  Cambodia, 53, 56, 112
  Indonesia, 53
  Laos, 53, 112
  Myanmar, 112
  Thailand, 53
  Vietnam (Doi moi), 53, 56, 112
Promotion of growth, 4, 5, 301, 306
  state institutions, 19
Property development
  Cambodia, 114, 115
  Indonesia, 100–102, 105
  Singapore, 101–102

Property rights, 6, 159, 301, 341
  reforms, 355, 359, 360
  See also Land-titling programmes
Protectionism, 42, 46, 50, 58, 62, 219, 326

R
Rational-choice institutionalism, 11
Redistributive policies, 6, 43, 125, 156, 161, 165, 170
  Indonesia, 101
  Philippines, 161
  Singapore, 98, 99
Reduced Emissions from Deforestation and Forest Degradation Plus (REDD+), 379
  limitations, 379–381
Reformasi, 25, 55, 92, 145
Regional governance, 183, 199–202
  anti-money-laundering regulations, 207–209
  ASEAN Economic Community, 212–220
  monetary governance, 205–207 (*see also* Regulatory regionalism)
Regionalisation of production and finance, 28
Regulatory regionalism, 204
  Asia/Pacific Group on Money Laundering, 207–209
  Association of Southeast Asian Nations; ASEAN Agreement on Disaster Management and Emergency Response, 212; ASEAN Community, 209–212; origins, 209; structure, 209
  Chiang Mai Initiative Multilateralisation, 205–207
  embedded mercantilism, 203
  governance institutions and rules, 204
  implementation, 204
  sovereignty, 202, 221
Representative politics
  populism, 156
Resistance movements, 46, 95, 125, 133, 143, 358
Resource extraction, *see* Extractive industries
Resource nationalism, 61, 62, 334, 375
Revolutionary Front for an Independent East Timor (FRETILIN), 143, 145, 150
Revolutionary left, 134–135, 151–152
Roundtable on Sustainable Palm Oil (RSPO), 358
  limitations, 380–381
  voluntary industrial standards, 378
Rubber plantations, 120
  regional investment, 350
Rule of law, 302
Rural poor, 166, 167, 169, 343, 344, 357
  See also Peasant farmers
Rural unrest, 342
  civil society activism; land-related mobilisation, 357; peasant rights and livelihoods, 357
  compulsory land acquisition, 357
  non-socialist countries, 344
Russia, 89, 307
  New Development Bank, 295

S
Sarawak, 138
Saudi Arabia
  international aid, 295
Semi-authoritarianism, 13
Service sector, 61, 353, 354
  Indonesia, 184; internationalisation of capital, 184
  Singapore, 21, 253, 262

Singapore, 37
  anti-colonial struggle, 95
  authoritarian developmentalism, 134
  civil unrest, 52
  compassionate meritocracy, 99
  consultative representation, 94, 97–99
  developmental state model, 20–22
  Economic Development Board, 43, 47
  export-oriented development, 43, 47
  expulsion from Malaysia, 47
  foreign direct investment, 51; export-oriented industrialisation, 47
  foreign students, 263
  high-wage migration, 262–265
  hybrid regime, 89
  inequalities, 37, 96–98, 105
  international aid, 295
  internationalisation of capital, 186–189
  leftist movements and parties, 138–139
  migrant workers; dispute resolution, 260; high-wage migration, 263; low-wage migration, 254–262; reliance on, 96
  Modes of Participation framework, 94–99
  open-led state capitalism, 12
  Our Singapore Conversation, 95, 97–98; five core aspirations, 98; phases of development, 97; policy reform, 98
  People's Action Party (PAP), 94; state capitalism strategies, 186
  post-WWII commodity boom, 44
  post-WWII economy, 44
  post-WWII political and economic instability, 47
  property development, 101–102
  quasi-authoritarianism, 20
  redistributive policies, 99
  rising social conflict, 94
  service sector, 21, 253, 262
  social care policy, 231
  state subsidies for export industries, 43
  technocratic elites, 95–96
  women; care work, 239–241; economic status, 233–234
Smallholder security, 358, 360
Smuggling, 47, 120, 121
Social care policy, 231
Social democracy, 92, 145, 149–150, 152, 156, 162, 171
Social inequality, 230
  class-based, 230 (*see also* Middle classes; Peasant farmers)
  gender-based, 230 (*see also* Gender inequality; Women)
Social power relations, 25, 93, 100, 105
  environmental degradation, 368
Social protection, *see* Welfare systems
Social reproduction, 231, 243
  anti-welfarist policies, 239–241; Indonesia, 241–243; Malaysia, 240; Philippines, 241; Singapore, 239–241
  depletion through social reproduction, 237
  gendered regimes of state power, 231
Socio-economic ramifications
  extractive industries, 330
Socio-environmental ramifications
  extractive industries, 318
Sociological institutionalism, 11
Soil contamination/degradation, 329
South Africa
  international aid, 295
  New Development Bank, 295

Southeast Asia Treaty Organisation (SEATO), 135
South Korea
  ASEAN Plus Three, 200
  Asian financial crisis, 237
  automotive sector, 68
  international aid, 295
South Vietnam
  land reform, 343
Sovereignty
  graduated sovereignty, 203
  membership of international bodies, 201
  regional governance, 220
  regulatory regionalism, 202, 221
Soviet Union, 43
  communism, 45
  international aid, 111, 142, 298
State accountability, 302, 332
State and bourgeoisie, relationship between, 89, 91, 177–181, 193
  Amsterdam School, 181
  Indonesia, 168, 185
  Murdoch School, 192
  Singapore, 21, 95, 96, 187
  Thailand, 163
  Turkey, 168
State autonomy, 8–10, 19
State economic groups (SEGs) (Vietnam), 117
State-owned enterprises (SOEs) (Vietnam), 117
States and markets, relationship between
  historical institutionalism, 5
  Murdoch School approach, 6
  Weberian approach, 5
State socialism, transition from, 111–113
  Cambodia, 114–117
  Laos, 118–120
  negative impacts on, 142
  Vietnam, 117–118

State transformation, 17, 183, 192, 254
  social reproduction, 237, 243
Strikes, 235, 259, 267
Substantive economic development, 36, 68
Suharto, 22, 136, 142, 143
  anti-Suharto movements, 149
  capital accumulation, 101
  cronyism, 23–25, 92, 101, 185
  end of rule, 24, 92, 145, 183
  extractive industries, 325
  land acquisition, 101
  logging companies, 352
  New Order, 45, 52, 55, 278;
    licences for property, 101
Sukarno
  August Revolution, 136
  end of rule, 45, 137
  Guided Democracy, 45
  Indonesian Communist Party, 135, 136
  nationalisation and forced acquisitions, 101
Sustainability certification schemes, 358, 381
Sustainable Development Goals (SDGs), 296, 300

T
Taiwan
  automotive sector, 68
  development state model, 10, 13
  environmental degradation, 123
  industrial-related resistance, 124
  mineral resources, lack of, 325
  status, 299, 303
Technocratic authoritarianism
  Indonesia, 160
  Singapore, 95–96
Telecommunications
  internationalisation of capital, 184

Terrorism, 207
Thailand, 24
  Asian financial crisis, 24, 237
  authoritarian developmentalism, 134
  automotive sector, 68
  conflict, 51
  economic ranking, 63
  export-oriented development, 43
  farm consolidation, 349
  foreign direct investment, 51
  hybrid regime, 89
  IMF assistance, 49
  industrialisation, 27
  international aid, 44, 295
  land-grabs, 352
  land reform, 343
  land-titling programmes, 356
  leftist movements and parties, 144
  migrant workers; high-wage immigration, 265; low-wage migration, 255; regularisation programmes, 259
  mineral resources, 323
  National Economic Development Board, 43
  oligarchic capitalism, 53
  populism, 155, 162; cross-class alliances, 165–167; drivers of, 162–163
  post-WWII commodity boom, 44
  pro-market reforms, 53
Thai Rak Thai (TRT) party
  cross-class alliances, 165–166
Thaksin Shinawatra
  redistributive policies, 166–167
  Thai Rak Thai party, 165
Timber industry, 51, 113
  Myanmar, 116
Timor-Leste, 150
  economic ranking, 63
  international aid, 299
  state-building interventions, 26
Toy manufacturing
  female labour, 231

Trade agreements, *see* ASEAN Free Trade Agreement (AFTA); Free trade agreements
Trade liberalisation, 56
Trade unions, 21, 126
  export-oriented industrialisation, 231–235
  migrant workers, 255
  women, 232, 233, 235, 243
Traditional livelihoods,
  disruption to, 123
  environmental damage, 123
  export-oriented investments, 123
    (*see also* Plantation agriculture; Rural poor; Urban poor)
  See also Displacement
Transition to market economies
  anti-Chinese feelings, 127
  business interests, 127
  Cambodia, 114–115
  China, impact of, 127
  commodities boom, 127
  industrial-related resistance, 123–124
  Laos, 118–120
  Myanmar, 115–117
  opposition and conflict, 121–126
  popular protest, 125
  poverty and deprivation, 127
  resource exploitation, 127
  traditional livelihood, disruption of, 122–123
  Vietnam, 117–118
Transnational investment and cooperation, 112, 120–121
  energy networks, 112
  transport networks, 112
Transnationalism, 178, 204
Trans-Pacific Partnership (TPP), 28
Transparency, 26, 186, 207, 302, 309
  Extractive Industries Transparency Initiative, 304, 331
Trump, Donald, 161
Turkey
  populism, 155

U

United Arab Emirates
  international aid, 295
United Kingdom
  international aid, 295
United Nations Conference on Trade and Development (UNCTAD), 36
United Nations Framework Convention on Climate Change (UNFCCC), 379
United Nations Intergovernmental Panel on Climate Change (IPCC), 371
United States
  international aid, 295
  populism, 155, 160–161
Urban evictions
  Indonesia, 231, 277–278
  Philippines, 283–287
Urbanisation
  agrarian relations, impact on, 146, 345
Urban poor, 273–274
  Indonesia; urban evictions, 277–278; women, 242
  insecurity, 282
  participation; Urban Poor Alliance (Philippines), 283–284; Urban Poor Consortium (Indonesia), 278, 279, 281–283
  participatory planning, 287
  populism, 281–283
  urban evictions; Indonesia, 278; Philippines, 283–287
Urban Poor Alliance (Philippines), 283
Urban Poor Consortium (Indonesia), 278, 279, 281
US Agency for International Development (USAID), 343
  Green Revolution, 343

V

Varieties of capitalism
  frontier capitalism, 12
  hierarchical market economy, 12
  inequality-trapped capitalism, 12
  oligarchic capitalism, 12
  open-led state capitalism, 12
  post-state capitalism, 12
Vietnam
  anti-Chinese outbursts, 126
  capitalist development, 92
  Centre for Industrial Development, 43
  Chinese occupation, 141
  collectivisation programmes, 344
  communism, 44
  corruption, 117
  crony capitalism, 117
  economic liberalisation, 112
  economic ranking, 63
  export-oriented development, 43
  farm consolidation, 349
  industrialisation, 27
  international aid, 298
  international investors, 117
  land conflicts, 122
  land-grabs, 352
  land reform, 343
  middle income trap, 62–63
  mineral resources, 323
  post-Cold War era, 117
  post-socialist transformation of property relations, 345
  post-state capitalism, 12
  post-WWII commodity boom, 44
  pro-market reforms (Doi moi), 53, 56, 112
  state control of the economy, 117
  state economic groups, 117
  state-owned enterprises, 117–118
  state socialism, 111, 117–118

Vietnam (*cont.*)
  transition to market economies, 117–118
  women; employment, 233; labour activism, 235
Vietnamese League for Independence (Viet Minh), 135
  August Revolution, 135
Vietnam Rubber Group (VRG), 120
Vietnam War (1955–75), 44, 51, 136, 139–140
  non-Maoist strategies, 139–140

W
Wage demands, 56, 259
Washington consensus, 301
Water pollution, 369
Water resources, 329
Weber, Max, 7
Weberian approach to state/market relationship, 5
  capacity concept, 8–9
  developmental state model, 8–10, 19
  ideal types, reliance on, 10
  institutional fundamentalism, 10–11
  origins, 7–8
  state autonomy concept, 8–10
Welfare systems, 236
  anti-welfarist orientation of states, 239
  Singapore, 239–241
Widodo, Joko, *see* Jokowi

Women
  anti-welfare policies, 239–243
  autonomy, 234
  economic status; Singapore, 233–234
  employment, 233; informal economy, 235, 236
  family policy, 236 (*see also* Gender inequality)
  labour activism, 235
  labour force participation, 243
  labour migration, 250 (*see also* Labour migration; Migrant domestic workers)
  low-wage factory work, 231
  Philippines; public health, 241
  social reproduction; class and nationality, 236
  trade union membership, 232
  unpaid labour, 236, 243
World Bank, 37
  anti-money-laundering compliance, 208
  extractive industries, reform of, 326
  international aid, 295
  land-titling programmes, 355
  land use policies, 348
  marketisation, promotion of, 27
  Performance Standards on Environmental and Social Sustainability, 331
World Trade Organization (WTO), 201, 203
  China, 16, 56